W9-CHO-120

The North Wind Knows My Name

July 10/17

Sydney:

I hope you enjoy
my book!
Thanks for all your
gifts to our College
and community.

Al McLeod :)

The North Wind Knows My Name

꼭

Albert McLeod

Copyright © 2016 Albert McLeod
All rights reserved.

Cover Photo by Dave Reede

ISBN-13: 9781533427281
ISBN-10: 1533427283
Library of Congress Control Number: 2016908501
CreateSpace Independent Publishing Platform
North Charleston, South Carolina

Contents

--- ⅋ ---

ACKNOWLEDGEMENTS: TO THOSE WHO LOVE AND SUPPORT ME

Thou hast clothed me with skin and flesh, and hast fenced me with bones and sinews. Thou hast granted me life and favour, and thy visitation hath preserved my spirit....wherefore then hast thou brought me forth out of the womb?

JOB, TALKING WITH GOD. JOB 10: 11, 12, 18

Sometimes I go around pitying myself, and all the while the great winds carry me across the sky. Ojibway saying.

⅋

FIRST, A CONFESSION: this book is not *my* book, and I am not a self-made man, as I once thought I was. I now see that our lives form complex, connecting webs across time and space. Our planet, mother earth, carries us all about, and her waters, food, and air flow through and sustain us.

Like most other creatures, we are herd animals, and our lives are profoundly shaped by others, even before conception. We arrive here with genetic imprints, carrying voices from our ancestors, hungry ghosts that desire to speak through us, that tease and call us.

In everyday life we overlook how our bodies, hearts, minds and souls are continually formed and tuned by others. We might embrace the fiction that we are *self-made,* that we've done it on our own, yet the reality is we are all connected by the waters of life. No one is an island. I did not form myself in my mother's womb. I am not the billions of genes and neurons that shape these words; *I* am carried and enlivened by them. We do not so much learn our native language: it is gifted, poured into us and we drink from a communal cup.

Our conscious awareness is not enough to know how we are hourly shaped by others. Here I recognize only those who've most consciously and lovingly woven themselves into my heart, and are the unspoken voices within and behind my words.

First to my wife Ruthie, and our adult children, Heather and Todd, and their spouses, Elliott and Jessica, who encouraged me to record the experiences of my childhood on the frozen, isolated prairie farm in Manitoba. Warmed by their springtime love, more stories thawed out and bubbled up. And here we are.

Like the love of God, theirs is a love that will not let me go, and for all love, I am grateful. Beyond the love we share, the books you've written, Heather and Todd, have motivated this old hunter to forge his own trail and travail of words. And Elliott and Jessica: your lives grace our planet with such gifts!

To my amazing, lovely wife, Ruthie: thanks for your daily, enduring and consistent love over the fifty-four years we've been together! Your love for me and most of what I write, reminds me over and over that I am not a lonely drop in the ocean of life.

To Kenny and Rich, loved friends and colleagues: over three decades, the soul sharing we've had, the tears and laughter, have been such a vital part of my life.

To the California State University Fresno: I have so much gratitude for the support you offered over thirty-eight years. I walked onto your campus in autumn 1968, and had no idea of how your hallowed halls would enrich and enliven me. To my 15,000 or so students during my tenure: I thank you for your ongoing curiosity, for sharing your warmth and wisdom. We celebrated and learned much from each other.

I am indebted to Joanie Herzon, for her editing skills, from beginning to end, especially during the birthing of my book at the end. Your love and emotional support was invaluable. To J.J. Anselmi and Beth Webster, each of you added something unique to what follows. Thank you for love and keen eyes that ferreted out my typos, kaleidoscopic tenses and more.

I'm grateful to my son, Todd, and Daniel Pompa for computer help when I neared my meltdown points.

To the legions of people along my path who opened and closed doors to me, time hath shown me that closed doors can be as decisively vital as open ones, and at this distance I have gratitude for both.

To my farm family who guaranteed my survival: you gave me life and all else I needed. I am grateful to and honor you who rocked me, fed me, held my hand for my first steps, and loved me through the challenging and fun times we shared. Most of you are fast asleep beneath the land you loved, yet I feel your presence in my life and hope that in the world of souls, you hear my gratitude. To you Mother, who left us much too early: your prayers have carried me my whole life through.

A special thanks to my sister Helen, and brother Phil, who during my writing of this book, have shared their recalls from the farm days, when Mr. North Wind tossed us about and ruled the prairie.

To one of the great teachers of my life, my eleventh grade teacher, Jean Solomon Moreau, who had a special love for me, and sent me home with the works of Shakespeare, science fiction and more. If you had not extended your heart to me, all would be different.

And to our soulful community of Fresno friends, thank you! You've heard and read a few of my stories, and like my family, have encouraged me to quicken my ink. A special thank you, Bruce Graves, for your continual interest and questions about how my book was coming along. And to Paula Costis, for your appreciation of my writings.

A special shout, more a hallelujah, to Esalen Institute, my sacred retreat for the past twenty-four years. My soul has been so enriched by your beauty, and your wise teachers and seminarians from around the world. I've nothing much to say about you, so don't get me started.

And finally to our grandchildren, in the spring of life, 2016: Somerset, now twelve, Oliver, two and a half, and our latest love, Lillian Skye, now six months and looking for legs. Each of you inspire and give us, give me, hope for the future of our planet. The holy moments we've shared, on the floor, crawling about, watching those first early movements forward into life, hearing your first sounds. Standing with you Somerset and Oliver, eyes closed, under our peach tree, listening to the thrumming bees work the blossoms. Such moments capture much of the relationship we elders have been honored to share with each of you.

In moments when I doubt the sanctity of life, all I have to do is walk or crawl about with any of you, and then I KNOW. Your lives lodge in our hearts as sacred scripture, and you are the fountainhead of all that was, all that is to come from your generation around our planet. May my day and night time prayers follow you as the prayers of my dying mother have followed me.

Somerset, Oliver and Lily: I bequeath to you, this late harvest of leaves, the memories of my childhood, hoping you'll feel delight and warmth as you think of your grandpa Al and what it was like to grow up wild on our far off, frozen farm, and to bring the harvest in.

Overview and Introduction

We shall not cease from exploration
And the end of all our exploring
Will be to arrive where we first started,
And know the place for the first time.

T. S. ELIOT

The way begins in the children's land, at a time when rational present day consciousness was not yet separated from the historical psyche, the collective unconscious.......life has grown cramped, crying out for the rediscovery of the fountainhead. But the fountainhead can only be found if the conscious mind will suffer itself to be led back to the "children's land," there to receive guidance from the unconscious as before. To remain a child too long is childish, but it is just as childish to move away and then assume that childhood no longer exists because we do not see it.

CARL JUNG: *INDIVIDUAL DREAM SYMBOLISM IN RELATION TO ALCHEMY.*

EACH OF US is a walking web of memories that make us who we are. Every day, like the spider herself, we catch some memories, carefully binding them for future feeding. Dreamy memories from childhood are the center of our web, and around these we weave ourselves.

As we move through the world we discard clothing, books, furniture, homes and cars, yet our memories remain, some precious, some horrific. If by accident or age we lose our memories, we are adrift in the world, uncertain about who or where we are, as lost as the spider without her web.

From the millions of moments that flow around and through us, only a few are captured, and these both nourish and impede our journey across time and space. We choose to remember some experiences, while others leave their marks without our choosing. Our cells, our faithful memory cells, apart from our willing it, insist on recording key moments of life. Memories show their faces in odd moments in the busy day and still of night.

For me: sweating at the gym, I take a drink of cold water and hear my father's voice: *sweaty horses won't drink 'til they cool down*. I see him and his horses, plodding in from plowing the east field. I put down my bottle, and decide to drink later.

We might wish to be something, someone other than who we are, to shake loose painful memories and bad habits, and start anew. We can do this with some success; however there is a boundary beyond which we cannot go, the ground of our being, cradled surely in childhood, secreted in our essence. Our long-term memories are a curse and a blessing.

This is our human story: we fall into the world soft and innocent, defenseless against the tides of life, and like it or not, we are soaked to our marrow by early caregivers. At birth our senses are open and primed for filling: our skin craves gentle touching, we thirst for mother's milk; sounds fill us, and our oceanic eyes seek comforting faces as we record inner maps of the startling world in which we find ourselves.

These eyes I peer into, can I trust them? Will they protect and ensure my survival? These are the unformed questions that sleep behind the eyes of every child.

Our first years in this surprising world form cellular memories, the infrastructure of soul and sinew, the foundation for the remainder of our days. Little of this is conscious, for we lack reflective minds until later in life, and try as we might, we can catch only glimpses of our early years.

The first few years of childhood are the best kept secret of all, for those millions of moments are rooted in our cells and beyond our knowing. Most of us have little recall before age three, and even though that time is marrowed in us, we cannot consciously summon it for inspection.

> *Through the unknown, unremembered gate*
> *When the last of earth left to discover*
> *Is that which was the beginning;*
> *At the source of the longest river*
> *The voice of the hidden waterfall*
> *And the children in the apple tree.*

T.S. ELIOT

We are pregnant with time: the past, present and imagined future stir within. If we think we finally know who we are, it is merely hubris, for are we not routinely surprised by ourselves and others? In odd moments we say and do things that are *out of character* and may shock ourselves more than anyone. We learn a friend has done something remarkable or tragic, and we are surprised and wonder how this could have happened.

Or perhaps we fall into envy, wishing to be like this or that person, yet we are bound tightly, held fast in the web of memory. We think of those few who appear to transcend constrictions and old habits as enlightened beings, and we stand in awe of them.

Memories and our sense of self are so vital we want to preserve them for those who follow, imprinting ourselves on rocks, in cave paintings, pyramids, monuments, music, photographs, diaries and books: *I was here! I passed this way and made my mark! Here I was birthed, here I lived and died. Remember us, remember me!* Who among us wants to disappear and be forever unremembered?

Our memory webs are more than personal, for we also like to know about the collective history of our family, our tribe and our species. Who are we and what does it mean to be us? How did my family get to be my family? These are the deep questions that haunt us and enliven our curiosity.

Seeking answers we look back thousands of years, puzzling over the mountain of memories of our shared history. When, in the mists of time, the historical trail disappears, we use our keenest intuition, constructing fantastic creation stories, involving gods and goddesses, imagining they breathed life into us.

Then, a moment ago in history, out of our curiosity, we birthed science as a way of discovering the longer roots of who we are. Science with its fidelity to material facts gave us a new creation story, as awe-full in its own way as the old creation stories. Unlike the religious creation stories, those of science evolve rapidly, challenging old beliefs, tempting us to stretch into something new.

Science tells us our cosmos was born in a giant explosion 13.8 billion years ago, insisting we originated from the dust of exploding stars, ejected long before we had memories, before we had history. Can we believe this? We are thinking, feeling stardust! Our mother is the cosmos, with an infinite womb, and every day she is birthing new life in us as cells die and are reborn, and in vast explosions light years away.

Our short and long history is easily distorted by the ways we embellish life events. However within us, apart from the whims of memory, we have astonishing librarians who fastidiously record and file detailed information for the long haul. We know now, that our DNA is a massive, permanent inventory of our past. Only now are we learning how to read ourselves and our journey, and like so many recent discoveries this one sets the apples rolling in the street.

Our ancient, inner manuscripts point to Africa as our first family, and from there we crossed land and sea. For reasons unknown, the stardust that fell over Africa, grew first legs, learned to feel and ponder.

The infinite scope of the scientific story can overwhelm, even numb us. The brilliance of our scientists and the light they shine on things, can blind us as much as the heavenly light blinded the old keepers of the faith. The web of life reaches from the heart of the atom out to the edges of space. Paradoxically, the scope of scientific accounts rivals those of religion, and for some makes it easier to fall back on faith and accept the older stories.

I doubted God: then I read about the big bang, and because explosions scare me, I ran back into the arms of God. Is not this the experience some of us have on the cusp of exponential science?

We've seen the pictures. We know our world is round. But what of it? The everyday earth on which we walk is flat, and that is that. Mountains are real because our everyday earth is flat. In the same way, our sweeping religious and scientific stories exist as background information, parked there for access, yet not always consulted or cherished. The realities of everyday life claim us: getting on and off the freeway, going to work, paying our bills, tending our families. And let's not forget to pay our taxes.

At some point in life, and in odd moments, we become dreamy, and wonder about the big picture of things. We become curious about the early days of our parents or grandparents. We look at old pictures, talk to relatives, or make a trip down memory lane to the place where we were born, pushing our hands into the earth, engaging in a personal archaeological dig, connecting the bones of memory to feel the skeleton of our lives.

And that is our journey here.

In what follows, I revisit my childhood, probing back into the mystery of my beginnings, wanting to make sense of the pieces, and so to understand who I am, and hopefully to shed light on the larger mystery of what it means to be human. Against all odds, each of us is unique, and simultaneously we have common souls, so each life sheds light on the whole. Every personal web is tied surely to the larger web of humanity and all life. The great tree of life excludes no one.

Wanting to be as accurate as possible with my story, I've consulted my father's diary, and a few kept letters from other family members, in addition to my own memories. My brother Bob, (sixteen years my senior) and my sister Jean, (fourteen years older) left memory traces in letters and stories passed down the line. My sister Helen and my brother Phil, both closer to me in age, have generously shared their memories, as have my nieces and nephews. I share some of their memories in the path that lies ahead.

I also write about the family pictures and other memorabilia I've packed around, from my first roots on the prairies of Manitoba, to my college days in Missouri and Nebraska, then finally westward to California in 1968.

Most days I have minimal awareness of the childhood objects with which I've surrounded myself in our current home. In writing about them, turning them over in my hand, in a few cases I've used a magnifying glass, hoping to find secrets hidden behind the surface of things. I fall back in time. With tender, nostalgic hands I handle my grandfather's powder horn, used during his hunting days. *Grandpa! Will I be lucky enough to find one of your fingerprints?* I peer through my magnifying glass back a hundred some years, and sniff for the last grains of powder. I see him crouched in snowy woods, blue eyes sighting along his rifle. Then the exploding silence, the quivering trees, as he fires a deadly shot.

My hope is that as you read my story you might reflect more on your childhood, noticing how it has shaped you. I hope too that, like me, you end up feeling more complete and integrated and have more gratitude for your early days.

From 2012 to 2016, as I've dug into my past in writing this book, images and emotions from the *old days* have re-birthed and enlivened me in the present. More than ever I've embraced my childhood in a conscious, more clear and reflective way, wanting to understand and honor the good and bad times we shared in our family.

I've laughed and wept in the writing, often with the recurring image of standing with my arms open to more fully embrace the shared times growing up on the cold prairies of Manitoba in the 1940's and 50's, carried along by my family and the north wind.

With my daytime writing, and awake at night, through the magic of memory I've flown back in time, letting images and emotions cascade through me. New reflections, insights and meanings have emerged. While writing my story, I've relived those days, and in certain ways have reformatted myself and our whole family, as images of the past have quickened in me, accompanied by moments of new insight. I've come to a deeper understanding of my family, of who I am, and of the flood of emotions that whisper though me. I am more aware of how similar I am to others in my family, and how each of us is unique.

Along with the new insights, I now have more appreciation and compassion for our family and all we endured during those frigid prairie years. Again, I hope everyone who revisits their childhood might experience the same. More than ever I know that each life is precious, is bequeathed to us for one blink in time.

As we go along, I share my awareness of the mental, emotional and spiritual features of our farm family, and the contrasts between it and our current family in California. Our farm family was tough, hard-working, tight-lipped, and our emotions like the land itself, were often chilled and silenced. Our present family has more sun and warmth—like California itself. Cold weather and snow was a preoccupation for dwellers on the prairies, just as warm breezes and the surf enchant Californians. Every family, each person, is stamped by a shared era and place.

For me, blowing the prairie snow off my memories of childhood is not about being stuck in the past. My extensive revisiting and writing about my birth family has added vitality to my present life, and I hope others will also have this experience. I believe it is possible for most of us—with exceptions for those with tragic childhoods—to think of our first family with kindness, knowing that each of us did the best we could, sometimes under terrible circumstances. Like us, our parents, siblings and other family members carried their own childhood scars. Unhealed scars are a primary source of the cruelty we perpetuate in families and the larger world.

I think again of Carl Jung, who has been a major influence in my life. Continuing with his quote at the beginning of this chapter, he goes on to say:

It is of course impossible to free oneself of one's childhood without devoting a great deal of work to it, as Freud's researches have long since shown. Nor can it be achieved through intellectual knowledge only; what is alone effective is a remembering that is also a re-experiencing. ....when, in later years, we return to the memories of childhood we find bits of our personality still alive, which cling round us and suffuse us with the feeling of earlier times.

As we gather up the threads of childhood we can reweave our lives in ways that work better for us. Recalling our inevitable wounds along with the good times, we can evoke the Buddhist practice of honest awakening to what lies within: we can step back, and as we detach we can have more compassion for ourselves, and thus for others. As we heal, we can heal others. Time, distance and wisdom can clear our eyes.

Based on my readings and therapeutic training, and on shared conversations with loved ones, reinforced by my own discoveries in therapy, reviewing and reclaiming our childhoods can help us transcend the hatred, anger, wars and greed that blight our human tribe. As we revisit our souls and heal ourselves we can tenderize our relationships, and extend our love into the world. The wisdom path is to tenderize, not pulverize.

The four years of writing my memoirs has been a Holy Grail quest for me, with the emotions that come with such a pursuit. At times I've lost the trail and given up hope. My mission has wakened me in the night, charging me with early morning chatter. Even when I've talked too long, my wife has been her loving, patient and curious self, supporting and encouraging me. She has slogged along my trail of words, palpitated dying paragraphs, camped out and warmed me.

I've drawn inspiration from my daughter, Heather and my son Todd, and how they've manifested in the world through their writings. I've also been uplifted by our three magical loves and fellow travelers, our grandchildren. With the rest of our family, we've watched the emergence of Somerset and Oliver (ages twelve and two-and-a-half in the spring of 2016) eagerly following open arms into the future. And half a year ago, yet another precious one has graced us, Lillian Skye, now learning to squiggle and coo into the forward reaches of her immense journey.

One of the great gifts children give us is that they allow us to review who we were before we had conscious memories. As we watch our children and grandchildren with all their firsts, we might hear forgotten voices dancing on the surface of memory: *Ah, this is the way it was for me! This is where I started, this the path I followed, these the sounds I made. This is how I learned to move, to get going, to launch myself into the world.* We see too, how much attention, love and help was extended for our survival and learning.

As we embrace our own childhoods, we can see in a new way how we arrived at this moment. Because of my interest in this process, I've written bits and pieces about our grandchildren as they've stretched into the world, putting this in a file for their future reference. Thank you Somerset, Oliver and Lillian for BEING, and for reminding us of who we were!

In addition to the more pervasive and unconscious impact of childhood, every few days I have recurring and precise incidents that fling open a sudden door to our prairie family. If I'm planning my calendar near the end of the month and am uncertain how many days there are in the month, I repeat the refrain our father taught us: *Thirty days hath September, April, June and November, and all the rest have 31, except February, coming once in four when it has one day more.* As I hear these words, I see my father's face and hear his voice as he shoves wood into our kitchen stove. *Thank you Dad for lighting our fires, for warming us.*

Occasionally I find my hand in my pocket, jingling coins around, and I remember our dirt farming days when many of us walked around with a handful of change in our pockets. As we talked with someone we might have a hand clinking our coins, making music in the secrecy of our pocket, as if to say, *Hey, I've got money. How 'bout you?* We didn't speak those words, but as I look back I think of it as our way of establishing status, of announcing we were not at the bottom of the pecking order, that we were someone to be reckoned with. Even small farmers want to announce their place in the order of things, and jingling coins can do the trick.

When I laugh deeply, I might slap my knee and have tears running down my cheeks, behaviors I trace to Grandpa Todd—the only grandparent alive when I was born. He'd sit on our north porch and offer us a nickel for every little pig we caught by the tail. We were fast little kids and so were the pigs, and it was preposterous fun for everyone, and Grandpa would snatch the pipe from his mouth and collapse with laughter, slapping his knee as tears flowed down his cheeks.

Often when I shave I think of our Dad and his article of faith that hot water was needed to soften a beard, and a blade baptized in hot water made a cleaner cut. He used a straight edge and often nicked his face and neck, and he'd dab these with a bit of cloth. Every few weeks, he'd ask us to shave the back of his neck; it had sun-darkened furrows nearly as big as our Riding Mountains, and I'd have to stretch them with my fingers to shave the valleys. Nostalgia grips me as vivid memories arise and I touch his neck: I wish I could have told him I loved him. We, I knew love, yes, but the words never fell from our lips.

Apples might fall in Eden, but words of love cling past season to our hoarding trees.

Our land was cold, farming was tough, and we slogged along with little time for sweetness. The loss of a mother cuts deeper than the north wind.

One of my most poignant memories is triggered when I smell flowers: I go back to the suffocating smell of flowers in our home during the funeral service for our mother, when I was eight. If I slow down and tune in enough, I can feel a ghostly lump forming in my throat, and an April thawing of frozen grief. The saddest chapter in my book talks about the cold secrecy surrounding her suffering and death, and the profound, life-altering stigmata driven into our souls.

Along with all their other chores, my grandfather and father both kept bees, and again this morning a warm memory arises, as I eat my toast and honey: I hear my father, encouraging us to eat every drop: *that last drop was a life time of work for one of our bees.* I peer into the last residue of golden honey on my plate, taking the last bit of toast, wiping my plate clean, honoring my father and the bees. As I do this, I might think of a more ancient father, Moses, and one of the commandments given to him, about honoring our parents. We heard that verse read many times in our home.

With my emotions of sadness and sweetness, my childhood memories often come with feelings of love and gratitude for each person. They appear in my inner movie, sharply etched, and as I look at their faces, they are born again in my present life. Are we not, each of us, indwelt by the faces and voices of others, however dimly felt? Some of my memories of loved ones are so clear it seems they live independently as renters in my inner house. In the attic of imagination, I hear their voices, and in odd moments have silent, imagined conversations with them. I get along well with all but the rowdy ones, yet keep extending their leases.

Some of my inner boarders arouse emotions of grief, rejection and abuse, and anger arises in me. I make a fist, I want to strike back. Then I return to what I've learned from my Christian and Buddhist teachings, imagining I'm them, scanning deeply to sense the suffering that caused them to strike out against others. When I do this, I can feel love and compassion for them and for the times I've angrily wanted to boot them into a dark alley.

Wise masters and teachers, past and present, tell us that to be whole we must embrace all of ourselves, all the darkness and light within our hearts. As we recall our childhoods, we have the choice to do this. There are parts of my childhood I'd rather gloss over and forget, especially when I write of our mother's suffering and death, and of her wee ones abandoned to time. Reviewing the details of her last years in the letters left by older family members has yielded a harvest of soft sadness, enabling me to shed hoarded tears.

I've experienced what many have when we let ourselves open to all our feelings: we can heal and open new doors of vitality in our lives. Out of darkest night, when the light comes, a springtime surge of compassion takes root and blossoms up.

While my diving into my past, in therapy and in my writing, has been marked with some anger, sadness and regret, mainly I view the past with wonder, astonishment, reverence and awe. I have the same feelings when I think of my college days and the other stages of my life up to the present time—something I experience every day as 4300 some photos dating back to the late 1950's roll across my computer screen.

When I see the pictures in my mind and those on my computer, a tsunami of emotions rolls through me: *I... we lived those days! I loved those people, and they loved me! We did those things! Look at how dark and thick our hair was! Look at us! Our clear skin and innocent faces! Look at us! There is the beach we walked with our children, and there the place we flew our kites! And there, on Vancouver Island, our favorite camping spot and our old blue tent!*

Is it not true that when we go back in time, along with everything else is the sometime wish that we could live those times over, knowing we could have loved more? In the night hours, do we not all know the feeling of wanting to re-wind the clock, to bring the past back, to embrace it more fully, to feel more love for each moment? We brace useless legs against the closing door of time. We make our pledges: *Lord, please let me do it all over again, and I will do it better. I promise! I will love and laugh more and complain less, if you just let me drink it all again.* Is this this not one of our un-cried universal thirsts?

Again, it is not a question of staying stuck in the past, for this can be as restricting as any of the many traps we create for ourselves. For me it is a matter of choice: living fully in the present is the wisest thing we can do, and if we can enhance our aliveness, our awareness of this moment, by revisiting the past, then let us turn back the hours.

Another clear image arises: Our kitchen clock has stopped and is showing the wrong time. To reset it, our father is standing on his chair forcing the clock hands backwards. I can hear the gears complaining, for like all clocks, it wants to go forward. Dad gets the hands set just right, then begins rewinding the spring that makes it run. Finally, with weathered hands he nudges the pendulum, and the clock begins its familiar tick, tocking, tick, tocking.

Resetting the clock: if we are feeling *out of sync* we can go back to childhood and re-imagine it, even do a reset. We can reach up and go back in time. We can gain new insights, and weave better stories about what happened to us. This has been my experience in writing my book, and I hope the same for you the reader. If we choose to feel love and gratitude for those who gave us life and enabled us to survive, we energize the present moment.

Finally, a few comments about my perspective and core assumptions in what follows.

My intense personal interest in people and what it means to be human began at an early age, and this led me to become a professional people person—a professor of social psychology and a counselor/therapist. I've made others and myself primary objects of inquiry. The more I know about humans, the more I see that two words are vital in describing who we are, and they color what follows. The first word is complexity, and the second is connectivity, and these are two sides of the same coin.

Complexity and connectivity not only apply to us as human animals. They apply to the larger web of life, to the atom and the cosmos, for at both these levels there is complexity and connectivity.

What I have read in science and selected spiritual traditions underscores the importance of complexity and connectivity in life. As science advances, the boundaries between disciplines have softened, for we see the connections between the atom, the cosmos, the cells in our body and all else. (I've attached as an appendix my brief essay that attempts to reconcile religion and science, entitled *The Last Perilous Particle.*)

Beginning in March of 1993, when my friend Trish gave me a book on Tibetan Buddhism, I've been fascinated by their wisdom, and married it with my Christian beliefs. One Buddhist teaching says that as we develop a more keen awareness, we see that everything has multiple causes and is connected to the entire web of life, both inward and outward. I revere this wisdom, and the more I contemplate life, the more I see that complexity and connectivity infuse every moment of our personal biographies and our collective history. Indeed, as we probe into life, we see every moment of life is impacted by many forces at once.

In the press of busy days, we take much for granted and surprise ourselves in moments when we question the familiar. Complexity resides in and all around us, and here I cite only one example from my childhood, involving a math riddle, given to us by our father. Every year or so, on a cold winter evening, he'd warm up the riddle and we'd have another go at it, to see if we might find different answers.

Here is the riddle: *If the third of six were 3, what would the fourth of twenty be?* I recall my fascination with the puzzle and how it turned mathematical assumptions upside down, asking me to see things in a new way. I had equal wonderment that Dad, Phil and I each solved the riddle in a different way, ending up with the same answer.

Just as interesting was that we could not be certain our answers were correct, and this left the riddle as open as the prairies, with cow-paths of inquiry leading in all directions. The fact we could not know for sure, opened the door of complexity. I realized that sometimes there are no final answers to things, and that this is just fine, and can even be fun. At the time I was not as aware of how much I was learning beyond the riddle—the lessons about complexity, and the open-ended nature of life. I've long thought of myself as a mystic, and for me that means that life is mysterious and replete with surprises, puzzles and unknowns.

These days I can also see the riddle encouraged me to question the *givens* of life, the things that are seen as bedrock beliefs, and along with this it showed me there were different ways to find the truth of anything. As part of the complexity of this example, I believe these traits may have been alive in me, and the number riddle was a catalyst that called them forth, opening a gate through which I could sense my way more deeply into my life, all of life.

A part of complexity is to note that some generalities are well supported by scientific research. For example, children who are abused early in life usually have more struggles and suffering in life, while those with stable, loving homes have an easier time of it. This is clearly manifest in the radiance of our three grandchildren, who are surrounded with predictable and unconditional love.

When we engage in complex thinking, we note that to some degree every child has a unique environment, even within the same family. Each family shares a common history, and each child in that family also shares a special place, and that is demonstrated in the research on the importance of birth order and how that stamps us. Childhood has universal elements that are similar for all of us. Some of us focus on how unique our childhood was, while others of us look at the common features shared by all children. Each of us lives along this continuum between uniqueness and commonality.

Connectivity is also a deep feature of the web of life. Philosophers and poets have reminded us that none of us are islands, that we are all interconnected in our history, and science now confirms this. We easily forget that we are one big family and share a common history, and to know the history of one of us helps us understand the history of everyone. Most of us have DNA inherited from many different peoples, tribes, races. My curiosity about this led me to order a DNA test in 2012, and it showed forty some countries where my ancestors had lived across thousands of years.

We see complexity and connectivity at work in the field of epigenetics, where we've seen we can no longer frame the debate between nature and nurture as either-or, for our genes (nature) are continually modified by the impact of our environment (nurture). Nature and nurture are an old married couple and have never lived apart or been divorced, despite our compulsive attempts to see them as disconnected. Even before we are born, the emotions and behaviors of our mothers are impacting our genes. The web of relationships that surround a mother, continuously modify her bio-chemicals, and her electrical fields, and these impact the child forming in her womb. Potentially, every experience we have, however small, alters us in some way, for that is how implicated we are in the web of being.

We've recently discovered that each of us have trillions of microbes that inhabit us, both on us and in us. These microscopic hitchhikers alter how we feel, think and act, all unconsciously. Not only are we not islands, each of us is a walking planetary system, teeming with life, much yet undiscovered. In the Everest of eyelash, little ones struggle for life.

We also see both complexity and connectivity in the science of microchimerism. We've discovered the placenta is permeable, and cells from the developing child can pass into the mother and vice versa. Our emotional memories of mother run deep enough. Now we learn that some of her cells are in us, just as ours are in her. This means too, that each of us likely carry cells from our older brothers and sisters, and these cells can impact us in both positive and negative ways, depending on where they reside in our bodies and other subtle factors. Given that cells from other family members dwell within, we can now see that the word *family* is not limited to the emotional and spiritual ties that bind us. Blood is thicker than water, yes, and this river of life ties us to distant ancestors.

The claim we've made, especially as men, that each of us is a *self-made man*, is preposterous in the face of recent discoveries. We truly might feel like an island, might feel isolated and cut off from others, but that is not factually true. We are each a bud on the ancient tree of life, embedded profoundly at the cellular, emotional, mental and spiritual ways at levels of complexity beyond comprehension. Our roots are ancient, and we are crafted by them, and in our night dreams they show surprising faces and voices.

The deeper we probe into life, the more we see that connectivity and complexity are the new pillars supporting the temple of life. Like it or not, we are sisters and brothers in a sprawling, sometimes rowdy family nearing eight billion in number. The air, waters and food of mother earth are continually flowing through us, along with much else below the level of awareness, including the gravitational and electromagnetic fields around and within us.

In only eight minutes, from 93 million miles away, the light photons from our sun arrive, energizing our entire planet, creating the life around us, filling our eyes with the forms and colors of all we see. The brain neurons that fire these words, and yours as you read my words, are charged by nothing less than solar energy. It takes more than a village to raise a child; it takes a cosmos. Each of us is a walking, breathing solar panel. (See my appendix: *Life, Light and Longing*, where I offer more details on this.)

Because of my experience of complexity and connectivity, as I've written this book I've come to see it is *our* book, a book about our farm family, and also in general ways, a book about every human. My brother Phil and I (he is the younger by 21 months) were truly two-peas-in-a-pod, inseparable until our college years, and as I write I often use *we* or *our,* rather than me or mine, and sometimes this includes our sister Helen, 19 months my senior.

Given that I carry cells from my mother, two older brothers and two older sisters, in imaginative moments I sometimes think my voice is a conduit for them. Our genes, our cells, especially the neurons in our brains, are loaded with information that impacts us in complex ways, influencing our emotions, thoughts and behaviors.

From this view none of us speak with only one voice, none of us are cut off from those who've come before. We not only stand on the shoulders of others: verily, they are in us, at the ground of our beings wanting to be heard, reaching out, speaking, dancing, chanting through us.

I'm reminded of a story told by my favorite Buddhist teacher, Jack Kornfield, who asked several writers where their words came from, and received a variety of responses. He concluded that none of us write our own material. As I've written this book, I'm puzzled at times where certain phrases come from, why they leap up unbidden, why certain thoughts wake me at night, insisting they are family and belong in *our* book. What pregnant ancestral voices cry to be heard? Our grandparents live surely within, and plead for resurrection and remembrance. I say, let them speak.

As much as I can I want to surrender to the grand host of ancestors, and to imagine I might be giving them utterance. I am only me, one small life, carried along in the great river of life. *Mother! Is that you who whispers here?*

I have moments when I believe I've walked around in, have been led and protected, by the prayers of my dying mother. I can doubt the efficacy of my own prayers, but keep the faith that the prayers of dying mothers fly surely into the bosom of the Divine One.

As I share my life, I hope you the reader feel gratitude for and see more clearly the complex connections that make up the gift of your life.

CHAPTER 1

———— ✑ ————

Return

Every one hundred years, as the story goes, the village of Brigadoon rises out of the Highland mists of Scotland, magically appearing for only one day. The story captures the way memories of childhood appear and disappear. If we want, we can call these memories to life, seeing again the mix of love and loss. Other memories have a life of their own, and in surprising moments, without our choosing, our past asserts itself, calling to us, reminding us: we see faces and hear the voices of ones long gone, we walk again the streets of our hometown, or reseed the plowed field that birthed us.

Sensing our way back to the fountainhead of our lives, retracing the shadows and lights of the great river that has carried us from highlands to lowlands, from aeries to valleys, can help us discover who we most are and how we've assembled ourselves over time. me.

Behold a sacred voice is calling you; all over the sky a sacred voice is calling.

Black Elk, *Oglala Sioux healer and visionary*

✑

Summer 2002

Thankfully, some things remain: the noontime sun, the reach of prairie horizon, the touchable sky, the hawk on high.

Under hearkening heavens, barely casting shadows, we stand upon the empty land. The north wind is as I remember it, is as restless as ever.

After long years I've returned with my son, Todd, and our good friend Kenny. I'm pointing a doubting finger into the wind, wanting to re-materialize a vanished town. Tentatively, barely believing myself, I wave an arm, gesturing to where the church was, then west to where the one room school house defied the winter blizzards.

The echo of children's voices, my playmates' and my own, ride the wind that blows through me. Across the decades and many miles, I've carried worn images of this place of first-beginnings, and I can see faces of those who knew this place as home. I slouch southward, gesturing to where the grain elevator, like a great buffalo, once heaved up into the blue. It was bold red in color and taller than the frost-crippled trees, and marked our town from miles away, serving as a lighthouse when blizzards cloaked everything in white. I hear our John Deere tractor, laboring as it pulls a load of prairie wheat up the ramp, into the dark interior. I'm surprised at how slim I am at twelve, and I smile remembering that at that age, I'd been driving our proud machine for over a year.

With our neighbors, we had muscled our way unto this land, yet forces bigger than us have wiped this space clean: time, gravity, winter blizzards and massive thunderstorms have reclaimed this part of the prairie, and I think they'll never give it back.

We believed the land was ours, but it was not. We plowed our sweat, blood and soul into the soil, claiming it as our own. We cast eyes heavenward, wanting to claim the sky and tame the weather. The time on our farm, like the prairie skies and horizons, seemed endless. The dreamtime of childhood, with its narrow borders, is like that. Our sacred plot of land with its clutch of buildings was the orb of life, and until late childhood, was all we knew.

Growing up on the farm we thought the cows would always come in for milking and the land would always be there for plowing. Our winters were as long as the prairies and we struggled through them one moment at a time, hoping spring would come, then summer, then bracing against late autumn that would usher in another bitter winter. We worked the fields, first with horses, then tractors, and the smell of freshly plowed sod, turned over and back again. The forever furrows: we assumed they were bigger than time, as we turned them over from season to season.

Now, standing under August skies with Todd and Kenny, I wonder if it was all illusion.

We've flown here from California, returning for my high school reunion in East Kildonan, a suburb of Winnipeg. In our rented car, we drove west, back in time, passing through Portage La Prairie, then Neepawa, then north like the geese of spring, winging it past the enduring towns of Eden, Birnie and Kelwood, Rising nostalgia claims me as we arrive at the intersection of decaying time where highway five meets the dirt road east to vanished Norgate.

Here we lived, worked, played and died, and now all is gone, gone. Everything gone except the land and the north wind. Gone are the trees that tried to buffer our one-room school house from the howling wolf winds. They bluffed and lost.

We are ghost chasers. We stand in the prairie wind, gazing into forlorn space. Under the noon sun, the three of us cast four shadows—one belonging to a cairn that marks the place. It stands as the latest native son, nearly as tall as we are. Still numb from winter, it's not talking. In silent reverie, we read the words from the brass plaque: *This cairn is dedicated to the memory of the village of Norgate, the church, the school and in memory of all the pioneers of the district. Also all the boys who left our community to serve in the two world wars, and in special memory of the ones who never returned. 1895-1971.* Then follows the birth date, the day the cairn was rooted to the sod: *July 27, 1985 AD.* I'm happy they put *AD* on the plaque, as that helps me anchor my spinning sense of time.

I'm pleased we remember those who die in war. I think of my older brother Bobby who returned from his time in the Royal Canadian Air Force, and then sadly of our neighbor lad, Alvin Jackson, who died trapped in a spiraling bomber. I feel upwelling tears, and the north wind helps me choke them down. I look west to the stable hills, the hills that captured our eyes and lifted us up in bygone days, calling me once again.

Our town is gone, but the map-makers don't know it, for it shows up on every map I've checked since leaving our farm in 1956. I was seventeen, with my life like a field of wheat stretching before me. I carried a bushel of guilt about leaving Dad and Phil with the work. The day I left for winsome Winnipeg, I heaved tears of sadness and remorse, then hiked a mile to the bus and my vast, unknown life before me.

Once gone I replaced our barns with books. When I browse bookstores, I check the latest atlas, hoping our town still appears, praying we are not stricken from official existence. Am I not like most of us in wanting our time and place to be remembered? I feverishly scan the latest map, finding Manitoba, then Winnipeg, then my eye flies west to Neepawa, then north one blink to Norgate. And there it is—still there, still there. A quiet voice echoes from holy roller church days: *Praise the Lord, Amen! Praise the Lord, hallelujah! The map makers of the world remember!*

Todd has pulled himself up to sit on the cairn, and I wrap an arm around his leg for another picture. I'm resigned to the fact that the church, the school, the elevator, the grocery store and post office are gone, but find it hard to believe the railroad tracks are also gone. Wooden buildings might crumble or blow away, but iron tracks strong enough to bear our shrieking steam engines—how could they vanish? Gone with them the gravel mound that held the rails above the land. I need something to hold onto, something real from that time so I can believe the wispy stories I weave for Todd and Kenny.

I'm puzzled why anyone would grade the railroad bed level with the prairie, and in a moment of whimsy wonder if it was flattened by the fierce thunderstorms and winter blizzards. The north wind, the betraying Mr. North Wind was our enemy, and we had no choice but to surrender to his power. Summer thunderstorms also humbled and devastated; they wanted their land back and righteously contested our homesteader rights.

I take inventory: the three of us are real, the cairn is solid enough, as is the sod that holds us. Something else endures; to the west are the gentle, blue hills of the Riding Mountains, and they continue to appear on all the maps, and presumably always will. Through my eyes of childhood, these were real mountains, big enough to scare me with ravines, thick forest, wild bears, moose, elk, and other real and imagined animals. These are the blue hills that daily lifted up our eyes, that enchanted us as we walked about, as we worked our fields, as we sat on our front porch. Out of the sheer flatness of prairies, the feminine curves of these hills were early loves, returning our glances, flirting with fog, rain and sun. I'm happy to share their beauty with Todd and Kenny.

We climb into our rental car, heading, finally, for the old home, the high point of our pilgrimage. We turn onto our beloved gravel ridge—the only road around that stayed dry in heavy rains. This ridge road carried several generations of us, on foot and with horse drawn sleighs, into the larger world. It stayed dry, but the north wind blew more fiercely across its face. I see myself crabbing north into the wind, with my sister Helen and my brother Phil, headed to school like prairie schooners tacking, feinting, weaving slowly forward, sometimes with frozen white spots on our cheeks.

We near the bridge and the pathetic grove of trees that hoped to shelter us. We stop and crawl under the bridge to check her timbers, deciding her legs can bear our weight, but just in case two of us walk across as the other eases the car forward, the bridge as silent as ever. I nod in passing as I see myself, decades back: wee Albert, along with Phil, lying on the bridge, peering into the little stream, working our snare wire as we tug it over the head of a guileless fish. Ah! I see the fish flashing like a mirror as we snap it into the sun.

On creeping tires we drive the dirt road through the trees, steering around the potholes—the holes my father filled with rocks the night before he died in May of 1969. As we emerge from the trees, the astonished house looks at us with dreary eyes, welcoming us, welcoming me after all the years away.

Home! Here I am, Albert, back again to see you, home from all my travels. You who sheltered us long ago, you the cradle of all we were, and are. Gratitude, sadness, loving reverence well up in me as I behold you again. HOME. *You with your crinkled eyes.* The giggles of children sound from your rooms. And then something dark: I don't want to think it, but there it is—the image of our mother suffering from cancer, embowered by you in your south bedroom, holding the silence, containing the holy space that finally launched her soul heavenward when she was forty-seven and I was eight. Your secret wood sings a song in the melancholy timbre of Mother's voice.

We park by the house, find the hibernating key under its rock, and gently open the door that has closed and opened since 1909, when our father and grandfather built our home. The old wood-burning stove is there and the old cupboard. I am waving my arm with confidence, for now I have something real to point at: *there's Dad's favorite tea cup, with all the stains!* With curious wonder we move cautiously through the house, and each discovery comes with a breath of exclamation.

When we discover some of my old clothes hanging in Phil's and my bedroom, I'm stricken again by a time-warp; I wonder if I've just gone out to get the cows and never really left. Then, in Dad's closet, a pair of shoes, some shirts and pants hanging in time, waiting his return. Fearfully, I touch his shirt to see if it's warm. My throat is full: I want to roust our family, to cry out: *Time to get up and milk the cows,* or another of Dad's rallying cries: *It's daylight in the swamps!* I remind Todd and Kenny that Dad left his home and body in spring of 1969. Yet, standing here, I can hear his voice, see the sparkle in his blue eyes.

Then reluctantly, into the dark, sacred and secretive bedroom where Mother battled her cancerous body, sheltered in silence, launching endless prayers for her children. Todd and Kenny put their arms around me as my voice breaks, and tears flow. *And over here, at the south end of our living room, is where she lay in her coffin....* I smell again, undiminished by the years and my forgetful hours, the overpowering scent of her funeral flowers that drenched the air and my shattered soul.

We take a few steps into the manly world at the foot of the stairs, as I point to the empty rifle rack where I re-dream the gleam of steel and wood of Grandpa's Winchester 45-75, our Lee Enfield, our shotguns and our .22 rifles. This time, instead of using my finger to point, I stick out my thumb, indicating the size of the bullet fired by Grandpa's rifle.

I surprise myself with a giggle as I note that the second to the bottom step was my favorite place to sit and eat bread and jam, with a glass of milk. The stairs beckon with tired arms, and we're not sure they can hold us. On tiptoes we go up one at a time, then explore each of the five tiny bedrooms. On this summer day, the breeze is gentle, yet it whistles the same tune as it did long ago around the north edge of home. I miss the lullaby of clucking hens scratching about.

In Bobby's north room, we find a few small pieces from the old Harvard airplane he bought after the war, along with bits of silver ribbon he'd toss from his plane to get Hitler looking the wrong way. And there! In the corner, covered with dust, our sled with the crooked runner. It looks eager to go, and I'm ready to fling myself onto its back.

From the large wooden box full of countless odds and ends, Todd pulls a pair of skates, waving them in the air. I know them as the hand-me-downs that carried my brothers and me through bloody hockey wars. The blades are rusty, but the yellow laces are stout as ever, and the black tape around the toe is ready to ward off the next assault by stick or puck. As we take more pictures, I feel skate blades under my feet; I'm taller, stronger, eager to hit the ice and mix it up. I crouch in position, looking as fearsome as I can, yelling at Todd and Kenny, *Okay guys, time to play hockey. See if you can get around me...!* I put a playful shoulder into Todd.

We pull out a few books from the book case, and I share memories of my favorites. The 1917 book on the sinking of the Titanic is still there, with the faded photos of that mighty vessel. I pull out the black covered book on hunting in Africa, and the brooding green book with the title, *Quo Vadis*. The title and the heft of that book spooked me. We laugh as we pull out a small copy of Shakespeare's play, *The Tempest*. On the cover, in the distressed hand writing of our brother Bill, are the words: *In case of fire throw this in!!* We agree this book must fly with us back to California.

As we descend the trembling stairs, I know our home will soon go the way of our barns, and of Norgate itself, vanishing into the soil and air. I imagine unborn grandchildren, knowing I want to pilgrimage here with them, fearful there might not be anything left to see and hold. *Who can believe this grandpa as he points his finger into thin air?*

Through the musky downstairs, we move toward the slant of light coming in the west door. We are musing about life and death as we escape into fresh air and sunlight, closing the door of memories, then putting the key to sleep under its rock.

The sound of our car engine calls me back to real time. Gravel crunches as we head north, around the curve and through the trees, easing across the bridge, driving meditatively through the airy town that was. I'm nostalgic, delighted that my son and friend have touched the life blood of clan McLeod of Norgate.

I'm honored, grateful they chose to come here on this brilliant, promised day that fills the sky and sings across the prairie.

ᑯ

Time and space, with some help from gravity, give us the stage upon which we live out our lives. Time and space are most elastic, and can be compressed down to micro-seconds and millimeters, then expanded to infinity. We mark our lives in terms of time and space, noting the dates of birth and death, and the places we've called home.

Bundled childhood with her baby horizons, and little creepings. We cling to home, fearful of strangers and open spaces. As we mature, our eyes, then our dreams reach out to real and imagined horizons. Each in our own way seeks roads that lead away from home, and today we have morning wings that let us fly to the uttermost parts of earth and sky.

Growing up I heard and read stories about the *Indians* who lived on our farm before we owned it. We played cowboys and Indians as kids, and we knew Indians were bad and wanted to kill good white people, so we wanted to kill them right back. As I grew, so did my knowledge and love of the first people who lived in our area.

Before the Europeans came, Manitoba was home to various people, mainly Ojibway, Cree, Assiniboine, and Dakota Sioux. Artifacts date them back nine thousand some years. They were descendants of the migration across the Bering land-bridge during the ice age about fifteen thousand years ago.

We had ghostly connections with them, from the arrow heads and other stone objects we found as we worked our fields and walked about. On a few occasions, Dad returned from a field, with pemmican, still in a worn leather wrap, with berries, nuts and meat inside. One of the most sacred objects from our farm, now in our Fresno home, is a hammer-stone that sleeps as a talisman under our bed. Every now and then I retrieve it, and it wakes me up with images: I see brown, caring hands forming, shaping it through sunny days, and by firelight from an unknown past that warms my mind.

About two hundred years ago, our ancestors, along with most immigrants, moved to eastern Canada, eventually moving west to homestead in the western provinces in the early and middle 1800's. Even though our farm days seemed forever, with long winters and forever horizons, only a hundred or so years later, much of the land had emptied out as the homesteaders died or moved to warmer climes, and young people fled to the cities.

Unlike our scientists and theologians, most of us don't spend much time thinking about vast time and space, yet with maturity some of us want to learn more about our roots. I have a passing interest in our family, and know the short history of clan McLeod traces to Scotland and Ireland. Some of us came from the Isle of Skye, off the west coast of Scotland, and with my romantic images of that place, I like to let people know I'm from Skye. On the golf course, as I prepare to hit one of my occasional straight drives, I often announce myself as McLeod of Skye, and my golf friends like to call me by this name. More significantly, we have a granddaughter who carries the name Lillian Skye.

Due to my interest in science, four years ago I had a DNA test to see where the McLeods lived in the expanded time frame of thousands of years. I learned that like most tribes and families, there has been much movement and intermarriage, and that clan McLeod has lived nearly everywhere. In the fifty or so countries through which we've passed, only a small portion of our genes are traced to Scotland and Ireland.

Never mind. In the face of science I still insist I am McLeod of Skye, perhaps because our clan motif is *Hold Fast*. To enhance my romantic ties to Skye, I keep a bottle of Talisker single malt, made on that fabled isle that houses Dunvegan Castle, the official home of our clan. In May of 2015, my wife and I are blessed to visit Skye, and I imbibe the fantasy that the Lord made this island from wind, rain and rocks left over from the first day of creation.

We the People: we the people of Norgate were small dirt farmers. Our farm was small, we were of modest stature, and often dirty. Small, dirty farmers. Whether we needed it or not, we bathed every month or so in a round galvanized tub, with water heated on our wood burning stove. Work clothes? Why wash them when they'll be dirty in a few hours? We had no telephone, no running water, no electricity, no TV, no refrigerators. We were our own distractions, and did a fair job of it.

With a mix of pride and lamentation, we often said we were surrounded by miles and miles of nothing but miles and miles. Poor we were, yet rich with clear air, northern lights, wild wind, bright stars, sweaty work and sweet sleep. Our lullabies: the cries of wolves and coyotes, the lowing of cows, the honking of migrating, wild geese.

We farmed with horses. Then in the mid 1940's, Dad made the scary leap to a green and yellow John Deere tractor, the pride of our family. Once he got over his anger with the stubborn gear shift, he'd return aglow from the field: *Heck, I can plow the east field in half the time I did with horses. Praise the Lord.* Before us our grandparents either *hooved* to town or used their horses to get around, until cars rattled into our lives, beginning in the 1930's.

Then came the magnificent flying machines, birthed in distant clouds, shredding the silence of the skies, alerting us with their distant droning and yammering pistons. Most crafts were military: young, gallant men, hunting Hitler, plotting their paths by stars and sunlight. Little me: I'd flee the house as I heard their first notes, and stand reverentially, awestruck, saluting as they passed. Our older brother Bob joined the mayhem of sky in 1942, as a navigator for the Royal Canadian Air Force. *The best darn air force in the world.* Bobby. Our brave brother. He'd find Hitler and bomb him good. That we could count on.

For we earth-bound younger ones, walking a mile to the Norgate School, store and post-office was a routine trip. If the snow was not too deep we'd cut across the fields to save time. Soon we wanted to head south five miles to Kelwood, then north eight miles to McCreary. Eventually I learned of the big town of Neepawa, home to a few thousand folks. We'd climb in our old Chevy and amidst an impressive cloud of dust, drive the thirty miles south. If the road was muddy, we might get stuck a few miles from home, and we young ones ended up in tears. Neepawa! Neepawa was our mythic city on a hill, for many of our clan, myself included, were born there in the brown brick two story hospital. Neepawa: city of life and death. There, in the arms of mother earth, rest the sacred bones of a few grandparents, along with our mother, father and brother Bill.

Still later, ninety miles away, even more mythical was the bigger city, Brandon. It led me to think less of Neepawa. Some of our first visits there, when I was six and seven, were saturated with sadness, for we were taking Mother to the hospital as she battled the monster cancer.

All the while, I heard rumors of our provincial crown, the city of Winnipeg, four hours away by car or train. Winnipeg. *The Peg:* Only big people ever went there, and their stories fired my imagination. I was about eleven when I first encountered that galaxy of swirling stars and flashing lights, and ever since I've been a lover of cities (and have been fortunate to visit many of the world's greatest). The road to Winnipeg was our escape route off the farm, and the roads from there led our family all over the continent, and as we grew collective wings, to other continents.

In the front of my Scofield Bible I've recorded every home and apartment I've lived in since leaving the farm in 1956. I tug it from the bookcase and am surprised: I've lived in 27 different places, with various friends and family members.

In what follows I go back in time, brushing the snow off the early days of our family and community of farmers. And for you the reader, this is your story too, for around our planet we share the same legs of childhood, the same big eyes, tentative stammers, the falling down and getting up. You may have taken your first steps on city streets. No matter. We started the same way, with lots of help along the way.

‰

CHAPTER 2

Nine Months of Winter

Hast thou entered into the treasures of the snow? .....out of whose womb came the ice? and the hoary frost of heaven, who hath gendered it?

Job 38: 22, 29

We have only two seasons: nine months of winter and three months of poor sledding.

A PHRASE QUOTED BY MANY IN OUR FARMING COMMUNITY.

‰

OUR HOT, HOLY roller religion instilled in us the fear of God and hellfires. The first snows brought fears of death by wind and ice. If I have to choose between eternal hellfires and death by ice, I choose the latter.

Manitoba winters blew us about and froze our bones. Biting north winds, birthed somewhere in the far north, danced on the fine line between life and death, and ruled our lives. Mr. North Wind, with his whistling and dancing could enchant with his romance and play. He was all fun as he blasted our sailing sleds across the frozen pond, but if you teased him too much, he'd kick snow in your face and throw you down to die. The driving, stinging snow created white outs with visibility limited to a few yards. The north wind loved the flat prairie, for it let him muster all his muscle, to coil up, snakelike, and strike at will. We thought we owned the land, and we were wrong. He owned us; he was grand emperor of the plains.

By age three we had mastered the art of walking backwards into the howling north winds. Our hooded parkas gave some protection, along with the woolen scarves wrapped around our necks, faces and foreheads. But the winter wind had relentless teeth, and when he clamped onto our cheeks and ears, they'd turn white. We called it frost bite. Once bitten was enough. When the blood ceased flowing through our toes, fingers, cheeks and ears, we'd attack the white spots with quick massage. We knew that left too long a frozen white spot on cheek or forehead would leave discolored and dead tissue as another reminder of the cruelty of winter. White ears were especially scary, for it took longer to get the blood flowing and return normal color. A well frozen, black and blue ear, would take days or weeks before the rose color bloomed again.

It was folly to walk alone in blizzard conditions, so we tacked across the prairies in twos and threes, checking for the dreaded white spots where blood ceased to flow, rubbing and blowing warm breath onto the frozen areas. We'd form a warming huddle, arms around each other, rewrapping scarves, perhaps exchanging mittens with someone who had warmer hands. Parka hoods were tied and re-tied as the wind worked them over. When too much snow sneaked into our heavy felt boots and woolen socks, we'd remove them, empty the snow as fast as we could, and give our feet a quick rub to keep the blood flowing.

Snow motion is slow motion, especially when the snow is deep. Blizzards demand a mix of faith and fool hardiness, dexterity and strength, along with team work. Like migrating geese, we'd take turns as leader, wedging forward, tossed about yet resolute.

Through the magic of time and space shifting you can see us there: you shield your eyes and fearfully watch our ghostly shadows: a crazy knot of chattering children, halting, feinting, backwards, sideways, forward, appearing then disappearing. Buffeted and blown, crab-like, to school, voices lost in the wind's larger voice. You fear we won't make it—wherever it is we might be headed. Just as you think we're done for, you hold your breath and watch as we near a fence, and hasten our pace as we move along the fence line. Then again, as we seem to sight a dim landmark, you watch us swerve across the bald prairie, through the riven snow, following blind instinct, drawing on faith and courage as we make our way.

Even when it's not snowing, prairie blizzards can start quickly and turn deadly in less than an hour. If the snow is dry enough, without a hard crust from a warmer day, the wind uses it as a weapon. To serve as some protection, snow fences, made of wooden slats, were built along our roads, and these would soften the wind, trapping snow on the south side. When the snow reached as high as the four foot fences, the fences were useless, and once again the wind blew as it would. Snow banks ten to twenty feet high could pile up on the south side of barns and houses, and these drifts were used for sledding, and for building snow tunnels and forts. Snowball fights, pushing and wrestling were part of our wild times in the snow.

Families passed down stories of individuals who'd died or had close calls, often in the early dusk of winter afternoons. In the middle of winter it would start to darken around four in the afternoon, even earlier if snow clouds were around.

The most tragic blizzard story for our family, told to us early in childhood as a cautionary tale, involved our great grandmother Sarah McLeod. As with many such stories, a furious wind erupted in mid-afternoon, October 22, 1890, as she was leaving home to visit her daughter, Annie, who lived near a small town named Toddburn, in western Manitoba. With limited visibility and her life on the line, she battled the slashing blizzard and found her way to a locked and vacant cabin. She no longer had the strength to break in, and next day they found her body on the steps. She was seventy-two. Mr. North Wind had blown out the light of another life.

Knowing this story alerted us to the risks of winter and may have helped save our lives. The fact that this blizzard came near mid-October served to keep us on blizzard alert from October until early May.

Our father had a close call one late afternoon. He enjoyed walking across the west field to the Sam Glover home, where Mrs. Glover would cook him bacon and eggs with toast and potatoes. He loved her cooking, and usually it involved something fried in the pork fat from the last butchered pig.

In mid-afternoon an impulsive wind kicked up, and Dad decided he could make it home. By the time he emerged from the wind shelter of their farmyard and hit the open field, visibility had dropped to a few yards with darkness coming on.

At first he could trace the footprints he'd made on the way over, but these were quickly covered with snow. He kept heading in what he hoped was an eastward direction as he staggered around seeking a landmark. Finally, out of the dark and snow, he ran into a fence line. He realized it was the fence south of our farm, for he recognized the repair work he'd done in the summer. He knew if he followed the fence it would lead him right to our house. When he stumbled into our kitchen, the white color of his face and the fear in his eyes, told an instant story.

Canada's largest export, not officially counted as such, is the cold weather that sends shivers into the southern states. The famous forty-ninth parallel that divides Canada and USA, like other man made barriers, is not recognized by the magisterial north wind; it moves as it will with no thought of passports and green cards.

The restless winter wind screams out of the arctic, freezing everything in its path.

I heard about the Arctic, and the Arctic Circle, early on. *Those Arctic winds! Coming in from the ice cap! They'll freeze your hands and toes off, and maybe your ears too. Better not let the cows out, they'll die for sure.*

The Arctic. We uttered the word with respectful reverence, for it, like God, had the power of life and death. The Arctic was mythic, larger than life. In my childhood images of the far north, I saw infinite plains of snow, with a great fan that never stopped blowing southward. I'd watch the birds winging north, then south, into and from the great white void. I knew the Arctic had no beginning or end. Our religion told us heaven and hell were infinite, and most winter days we knew for sure our north wind was infinite.

As a grown-up, fully mature college student in the summer of 1961, I have the chance to fly into the mysterious north, into the mouth of winter.

I'm no longer a kid backing into the wind on his way to school; I'm aboard a hammering, vintage DC3 flying directly into the birthplace of blizzards, headed north to Churchill, then farther still, into the throat of the arctic. Officially I am on Canadian Government business, but unofficially—just between us—I'm hoping to discover the source of the winter winds, and if I'm lucky, maybe a glimpse of Santa Claus.

I'm in a left seat with a handful of other daredevils, foolish or perhaps brave enough to trust our antique craft. The fulminating engine outside my window is dancing, shaking, rocking and rolling, as though it is ready to abandon us and leave all the work to its starboard brother. I'm a nervous flier and my heroic duty is to hold our craft together. I clinch my hands more tightly to the seat, and at times grab the vibrating seat in front of me. No one else seems to care if our craft flies apart in thin air. Trans Air, the airline that carries supplies, and desperate souls, into the far north. *If you don't care, fly Trans Air:* that is the phrase we used as we loaded boxes of equipment into the plane.

As we bump and sway toward Churchill, under the wings, trees grow spindly and ghostly, then disappear. This is the tree line I've heard about. Now all we have is flat, frozen tundra, thousands of lakes and rocks. The silent, soulful north: not only have trees given up; here civilization wearies of progress. We enter an untrammeled, ethereal world of light.

I'd like to tell you our mission is top secret, headed as we are toward the Distant Early Warning Line (the DEW line), consisting of a string of radar stations, garlanded around the north pole, each a wakeful eye watching in case the pesky Russians launch a missile. I want you to believe we're on a mission to save civilization as we know it. I'd like you to fancy me a highly trained commando type, skilled in the art of secret raids and night time skulking. As with most of the myths we use to embellish life, this would not be entirely correct. I hope the truth does not send you crashing to earth, as it seems our plane wants to do.

As is often the case, the truth is mundane: we are a land survey crew of three, laden with equipment, ready to run some lines, shoot some angles and measure elevations. At Churchill, we board a bus into town for the night. At the second stop, Donna Seeley, the woman I almost married two years earlier, walks out of time and sits down a few rows in front of me. In this land where trees have gone to ghosts, and the sun forgotten how to run, she can't be real. I strain in my seat and look again. Her black hair, her nape of neck and turn of nose. That's her alright. That's Donna. Do I really smell her perfume?

I too, walk out of the past, out of time and stand before her. She shrieks. Between the seats, in the aisle, we're all a-tumble with hugs and tears. Let the sun stand still; we stand in the gobsmacked, godsmacked bus, dazzled by magic. Her black hair touching my cheeks, and, yes, the same perfume. After dinner we sit on the shore of Hudson Bay, watching a wayward sun seeking a lost horizon in the west.

Our *chance encounter* shatters all logic, and my companions tease me the rest of the summer about being fast with the ladies. They drink and I don't. They play poker and I don't. I have serious religion, they don't. Yup, for sure, I'm a ladies man. I let myself be flattered, hoping to forget my pimpled insecurities.

Next, eager morning we scramble into the new Royal Canadian Air Force C-130. Fearfully, I look at the massive tires, flattened by the bulldozers and snow equipment aboard. This shiny monster has four engines, each with proud, large blades, ravenous for air. The C-130 is better known as Hercules, and the name really fits.

The runway stops at the edge of the bay and I worry we'll go into the drink. Aboard the plane, at the south end of the swath of concrete, we pivot north, poised for what might lie ahead. I hear the powerful music of our engines as we go to full power. The plane shudders. I have goosebumps and a rush of adrenaline as we race ahead, feathering into sky. This beast of burden was made to fly. The front cabin door is open and the young pilots, proud of their new wings, are laughing and cheering as we climb aloft. No more wind-worn DC-3's for them.

We wing into endless day. Instead of setting, the sun holds steady, and at times appears to float upward in the west. Here where time plays tricks, if the weather holds we plan to land at Alert, on the northern tip of Ellesmere Island, five hundred miles from the pole.

Santa Claus country. I fancy this is the spawning ground of the brutal weather systems that blow frost all the way to Florida. The pilots tell us that if Alert is socked in, we'll lay over at Thule, Greenland.

There are a handful of us with *the rest of the equipment* in the cargo section. Men and their machinery stacked up, ready for whatever. The doors to the pilot's cabin remain open and we stroll in and out to chat and check things out. The pilots eagerly talk about their new plane; the power, the carrying capacity, the advanced technology. Flashing lights, switches, levers above and below. The radar screen paints a shimmering picture of something, but of what I cannot tell. Enviously I eye the throttles and imagine myself pushing them forward, unleashing the power of the four massive engines.

I return to the cargo hold putting on ear phones, listening to the chatter of our pilot to ground control, warning us not to land because *we're socked in.* Our pilot reports he has a hot date in Ottawa and needs to land, unload and get back to civilization. Meantime he tells us he'll circle around, waiting for the fog and snow to clear.

We throttle back, carving large circles, sunlight splashing our wings. It is nearing midnight and the sun shows little sign of resting. Ground control checks in, informing us of the snow and fog that persist below. Rather than risk losing his girlfriend, the pilot announces his plan to all interested parties: *Okay, I'll take my chances. I'm coming in over the ocean so I won't hit the mountains. Be landing in ten minutes.* He bleeds off more power and we settle into clouds for a lazy prelude to a certain crash. I clench my jaw along with my hands. Time, a lot of time, and finally we break through clouds into a shaft of light with ocean and jagged ice a few hundred feet below. A light snow is falling as our tires crunch the dirt runway.

We are down, scared, safe. As we come to a stop I see a scowling man with ear phones on. He's shaking his head in disapproval at our landing. He's the tower, he's ground control. He's the guy who warned us not to land. This is the far north, where the wind shatters the rules. This is the Arctic, the dreamy white, the fabled land of the midnight sun.

It is one-thirty in the morning. We stand in disordered sunlight, scratching our heads, peering about. Beneath my feet the snowy tundra feels solid, yet in this mystic place I wonder if I can trust it. We've landed at Alert: nothing but a military and weather outpost, and a handful of men. I see some military orange buildings and not much else. A sign tells me I'm closer to Moscow than Minneapolis. I feel abandoned, small, adrift. *Alert. We are in Alert.* I say the words softly, and this helps wake me up. *I am only five hundred miles from the pole, five hundred miles.* This fact becomes a summer mantra, alive in my head during our sun drenched days.

For the next two months we blanket our windows against the unyielding light so we can sleep. For bragging rights we run survey lines at two in the morning. Atop the world we help the weather guy release balloons, peering at them as they grow smaller and smaller.

One midnight day, we stand frozen as a black conning tower rises in a stretch of open water a rifle shot away. Russian for sure! The guys aboard have binoculars and wave at us, and we wave back. One of our unruly crew yells: *can we get some vodka?* He pretends to tip a bottle to his mouth. We laugh and wave some more, inviting them to join us for a meal. We can't hear each other, but we are ready to embrace them and party. Here on top of the world, brains addled by the pure thought of it, we recognize we are humans first, and face the cold as our common enemy. Our new friends soon leave the field of ice, and descend again into their secret, watery place under the polar cap.

Mid-August, with the summer sun sinking lower and lower on the horizon, we fly south to another small base, hoping to get a dead engine fixed. After a couple of hours, the mechanics give up, and we fly out on three engines to Edmonton. We grab a van to our hotel. Everything is paid for, and it is hard for me to comprehend that I don't have to spend one penny on anything. The hotel has comfortable beds and real showers, and we start to humanize. I shave off my first tentative beard and join my crew for a special dinner.

The next day, east to Winnipeg. Home! I've earned double overtime pay for hardship duty, and have money in the bank for a year of college. A week later, my brother Phil and I pile into our green, fluid drive, '47 Dodge, and head south to Springfield, Missouri for the fall semester at Evangel College. I'm pregnant with stories of the far north.

∞

With a mix of humor and toughness, we said that our prairie weather was sliced into two seasons: *nine months of winter and three months of poor sledding.* Late April and early May teased us with spring, yet might collapse back into winter with a snow. Snow could return on the heels of growling thunderstorms in late September, slamming the door on aspiring autumn and delaying or ruining harvest.

One story our father told us: *I heard of a farmer who'd buy hammers for fifty cents and sell them for forty-five, because it sure beat farming.*

The days of poor sledding from June through August were rarely above eighty degrees Fahrenheit, and we had many days of slashing cold rain when our mercury plunged into the mid-fifties as though it couldn't wait for winter. Winter, like a troublesome ex-lover, was always on our minds. From those who'd moved to Alberta, we heard about the Chinook winds, and how in a few hours they could stomp a winter day, making it all summery.

In January I'd pray for Chinooks, and think of flowers blooming in Vancouver. The tales of the warm west aroused lovely images of walking about in short sleeves and picnics in some imagined meadow with lots of happy families around. Mainly I believed the stories, yet caught fast in winter, I wondered if the warm weather thing was exaggerated.

In a good year, after a cold snap in late September, we might be blessed with a week or two of Indian summer—golden sun-splashed days with radiant fields and the cries of the last meadowlarks.

These last warm days were subtle and settled in on soft wings, leading to times of celebration. We'd shed our jackets and spend hours outdoors, hoping for just one more sunny day before old man winter blasted his trumpet. Thousands of flies and mosquitoes reappeared from their mysterious hiding places. If the warmth held, we might take a September trip into the hills to mythic Clear Lake, twenty-five miles west. Indian summer was perfect for flying kites, playing in the creek, and pretending that winter would never come. *Hey! Maybe we'll have a short winter! We can always hope!*

In the dying days of autumn we scanned the skies with practiced eyes for telltale wisps of clouds, noting the way they stretched across the hills, the spread of fingers, the blush of face, listening to the secrets of the whispering wind. From our garden, the potatoes were often the last harvested, and as we turned them up, the ground had already given up its warmth. The ground knew, we knew, what was coming. *God help us.*

Survival demanded many things: firewood, one of the most important. Our brother Bob and other men would head into the Riding Mountains to cut trees, none with trunks thicker than six or eight inches due to the stunting of the cold. If we ran short of wood we might borrow from a neighbor. The trees were cut with axes and saws, and carried home on big horse-drawn sleighs. I have a picture of our brother Bob as a young man, seated atop a load of logs, pulled by a team of horses, on a road with snow banks as high as the load.

Once the load was home we'd use a two-person bucksaw, cutting the logs into short pieces to fit in our stove. By age eight or nine we boys were working the saws. We'd split some of the larger pieces with an axe, careful, careful to not miss the wood and hit our feet. A few times the axe would slice into our boots, but luckily our toes were spared.

In the late 1940's, we acquired a large rotary saw, driven by a belt attached to the pulley on our John Deere tractor. The saw was three feet in diameter and mounted on a heavy wooden platform to give it stability. The foundation of the saw had two large runners which allowed us to pull it from home to home. Cutting wood required several men to pick up the logs, and hold them straight while they were being cut. The ripping sound of the saw was frightening, like the sound of a million angry bees swarming after we'd ruined their nest with rocks. The man who stood the closest to that singing blade, feeding the wood into it, seemed brave and also foolish. Injuries were common; the most serious, a piece of wood that flew into the eye of our neighbor, Mr. Beairsto, blinding him and creating other health issues.

After the wood was cut into short pieces, we'd feed it into the kitchen stove, replenishing it every hour or so. Some wood burned faster and hotter, and we'd use the stove handle to remove the top grate to check on the fire level. We took turns bringing in armfuls of wood, and cranking the grates of the stove to shake the ashes down into a pan for dumping outside.

We'd fill the stove prior to bedtime, hoping to keep our home warm all night. It rarely worked, for our indoor morning temperatures were often near freezing, and during a cold snap, we'd find ice on the water pot atop the stove. To help us cope with the cold at night, we'd heat a few of the irons—used to iron clothes—wrap them in paper and take them to bed. These would give off heat for a few hours until like everything else on the prairie, they too would fall under the spell of Mr. Frost. We also used large stones or a hot water bottle to help keep us warm in bed. Phil and I slept together and that was the best way to ward off the cold. Dad or Bob would rise early and get the fire going. Snuggled in bed, I relished the sound of popping wood as it flamed up, then the warm air as it spread through our home.

Early storms might dump a foot or more of snow, and if the wind blew, the shifting snow would form drifts on the leeward side of buildings and trees. By November some snowdrifts could be ten or more feet high, ideal for snow caves, forts and tunnels. The bigmouthed shovels, used for shoveling grain, were perfect for moving snow around. Cold temperatures meant the snow was light and in a short time we'd have a cave ten or more feet into a drift, with tunnels and connecting rooms. We'd make a skylight by digging near the top, and the light that shone through the snow was a soft blue color.

With some snow caves we'd make an entrance from above, often hiding it near a tree as an escape route if Indians, rustlers or robbers attacked us. One of my scariest memories was getting stuck, head down, in a roof tunnel. I was terrified, knowing I would freeze to death, upside down in the cold. No one heard my screams. I wiggled and turned with all my might, desperate to live, finally falling out the bottom, free as a newborn. I sat there dazed, crying, sucking in air, thanking Jesus, happy my life would go on. *Thank you Jesus, thank you Jesus. Now if you want me to go to Africa I will, I really will.*

High snowdrifts were great for sliding, and in addition to the one sled we had, we used scoop shovels, sitting with the handle in front of us. Any piece of smooth wood could serve as a sled. One of my favorite improvised sleds was a top from an old school desk that I found in the basement of our school house. It was a beautiful piece of shiny wood, and had a nice curve to it, and I called it my Star Express, after an ad I'd seen somewhere for a trucking company.

We spontaneously created the fun things that kids do when sledding, engaging in races, seeing who could pile the most kids on one sled, trying to throw someone off their sled as we raced beside them, forming tangled, laughing, screaming knots of flesh and limb.

When blizzards came we'd be snow bound for days. We had no phone, so one of us would hike to the neighbors and help organize a work crew to clear the roads. We'd spend hours shoveling a narrow passage barely big enough for a team of horses or a car. When the snow was very deep it was easier to dig a low tunnel, rather than remove all the snow. When the next storm blew in, the snow would blow over the tunnel, rather than filling our roads again.

Once we shoveled out to the main road, we'd wait for the big snowplow to come. The snowplow was a large dump truck with massive tires and chains, and a big V-shaped snow blade on the front. The monster plow with a gleaming red mouth. I loved it. To give it weight and better traction, the truck was loaded with rocks to help it bust through large snowdrifts. When we saw the snowplow coming down the road west of the school, we'd beg to go outside and cheer it on. We'd run around waving to the driver, sometimes tossing snowballs as the powerful engine snorted. With the larger drifts, the machine had to back up and take several runs, like a great bull, finally smashing through. When snowdrifts were high, it might break down and could sit for several days until parts arrived. We children loved this, for we could climb into the abandoned machine and pretend to drive it.

When rotary plows arrived, beautiful snow fountains erupted across the prairie. They could crawl through the deepest drifts with only the roof showing, creating a rainbow of snow that touched the heavens. As farm boys we were excited by machinery, especially if it was new and different, and the rotary plows caught our fancy. While the diver yelled at us to stay away, we'd run madly through the cascading snow, hit sometimes by pieces of ice or stone.

The most fearsomely magnificent snowplow on the prairies was mounted at the front of the mighty C.N.R. (Canadian National Railways) steam engines.

With their tons of weight barreling along at high speed, the Lord Himself must have feared for His snow. We'd hear the iron steeds coming from miles away, shattering the silence with their shrieking and jangling bells, and as we rushed outside we'd see the foam gushing from their nostrils into the prairie blue. They'd pass with a roar of wind, and the smell of coal. The clear tracks meant we could once again walk the rails, doing our pirouettes and competitions. We were especially challenged when the rails were coated with ice and snow.

The railway snowplows with their hissing steam, their smoke and screeching seemed impervious to any threat, but Mr. Winter knew how to break their backs. On one occasion, when snow had turned to ice on the tracks, one of the beasts jumped off its path and fell on its side, dazed and heaving. A large crane had to be brought in to hoist it back on its feet.

The smallest snowplow of all, was a war surplus, four wheel drive Jeep purchased by a neighbor in 1946. He'd welded a small snow blade on the front. The first time I saw it was from upstairs in the boys cloak room at school. I stood barely breathing, eyes glued to the window, enraptured with the power of that jeep. The driver would gun it with snow flying from all four wheels, then plunge into a large drift. When the snow won the battle, instead of being stuck, he'd back out and take another run at it. If the drift was too big, he headed into the open field kicking up snow all over the place, creating a new road for us to drive over. It was not long till he had chains on the wheels, and he could drive most anywhere he wanted and not need a tow. As the word spread, he became the official tow guy. He was proud of his Jeep, and refused to be paid for his work.

Winter brought other exciting events. As soon as the creek froze, we'd put on our skates. If we had a few warm days early on, the creek could flood and form a perfect pond for hockey games. If it did not flood then we'd spend hours carrying buckets of water from the creek to make our own rink, forming a border of packed snow and ice around it to hold the water in. We'd spend hours keeping the surface clean and expanding it in size, and filling cracks and holes with water. Because we had no boards along the sides, pucks would disappear in the snow. As we looked for them we'd walk through the snow on the tips of our skates, to keep from dulling the blades. We had only a few pucks, and the lost ones would show their faces only when the snow melted in April or May.

Hockey wars rage across the Dominion during winter months. Canada is a peaceful country with a small military, and favors hockey wars over all others. Money not spent on tanks and bombs goes to skates and sticks, and these are formidable weapons, as we learned by age five or so. Invasions into the territory of others, consists of crossing red and blue lines, even in the face of those out to slay you.

When we spoke of *the draft* we were referring not to any army, but to the wind, or else the hockey draft system. Canadians are known to be gentle people, and this is so because all resentments and anger bleed away on the ice. I believe we could do away with the United Nations and other peace loving groups, if the world took up hockey. Hockey, it must be said, is an artful healing practice, painful in a way, but with widespread salvific effects.

Hockey wounds were common: broken noses, cuts, bruises, shattered teeth and occasionally a fractured bone. Most games had a few broken sticks along with the teeth. We could forget about the teeth, but had to keep our primitive sticks in shape, to *play up and play the game.* Massive amounts of black hockey tape were needed, along with splints and baling wire. At the end of a really ferocious game, the icy battlefield was a pleasing scene: bits of tape, wood, blood and teeth.

Our most memorable hockey stick could not be fixed, for the handle broke about a foot above the blade, and tape, screws and wire would not hold it together. One of us remembered we had a round piece of aluminum from the Harvard airplane that might do the trick. As soon as our idea breathed itself into the cold air it solidified, and we ran to the plane. (More about the Harvard plane later.) It took only a couple of minutes to shove the hockey stick into the bottom of the hollow pipe, then we taped the sucker together, and entered the fray with more fight than ever. Not only was the stick durable and created wicked shots, it came with a funny side effect. I was not a good skater, and when I fell or got knocked down the whole country knew, for the aluminum handle created a sharp pinging sound as it hit the ice. Along with my embarrassment, I hoped the other team might hear the sound as a cavalry trumpet, blown at the beginning of battle.

Dad would occasionally watch us play hockey, but never joined in, and I don't think he ever learned to skate. When he was done with farm chores, he loved to read and passed this gift onto us. As with most children I don't recall learning to read, for like so much else it seemed to just happen to us. Words were in the air, and we breathed them in with much else. We drink in our native language like mother's milk, and this milk never runs dry, for it nourishes us though our life, bonding us to our tribe.

Reading occupied many evenings, after the cows were milked and the pigs fed. Short winter days meant long evenings, usually spent in our kitchen huddled around the wood burning stove. It is easy for me to visualize a typical winter evening: I feel the comfort of touching shoulders, as I sit between my father, Helen or Phil, with our feet in the oven, braced against the invasive cold. We are wearing our knee-high winter boots, made of thick felt material. Only three of us can get our feet into the oven at the same time, so we keep rotating spots.

Cradled together, immersed in our reading, with the wood fire popping, another winter night slides through and around us. In harmony with the fire, two coal oil lamps buzz behind us, shedding light on the words that flicker from our pages. The smells of burning wood and lamp oil mix with the scent of boots drying in the heat. A distant coyote cries, and I have images of her and her family, pointing their noses skyward in the woods along our creek.

The opened oven door supports our legs, and as our eyes prowl the word trails of a book, we are in our own worlds, far removed from the prairie icebox. When our feet get too hot we pull them out, steam rising from our felt boots. Our feet cool quickly on the chilly floor and soon we have them back in our toaster.

Occasionally one of us walks over to take a drink of water from the metal pail used to haul water from the creek. At this remove, I still can feel the long handled metal ladle as I push it into the pail, water and ice running over the edges as I fill a cup. Then I return to my spot in the warm circle, jostle into position, joining my brother, sister and father in a flight into the magic world of words.

Smoke from the burning wood would ascend up a metal stovepipe, into the brick chimney in Bob's room on the second floor. The stovepipe had a couple of elbows, giving it a zigzag shape, so that the smoke and heat would move through it more slowly, while releasing more heat into the room. Farms are held together by wire and tape, and we used wire to lace our stovepipes to the wall and ceiling to hold them in place. I recall one incident when gravity, in defiance of our wire, yanked the pipes to the floor. There were a few moments of panic as hot embers fell on the linoleum and smoke filled our kitchen. We tossed water around and put out the embers. Our linoleum already had black, burned spots around the stove, now we had more. Nothing to worry about.

Even more, our chimney fires were a source of true panic. The smoke would leave heavy resin deposits in our stovepipes and chimney, and we rarely cleaned them. Climbing up our steep roof was dangerous, especially when it was coated in frost and snow. The few times we did clean our chimney, we used a home brewed, cleaning method: an adult would make the assault to the roof top, bearing a heavy logging chain, then drop it into the chimney, moving it up and down, and the black deposits would end up in our stove.

Because we were farmers, not chimney sweeps, we let the chimney clean itself, not by design, but with random and roaring flare ups. I can tell you, chimney fires are a fine cure for boredom!

Chimney fires started with a vague sigh of discontent, a complaint about being dirty and forgotten. Before we could be sure what we were hearing, the murmuring would ignite into a full throated moose roar. We'd fly out the doors, screaming with fear, and from our snowy yard, look up to see flames rocketing skyward from our chimney. In a few short minutes, as suddenly as the fire began, it would stop, having cleaned the chimney much better than any sweep or logging chain could do. Once calmed down, we kids would reenact the fiery spectacle, using sweeping arm movements, and loud whooshing sounds.

After the cleansing fire—as with a good altar call and prayer session—we felt relieved, knowing we were safe for a while. We didn't worry about future chimney fires, just as we didn't worry about most other things. Farming is a risky business, with new challenges and risks every few days. We lived with this reality, and there was little need to think or worry about such matters, for we knew unexpected events would happen.

Happily, our fires did not result in injuries of any note. Sadly, Mr. Satterthwaite, who lived a few miles north, lost his life one March night when his home burned. Because of our flirtations with fire, we could imagine many ways his fire might have happened. Like our dad, he was a violin player, and out of the ashes of his home, a rumor rose up and claimed us: *His violin was a Stradivarius! That was the fact of the matter. He owned a fine instrument of precious wood, worth millions of dollars. Yup, he'd carried it with him on the boat when he crossed the Atlantic, and kept it a secret all these years. I always suspected it might be a Strad. Just the sound of it! Well, he's gone to a better place, and playing music in heaven. God bless him.*

Now we could think more highly of Mr. Satterthwaite. Nothing Norgate: believing we had a famous violin in our area gave us bragging rights, in a place where humility ruled. Thinking we had a famous violin gave us a sense of pride. *If you could only have seen it! The burnished gold of his violin was soooooooo beautiful. And the sounds it made as he played it. If only we had known. Yes, of course we suspected but now we knew for sure.*

Our first school, for us and the generations prior to us, was a one room schoolhouse, for grades one through eight. In warmer weather we'd walk the mile to school, taking a short cut by hiking across the fields. When Mr. North Wind was howling, facing him for a mile was too much and on such days our father would put Helen, Phil and me in the homemade toboggan and take us to school. The toboggan was pulled by one horse, and we'd harness the one that had the experience and courage to face the fierce winds. Hating blizzards as I did, rather than seeing our horse as brave, I thought he was simply dumb to head into the maw of winter.

The world of childhood is an inherited world, and our rough wooden toboggan was part of our legacy, presumably made by a prior family member.

It was a basic box, twice the size of a coffin, and there were moments when I thought we might die in it. It had a sloping front end, was about ten feet long, three feet wide, and three feet high. For comfort and insulation we covered the bottom with a layer of straw. The width was perfect for Phil and I to sit snuggled together, leaning against the back of the toboggan, covered with a heavy rug from a bear killed by our Grandpa McLeod. As I write, the weight, the wet fur smell of that rug haunts the spaces between these words. Helen sat in front of us, facing us, huddling with the leftover part of the bear skin. The stronger the wind, the deeper we'd burrow under the rug and any other blankets we had along, while Dad and the horse bucked into the howling gale. When Helen was properly chilled, one of us would take her spot, and let her in under the bear rug. Survival, staying warm depended on looking out for each other.

The assault of the north wind was softened, but not disarmed, by our barns and the small grove of trees by our creek north of the barn. After crossing the bridge over the creek, as we moved along the bare ridge into the open prairie, each driven snowflake pierced and stung, much like the pellets from our BB gun. Once into the open, our horse might stop, turn his head and refuse to go on, rooting himself like a statue to the ground. On these days we'd head back to the barn as fast as we could, standing around stomping our feet, and clapping our hands to warm them up. Leaning back against a quiet cow was a sure way to warm quickly.

A winter's day with no school meant we could listen to some morning radio shows, play games and do more reading. There were always chores to be done, school or no school.

On most days we made it to school, and would tether our horse with others in the school barn. Because of the low ceilings the barn was surprisingly warm, despite some cracks between dried out pieces of wood.

The north wind and snow were not the only context of winter, for the northern lights were often out, spreading their colorful wings over us, changing from pink to purple and green.

On a couple of nights, when it was forty or so below, they were so close we could hear the subtle sound of static electricity as they danced above our heads.

One winter evening shines bright in memory: in November, Dad had given Phil and me a few dollars so we could buy Christmas gifts for the family. By mail, we ordered socks and a few other items from the iconic T. Eaton Company. We hiked across the snow-covered fields to the post office and loaded our little hand-pulled sled. The northern lights had softened, and with no moon, each star was as piercing as the Christmas star. Except for the some-time squeaking sound of our sled runners, and the cry of a coyote by the creek, the fields were hushed. At one point a jack rabbit startled us when he leapt up from his bed behind a clump of weeds, springing across the field. I imagined us as wise men, bearing gifts, as we trudged home to our family.

And, like kids around the world, we might skip school without telling our teacher or parents. We called it *playing hooky,* a term I don't hear much these days.

My clearest memory of sneaking out of school for a day was when I was twelve. Our teacher was unusually late to school, and after an appropriate wait, a few of us convinced ourselves he was sick. Besides, it was bright sunny day, after a nice snow fall. We were ready to kick up our heels. A naughty band of four of us grabbed our lunch pails and headed south across the snowy field, running along the fence line under the cover of weeds and small bushes, heading for the trees sheltering the creek.

When we reached the bush we were uncertain what to do next, and not sure if we'd made the right move. After our run across the field, we started to get chilly and some guilt blew in. Breaking little rules was familiar territory, but this time we'd broken a big rule and were uneasy about our run for freedom. It took a few moments for our imaginations to catch fire. Why not light up a cigar like grown-ups? We picked some dead ragweed stalks, lit them up and sucked the smoke through the hollow stalks. We lowered our voices and the topics of conversations, pretending we were big people, blowing smoke around. With lots of laughter and exaggerated postures we talked about the price of wheat, and our Prime Minister, making up big people talk.

We crossed our legs as we stood tall, jingling coins in our pockets. As we sucked our weeds, we started coughing like real grown-ups.

Bored with our fake cigars, and the nasty taste in our mouths, we followed some rabbit tracks to see if we could find their homes. We played cowboy and Indians, being careful not to hoot too loudly, had snowball fights and wrestled in the snow. With the sun at high noon, we built a fire and warmed our sandwiches. Shortly after lunch the sun began an early slide down the western sky. The day was dragging; cold, fear and guilt were claiming us.

Finally, relief: the prairie-piercing whistle of the four-o-clock train headed north out of Kelwood! We ran as fast as we could through deep snow to scramble under the bridge so we could hear the train roar over us. The bridge shook and we yelled and trembled with it. I could feel the heat of the steam engine and smell the coal as it passed, then hear the whistle cry as it neared the station.

With mixed emotions we split up and went home. We'd had some fun, but I missed the warm classroom, the other kids and hot chocolate at lunch. (That was the last time I played hooky until 1963, *senior sneak day,* when our class left our Evangel College campus, in Springfield, Missouri. At dawn, we snuck away for a day in the Ozarks.)

A few hundred yards east from the school, past the grocery store, stood The United Church with a classic white steeple, like folded hands pointing to heaven. Going there to light the fire for our Christmas concert rehearsals was another badge of manhood. As a younger student, I sat in my desk, envious of the older boys who left an hour or more before the rest of us. They held their heads high and stomped noisily down the stairs, as they went on their mission.

Soon enough the time came when, as an older student, wise to the world, I took the honored, manly walk to the church and entered that hallowed, cold and quiet place. Two of us were sent on this important mission. I took longer steps than normal as I made my first fire-lighting walk, doing my *real man* swagger I'd seen grown-ups do, swinging my arms in proper time. Amidst tossed snowballs, we took a quick detour to get some candy at the store.

After lighting the fire, as we waited for the church to warm and for the sissy kids to join us, we played a cowboy shoot-out game. Our guns were leather mitts, our pockets our holsters. We put a mitten in each pant pocket, then facing each other across the room we'd walk slowly towards each other, bowing our legs, scowling, taunting our enemy with dastardly jeers, daring the varmint to *slap leather* and draw his gun.

We used slang words from favorite western novels and movies: *You cowardly horse thief, I'm going to gun you down here in the street,* or: *You cold blooded murderer, your time has come! I'm Sheriff Gene Autry, and I'm here to take you in, dead or alive...which will it be? If you go fer your gun, yer not gonna leave Dodge City alive...! You can surrender now, or slap leather and we'll haul you out in a box!*

Surrender? We didn't know the word. None of us wanted to be taken alive so we fought it out, throwing our mittens with fiery arms, dodging and ducking for cover behind the pews. The cowboy who drew his mitten first and scored a hit lived to fight another day, while the gunned down varmint flailed about with dramatic death sounds, and lots of blood in the church aisle. A holy melee, a brave death, noble and fitting. To add to the drama we might run to the church organ and pound a few low notes.

If the first shot was not direct enough we could claim we were only wounded, and fire a mitten from the floor. Real anger might erupt as we argued over what was a wound and what was a killer shot. This would be followed by a hot, ferocious shoot out, sometimes ending in a boxing or wrestling match. If there were three or four of us in one gun fight it was a lively time, with the sound of gunfire and the groans of dying men in the streets of Dodge.

As soon as we heard the voices of the younger kids approaching, we'd go back to stoking the fire. By the time the teacher walked in, Dodge City was an orderly, law abiding town, with all the hymnals in place.

Unlike our church battles, snowball wars were actually dangerous and began about the same time as hockey. By age three or four we were wild about both. Goaded by the older boys, we thought that snowmen and snow angels were for sissies and girls.

Early fights were innocent affairs, for our arms were still finding their way in life, and our throws were soft, with a rainbow arc. Kid stuff. By seven or eight we could make Hitler dance. After thousands of throws our arms were stronger and our aim more deadly. By eleven and twelve we threw darts, flat laser shots that could rock you. We were born to throw, and this included stones, bread rolls and each other. Barns, tractors, birds and other living things were fair game. Anything that made a ringing sound when hit was especially appealing. In late summer we sought out wild bees nests so we could pulverize them with vehement rocks.

We skipped stones in the creek, and a few times broke the glass insulators on the telephone poles. This was especially exciting for we knew it was wrong, so watching the green glass fly had a particular thrill. If we were lucky we could break the glass insulators with an ice ball, made from repeated rubbing of a snowball and lots of spit. One harvest season we had fun hiding in the dimming light as the last racks of grain came in, throwing plums at the tired guys up on the load. Our arms were not officially registered weapons but they should have been.

I'm thankfully astonished as I look back and think that no one suffered serious injury from the snowballs we threw as we moved into adolescence, with our hormone fueled, rocket arms. We crafted snow into icy, orange-size balls, firing them with deadly aim at most anything. We'd hide around corners, ready to fly away in a second, as we pelted unwary adults. Loud screams with curses gave us pride, for we knew we'd scored a brilliant hit.

The teachers that came and went most every year were usually male and not much older than us, and we'd goad them into snowball fights. They were not prepared—no one could really be prepared—for the hellish torrent of ice balls zinging around as several of us let loose. I can still hear the sharp sound of our missiles exploding into walls, or the sides of moving cars. Firing a snowball into the open window of a car or truck gave us special satisfaction. Occasionally someone would slam on their brakes, and give chase. That was a joke, for we were fast like the wind, and knew lots of hiding places. Our arms were not only strong, they never tired. It was advisable for babies, women and chickens to take cover.

Despite the irrepressible snowball wars, I recall only a few bloody noses and black eyes. Direct hits to an ear was worrisome, for we'd have an odd buzzing sound for a few hours or days. Like kids around the world we didn't think of the future, but lived wildly in the moment. Farm days were charged with lively action and little thought of the consequences. Risk was our companion.

Winter was our main hunting season, and by age ten or eleven, using our .22 rifles, we were killing rabbits and the occasional bird. We inherited our hunting practice from our Grandpa McLeod, for he had earned part of his living killing bears, elk, moose, deer, fox, coyotes and wolves. He also had a trap line in the wooded hills a few miles west of our farm. At one time his trap line was twelve or more miles long, and he had a small cabin at one end where he could spend the night. Using his small traps he'd catch mink and weasels, and with his large trap, the occasional bear. He'd skin these animals and sell the hides. Grandpa and his family would eat bear meat, along with elk and deer.

After hearing the stories about Grandpa, Phil and I naturally wanted to have our own trap line. For a few winters, we set our snares and traps in the woods along the creek, and would check them on our way to and from school. Mainly we caught rabbits, along with a few mink and weasels. One time we caught a skunk, and due to his smell, we left him many days before taking him from his trap. Sadly, we did all our trapping and hunting only for sport, leaving their bodies in the woods for the coyotes, foxes, hawks and owls.

CHAPTER 3

Holy Roller Days with Sister Rachael

From this broken hill I will sing to you. From this broken hill, all
your praises they shall ring, if it be your will to let me sing....
...If it be your will, if there is a choice, let the rivers fill, let the
hills rejoice
Let your mercy spill
On all these burning hearts in hell
If it be your will to make us well.
And draw us near and bind us tight
All your children here in their rags of light
All dressed to kill and end this night
If it be your will
If it be your will.

LINES SELECTED FROM LEONARD COHEN, IF IT BE YOUR WILL.

IN SUMMER 1946, Sister Rachael blew into our lives like a summer storm, with
flashes of lightning that seared our souls. She was not a blood sister; she was
more than this, a sister in Christ, tied to His soul and ours forever.

She was our first housekeeper, come to help out after Mother was diagnosed with cancer. Those of us who fell under her religious spell called each
other sisters and brothers, for we were part of a tight family, a robust band of
holy warriors, saved by Jesus and engaged in battle with the heathens around us.

We had a scorched earth policy: either you believed as we did, or you'd be wiped from the earth and thrown into eternal hellfires. Yes, Hellfire. Not for a day, or a year, but for eternity. Praise the Lord!! God is love, but hates sin, and hates sinners.

How one could remain alive after even a moment of hellfire was a mystery, but our guarantee had no restrictions. If God had any love at all it was, like much else, a well kept secret.

Our militaristic religion instilled a fearful loyalty that banded us together as happens with soldiers in the bloody trenches of war. We were a devoted army of true believers, and you better wave the white flag of surrender, or run for cover. The bonds of our holy and unholy alliance helped us through our dark valley of suffering when Mother died in July of 1947.

When Sister Rachael marched in, Bob was twenty-three, Jean twenty-one, Bill eleven, Helen nine, Phil five, and I was seven. Verily, we were not prepared for her coming. We were hand maidens to the cold tricks of Mr. North Wind, but the heat of hellfires alarmed and surprised us.

ço

I learned about tornadoes on the plains of Kansas, from reading *The Wizard of Oz*. On the prairies of Manitoba, we never had tornadoes. We had Sister Rachael. She blew into our lives like a mighty wind, on fire for Jesus, full of good intentions, heaven-bent to sweep the dirt from our lives.

In her person she combined the frost of winter, the boom of prairie thunder and the heat of lightning. After she came, nothing could ever be the same. On days she wasn't heaven bent, she was hell bent to clean things up, to set the world aright and the Lord help anyone who stood in her way. During her reign, we were carried up and away, further than the Land of Oz, to the cross of Jesus, where we fell on our knees and begged forgiveness.

Following the arrival of the juggernaut of judgment, the tranquility of the prairies, the sound of meadowlarks was replaced by shouts of *hallelujah* and *Praise the Lord!*

Prior to Sister Rachael, we thought our home, yard and souls were clean enough. After she arrived, we saw how blind we were. After being belted with a few scriptures, we discovered, too, how wrong headed we were to think we were decent folk, leading good lives. Her laser eyes saw right into the essence of our souls and did not like what they saw. We were smart enough to admit we were sinners, bound for hell. She was possessed, and in short order, our tiny clutch of fifteen or so true believers were all on fire for Jesus. We were eager to roast you, or anyone, with a memorized verse of scripture, letting you know in absolute words you were a sinner headed for hell.

Sister Rachael was a big boned woman with large arms and bulging eyes, and as an eight-year-old, I was scared and fascinated by her. While physically strong, her true power came from Jesus. Hers was the gift of fanatical energy, and like many gifts it came with a dark side: a cloud of shame, guilt, anger and damnation which claimed all of us.

She was not satisfied with just saving our souls; she wanted to save everything. Dirt was of the devil, and was purged out of our home. Clean hearts and homes were signs of being good disciples of Jesus. She'd rise early with a shout of proclamation, rousting the rest of us out of bed for a day of work. With her enthusiastic cajoling we began scrubbing the house, cleaning the cupboards, painting, wallpapering and hanging new curtains purchased from the T. Eaton catalog.

Yea verily, the hollow places were made flat, the dull spots made to shine. Like us, our home was saved and reborn, and we took much pride in the sweat of our labors. Her eyes were like the great eye of the Lord, sweeping hither and yon across the earth, and not a speck of sin or dirt escaped notice. She could see dirt in hidden places, and her eye could pierce the armor of all who pretended they were good and innocent, seeing the dirt in their hearts.

The yard was blighted with sin and dirt, like the rest of us, and under constant surveillance, we proceeded to rake up twigs, sinful stones and pieces of glass and metal. We pruned trees, planted flowers and began cutting the grass regularly. Our inner and outer worlds were reborn, Hallelujah!!

The rebirth of our home and yard was easy work compared to cleansing the inner dirt we discovered from her fiery proclamations. The inner dirt of the heart. There was no broom big enough to get it all. And one lifetime was too short. We swore vows to the Holy Trinity: God, Jesus and the Holy Ghost—though I confess I was never sure which was which. I played it safe and loved and prayed to them all.

It is not that we were hellions prior to her coming, for our father and many of our neighbors were faithful members of the United Church of Canada, housed in a classic white building with a steeple pointing, we had thought, up to God. The United Church had a long and sane history: on Sundays we'd greet our neighbors outside, move solemnly inside, and sit, stand, sing and pray together on cue. When the final Amen sounded, we'd shake hands again and head home. All good. Some of us were even baptized with sprinkled water, which after seeing the truth, we learned could only *save us in spots*. The new truth: real baptism meant full immersion under water, and long enough to make you think twice.

Before her feet touched the ground, Sister Rachael blew a great blast on her trumpet, proclaiming the United Church was of the devil and Satan ruled our souls. We were headed for hell if we did not accept Jesus into our hearts, and confess to Him every bad thought and deed we'd ever had or done. And the Catholics! They were really evil, and we knew their nasty secret: the priests and nuns had babies and buried them behind the church.

It was a riveting, militaristic message, and those of us who valued our lives fell to our knees and cried to Jesus. Sister Rachael loomed above us with her menacing voice, her big eyes and arms, and in an eye-blink, we agreed we were little sinners and started confessing our all our sins, asking the blood of Jesus to cleanse us. Water could clean floors, but the blood of Jesus was the only cure for sin.

To help herd us into line, we were continually reminded that Jesus could return at any moment. *In the twinkling of an eye,* the sky would split open, the archangel would blast his trumpet and Jesus would appear in clouds of glory. Hallelujah! Oh, Praise Jesus! Most of us would be cast into fiery hell. Forever, and ever, and ever, and ever, unending to infinity. Thinking about it gave me a headache.

She often quoted the biblical passage that *Two would be working in the same field, and one would be taken, the other left behind,* and this would happen when the trumpet sounded, and Jesus would descend in clouds of glory. Such admonitions and fears were the fuel that kept us vigilant, and gave us the scanning eyes, too. We learned quickly to spot the *beam* of sin in the eyes of others, as revealed by their dress, their shifty gaze, their language and more. It was our job to cajole and guilt sinners into owning their wicked ways and confessing to nothing less than everything. Sin spotting and naming, along with extracting confessions, meant more stars in the crown we'd wear in some promised heaven.

When we were beaten down enough with our sins, when fear and depression became too dark, we were reminded that God was a God of love, Praise the Lord! Once resuscitated, the God of love was easily forgotten, as the cloud of doom and damnation, darker than our thunderstorms, settled over and into us.

With Sister Rachael in command, we quickly came to see how sinfully frozen were the souls of the United Church folk. They were an orderly and predictable bunch, sitting, standing and singing in unison. They started on time and ended on time. By contrast, our services and prayer meetings were often chaotic, with people leaping to their feet, shouting, confessing sins and praising God, often in other tongues. We'd start services on time, and no one knew when they'd end. If the spirit fell in a special way, followed by long prayers at the altar, we could go on for a few hours, me with my headaches.

During worship services, random sisters and brothers would fall and spasm on the floor, while others might erupt with hysterical laughter. Always there were shouts of praise to Jesus, with arms waving in the air. We were everything the United Church wasn't. We were, Praise the Lord! on fire for Jesus, and wanted everyone to know it. Hallelujah, Hallelujah!!

Falling and jerking about on the floor would sometimes lead to rolling around, while speaking in tongues or loudly praising Jesus. We knew we were holy rollers, and that's what the other kids sometimes called us. Other names were used to shame and belittle us. We thought of ourselves as Pentecostals, for we believed in speaking in tongues based on the day of Pentecost in the book of Acts, in the New Testament. Speaking in tongues was a definite sign that one was saved and in intimate relationship with Jesus.

When others mocked us, we learned to turn the other cheek, even to appreciate any damning words, for this proved we were right, that we, like Jesus, were persecuted for being righteous, for speaking the truth and nothing but the truth, so help us God. I felt shame at the names we were called, but on the surface pretended it was a good thing. We were warriors in the Lord's army, and the more wounds, the better.

The world of Sister Rachael became our world, and that world was cleaved into two parts, as neatly as a knife cuts winter butter. People were either saved or damned, either loved Jesus or hated Him. The world and the actions of people were either good or evil. Things were either clean or dirty. We despised anything gray, anything in between, anything not either-or. We often quoted the scripture found in the book of Revelations warning us of what could happen if we were like the church at Laodicea, for they were neither hot nor cold, but only lukewarm and God spit them out of His mouth. In addition to the terrors of eternal hellfire, we were now on high alert to the dangers of being spewed from the mouth of the Almighty. Such fears kept us vigilant, and when I feared testifying for Jesus, all I had to do was think of God spitting me into hell. That would fire me up, and get me to my feet to testify. Our God, the ruler of the universe, the recorder of all our thoughts, was a hellfire God, a spitting God, with little love.

If the Bible says it, it's true, and that's enough for me!! This was an oft repeated and basic part of our belief system, and followed by a scripture to prove it. All the warnings, the red flags and danger signs preached to us: we must never change a *jot or title* of any of the words in the sacred King James version of the Bible. It behooved us to trust the spirit in all things, especially when it came to discerning what the Bible really, truly said, and if you challenged the truth of any scripture, you were a reprobate and given to *unclean spirits.* We never, ever thought that anyone interpreted Bible verses, assuming that we read them just as they were, apart from any opinions we might have.

We knew what the Bible said, no questions asked. And so help me God, if you disagreed or doubted the truth revealed to us, you'd go to hell. Our God was a God of justice and that was that.

In an effort to dampen the attraction of women and men, the women were required to wear long skirts, and to conduct themselves in a modest way. Dancing in the spirit at church was a fine thing, but all other dancing was taboo. Cosmetics, sinful dresses, pants and slacks were forbidden for women; they were signs of the fallen nature of women dating back to Eve in the Garden of Eden, or the whores of Babylon. There were good, chaste women, and the rest were sinners, *loose* women or prostitutes.

The list of evil doings kept growing depending on Sister Rachael's mood swings and new, ongoing revelations from scripture. Dancing, going to movies, reading comic books, Christmas trees, makeup, cussing, fancy clothes, idle thoughts and more were on the list of stuff that was *of the devil,* and strictly forbidden.

Along with the many Bible verses we memorized, we learned the idle brain was the devil's playground and were encouraged to stay busy with chores and religious activities. Most books were now off the reading list for they were *of the devil.* Prior to the purging revolution by Sister Rachael, we might see a movie every few months in Kelwood or McCreary. After the revolution, movies ranked right up there on our list of evils.

Christmas trees were somehow evil, and my sister Helen recalls how heartbroken and embarrassed she was when she had to tell our teacher, Mrs. Koop, that we could not be at the Christmas concert. Because we sang gospel music in church and as we worked, we had good singing voices, and our little school choir missed us.

As much as any puritan, Sister Rachael was profoundly suspicious of most forms of fun, and this spirit of sobriety carried over to all of us. We four younger kids were gifted with creative imaginations and a sense of play and mischief that we could turn off around intense looking religious adults, including Sister Rachael. When we were by ourselves, our imaginations and play were boundless, partly I now think, in protest to the straight jacket of our religion.

While we were free to roam and play, if we crossed the boundary into sin, as defined by an adult, we'd be in trouble. One example is stamped in my mind: Phil and I were excited about going to Kelwood on Halloween night, with our friends Nels and Bill Arvidson. We'd heard stories for years about the pranks we might play in the back alleys of that town, and in the late afternoon we walked the two miles to their home. Nels and Bill had dressed up for Halloween before, and with much giggling we began suiting up to fill our fantasies. I decided to be a hobo and had a stick with a small pack on the end. As I started having fun with it, beating the heads of Phil and our buddies, they got their water guns and went after me. We were having the most wild and wonderful time, when an elder from our cult showed up. His conscience was finely tuned, and he could smell the levity in the air the entire way from his farm, and decided to patrol the area. The fun and dreams evaporated as he scolded us, demanded we take off our silly costumes and ordered Phil and me into the car. I was shattered, and as we drove home, had another shame attack as I realized the error of my ways. We begged forgiveness and shed appropriate tears. Yet, thankfully, despite many incidents like this—or perhaps because of them—my puckish, prankish and playful nature endured, and continues to flourish.

With the exception of Dad and our brother Bill, the rest of us agreed we were terrible sinners and gave our hearts to Jesus. Dad was loyal to his United Church and the people who went there, so at first he would not line up and salute Sister Rachael, and there were many fights over this. We launched repeated prayers on his behalf, crying to the Lord that he might be saved, and eventually, after a serious illness, he joined the Lord's Army and started marching in step. We gave thanks to God, and turned our full sights on Bill.

Bill was in the early stages of puberty when Sister Rachael stormed in. With his down-to-earth logic, tough mindedness and newly acquired hormones, he decided he wanted nothing to do with our loony religion. And being true Christians, we spat him out of our family. He became our black sheep, our targeted sinner, and the object of even more fervent prayers than we had for Dad. Bill and Sister Rachel would fight, then our sister Jean, another firebrand for Jesus, would fight with Bill, calling him a reprobate and worse. A few times Jean chased Bill out of the house, swatting him with a rolled up newspaper, running into the field after him. She never caught him and it ended badly for her. She spent a long time picking the thistle stickers from her hose, and tending to assorted scratches. It was a liberating sport for Bill.

Sadly, our love for Bill was covered over with our self-righteousness, and our absolute truth that had no margin for error or human frailty. In the face of the eternal truths of the Bible as taught by our elders, we younger ones, Helen, Phil and I, were afraid to stand up for Bill. Had we expressed concern or love for him, we too might have felt the weight of our Biblical juggernaut.

Bill was emotionally ostracized from our family, and increasingly began spending time with his friends. With plenty of help from us, he became a rebel with a cause. He started smoking and drinking in his middle teens, fleeing the farm to do construction work in Alberta and British Columbia. Over the years, when he returned with fabulous stories, I had moments when I wanted to head west with him. A few times I stole a sip of his beer and knew for sure it was of the devil.

We three little ones made up for all that Bill lacked in the soul realm. Helen, Phil and I caved in to the dark cloud of conviction. We'd lie awake at night, full of terror believing the trumpet would sound and we'd go to hell. Jesus, we were told, could come in the twinkling of an eye. Helen had the mixed blessing of sharing her bed with Sister Rachael, and remembers gripping her night gown, believing that at the first trump, Sister Rachael would carry her up above the cold and sinful prairies through the pearly gates into heaven. The daytime sweat of hard work was trivial compared to the terror sweats at night.

When religious fervor burns so hot, those standing close are scorched, and often the weakest, the children, are the most scarred. Adults used the phrase, *Spare the rod and spoil the child,* and while I don't recall any severe beatings, the old leather strap was a threatening wall decoration, used occasionally depending on how the spirit of discernment was roiling our caretakers. Repeatedly, we heard it was necessary to break the will of children, and not let them have their way, or sass back. A few times we had our mouths washed out with soap as punishment for uttering God's word in vain, or when we told a fib.

Certain adults, as a sign of true faith, told stories of how it pained them to whip their much-loved children, *for their own good.* Children, it was clear, were fallen little critters, conceived in evil dating back to the sins of Eve in ancient Eden.

Prior to Sister Rachael's appearance, Bob and Jean had already prepared the ground for seeding, for they had already accepted Christ into their lives, but not fully enough. Sister Rachael's gospel demanded a total infilling, a complete surrender to Jesus, and her arrival ignited a hotter fire in them too. The three of them joined a handful of others, forming our little brood of true believers. Brother Ed, Jean's husband, and Sister Rachael were the captains of our army, and carried the torch of truth into the benighted prairies.

We were imprisoned by rules and Biblical doctrine. One of our rules was to eat the food set in front of us, while we thought of the starving kids in China. Before every meal we said grace, expressing gratitude to God for the food, and asking it and our lives to be blessed. This was a solemn ritual, and if we were giggling about something, we were roundly warned of what Jesus might think, and how at any moment we could be lead astray by idle talk and play. God, with the ever roaming eye, God the accountant who recorded every bad thought, feeling and action, all to be used at the day of judgment.

As kids we shared a dislike of hard bread crusts, and began hiding them under the table, where we'd discovered a secret shelf where the legs joined the table. This worked well for many weeks until one day someone moved the table and an enormous cache of bread crusts fell to the floor. Worse, was the infamous boiled egg placed on one of our plates. When the egg was cracked open it was a hard, sticky black mess that looked like a chicken getting ready for the barnyard, and one of us suffered the ignominy of having to eat it. Eat what is set before you. Other children are starving. Thank God for what you have.

Our fiery gang of true-believers met in a modest church building, located fifteen miles south in the town of Riding Mountain. A small manse was part of the church property, and served as a home for Jean and Ed—a place where we enjoyed many delicious meals after Sunday morning service. Feasting at the Lord's table was fine and all, but Church time passed faster when I let myself dwell on the lunch to come, and my headaches were tolerable. Once out of church, my headaches would go away.

Our modest church was a hangover from the past, built of logs, with a few rows of wooden benches that might hold fifty people, and could easily accommodate our band of true disciples of twelve to twenty. The United church had an upward pointing steeple that was a sure sign of apostasy; it was pristine white, but that did not fool us.

Our humble log church consisted of one large room with a small room in the back, both heated by a round wood-burning stove with a black pipe that, like us, pointed hotly toward heaven. Inside the church, round, hand-hewn rafters held the roof on, and when I opened guilty eyes during prayer, the axe marks on the logs interested me. I escaped into another world, imagining the pioneers who had chopped the trees, leaving their axe marks on the wood.

Just south of the church was a small creek rippling down from the hills, and that is the creek where Helen, Phil and I were properly baptized—held under the cold water while prayers for us went on and on. We learned that baptism by sprinkling saved only a few spots of our poor souls, while full immersion, real, honest-to-God spluttering baptism, was another sign of dying to our old lives and being born again. When I sucked in my first breath of air after being held down to my breaking point, gasping my love for Jesus, I did indeed feel reborn. Fifty years later, I return to that creek, with our son, Todd, and he takes a picture of me standing there, with hands folded in supplication.

My wife, Samona Ruth, was also raised in a similar tradition, in Houston, Texas, nearly 2000 miles south of Manitoba, and when we met in 1963, I could seamlessly blend into the services she attended. Her father was a Pentecostal preacher, and he and many of his congregation spoke in tongues. At first I had trouble understanding some of the thicker Texan accents, which for me sounded like a slower form of speaking in tongues.

Most Pentecostal churches have two meetings on Sunday, one in the morning and one at night, and if the spirit is moving, services can be two or more hours long. Sunday night services end with an altar call, directed mainly at visiting sinners. Altar calls consist of an invitation, often more like a demand, that sinners identify themselves, and come to the altar and accept Jesus into their hearts.

In our band of believers, when Brother Ed, or Sister Jean and Rachael fixed their laser eyes on you, it was wise to get down to the altar, or hit the road. After the weary sinners had made their way to the altar, those of us who were friends of Jesus would be on our knees next to them perhaps putting an arm around the sinner. Male elders would often slam their hands to the foreheads of unsuspecting folk, with a victory yell: *In the name of Jesus, I order the devil out of you!!* This initial outburst would be followed by other orders and imprecations, hollered in a loud voice, similar to a circus barker. A good hand slam to the forehead was enough to drive most folk to the floor. As with medicine, sometimes sinners needed to be well shaken.

We rarely had visitors, I suspect because the word spread about the heat we generated.

Altar calls were still vital for believers, and we were encouraged to get on our knees, wave our arms round and ask forgiveness for our latest sins. When our sins were washed away, we'd break into words and songs of praise, with more hand waving, and sometimes dancing in the spirit, along with speaking in tongues.

The prairie devil was deemed especially malicious, so we needed a mid-week insurance rally. Wednesday night services included much the same content as the Sunday services, with a longer prayer session at the end.

We believed it was necessary to *tarry before the Lord*, to pray through our doubts, shame and sin. Only then would the *showers of blessing* fall on us. If I had college credits for every hour of tarrying, I'd have a rant of Ph.D.'s behind my name.

Here I speak only for myself, however I believe that my prayer pattern applies to many who cried at the altar. First of all, I'd beg forgiveness for all my many sins, large and small. Most of my sins were bad thoughts towards others, an impressive list including hatred, anger, bitterness, judgments, and after puberty, my surprising interest in women. The shame and guilt I carried was almost too much to bear, but after a confessional outpouring I always felt better, believing I was cleansed and right with the Lord once again. The sweetness and hugging that followed our intense prayer sessions was worth the cost of confession. Once my hormones got rolling, it was exciting to hug the sisters.

Whilst confessing my sins, after an intense focusing on my own soul, I'd take a break and engage in guilty moments of voyeurism, tuning in to the high decibel sins others were voicing. At such times I'd fall into the sin of judgment, thinking they were putting on a show for the rest of us, trying to convince us they were the greatest sinner in the room, and at the same time the most on fire for God. Once I'd heard the same confessions over and over from the same brother or sister, I'd be bored and make sure to go and kneel in a different part of the prayer room to hear new dirt.

As I confessed my sins, I had the image of myself kneeling at the cross of Jesus and his blood cleansing me. The line from The Old Rugged Cross was my favorite mantra: *I will cling to the old rugged cross...* My brain, heart and soul were imprinted with that image thousands of times over the years, and it remains with me still, echoing in my head as I write.

Heaven and hell were not passing fantasies, but were real, eternal places and taken seriously. We were often reminded it was a terrible thing to fall into the hands of a living God, and this made sense, considering the angry God we worshipped. I went faithfully to the prayer room because I wanted to save my soul, and additionally I wanted others to see how committed I was. Anyone who shirked the prayer room, or who did not stay long enough, might be suspected of backsliding—of falling back into old, sinful ways.

After fifteen to twenty minutes of feverish confessions and pleadings, I would fill with the most intense sweetness and love for Jesus, and for those around me. When I finally got to my feet at the end of an altar call, I felt cleansed, forgiven, fully alive and ready to save the world, or to go to Africa as a missionary. That was the big one. Had I surrendered enough to Jesus, had I laid my all on the altar of sacrifice to even go to Africa to save the wild, heathen natives, the *darkies?*

The sweetness, the afterglow of intense confessional prayer accompanied by the gratitude that follows, cannot be captured in words.

Altar times were a sensory overload: the smell of sweat, the whispers, shouts and tears, the release of laughter, the old hymns in the background, the sight of people standing and waving their arms in victory, while others were curled up on the floor. If a true revival was happening, the prayer room might be so crowded we'd occasionally be bumping shoulders or legs with someone. After puberty, I'd pick a spot next to a pretty sister and hope we might touch shoulders, even legs, as we prayed. Fleeting contact with a lovely woman generated a shot of electricity more potent than prayer. Such contact led to shame and guilt, and another round of confessions. When my guilt for this reached a certain threshold I'd move next to a holy elder, hoping I might catch some of his blessings.

While we cried out to God, certain old hymns, usually played on an organ or piano, would help us melt down and surrender. Some of us would sing along with the background hymns, and those standing would move their bodies or upraised arms to the music. These old hymns ring clearly in my mind even today: *Just as I am without one plea, but that thy blood was shed for me, oh Lord, I come, I come to Thee.... And: I surrender, I surrender all, all to Jesus I surrender, I surrender all. Is your all on the altar of sacrifice laid...*was sung over and over. It was common that the room would fall into harmonic parts, and that was especially beautiful. Our prayers were a vital tonic for our souls. After intense confession, our grief, sadness and guilt, found sweet relief during our prayer meetings. Intense prayer can be a potent therapeutic experience, whatever the religious context.

More times than I care to admit, I was mistaken as a sinner when I went to a different church. I'm still uncertain if this was due to excess ambition on the part of other believers or due more to the sense of guilt I carried from imbibing so many hellfire and brimstone sermons. I recall one incident where an especially focused believer, intent on bringing a lost sheep home, refused to believe I was saved and kept exhorting me with words and arm tugs, wanting to drag me to the altar so he could get a star in his crown. But I stuck with my story. I learned that when someone laid holy cuffs on me, I'd be freed if I gave the precise date when I was saved, where it had happened, along with the name of the pastor of the church. It was like being in court. Much of our lives felt this way, as we were cross examined by elders, and as God patrolled our conscience.

As a child, I was never clear, and remain confused today, about the distinctions between Jesus, God and the Holy Ghost. When I prayed, I had an image of Christ on his wretched rack; that was the dominant image of my prayers. In the back of my mind I had wispy images of God and the Holy Ghost, somewhere in the area, around the cross and in our prayer room. It was difficult to think of Jesus or God being inside me, for we had been brainwashed into thinking we were born evil, and that evil was our certain nature.

So many of the actions of our cult elders were scary and bewildering. Seeing adults leaping to their feet, then speaking in tongues was frightening and mysterious. I couldn't understand how an adult could suddenly speak in a totally different language. An ecstatic ripple of energy would flash across our little band of believers when someone spoke in tongues. Folks would leap to their feet, praising God, yelling, crying, laughing and waving their hands, especially if this was a first time baptism. I wanted to fit in and to be seen as a true Christian, so I'd leap to my feet, even though at times it seemed I was just being a copycat, desperate for love and to blend with others.

I prayed earnestly, endlessly, for the gift of tongues, as I wanted not only to be closer to Jesus, but to also let others know I had fully surrendered my life to Christ. A few other kids had spoken in tongues, then my sister Helen received the infilling, and I felt like a second class citizen and became even more eager to receive the blessing. I prayed and cried louder and longer for the Holy Ghost to take my tongue. The adults around us were eager to help and would place their hands on our heads shaking us, yelling and pleading to God that we'd surrender to the Holy Ghost. When the intensity of seeking reached a fever pitch and my head was being rattled excessively, I realized I could fake it, and a couple of times did this to escape the emotional intensity and the pressure to *let go and let God*. My faking was followed by shame and guilt for which I never confessed, for I thought it would lead to deeper problems, and might in fact be the ultimate sin against the Holy Ghost, something we were warned could never, ever, ever be forgiven or washed in the blood.

We were repeatedly told that the blood of Christ was the only way to purge sins, and that it would wash away all sins. Except one. There was one sin the Bible talked about, and this too, was held over our heads as a fearful thing: the sin against the Holy Ghost. No one seemed to know what this was, exactly, though different preachers had different revelations to offer. The fact no one seemed to know meant it could be many things, and thus the fear was increased. When we fought as kids, we might hurl this threat against another.... *Be careful!! Don't sin against the Holy Ghost!!*

As on fire as we were, inevitably a certain lethargy would settle over us. Lukewarm was a dangerous trick of the devil. We'd become a bit tired of the same sermons from our pastor. As the devil breathed down our necks, we might miss church a few times. The cure for this was to bring in a genuine fire-breathing preacher from parts unknown. Stories of the miracle worker coming to set us on fire would spread quickly among us: his true powers of healing, his direct anointing, and the thousands slain and saved under his ministry. By the time he landed in our church, our pump was primed.

Lukewarm be gone! The electricity during the first meeting of our visiting preacher filled the air. Showers of blessings would fall in rich abundance and for a few days, we'd shout louder, shake and shimmy more, and have longer services and altar calls. If the revival fires were especially hot, many sinners would be saved, and the offering plates would fill. Some believers would be moved to a remarkable level of charity, giving more than they could afford. Occasionally, gripped with a special sense of guilt and love, someone might put their wedding ring in the offering plate, and later, when they testified to this, they'd earn applause and many stars for their heavenly crown.

We ushered in the new year with special *watch night* services. No drunken parties for us. We were a called and separate people, and proud of it. We'd assemble at ten in the evening, hear about the wretched conditions in the world, fall on our knees around eleven and pray well past midnight, pleading with God to purge the world, and for the second coming of Jesus to snatch us away from the black tar pit around us.

As soldiers in God's army, it was vital to have *sword drills*. A sword drill was a fierce competitive event, similar to a spelling Bee. Bible verses were swords of truth that could cut to the quick of things. The rules were simple: an adult would give us a question, and we'd raise our hands if we knew the Bible verse that fit the question. The last one standing was the winner, and Lord help the slackers. At one time, without taking a breath, I could rattle off the books of the Bible in order, along with many verses, and when Phil or Helen were quicker with their swords, I'd practice harder for the next dual.

We continued sharpening our swords at the Golden Branch church, located in the town of Sprague, in the south east part of the province, where we lived for several months after Mother died. I can see the faces and remember the names of many of the poor, hardworking people of faith who regularly showed up for midweek prayer meetings, and the Sunday morning and evening gatherings. We'd heard they were even more on fire than our Norgate group, and soon I believed it.

Most churches had summer camps, a week or two long. When I was nine or ten, we had one such camp at our Riding Mountain church. These were organized by my sister Jean and her husband, Ed, the pastor. The camp was held next to the church, where Ed had constructed temporary sleeping cabins and tents for the fifteen or so children who attended. The eating area was covered with the two yellow wings from our Harvard airplane, and at mealtimes we'd sing the old hymn, *Under His wings, Under His wings, we will abide forever.* We were a spirited and devoted group of kids, and we spent hours memorizing Bible verses for sword drills and learning craft skills with leather and wood. It was great fun.

One unholy incident remains clear in my mind: we boys found we could peek into the changing area where the girls were. We were soon found out and required to have special prayer sessions, asking to be forgiven. Walls were built to block the view of our curious eyes.

As an example of our religious view of things, I quote from a letter written by our sister Jean, (deceased in 2002) dated October 15, 1985. Her life, as revealed in her words, is a powerful example of someone who had an abiding faith, unblemished by doubt. She was eager to witness every chance she had. We learned to begin many of our actions, including our letters, with the phrase, *In Jesus Name,* and Jean was especially vigilant in this. The following catches the essence of many of her letters.

Dear Albert: In Jesus Name!! This is followed by a bit of news, then she writes as follows:

Jesus' life gripped my heart—His tremendous Love in laying down His whole being for wretched, miserable me, and this walk of true humility, always giving up his own will to do only his Fathers will!! (St John 6, and all of St John) became so living and real. My heart craved and panted after this NEW LIFE of Jesus—this resurrected life to become my life too! (Romans 12:1-2) True transformation from carnality and human tendencies into genuine holiness and godliness became my fervent goal that consumed my heart day and night! Psalm 1 became so precious too, as well as multitudes of other glorious verses (far too numerous to mention).

The lines from this letter reflect a continual theme of most of her letters to me (and from what I hear, to the rest of the family).

Her letter reveals her loving nature and generosity of spirit, her bedrock religious convictions and hopes. I notice too, her love of humility in others, and her practice of not thinking too highly of self. Her letter conveys the near universal human theme pervading most religions: the positive shift in life that accompanies certain religious experiences.

As I type her words, noticing how often she uses exclamation points and etc. I smile and wonder if that is why I use them when I write etc.!!!! I can picture her smiling from heaven each time my fingers use these phrases, and based on the science of epigenetics, my inner scientist imagines one of her cells nudging my neurons, unconsciously living her life through me!! Etc. Amen!

Reading her letter, I cringe as I see her shaming herself for being such a terrible, sinful, wretched human, in part because I've often felt this way in my own life. I've spent decades shifting my view from seeing human nature as evil to believing we actually prefer making loving choices if given a chance.

And I want to say to my sister Jean: *as much as I struggled with what I saw as your severe religious beliefs, I honor and love you, and cherish my memories of you. If you or Sister Rachael were to walk back into my life, I'd jump up and hug you both with tears of joy.*

Testimonies were another core event in our Church services. Most services would include testimony time, giving everyone a chance to stand and share gratitude for blessings, answers to prayers or to ask for prayer.

The following is a composite of the kind of testimony I often heard and used myself: *I thank Jesus for saving my soul! I am so happy I found him. I used to live in sin, and the devil had me, and now praise God, I'm saved by the blood of Jesus. If there is anyone here who has not repented from your sins and found the love and peace I found in Jesus, I pray you do so. Hallelujah! Praise Jesus, Praise Jesus! Amen and amen!* The repetition of key words added clout and rhythm to what was being said. If someone testified to a healing from illness, special thanks was rendered to God.

Under the reign of Sister Rachael, another decree went forth, to be obeyed as closely as the others. Each night before bed we'd be required to confess our transgressions to our sisters, brothers and adults. If we had a hateful or angry thought against someone, it needed to be confessed before bedtime, for Jesus could snatch us away in the night—but only if our souls were cleansed in the blood.

My sister Helen recalls the time she hid the remnants of her lunch in the pail that held the pig's slop, thinking she'd get away with it. However, she could not hide from her acutely tuned conscience, and, gripped by guilt, she tearfully confessed the sordid episode, asking Sister Rachael and Jesus to forgive her.

Encouraged by Biblical instructions, we were continuously encouraged to let our little light shine, to not hide it under a bushel, and we had a song expressly designed to remind us of this: *This little light of mine, I'm going to let it shine...let it shine, let it shine, let it shine.*

After we'd been with other kids, Sister Rachael and other adults would grill us to see if we'd witnessed for Jesus. If we had, we were so proud, and if not, we felt like failures and apologized. Such surveillance encouraged us to either lie, or embellish the truth: had we really stood up for Jesus, and did we make it clear that we were saved and loved Him? Had we reminded our friends that they were sinners? Had we talked with them about coming to Jesus? Because of my shame due to the name calling and teasing, I covered my tracks as best I could, and I think Helen and Phil did the same. Anything to avoid the wrath of God and his vigilant followers.

Expected to verbally witness for Jesus every day, Helen, Phil and I were made to carry religious *tracts* to school. These were small pamphlets, a few pages long, and like our verbal messages, they warned the reader of the dangers of sin and hellfire, and of the necessity of finding Jesus. The tracts did not mince words and had large, black words on the front: *Are you saved? Do you know Jesus? Hell is real! Does the Devil own your soul?* Stuff like that.

As with much of our religion, I had profound shame connected to our religious tracts, and after enough biting comments when handing them out, chose to hide them in my desk at school. One night when a social function was held at our school, my tracts fell to the floor, and a few students were happy to taunt me with them the next day. Kids were throwing tracts around, tearing them up and laughing. I was mortified and wanted to disappear.

We discovered a way to distribute tracts anonymously, and thus avoid the shame of handing them out, face to face. As we drove through Kelwood, in the back of Brother Ed's new Austin van, we threw tracts out the window, as a way of impersonally letting others know of their sins, and how to get right with God. This felt like such a clever solution to the witnessing problem, for we could witness and not be found out. Or so we thought.

We shared many shameful and embarrassing moments, but one stands out as especially excruciating. We had been invited for dinner to the home of Mr. and Mrs. Bieresto. We felt honored to be invited, for we saw them as the rich family, and they lived in a large white home that stood facing the road to Clear Lake. They drove a fancy, green Oldsmobile and were pillars of faith in the United Church.

We dressed in our go-to-church suits and put on our best manners. I remember the delicate china dishes and how we imitated the way our hostess held her fork and tea cup. Napkins were used and folded just so.

Then the party exploded. After dinner the two elders with us reflexively began witnessing to our hosts about the dangers of hell if they did not accept Jesus as their personal savior. The heat was on, and our hosts were being hammered on the anvil of truth.

Our hosts did not take kindly to this show of superiority and began arguing back, and a shouting match broke out. I was fearful someone might throw something, as I had seen happen in our home. Fighting with, and humiliating our hosts seemed so wrong, and again I was mortified in my bones. I lowered my head to hide my shame. As we drove away into the night, I hoped we'd never have to face them again.

Our zeal for saving others reached its peak during our Saturday night street meetings, held eight miles north, in McCreary. Witnessing to our school friends and handing out tracts was important, but Sister Rachael, Brother Ed, Sister Jean and a few other pillars of fire felt the need to turn up the heat even more, and to this purpose we started our street meetings.

What was clear to us, and not so obvious to others, was the fact we were the only true believers on the cold dark prairies, and as such, we had the holy duty to spread the truth of God as quickly and loudly as possible before the second coming of Christ. We were mightily encouraged by the song, *Bringing in the sheaves, bringing in the sheaves, we shall come rejoicing, bringing in the sheaves*. We knew the *end times* were near, and the evil world was in the autumn of life, ripe for harvest, and we were heaven bent to bring sinner sheaves to the altar for a good threshing. We were motivated, in part, by the truth that every sinner saved meant another star in our crown of glory when we passed the pearly gates, and Lord knows we craved those stars. Hallelujah!

Our street meetings did not meet the standards of modern rock concerts with booming sound systems, flashy lights and screaming fans, and yet we staged a fine show in our own way, with a few twists unseen in the flashiest concerts of today.

Saturday nights, under cover of darkness, we brave soldiers of the Lord, a committed invasion force equal to Seal Team Six, would pile into a couple of cars and head north to rescue the heathens. McCreary was full of infidels, and the worst were the Catholics. It was imperative that we introduce them to the truth of the Bible, and lead them to Jesus.

As we drove north into the night, we'd fortify ourselves by reciting scriptures and singing the song: *We're in the Lord's army.... We march in the infantry, ride in the cavalry...* We lined up and marched to this rousing song before we piled in the car and headed north for battle with Satan's legions. Our sword drills meant we were sharp and ready to attack the enemy.

The battle ground between saved and sinners was staged on a vacant lot between the hardware and drug store, watched over by a puzzled maple tree.

We'd set up our microphone and speaker, holding hands and forming a holy knot as we readied for battle. Jean and Helen would work their accordions into a frightful wheezing state, and the rest of us would sing along with a selection of old hymns, always including *The Old Rugged Cross: On a hill far away, stood an old rugged cross, the emblem of suffering and shame: and I love that old cross where the dearest and best, for a world of lost sinners was slain…...I will cling to the old rugged cross and exchange it someday for a crown.*

After softening our target audience with some sweet music, in turn we would walk to the mike, proclaiming our testimony of how we found Jesus, how he'd washed away our sins, and we were now bound directly for heaven. The entire proceeding left me confused and stricken with shame. I was terrified to take the mike, and scared not to, lest I be seen as not truly on fire for Jesus. As the pressure mounted, I'd lunge for the mike and as quickly as I could, fire out some scrambled words, about how I loved Jesus, then dart behind my sister and her accordion. From my hiding place, I'd scan the crowd to see how many of my school friends were watching and prepare for the ridicule I'd take the next day at school.

After our testimonies, Brother Ed would grip his red Bible, and stand tall with the mike. Words would gush from him as the spirit seized him to preach about the love of God and the necessity of accepting Jesus to avoid the fires of hell. I'd shrink away as the volcano of truth erupted, hiding behind my sisters and brothers, peeking out at the crowd while feeling pity for them. As brother Ed preached, we'd back him up with encouraging shouts of, *Amen and Amen* and, *Praise the Lord!*, and a litany of *Hallelujahs.*

Our show was electric enough, and the Lord often helped us by adding the drama of a massive lightning storm. Was God angry at sin and sinners? Of course He was. Jesus sent the storms to cleanse the town of sin and to show the general power of God to do as He pleased. We knew we would not be hit with lightening, for we were his children, but sinners look out! I secretly hoped God might singe them a bit, giving them a taste of hellfire, so they might find Jesus and join our group.

Both violent storms and cults pack a lot of heat, and can burn you. Luckily, both pass quickly.

After the storm passed we'd rush back to the front line, drenched, but still on fire for the Lord, singing the old hymn, *Showers of blessings, showers of blessings we pray.* Wet from the rain I'd think of old Jonah, and how he must have looked after the whale puked him out.

Invading forces inevitably create resistance, and one night the local boys surprised us with fire crackers, tossing them among us from the roof of the drug store. We scattered into the shadows, except for Brother Ed who held fast to his microphone, gripped mightily by the spirit, uttering words of damnation to the sinners. His courage in the face of direct fire made him a hero in our eyes.

The town kids had imaginations as active as our own. If fireworks would not drive us out of town, other things might, and soon we were pelted with eggs slung from the dark alley behind us, while the audience roared with ungodly laughter.

I felt much shame, but was not afraid, for I'd been on the front line of egg wars on our farm; I skipped and darted about to keep my Sunday clothes clean. The kids who threw the eggs at us had the usual slingshot arms, and direct hits smarted for a few seconds. Given the rifle velocity of the eggs, some would fly above us, striking our curious audience.

And once again, Brother Ed was our hero: he never ran, but held his ground, yelling more loudly as each egg hit him. He was no coward, nothing yellow about him—at least at first. As he took more hits, his suit and white shirt bore the orange and yellow colors of battle.

Phil and I hatched a plan of a counter attack, for we too had rifle arms and pails full of organic, free range rotten eggs from our hens. As we giggled about revenge, we knew it was only talk; our marching orders were to turn the other cheek, to grin and bear it, and to smile sweetly for Jesus.

As I reflect on those days I imagine the good farmers, come to town for Saturday night shopping and a beer, must have been astonished to learn they were sinners and headed for hell. Over the summer the size of our audience increased, and we rejoiced in our victory. The stale movies at the theatre were no match for us. For most, our Saturday night circus was the best show in town.

Helen, Phil and I were much impressed with the powerful electricity of our pastors, and drew on our active imaginations to form our own church in the woods, far enough from our house so we could not be heard. We built a small preacher's podium, similar to the ones used by big people, and would sneak the large family Bible from the house, delivering our version of fire and brimstone to each other, and to any birds and wretched worms that cared to listen. We took turns being preacher and congregation, and after each sermon those in the role of audience would rush to the altar and fall to their knees, where the preacher would lay on hands and pray for deliverance. We'd dance about, and roll on the ground, consumed with healing laughter. At first we feared God would strike us dead with a lightning bolt; when that did not happen we took it as evidence God approved our fun.

Those of us who knew Sister Rachael saw her as a wonderful example of the power of Jesus to save and cleanse sinners, for she had been saved from alcoholism. Because of our shame and secrecy about most everything, we children did not learn till years later she had also been *a woman of the night* living in *the gutters of sin*. She was saved at the Lighthouse Mission in a seedy part of north Winnipeg, under the ministry of Sister Margaret Sinclair who was also a firebrand for Jesus. Helen, Phil and I visited that church a few times, and I was intrigued and frightened by the poor people who lived in that part of town.

When I first heard that Sister Rachael had traded away her feminine charms, the anger I had toward her felt more justified, for I could see her as a hypocrite. As I've matured I remember the love Christ had for street people, including those who sold their bodies to put food on the table, and I have compassion for her. Based on what I've read of other cultures and religions, I know that in some traditions, prostitution can be a holy calling. If I were raised in such a culture, I'd believe this along with most other traditions of that culture. At this point in my life I have only residual judgments of Rachael; mainly I honor her soul's journey, and her astounding and enduring faith in her Master.

In passing, a note of irony if not synchronicity. Margaret Laurence, a much read Canadian author, and born like me in the Neepawa hospital, and in her early years a resident of that town, wrote a novel entitled, *Rachael, Rachael*. Her book was published in 1966, and like the lives of many of us of that era, shame and secrecy play a central role in the life of Rachael, the heroine. I'm sure Laurence never met or heard of our Sister Rachael. If only she had known.

Sister Rachael died only a few years after leaving our farm. I heard from several believers she suffered a heart attack while witnessing for Jesus on the streets of Sprague, Manitoba. I can readily believe this, for she witnessed every chance she got, boldly speaking her love of Jesus. I can see her testifying, then suddenly leaving her body and flying straight into the arms of her beloved Savior. Jesus was in her blood, was the air she breathed, the ground she stood on. It is fitting as I see it, that she died in the street, for that is where her Master did much of His teaching.

Her body reposes in the good earth in the diminutive Golden Branch cemetery, next to the church. One brief eulogy away rest the bones of our brother and flyer, Bob, grounded at last, and his wife Donna.

CHAPTER 4

—— ✤ ——

Hockey Wars and More

*A very long time ago on the wind swept Isle of Skye, after years
of depleting wars, the clan chiefs got together to see if they could
find a substitute for war. Their other game, curling, they knew
would never do, for it was far too tame. They needed to satisfy their
ancient lust for blood, broken bones and flying teeth. During a
few days, as the whiskey flowed freely, it was agreed that the most
terrible effects of war would be less if only a small group of men
armed with clubs would bat around an object in a confined area
with a few rules to temper the bloodletting. Swords would be banned
in favor of knife blades used only on awkward feet. After drinking
even more whiskey it was also agreed that this new sport would be
played on a pond, on the small sheep farm of Ian McLeod. Ian's
wife had a very old, small and hardened ball of haggis, and it was
decided this would withstand the rigors of being batted about. Only
a few months later Ian McLeod and all the haggis hitters shipped
off to Canada, taking their violent game with them. Because a ball
of haggis was not hard enough, a disc of round and flat hardwood
was chosen as a way to guarantee more bruises and blood. Thus was
hockey invented as a moderation for clan war.*

From a document found in the basement of Dunvegan
Castle, well preserved because it was nestled next to a
bottle of Tallisker Scotch Whiskey.

✤

SONS AND DAUGHTERS of the true north lace on skates in the first three or four years of life, and it is a big step in life. We had barely put our bottles and rattles down when hockey sticks appeared out of thin air, along with skates. Creeks and ponds had ice much of the year, and we were excited to enlist in the hockey wars that raged across our great white Dominion.

Before hockey we started throwing things, in preparation for the baptism into hockey. Our farm was on a gravel ridge and we had an endless supply of stones perfectly sized for throwing. Our two large barns were built on the ridge, and we played baseball between them, using them as backstops. The pitcher would stand near our west barn, throwing stones east to the batter standing a few feet lower by the east barn. Honed pieces of boards served as bats.

At mealtimes, when a brother or sister asked to have food passed, we liked to toss the requested item, including bread, rolls, hard boiled eggs and small jars of jam. Baseball soon followed, along with soccer, then football, with the oval ball that was tricky to throw. Because granite curling rocks weighed forty pounds, we waited until the fifth and sixth grades before testing ourselves with curling.

The flat lands and tempting horizons of prairie invite movement, and we were usually on the move—-walking, running, hunting, playing sports, chasing cows and doing other forms of physical activity. Along with the formal games bequeathed to us, we also made up games on the fly, improvising rules as the game evolved. Because our winters were long, many games centered around snow and ice. Building snow tunnels, forts and games on ice offered endless, cold fun. But hockey ruled.

Everything Canadian can be traced back to hockey in less than six steps. Canada, for example, has little interest in military matters, and rarely goes to war. Why? Canadians, God bless us one and all, leave it on the ice. The urge for war dissipates in the mayhem, the rage, the bloodletting of hockey. Sharp skate blades are as close to sabers as the law allows. Of course, we are gentle people! We play hockey. Political discourse is polite and decent for the same reasons. If tempers flare, they can be calmed by playing, or merely watching a game, while quaffing a Moosehead and more. The entire national character of Canadians rests on THE GAME: thoughts, emotions, literature, music and all the rest, finds inspiration on the bloody ice. The hockey stick graph is so well known, it needs no further explanation here. Not so well known is this: if you look carefully at the maple leaf on the flag, you can see a hockey stick embedded therein. It was not done consciously, but inevitably emerged into the leafy structure. Hockey is the root of Canada; hockey rules. And it is mainly a good thing, for it dissipates all vile, and renders its people harmless.

When The Great Gretzky left Edmonton, Canada collapsed with death spasms, as her breath was sucked southward to Los Angeles, the land of angels. How can hockey exist alongside angels? Hockey is closer to hell than heaven, and Gretzky should have known better.

Most Canadian kids play their first hockey on ponds, lakes and creeks, and that was true in our area. The only proper skating and hockey rinks were either five miles south in Kelwood, or eight miles north in McCreary. Getting to town was tricky, because of the challenges of getting our cars running in freezing weather, and so we spent many hours creating rinks, and playing the game on creeks and ponds. We'd talk with neighbor kids and find out who had the best ice, and gather there on Saturday mornings to clean off the snow, using it to construct a boundary for our rink. Many hours were spent shoveling and brooming snow from the ice. After it was cleaned we could see easily see the cracks, which we'd fill with water poured from our milk pails.

Neepawa, thirty miles south, had a covered rink, but you had to be part of a winning team to play there. Our games were played in the open and freezing air. When it was colder than thirty below, our throats could bleed from sucking in freezing air at warp speed. Not that this was the only blood around. Hellion hockey: the madcap days before masks and helmets, and no referees to calm the insanity. Until high school we had no shin guards. This is why Canadians can travel freely without passports or visas: all you have to do to ID an ex-hockey warrior is to lift up a pant leg, either one will do, and you'll see the scars, bumps, bruises and other curiosities from the ice wars. Airlines are known to offer free rides to hockey players in case trouble breaks out, and some provide sticks along with beer.

When people hear I actually survived hockey they are curious about which position is most dangerous, and I cheerily tell them that playing defense and being a forward shooter involve continual hazards. Then I deepen the story by noting that the job of goalie is a dead-man skating affair.

When their faces drop far enough, I deliver the good news to cheer them up, informing them that playing goalie can lead to miracle cures. My example is this: if you are an easy going guy with never a paranoid thought and too optimistic for your own good, a few seconds in goal will remedy that, for you'll know the guys on the other team really are out to kill you. What else are you to think when black missiles are fired at you, over and over, along with screams, the board banging, the bared teeth when they shoot? In the few wars Canada fought, hockey goalies, familiar with the ice trenches, were slow to sign up, and in fact were often granted exemptions for this very reason. *You were a goalie, eh!!?? Just sign here and go back to the farm. You've paid your dues.*

What could ever motivate a young kid to play goal? Those of us who tried it just weren't thinking. And that is the main answer I can give as to why I played goalie for half a game in high school. I was inspired by tales of the famous Turk Broda, who we were told was raised *up in the Clear Lake area,* and hence a local boy who became a professional star. As I strapped on my oversized pads I had images of being the young Turk, playing Saturday night hockey in the Maple Leaf Gardens. I was ready to face the black plague of pucks.

All padded up, as I sloshed awkwardly toward the net, I remembered that at forty or so below, a slap shot can shatter a puck if it hits the goal post full on. We joked that the pieces that went in counted as half a goal. As my panic mounted I spun around once and nearly skated back to the safe harbor of our dressing bench, rousted from my retreat only by the friendly jibes of my team mates. A few of them had tried goal and quit early, and they wanted to see how McLeod would stand up under fire.

Just to prove that God had turned his head, that night we were playing against the adult team. In the first period a wicked shot fired from my blind side by Delmar Kyle, Mr. Rocket Man himself, missed my head by a few inches. He told me before the game he'd be gunning for me. He was. And so were his teammates. They all had a thousand or so shots in the first period. *Gotta test the new kid in net. See what he's made of.*

Thanks to our religion I had a proper fear of God, but this was something else. This was down to earth, real fear. My legs felt shaky. I was screaming at my cubs to protect me from the lions. A few minutes later, another hateful shot hit my bare ankle below my shin pad. I was familiar with pain, but this was hellishly excruciating, and I limped off the ice, shielding my tears, and never played goalie again. Delmar looked pleased as he whipped his stick around, snarling at me with his lion teeth. He and his muscled-up, plowboy wingers killed a dream that night and were pridefully gloating as they circled around the ice. *Get back in net, McLeod! Come on. We dare you. Your team needs you!*

Whimsically, I look back and am amazed and thankful that we survived the hazards and full bore insanity of hockey. I was one of the lucky guys who came away with all my teeth, and without broken limbs or serious scars, and this due to luck and the fact I was a less-than-average player, and avoided most fights. Truth be told, my shame about my skating ability led me to try goal. All goalies do is stand there, right? Wrong. Just stand there as you would before a firing squad. Nothing to it. And don't forget to breathe.

In addition to deepening my respect for the hazards of hockey and war generally, I became and still am a proud member of OHGOD: the Ottawa Honorable Goalie Order. Sadly, I still have passing, usually manageable periods of paranoia.

Church leagues were especially ferocious, and it seemed that excess knee time at the altar bent us toward an icy anger. You might think players in church leagues would be more compassionate and decent. If anything they were more vicious, as the chaos shattered our halos, and helped the old devil exploit our killer instincts. Before games I prayed that my teammates and I would not be injured. I imagined Jesus as our seventh man, as our protective spirit. Jesus, I figured, was a great skater and my winger. But I knew how clever the devil could be and how he could sneak around. One night in a church league, two of my friends were taken to hospitals, ten minutes apart, both with several teeth gone, and the usual fountains of blood. You might think helping a teammate rummage through the bloody slush, searching for missing teeth, could lead to contemplating the risks and rewards of the game. Wrong again.

In another church league game, my buddy Ray Unger was in goal for our team, and we were losing to a Mennonite team by about eighteen and a half to three. On a face-off in our end, one of their snipers chose to slap the puck before it hit the ice. The black missile flew straight to the goal, and broke Ray's stick. Already upset that we were not protecting him, he angrily stalked off the ice. The dreams of another goalie, shattered on the ice. We his useless teammates, snickered behind his back: *I guess ole Ray couldn't take it, eh?*

Sane thinking and logic are foreign to the so-called brains of hockey players. Think again of Gretsky's reflexive move to Los Angeles. Hockey terror is fueled by pure testosterone. In fact, when one reflects on the hazards of the game, the mind drifts across the red line into the realm of physics, and you're tempted to think of hockey as a parallel universe inhabited by angry aliens. But we must not go there, for even to suggest this is an act of blasphemy against Canada itself.

On another memorable night, my metal protector cup decided to make a break for the goal on its own and raced down my leg onto the ice. It made a fantastic ringing sound as it skittered across the blue line, hitting the boards and ricocheting back toward me. I was mortified. As the fans erupted, with laughter and applause, I put my head down and retrieved my errant protector, and all crimsoned-faced, skated to the bench where I shoved it back into my pants. In defense of all things hockey, I must note we were not completely insane: we had the good sense to wear cup protectors before we wore helmets. As hormone crazed teenagers, we had our values right.

What is most needed is a twelve, or maybe eighteen-step program to help retired hockey players recover. Post traumatic stress syndrome is a real thing for warriors of all stripes. My recovery from hockey madness is ongoing.

I watch playoff games and wonder why the injury rate is so low and no one dies out there. A computer search tells me several players have died over the years. Also, on my computer I've seen pictures of players where their faces display the accumulation of decades of scars, as though they are all still present. Not pretty. I sadly remember my high school friend, Bill Masterton, who died while playing hockey. Bill was a gifted player and went on to play professionally with the Minnesota North Stars. He suffered a massive concussion during a game in January, 1968.

As I've hinted, Canadians are compelled to play hockey due to a peculiar genetic trait, and this rare affliction helps us understand most everything Canadian. In part, due to the bitter weather, each of us was cursed and blessed with the recently identified hockey gene, (known to scientists as Pucknut 666). We could not just sit around when formal games were over. Just as we were born to breathe, breed and walk, we were instinctively driven to join the bloody fray. Girls and women were also born with the gene, though in diminished form, and could express this by playing broom hockey, wearing shoes rather than skates.

If there was no ice around we'd play snow hockey in our yard, wearing our snow boots. In 1949, after we finally got electricity—all 110 volts of it strung between poles in our west field—we now had a dazzling yard light on the pole between our house and barn. Along with our neighbors, it was a source of pride to leave our yard lights on, signaling, *here is where we live. We are modern farmers. We have electricity!* When we walked across the fields at night, it was comforting to know where everyone lived, for each light was a beacon in winter storms.

Manitoba suns tire early in winter time, and as our yard lights extended short winter days, we were quick to use the new light for various games. The games of tag and hide and seek took on a new dimension, as our long shadows darted around us, trying to keep up with our fast legs. Hide and seek offered new hiding places, as we learned to work with the new mix of light and dark.

When the first snow came in October, every night became hockey night in Canada. We grabbed our sticks, put on our overshoes and joined the fray of yard hockey. Loose snow packed quickly under our melee, and the silence of the prairie nights yielded to our screams, laughs and yells of exclamation.

We had one problem, and immediately turned it into fun. After only a few minutes our puck would disappear into a snow bank. They were hard to find in deep snow, and soon, like the bears in our hills, they'd hibernate, waiting till spring thaw to show their faces. The good news was we always had a generous supply of frozen horse turds, and never lost a moment before upgrading our game. We discovered the durability of frozen horse *pucky*, along with how easy it was for the goalie to catch with his baseball glove. When they hit our legs and ankles, they hurt less than a regular puck, and this was especially true when we took one to the face; they'd bounce away leaving a bit of fragrant residue on our cheeks or foreheads as badges of honor. This was nearly a blood-free game, but it was still fun. And we had lots of jokes: *That shot stunk! We're just horsing around.*

When Mr. North Wind drove us indoors with his angry outbursts, the lethal hockey gene led us to play in our kitchen, while Dad read his paper. He must have realized early on that we had too much wild energy for him to monitor and control, and this was especially true after Mother died. Increasingly, he chose to ignore us and only rarely would ask us to calm down. He was often working in the fields or the barns, and that made it easy for us to celebrate our primal instincts.

And so it came to pass that during blizzards and random times, we'd play hockey in our kitchen, with a real puck and real hockey sticks. Like most Canadian boys we wanted to be great hockey players, and kitchen play gave us extra hours of practice. If Phil started out as goalie, I'd be the shooter, while dad sat with his nose in the *Family Herald* or *Reader's Digest*. The goal was in front of the low coat rack where we hung our heavy parkas and overpants; they hung to the floor, and we hoped they'd protect the wall from our hard shots.

After feinting and faking to fool the goalie, we'd zing a shot at the clothing rack. Most of the shots were blocked by the coats, but some would zing through, and we ended up with holes in our plaster walls. The linoleum had black marks from the tape on our sticks, and every few weeks we'd get baking soda and scrub them as clean we could. We were wild because we were raised in the wild.

Our games were punctuated with yells, the most common, *he shoots, he scores!* using our best imitation of Foster Hewitt, the famous Toronto Maple Leaf radio announcer. Our father sat only one hockey stick away, his feet warming in the open oven door, unblinking and unmoved, far away in his reading. When a puck hit him, he'd ask us to tone it down a bit. It was all good. He'd go back to reading, we'd go back to hockey. He knew boys would be boys.

Kitchen hockey, due to the small rink size, had even more contact than regular hockey, and this led to regular fights, as Phil and I pushed and shouldered each other. Dad decided we might as well learn to box properly, and came home from the post office one day with two sets of purple boxing gloves. He was a big fan of Joe Lewis, and saw how easy it would be to harness our hockey gene into a boxing career. Both the noise and bloodletting increased, as we sparred around, popping each other. Dad would instruct us, based on the fights he heard on the radio, and he'd occasionally put on the gloves and go a round or two. He was a lefty, and got in some good shots. Kitchen hockey and boxing helped winter pass more quickly.

When Phil and I visited our relatives, the Confreys, in Winnipeg, we played hockey with their son Dave, on the icy street at 84 Leighton Avenue. Dave was younger than us, but gifted with more hockey genes.

⚬⟁

In addition to hockey, baseball and soccer, we took up curling in the first year at Kelwood High, five miles south. The town had an enclosed building that housed two curling rinks. Compared to most games we played, curling was tame, without body contact, and slow in tempo. Curling required a meditative approach to the world, and as hockey hellions we struggled with this. We added excitement by throwing high speed bombs and runners, to knock out other rocks, and sometimes a few would jump the rail, causing mayhem for players in the adjacent rink, amidst our laughing fits.

In winter, when the living room was warm enough, Phil and I played football, facing off on our knees, using the patterns in the linoleum as field markers. We'd hike the ball, snapping it up from the floor, and slam our shoulders into each other, pushing and feinting, trying to get past each other to score. Scores were always low as it was difficult to move quickly on our knees. Occasionally our hockey genes would fire up, and we'd punch and wrestle, sometimes ending up with a bruise or bloody nose.

At school we were not supposed to play rugby, and this of course was an incentive to do just that when the teacher was not around. While I never learned to skate well, on the ground and snow I was fast, and excelled in soccer, baseball and touch, or flag football. When we played soccer in winter, Mr. North Wind was the strongest player, stealing and curving the ball at will. When he was howling, we'd often chase a soccer ball half a mile into a field, and that was part of the fun. Soccer for us was played by hockey rules, and we loved to trip, body check and mug each other as we did on ice.

In our family, until age twelve or so, most of our baseball was played with stones, using boards for bats. We played on the gravel ridge between our barns. We'd gather a milk bucket full of stones, and the pitcher would stand on the ridge, using it as an elevated mound and pitch downward to the batter. Phil and I, sometimes with friends, spent hundreds of hours taking turns pitching and hitting. Our humble Yankee Stadium was blessed by the famous players who appeared: Satchel Page was a regular, and he'd face batters including Mickey Mantle, Duke Snyder, Jackie Robinson and *Joltin* Joe Dimaggio. Our field of dreams was complete when Roy Campanella showed up to catch. The stadium was always full, and we'd announce our games to the millions of radio fans.

When a dumb cow or pig walked onto our diamond, or Dad walked through with a bucket of milk, *The Mick,* (Mickey Mantle) would pause for only a few seconds before belting another homer over the barn. Sometimes Dad would join in for a bit, and I can still see his awkward left handed throw, his stiff arm cranking like one of the levers on our threshing machine.

Because of the hundreds of hours with sticks and stones, Phil and I had keen eyes and were gifted ball players. Our country high school had only a dozen or so players, and we played several different positions, depending on who showed up for games. Phil and I took turns batting third and fourth in many games. While we rarely hit long balls, after years of swatting stones, we rarely struck out.

I experienced seven seconds of fame in one ball game, and in 2008 wrote the following account of my exploit:

On that summer day in 1955, my first year of high school, I was back on base. I was a decent hitter, but my true, God-given gift was my speed.

Whether playing tag, racing, soccer or baseball, I was fast and knew my legs could blur the air, but coach did not appreciate my speed. He was a balding, overworked farmer, and had appointed himself coach. This is how it worked in Kelwood, our little town on the frozen prairies of Manitoba. When we needed a coach, someone would step up. There were no committees, no advisory boards, no lawyers for advice and recourse. Everything was unofficial. We had no uniforms.

All of us on the baseball team were hockey hellions, better on ice than dirt. The lethal mix of hormones with hockey guaranteed we were an unruly bunch, full of mischief and sudden moves. Playing hockey, we learned to lunge in any direction at any moment, quite unlike baseball, with its rigid rules about base running.

Coach was often testy. Thirty below and hard work on the prairies can do that. He'd ride us for our errors, rarely saying anything positive. And on this day he'd been riding me, and I was plotting revenge. The only thing faster than my legs was my imagination. Standing in the prairie wind, my feet comforted by the bag, images tumbled through my head like a runaway slot machine. I was in a gambling mood.

I was going to risk stealing second without any lead off. Coach always insisted if we were going to steal, we must take a long lead-off. He saw most of us as slow, and often said we "lumbered" when we moved. I could easily see that some of my teammates lumbered, and would get cut off and sanded in that dangerous space between bases. But not me, not today.

We were facing another scrubby farm team, and the catcher with the long-sleeved shirt was slow and had a spaghetti arm. This was not a guy who could throw darts to second base. By stealing second without any lead-off, I'd again prove my speed, and coach would get red and roar around. All good. It was bottom of the eighth, and we were a dozen or so runs ahead. No way to lose this one.

Best of all, my buddies would fall down laughing at what I was about to do. The only risk I could see was that I'd never actually seen anyone steal second from third. I'm ready to rocket. The pitcher checks third, sees I'm rooted there and unloads the rock to his catcher. In that moment I launch myself toward second. I'm a blur, another crazy kid headed the wrong way. A cloud of dust, and I'm safe on second. My heart is on fire, and life is tearing through me. My toes grip the bag like talons. From out of the blue I've pounced on this bag and it's mine.

Around me, chaos: I see the catcher wringing the ball, looking around for help. Coach's face and bald head are crimson, and he's leaping about, roaring, pointing. My teammates are collapsing with laughter. I'm feeling wild, giddy.

Then the fear hits me, as I realize what I've done. Maybe this time I've been too crazy, lunged once too often.

Inevitably, amidst the confused voices, I see first base has been abandoned, and for a brief moment another mad impulse grips me.

The Confrey family graciously invited me to live with them for my final year of high school in Winnipeg, where Dave and I continued night hockey, playing on packed snow in the street. Dave developed into an excellent player and received a hockey scholarship to play at Michigan Tech University, and they won two NCAA championship during the years he played with them. I like to think our hours of horse-pucky games helped develop his skills.

I note too that during our first trips to Winnipeg, Phil and I traded baseball cards with some other kids. One of our bubble gum chewers and card traders, Pete Stemkowsi, went on to a solid professional hockey career. I carried about forty cards back to the farm, and they were lost for over thirty years. Then, in 1992 I received a call from my brother Bill. He had found my cards in a corner of our farm home. Hearing the news it felt like my childhood had again sprung alive in me, and I had goosebumps, tears and laughter as we talked. In my stash were cards of many of the stars of the 1951 to 1953 era, but sadly they were all in poor condition, thus not collectible.

A last note on curling: my brother Phil kept honing his skills and as an adult played in national bonspiels with a team from Omaha, usually as the skip, (the captain.) He played in three national championships. Over the years he managed to score two eight-enders, meaning his team had all their rocks in the circle, and the other team had none—a feat that is statistically nearly impossible. He may be the only guy walking around with two eight-enders in curling and a couple of holes-in-one in golf. He tells me his team drank excessive Scotch after one of the eight-enders, and swore never to score another.

CHAPTER 5

— ❦ —

Spring, Summer and Fall: Three Months of Poor Sledding

*Who hath divided a watercourse for the overflowing of waters, or a
way for the lightning and thunder.....and to cause the bud of the
tender earth to spring forth? Hath the rain a father? or who has
begotten the drops of dew?*

JOB 38: 25, 27, 28.

❦

IN THOSE FAR away days, fickle spring wafted in and out, on the wings of robins and crows. Sunsets would slow, and the three-foot icicles on the barn and house would surrender to the north-creeping sun. With others around the world, we had our rites of spring: we'd hang up our winter parkas, let the fires burn low, open our barn doors, paroling the animals out to greening pastures. Dancing around a maypole? We'd never heard of it, but we kids would chase around after the calves, pigs and chickens, all of us made merry by the sun.

The sound of a crow at sunrise, followed by the sighting of a robin helped scare winter away. April and May, uncertain about the dramatic shift from snow covered prairie to dark soil, would sometimes bring inches of snow stunning us back to the middle of March, and the robins and crows would vanish.

As spring came on, the rabbits we hunted in the trees along the creek gave up white winter coats for summer brown. On the day when the setting sun shot his first beam through our north kitchen window onto the east wall, Dad would excitedly proclaim the end of winter. *There it is! The light is coming in our north window, spring is here! Run and tell Helen and Billy to come see...praise the Lord, thank you Jesus, spring has come.*

We'd stare at that magic light beam, touching it with our fingers where it struck the wall. We felt relieved to have survived another winter, and celebrated the coming spring.

As the snow and ice melted, the creek flooded into our field on the west side of the gravel ridge, a stone's throw west of our house and barns. As soon as the new pond was big enough we'd drag out our old wooden raft, find a couple of boxes to sit on, and pole our way around the pond. When winter blew back in for a few days, the pond would ice up and we'd strap on our skates, zipping across the open ice. The pond was many times bigger than a normal rink and during hockey games we could make long passes, with the puck echoing and singing across the ice.

Under a full moon, at the north end of the pond, we'd skate along the swollen creek, shimmering like ghosts in the dim light, flashing between trees, appearing and disappearing as we darted about. The northern lights regularly blessed us with a colorful light show, and we'd try to touch them with our hockey sticks. A few times we actually heard the soft static sounds of the lights as they pulsed above us. Even with our passion for skating, we could not ignore the heavenly lights for long. We'd stand motionless, supplicants awash in the beauty, silently breathing in the reds, pinks and blues.

As we darted around on our skates, we listened closely to the song of the ice: dangerous, thin ice had a sharp, ringing sound, while thicker ice made a dull roar beneath our blades. Our survival training had taught us to avoid thin ice, but our pond was not dangerous, for it was only knee deep. When we fell through thin ice it added screams of excitement. After we pulled each other out, another one of us might collapse into the water, and that was part of our wildness. We kept a plank of wood nearby, and if needed, we'd balance on it to keep from breaking through the ice as we engaged in rescue operations. While balancing on the plank, we could use our hockey sticks to extend our reach and complete our rescue. Ice water didn't slow us down. Our freezing, wet socks would warm in a few minutes as we kept circling around like the hawks of coming summer.

Our faithful little creek supplied much of the drinking water for us and our animals, including our busy bees. Our animals, and those of the neighbors upstream would wade in, doing what animals love to do. This guaranteed an organically enriched supply of water for everyone. One clear exception to the organic infusions happened when a gas truck crashed into the creek a mile west of us. We learned of the accident after I had swallowed a few mouthfuls of creek water, and ended up retching from the taste.

For washing and drinking we also used water from our well, and the rain-water that filled our large, basement cisterns. Well and cistern waters were also enriched with dead mice and rats, and various flying insects.

Around the middle of May we'd harness our horses—and after 1946, our new John Deere tractor—to the seeder, fill it with grain and hit the fields. If we didn't have enough of our own seed from the year before, we would order more and the train would drop it at the Norgate station. Rains were common and often heavy, and the muddy fields might delay us for days or weeks. A late May or early June snow could freeze the crop already planted and we'd have to reseed the field. The ancient marriage vows of farmers and Mother Nature cannot be broken despite the stormy times.

In late April to mid-May, the meadowlarks, owls, hawks, magpies and other birds would return, along with bees and butterflies. We welcomed birds as warm weather friends, though at times were overrun with sparrows and barn pigeons. A few times, using our 22. rifles, we shot pigeons and cooked them up. Their meat was bitter and tough. We never tried sparrow.

Spring sun meant hundreds of gophers would show their faces, dig new holes and scamper about. Some of them had short lives, for Phil and I would go after them with our .22 rifles. Their holes were dangerous for our cows and horses, and our dad wanted to us to kill as many as we could. This gave us another happy chance to turn into Indians and cowboys, sneaking up on the wily critters and firing away. If one of their dens was close to the creek, we might drown them out with buckets of water. When, soaking wet, they finally fled their homes, we'd chase them about with sticks and a baseball bat.

In mid to late May, we'd plant carrots, corn, potatoes, turnips, onions, peas and beans in our garden, and one year Phil and I decided to try our luck with watermelons. We'd never heard of anyone in our area growing them and we felt like pioneers. By mid-September we had several dozen watermelons, all small and moderately good tasting. The pride we had in our melons added sweetness to their taste. We had enough to share a few with our neighbors, with some left over to store in our basement with the potatoes, turnips and onions. By mid-January the few remaining watermelons had rotted, and became pig fodder.

Rhubarb plants flourished, and Jean or Helen, or one of our housekeepers would make delicious pies and rhubarb sauce. Some years they would cook a pot of rhubarb on the stove, and put it in glass jars for winter eating. On at least one occasion we found wild horseradish growing in the bush east of our house, and ended up with mouths on fire.

Come July and August we'd roam the countryside to pick wild strawberries, raspberries, chokecherries, plums and saskatoons. If we found a large patch of berries we'd let our neighbors know and they'd do the same with us. Word would pass around at the tiny post office: *Last Tuesday we found a great batch of saskatoons, just west of Finnemore's farm. Those berries are bigger than my thumb. Take their cow path and you only have to walk for five minutes. There's enough berries there to feed an army.*

As with the rhubarb, some fruit would end up in our copper boiler atop the stove, to be preserved in glass jars. Helen, Phil and I loved to stand in the dark basement, staring at the shelves of preserves, and picking one for a winter dinner was a special treat.

In June, the first thunderstorms rumbled in; jealous of our winter blizzards, they'd dazzle and overpower us. The hotter the day, the greater the storms. On milder days gentle rain would steal in without any fireworks. Cloisters of clouds would release hooded monks to walk softly down the hills and baptize the land. Some rains overstayed their welcome, saturating our fields over long days. We'd hunker down in our house, reading, listening to the radio, and playing in the hay loft.

One of the early signs of a coming storm was the sheet lightning that sent uncertain flashes into the clouds. We knew what was coming, and would watch larger clouds boiling up, higher and higher, filling their quivers with fire. Eventually, the sheet lightning would give way to fiery bolts, as the rumble of distant thunder changed to explosive cannon cracks.

Usually we'd not risk being caught in the open, and would take cover on our front porch, welcoming and dreading the coming onslaught. The feeling in the air would begin to shift as the storm moved closer, and we kids would start to shiver, dance and scream. At night the flashes were bright enough to light up the hills several miles west. When night storms were violent enough, we'd wake and go out on our front porch to watch the show. We kids might dare each other to make a run for the barn, or maybe the outhouse. We'd be soaked to the bone: *Helen, you look like a drowned gopher....look at her! Her eyes are popping out just like a drowned gopher.*

Thunderstorms were chaotic, reckless, warlike, full of promise and danger. The roar of thunder, the staccato flash of lightning, were a startling contrast to the blushing northern lights that seduced in all seasons. Summer thunderstorms roared across the land like angry hockey players, board-banging in sudden death overtime. If we stayed too long in the field, we'd streak, hands over ears, seeking asylum anywhere we could find it: a tree, a nearby shed or granary, an outhouse. A large boulder would not keep us dry, but would offer shelter from the wind. If the rain changed to hail, having cover was vital. If a stable refuge was not near enough, crouching on the sheltered side of a cow or horse offered protection from weather onslaughts.

It is worth a trip to any of the midwestern states or provinces to see the sky shatter, to feel the earth tremble. Those of us who've been hammered by such giant spectacles can understand why storm chasers risk their lives. Who can resist the roaring cry of a massive storm? Brutal beauty. Under bombardment, we joked about God being angry.

Beyond their muscle, massive storms are also spiritual, driving us into the far corners of soul, exciting reverence, fear, gratitude, ecstasy, adoration and other emotions often linked to the divine. Many cultures have thunder gods and goddesses, and Zeus is perhaps the most well known in the west.

When the rain turned to hail I'd watch our dad, knowing his crops would be wiped out in minutes. While Dad shook his head and looked about, I'd sneak behind the house and hide my tears. At other times my hands would curl into useless fists, and angry at God, I'd not pray for days.

We lost two workhorses to lightning, both close to our house. The sizzling, snapping sound of close lightning, simultaneous with a soul shattering boom, is something I won't forget. As a six-year-old, one of the horse-killing strikes sent me screaming to my parent's bedroom. Our horses were powerful animals, but no match for the fire from heaven.

I fell in love with the wondrous power of summer lightning storms, and the storms loved us back, dropping in with surprise visits. (In the central valley of California, where we've lived for over four decades, we get little rain, and only rarely thunder and lightning. However, on hot days, above the High Sierra range, massive clouds pile high, like angry lions reaching for the heavens. My wife and I watch them with the same wonder, and sometimes drive into the country to feel our ancient adoration, well known to people around the world.)

If we had a good spring, by mid-May the snows would melt, and the land might be dry enough to hold up the tractor so we could begin cultivating for spring crops. When we had a dry spell, volumes of dust would mark our paths as we rolled across the fields with our tractors. Our tractors had no dust-protecting cabs and the good earth became part of us: we breathed it into our lungs, it filled our ears, matted our hair, lived under our fingernails. We owned the farm and the farm owned us. We'd accepted Jesus as our savior, and He was in us, and so was the prairie dirt.

Going downwind on the tractor was a curse, for we'd be enveloped in a cloud of chasing dust. At the end of the field as we swung our machines around in a wide and happy arc, heading into the wind was a moment of salvation as the dust flew away behind us.

Driving tractors up and down the field was fun for a while, then boredom would claim me. Up and down, up and down. Watch the front wheel and stay on the right furrow. Turn smartly at the end of the field, so as to avoid hitting a fence, then watch the front wheel again along the proper furrow. Up and down. Go west young man, then go east, then west again. Back and forth. Watch the front wheel. How could anyone do this and not go bonkers? I was easily bored, and if we'd had shrinks in those days, I could have been diagnosed with learning challenges, attention-deficit disorder and who knows what else.

Being easily bored, like all things, is two sided, even on merry-go-rounds. To relieve the tractor boredom, I used various strategies to liven things up: I'd sing very loudly, usually old church hymns. I imagined myself as a great opera singer, and I'd stand up and raise my arms and take my bows. The gulls were my off key choir, crying as they followed me up and down, up and down, picking up the earthworms from the fresh soil. I'd scream and laugh at them, and hit one of my Irish tenor notes, blasting them back into the sky. I imitated their talk, hoping to crack their odd language code and learn their secrets. I'd stop and chase the field mice, their nests ruined by our plows and discs. And I'd think of mealtime, of going to the creek and feeling the cold water flush out my hair, mouth, nose and ears. If my tractor route was close enough to a creek or pond, I might throw myself in, clean up and cool down, then back on the darn machine for more up and down, up and down. After several hours my ears would ring from the sound of our John Deere, rousing me from sleep: the steady drum roll, pom, pom, pom, pom, the beat slowing down in soft ground as my wheels sunk in the mud and the plow went deeper.

The birds of summer happily proclaimed their reality with cries and flights. The most magnificent were the Canada geese, honking as they winged south and north, in their clever V patterns. They know much about aerodynamics, and we'd be mesmerized when a tired leader would fall back and another bird would move to the front. As they flew away, we might see this happen again, close to the northern horizon, their honking now silent.

Yet, the bird that haunts me was mythic, inflated by my imagination into the realm of all mythic creatures. I never saw or heard a sandhill crane, and yet they fly and pipe in the higher reaches of my heart.

Our father would return from the fields, reporting that he had heard them crying high in the unfathomable blue. His blue eyes would luminesce and move heavenward as he spoke of them with wonder and reverence. I'd be frozen in place, spellbound by his emotions, opening all my ears to hear of these high-flying birds. I could see them flying just below God's throne, way up above the clouds, in the realms of glory talked about in the Bible.

I prayed, I hoped to hear one of the cranes, but never did. At work in a field, we'd pause, stopping our tractors, putting down our forks, to listen, listen, eyes and ears skyward. The silence of the prairie was deep; our ears and eyes were sharp, and yet no sightings, no sounds, and so my longing remains.

We did not like or welcome the plague of flies and mosquitoes that filled our home, barns and the entire countryside. To give the cows relief we'd build smudges, first collecting small pieces of dry wood to get a hot fire going, then piling damp straw on top. As the damp straw smoldered it would create heavy smoke and drive off the flies. The cows quickly learned to stand down wind in the smoke, for respite against the insects. They didn't want to go back in the barn with all the flies about, so we'd milk them outside as they stood in the smoke. As we milked, our eyes would run and we'd cough so much we'd have to take a break and walk out of the smoke.

We children loved to run through the smoke, and we made up a little rhyme we sang as we did so: *if you want a good joke, run through the smoke.*

The flies were bothersome in many ways. When they bit our cows they'd plant their eggs in the skin, and in a few weeks the bite would result in a pronounced bump on the cow's skin. We called these *warbles* and when the bump was large enough and red on the tip, we'd squeeze them with our fingers or the top of a pop bottle, and an ugly, white worm an inch or more in length would pop out. The worms had black eyes and would squirm about as we flung them at each other and stomped them into the ground.

Wild mustard was also a curse, and if not picked, it would take over a field of grain. We hated this bright yellow weed. Barely awake, with an early sun making the yellow stalks glow all the way to the horizon, I felt tired before I picked my first stalk of evil weed. Mustard stalks have deep roots, and pulling them tested our strength. Our hands would get raw from the small barbs on the stalk. We'd pick a few hundred plants, stacking them in piles, eventually carrying the stacks to the road. After they dried we set them afire, hoping to kill the seeds. We knew next year the plants would be happy to show their yellow faces again.

In 1948, weed chemicals came to the prairies, with the promise of making our lives easier and better. One day we saw an airplane flying low over a neighbor's field, and we thought it might be an air force plane practicing bombing runs. As we watched the plane making sharp dives and climbs we noticed white fog coming from its wings. We ran to our neighbor's home, to learn they were having their crop sprayed for mustard and other weeds. A week later the plane was dusting our fields.

About the same time, we learned that DDT was available for killing flies and other insects. Dad came home with a gallon of the stuff, and a hand pump sprayer. We were excited to spray away and create a fog of DDT in our house and barn. The fog in our kitchen would be as thick as the smoke from our smudges; our eyes would water and we'd have coughing bouts. The spray was quick and deadly, and soon thousands of flies would be fluttering on their backs, buzzing furiously as they died, creating a bizarre orchestra of sound. We hated those flies so much; as they thrashed about we'd stomp them: *there be double dead, double dead!* We'd sweep them up with our broom, and pile them in the weeds. The next day we'd repeat the satisfying process, spray and stomp, spray and stomp.

A couple of times each summer we'd drive thirty miles west, on the gravel road, to Clear Lake. It was also exalted in our minds, as mythic, as bigger than life. As far as I could tell, the lake had the usual wet water, but the images of the place, woven and honeyed over the years in our hearts, elevated the place above all other lakes. There was only one Clear Lake, and years later when a college friend talked of a Clear Lake in his southern state, I assumed it was named after our lake. That's how mythic our lake was.

Highway 19 ran west from Norgate into the blue hills, slowing only at the official entrance, a wooden gate that was itself famous. Chuffing, cheering up the dusty, gravel road we'd see deer, elk, and the occasional moose and bear. The ride into the mysterious hills was an exciting prologue to the lake itself. Finally, after all the cries of delight at spotting wild creatures, we'd glimpse the east end of the lake: *We're here, we're here! I see the Lake! And there's the golf course! Look how green it is!*

As we walked and drove around the town, we delighted in taking note of the license plates. *There's one from Minnesota. Look! Michigan! And that blue one is from Missouri!* We'd also see plates from many provinces. We knew our place in the order of things: yes, our Norgate was a nothing town, but we could feel important just because we lived next door, heck, just over the hill, only a few miles, from the most famous lake in Canada.

Clear Lake was surely the most beautiful lake ever known, with her dazzling blue robe fluttering against green pine trees, shouldered with clouds of satin white.

Rich, city folk had proud signs along the street, with clever names for their cabins: *Dew-Drop Inn* and *Pair-a-dice,* with two dice hanging on the sign. *Tea with me? Gone fishing.*

Even more mythic than our famous Clear Lake was Bald Hill, for we could see it on clear days, and visited it more. It was a sand color, and amidst the blue green of the hills it stood out and called to us. In our imaginations Bald Hill was bigger than life. In reality it was a diminutive mound, perhaps five hundred feet high, composed of shale, and treeless. Now, having seen some great mountains of the world, as I look back I feel the loss of our adulation, our exaltation of Bald Hill.

Hiking to Bald Hill was a highlight of summer, planned days in advance. The morning of our hike we'd cut the barn chores short, jump in the car and drive to the end of the road, then hike cross country, through the bush, around the swamps and small lakes. We were careful to hold the green branches as we passed, so they'd not slap the person behind.

Bob, sixteen years older than me and home from his high-flying days with the RCAF, would usually lead our group. He was our hero and we never doubted his navigation skills, even in thick bush. Occasionally, to confirm our heading, he'd shinny up a tree, yelling down to us, noting where we were, and how far we had to go. Usually we'd be a group of five or six, and our racket proceeded us, scaring away most wild game. If we went into stealth-hunter mode we might see bears, deer, elk, coyote or small animals. Because I was afraid of bears, I liked all our noises, for I knew they'd run for cover long before we were close to them. *Those bears are running for cover! They'll have scary dreams tonight.* The hills would fling our screams and laughter back and forth.

Once we reached our destination, we'd run up and down old Baldy, creating clouds of dust, falling, rolling, screaming. Victorious atop the crown, we'd eat our sandwiches and admire the blue vista of farmland east of us. We could pick out the white Norgate church, our home and other landmarks. On the edge of the eastern horizon shimmered Lake Manitoba, some forty miles away.

Much has been made of what to do when we come to a fork in the road. Cutting through bush country we never had that problem: there were no forks, no signs, only the pushing forward and the ducking of branches. We could not lose our way, or go off trail, for there was no trail. Heading through rugged bush country was great fun. We'd arrive home brandishing scratches, muddy clothes and boots, and wild stories to recount on long winter nights as we sat with our feet in the oven. If we were lucky, our lunch pails would be filled with plums, saskatoons or choke cherries.

Most years by mid-September, our wheat, barley and oat fields were ripe for harvest. We used a McCormick binder that was part of our genetic inheritance, as rusty and old as a bad memory. It was pulled by a team of horses, and the wheels of the machine would run the cutting teeth and the horizontal *windmill* that swept the grain onto a conveyor belt as it was cut. The grain would then be compressed and tied with binder string, all done within the machine. Bundles of grain called sheaves, would then be kicked out and fall to the ground. Bringing in the harvest was Dad's crowning achievement. He'd sit atop his clanking machine, on a high seat, like a king, moving back and forth across his golden field, holding the horse's reins in his hands, ordering his serfs about with various commands: *giddy up, giddy up. Whoa boys, whoa. Only an hour to quittin' time.*

The binder was a work of pure genius. I'd marvel at it, and the way all its parts rotated, turned and flashed, and slid back and forth. Because it was complex, it often broke or required adjusting, especially the finger-shaped metal hook that tied the binder string. *How could anyone devise something to tie a knot?* My childhood curiosity led me to examine that finger carefully, both at rest and in motion, and I never did figure out how it performed its magic. Over and over it would thread the needle, a small opening through which the twine was fed. Using my own hand, I'd imitate the motion of the knotting mechanism, and hoped that would help me figure it out. As I worked my hand and arm I'd make a clanking sound, hoping that would help me unravel the knot.

The finger mechanism would consume a large ball of twine every hour or so, as it wrapped up the stalks of grain. The binder twine had a distinct smell, hard for me to describe, yet clear in my memory.

Our new John Deere tractor gave the binder a more consistent source of power, for it was driven by a *power takeoff* from the tractor. This consisted of a shaft, under and at the rear of our tractor, and this connected to another shaft on the binder. The binder ran more reliably with this stronger, consistent source of power. Compared to horse care, the machine management was easy: fill her with gas and an occasional greasing and oiling. It never tired or complained like our horses, and there was no barn to clean up afterwards.

After a field was cut and the wheat bundled, our next task was to pick up all the sheaves with pitchforks, and lean them together in clusters of six or eight. This let the grain dry, prior to hauling them to our threshing machine. The cluster of sheaves was called a stook, and the process of standing them in clusters was stooking. In addition to drying the grain, this provided hundreds of little houses and forts where we could play. In a few days mice would see the possibilities, and move in. We had great fun chasing the mice around, using our feet and forks to kill them. They ate our grain, and the adults encouraged us to kill as many as we could, so it was all fun to us.

Walking into an early morning field to begin the stooking was, like most field work, intimidating. Some of our fields were nearly half a mile long, and in the early morning light, we knew there were thousands of sheaves to be stood up, over and over, the same process. Stick the fork in the sheave close to the binder twine, lift it up, hold it firm so it doesn't turn, then prop it against the sheave just picked up by another member of the stooking team. Stooking alone was nearly impossible, for it was tricky to stand one sheave properly, until the next one could be placed against it. Often, when placing the second one against the first one, it would collapse to the ground, and the entire process was frustrating and time consuming. Stooking required close teamwork with a high degree of synchronization, and properly rooting the first two sheaves was vital, for they anchored the ones to follow.

In a good year the rain clouds hid behind the hills and did not show their faces, allowing our stooks to dry. After drying in the sun for a week or so, we'd let our neighbors know we were ready for threshing. We owned one of the few threshing machines in our area, and it, too, was made by McCormick Deering. From the viewpoint of a child's eyes it was a monster, a belching dinosaur, spitting straw from its long neck, and making terrific noises.

Our dinosaur had four large wheels, and we'd move it from farm to farm, depending on which crops were dry and ready for harvest. The word would go forth: the Glover's west forty is ready for threshing. Several families would share our machine on a given autumn, and each farmer provided a team or two of horses, with a hay rack for hauling the sheaves in from the field. One or two men were responsible for setting up the beast, making sure it was level, greasing and oiling it, then cranking out and rotating the large pipe that blew the straw out after it was separated from the grain. A tractor would be set up fifty or so feet from the threshing machine, and a belt would extend from the pulley on the tractor to the pulley on the monster machine.

The first load of wheat in from the field, and the starting of the machinery with all its noises, was a celebration accompanied by smiles, laughs and whoops. We'd made it through the mad thunderstorms and were bringing in another crop! This was the payoff for all of us, and we were proud of the teamwork between God and man that provided the blessing of harvest. If the Lord smiled on us we'd avoid rain, hail and frost, and reap another harvest.

Our dinosaur also had scary teeth: large, flashing blades that ripped the twine from the sheave as it moved quickly into the belly of the beast. The straw that belched from the blow pipe emerged like golden fire, and soon we'd have a stack of straw from ten to twenty-five feet high. Nothing was more wondrous than watching the men coming and going with their loads of grain, competing to see who could stack their rack the highest. Occasionally, an overloaded rack would break a wheel or axle, and that reminded us again that our strong arms and ambition had their limits. An overloaded rack might also drop its wheels into a soft spot in the field, and would have to be offloaded and towed free.

Before blowing the straw onto the field, we'd set up our machine near the barn, positioning our blow pipe into the loft. The straw was used for bedding and feed for our animals during the winter. Dad would risk his life, as I saw it, by climbing into the loft as our threshing machine blew in the straw. Every harvest, he performed the same scary ritual, disappearing at the top of his ladder into the dust storm, balancing a fork to move the straw around. To help filter the dust, he'd cover his nose and mouth with a small towel, and sometimes wear goggles. I feared he'd be buried in the straw, and because of the noise of the machines we would never hear his cries. For me this was the scariest part of harvest time. I'd stand fearfully, as time slowed, barely breathing, thinking I might never see him again.

Eventually his hands would emerge from the dust, and with fits of coughing he'd crawl back down the ladder. Could this be a human, could this be our dad? He looked more like a dust ball from a comic book. As happy as I was to see him, I'd run clear as he shook the dust from himself, sending a dust storm across our barnyard. After rinsing his mouth, and snorting water up his nose, and spitting all about, he might have a cup of tea, then crawl back into the dust inferno. The other men stood around shaking their heads, worried and wondering about his behavior. Because he had never gone to war, I figured this was his service on the front lines, and the loft a kind of trench.

We kids would run about, keeping an eye on everything, and hustle tea, coffee and sandwiches to the sweaty men. The men consumed nearly as much raw product as our roaring machine, and when we all came in for dinner, the real eating occurred. The standard fare typically included a beef vegetable soup, boiled and mashed potatoes with gravy, sliced hot beef and corn on the cob. Most men would eat five or more cobs of corn along with the rest. Dessert would consist of a berry pie, depending on what berries were in season.

As devoted holy rollers we were careful to avoid anything that smelled sinful, including the evil alcohol. However, the sinners among us would head to the field and drink beer after dinner. Come morning, Helen, Phil and I loved to go into the fields looking for empty beer bottles. They were forbidden and secretive, and that added much excitement to our finds. If we felt especially impish, we'd drain the lasts drops from a bottle and play drunk, staggering around in the field and slurring our words.

By age ten or so we were helping more actively, at first by driving the tractor with a load of wheat to our United Grain elevator, a mile away. I felt so grown-up on the first trip I made. Dad had promised me in the morning that I could take a load of grain, all by myself. I stood impatiently on the tractor, as the golden stream of grain fell into the wagon. Once the wagon was full, I headed out across the little bridge over the creek, and then along the ridge, north to Norgate and the skyscraping elevator. Being alone with our brother, Johnny, snorting away, heading across the wide open spaces, gave me a rush of freedom, a feeling of power. I started to sing in tune with our tractor, silly songs to help carry us along. Finally, I was a real man, part of the working crew, trusted by my father and others to take our golden treasure to the elevator.

It seemed like a long ride, a rattling ride from boyhood into manhood, with Johnny faithfully carrying me along. I recall the look of surprise in the eyes of Mr. Cripps, the man who ran the elevator. He knew I had come of age, and I knew it, and my pride was bigger than his surprise. I was glowing and he could feel it, and honored my glow. *Well, Albert, what a nice surprise! And all by yourself, oh my! Happy to have you bring the load in. Now let's weigh it, and check it out.*

Ever so carefully, I follow his hand signals and voice commands, edging ahead and parking on the giant scale. He unhooks the tractor and I pull it forward so we can weigh the load. He steps to the arm of the large balance scale, sliding the mechanism back and forth, noting the weight of my load.

I've joined the company of men, and feel six feet tall. The buttons on my shirt are ready to pop, along with my eyes. The ritual unfolds as he takes a couple of scoops of grain and disappears into his small testing area, checking for dampness and measuring the amount of debris in the load. In addition to being a hauler of grain, I am a milker and am familiar with the odd farm debris that infests our milk. In the load I've delivered, my eyes see the truth: among the golden kernels are a few dead mice, wild oats, thistles, flies, crickets, motley dead bees, a few toads and more. He pulls out a hand full of grain, letting it run to the floor, blowing on it, watching with measured eyes. He puts a few grains of our prize wheat in his mouth, and chews on them, feeling the hardness, the wetness, then spitting it all out. Finally, he rattles off some numbers and writes them down on his official, yellow pad, with a copy for Dad. I'm nervous and fearful that my first load of wheat might not get high marks.

Then the closing act, the crescendo. He yanks a mighty lever, and like our horses in springtime, the entire front of the trailer bucks upward, and its rear gate snaps open, sending our treasure into the dark pit below. Ever so carefully I back Johnny up, and he hitches me back to the wagon. Down the ramp I fly, homeward, on wings of excitement, Johnny pom-poming and the empty wagon jumping behind me.

Johnny might roar out at eight miles an hour or so, but we'd learned that after reaching flight speed, we could squeeze the throttle rod against the frame of the tractor and gain an extra few miles per hour. I reach out with practiced hand, forcing the throttle, pouring more gas into our tractor. Our Johnny is not designed to break the sound barrier, and it sounds very odd with its pistons spinning faster than Mr. John Deere ever intended. I hit full attack hockey speed, cheered on by the rapid pom-poming tractor,

Once parked in the barn yard, I race to Dad, waving the yellow receipt. *There! I did it! I took the load over, and I think it was a good load!* Dad examines the paper, turning it over in his scarred hands, holding it up to the light, smiling. *Well, Albert! I knew this was good field of wheat… even better than I thought. Now let's get another load over.*

If Mr. Cripps and the United Grain Company docked us too much for damp grain, we might start harvesting another part of the field: *let's work along the creek this afternoon, for the wind is stronger there, and the grain will be dryer. If that grain is too wet, tomorrow we can move the rig to Arvidson's for a day, then come back.*

Autumn and harvest ended between late September and mid-October. If we had heavy rains some crops might stand in the fields until May, when they'd be plowed into the ground. Our potatoes were the last thing to be harvested, often after the first frost. The frozen, top layer of soil would resist the first impulse of fork and shovel, then as we probed deeper, we'd find our sleepy potatoes, with their promise of food for a winter already blowing at our door.

ℭ ﹑

As I write about our famous Bald Hill and Clear Lake, I notice the mythic element falling away, and the emergence of thoughts I don't like: *after all, the lake was just a little lake and blue like millions of others. And Bald Hill? A pile of pathetic shale and no more.* Now that I've seen real mountains, our little Riding, so-called *mountains*, seem small indeed. I play with my skeptical, tough reality voice, noticing I am stripping away the years of careful and collaborative magic created in our farm family. *Blasphemy. I recognize you, my old friend.* In me, another dialoguing voice, one that fits the Buddhist teachings: *I can tell myself whatever story I want, remembering some stories are better than others.*

I tamp down my jaded voice, and see myself standing in our barnyard, milk pail in hand and ready for filling. With open arms, I face the setting sun in the west: *I salute and honor you, you Riding Mountains with your Clear Lake and Bald Hill. You may be small, blue hills, but you are mighty. I look at you with the eyes of all of us who loved you, who still love you. I thank you for your gifts of beauty and of weather. I am wee Albert, returned now to embrace your magic. I pray you, fill my cup to overflowing.*

CHAPTER 6

Lamentations: I'm Chained to a Dying Body.

I feel like I'm chained to a dying body. Uldene McLeod, our
mother, 1899-1947

The moving finger writes;
And having writ, moves on:
Nor all your piety nor wit
Shall lure it back to cancel half a line
Nor all thy tears wash out a word of it.

OMAR KHAYYAM (1048-1141)

For I know that my redeemer liveth, and that he shall stand at the
later day upon the earth: and though after my skin worms destroy
this body, yet in my flesh shall I see God....

JOB 19: 25-26

SOMETIMES I THINK we made it all up. Mothers don't die. Mothers can't die.
Nights can't be so dark and long.

Yet truth and reality prevail; my memory strikes a knell. She really did
die, and we her family, scattered here and nearly everywhere, carry still the
wound and all that decays and blossoms there.

I can't remember her face, hear her voice, or recall the warmth of her arms. Like you, I must have had a mother, for how else do we get here? I know what she looks like only from pictures, and my sister Helen who seems a twin of her.

She exists as an abstract and imagined entity, a wraith that floats in me, behind my eyes in the waters of soul. No clear mind pictures, yet her cells, her life lives on in me. Mothers are like this. They never truly leave, even when their bodies go down to dust. We come from our mothers, and even in the worst storms of life, they are anchored surely within.

Yes, there are, in odd moments, a smattering of possible memories that stir up questions. Possible memories: I want them to be real, I want to trust them, yet I can't be sure. My longings for Mother take me up and down the holy roller coaster of life.

Life flows around and through us with her tastes, sounds, sights, smells and touch. Every day, innumerable small sensations, each igniting an image, an emotion. And dreams that haunt our nights. From this river of life, we carry only a small cup into the future. We cherish the beautiful waters, the memories of joy, love, family. Yet, for each of us some bitter waters darken our souls with a stain that longs for cleansing.

The Buddha says: *Life is suffering.* That, his first noble truth. Stark, unflinching: an arrow of truth that cuts inescapably deep. And I don't want to hear it. Buddha! If you don't hush up, I'll walk away.

I'd rather listen to the words of St. Paul: And now abideth faith, hope and love, and the greatest of these is love. St. Paul, you can talk this way all day, and I will listen.

Most of us can recall that day when flowers filled the meadow, and love was all abloom. Lunch was perfect and the ants stayed away. We treasured those sun warmed days when heaven touched down. But let us agree to not talk about our clouds of suffering, our pain. Let's not talk about that, for it is too dark and takes us down. And yet, pain remains. Life and the eyes of the Buddha pierce us: suffering is.

The billions of us: some alive, some gone down to grave. We've all known shades of light, shades of dark. Joy and suffering are universal, and each of us carry and blend them in our own way. Each life is important, unique, universal and precious.

There are spiritual warriors among us who pack around their pain, scarce giving it a glance. Off to work they go, tilling the fields, milking the cows, running numbers, getting on and off the freeway. They carry their pain as though it were a trifle.

And we have warriors who dive into their pain, hoping to uproot and make an end of it, as I have done. Pretense helps. I want to pretend our mother did not die when we were lost and tiny. Maybe she didn't get cancer when I was six. Two years of silent suffering in our south bedroom—maybe that's just a ghost story after all. Maybe she did not in summer die, when fields were gold with summer wheat.

How can mothers die and leave a nest of little ones? When mothers die, how can life go on? I'd like to tell you I've forgotten all about it, and her. Yes, we are all wounded. Weeks go by and we don't consciously think of the event that changed everything. Yet, such events color our hours, and echo in our cells, below our level of hearing. We are our history. Our history lives in us and through us, consciously and unconsciously.

Our car mirrors remind us: Objects in the mirror are closer than they appear. It is this way with our childhoods. They may look far away, yet those days are always with us, moving closer then dropping back, but always with us.

Mother: I began writing this chapter the first week of July, unaware until several days later, that this was the week of your death. If indeed you and your prayers have been with me, in me all along, you know how hit-and-run this chapter has been. I write for an hour or so and feel so blue I can't go on. I move on to something else, returning a day or two later for another burst of words. Trying not to feel, I let my fingers do the talking.

I grasp at words, wanting clarity, and honesty, wanting to mark your place in history, to carry you forward to help us remember. Elusive words move through me, my fingers choosing the ones that sing the right chords, marking them on my keyboard.

Words! I love you and you love me; why then our lover's quarrels? Words! Stop running away from me! I want to find you, to find the perfect you that captures the blood, the soul of me. *Mother: I want to find the words that enclose the hole in my soul created by your sudden leaving. Forgive me that I don't call you Mom, for that carries an intimacy I can't recall with you. As I write of you, Mother, more than ever I see that papered words can't fully capture the heights of love, the depths of pain.*

That which is most us, seeks (sometimes desperately) an articulation that might capture the cellular whispers arising within. Sentences fail, utterances fall away. Who dares to speak of love and loss, thinking our words are real?

Mornings: I walk into the word bank at the intersection of heart and soul, hoping to leave with a clutch of dollars, leaving with only pennies and nickels. Still, lines arise from within, wanting the light of day:

I want to say all this as well as I am able.
Like horses cold my words seek something stable.
Round them up, all undone.
Through pen and ink let them run.

If a word smithy I must be
Let my words ring out for thee.
Stoke up, stoke up the fire,
Send them into fields for hire.
Shape sharp the shears
Plow up the sod with tears.

Bring me milk, bring me cream
Shine my light out like a beam.
Pound the milk till it is butter
Drink it all and end my stutter.

Pray thee Lord, let nothing here be hurried
Sound thy trumpet, summon those long buried.
Words disinterred, wanting out, wanting heard.

Mother: *my busy world claims me, and the hours pile up when I think not once of you. You are really gone. I hum along with all creation, buzzing with my life, then comes that odd and surprising moment; you spring to life in me, and I'm back on the farm with a cold wind blowing.*

Flowers, for example. With decades stretched from frozen farm days to sunny California, the smell of funeral flowers can still take me back to eight, and I'm sitting in our living room, with you dead in your blue box and I'm nauseated with the smell of dying flowers. Flowers of many hues, all forget-me-nots, forget-me-nots. As if I could. Who among us can forget our mothers?

Oddly, she has never shown her face in my dreams. I've been fascinated with dreams from early on, my first written down at sixteen, and several thousand since. For over twenty-five years I've helped clients understand their dreams. You'd think, I'd think, that Mother might have shown her face to me. Others who've died have found their weary way to me, have come to life in shocking, soulful nights. *But not you, Mother! Where are you, where did you go? Why not show yourself to me? You must know, in your ascended wisdom, my soul would sunder if one mirror glimpse of you arose in me.*

And if you spoke, if you reached out and touched my face, what then?

Dreams, like life itself, are mysterious and bring surprises. Last night, this surprise: after penning these words, in my dream I find your diary and a couple of photos of you. I can't see you clearly, nor can I read your words. That is as much as you want to show me now, perchance as much as I can bear. The first steps for wee Albert. In some future terrible, wondrous night, will you reveal your face? Methinks you'll take your own sweet time, as mothers do.

And Mother, just in case you're missing me: I must tell you that you've been devastatingly present several times in the individual and group therapy I've done. My frozen grief, like the icicles of winter, thawing, melting down, tears running out, followed by the meadowlarks of spring.

Since my thoughts and words have evolved into an unplanned, dreamy talk with you, I want to also say this: I was more or less successful in forgetting you and your suffering until in my early thirties, when my grief for you insisted on being heard, seen, felt. In an early therapy group, from my marrow a flood of emotions surge up. I can stammer only a few words to let others know what I'm feeling. I sit there and shake, shake, shake, embarrassed that my so-called adult body is curling into a fetal position. My body remembers what I want to forget with my mind.

Our bodies and cells are libraries of information with volumes to speak, molded especially by the falling downs, the getting ups of our first days.

The inner dance of life: the interplay of consciousness with the cellular unconscious. *You might smile at this, Mother: there are times when I feel like such a baby with "my mother stuff," thinking I should have been over you long ago. You died, life went on, and that was that. It was, after all, a long, long time ago. Why can't I just pretend it was no big deal and act all grown-up as others do? Can you help me here? Why can't I be that kind of warrior and just get on with life, forgetting how you might have been and then were not? What, after all, is wrong with a final forgetting of you?*

My inner, scolding voice sounds off again: *Albert, don't be such a cry baby! Get over it! Let it go! For God's sake let it go! Brace yourself. Buck up, man! Then I remember we are our history—our hoary, haunted history with all the hungry ghosts, the faces, times and spaces from the past.*

I'm emboldened by the words of Margaret Laurence (1926-1987), who was one of Canada's most loved and heralded writers. Her thoughts are especially compelling, for we were born in the same Neepawa hospital, and raised only thirty miles apart. Really, almost siblings! In her book, *Dance On The Earth*, she relates that her mother died when she was only four. At age fifty-five her grief at her mother's death suddenly erupts like a volcano, and she sobs so deeply she thinks she'll never stop. And this: three friends are holding her as her heart breaks, and her soul floods outward.

I say to myself: *here is a gifted and mature woman, stunned by the pain erupting from a fifty-one-year-old wound.* Hearing her story helps me feel normal. Maybe I'm not such a baby after all. These days I look for support and help anywhere I can find it.

I know from working with clients and my own self-work that when the going gets deep, when we touch into fearful cellular memories, often we can't go on alone without the hands-on support of others—touching, holding, stroking, kneading.

Mother: During the long days of your suffering fear gripped us. Fear and silence. Fear that if we grieved an inch, we too, might go down to grave. Fear that if we slowed to talk about you and your cancer, work would not get done. Sepulchral silence within, without, as shadow-like we moved from house, to barn and field. Our shallow breathing; the prairie air as thick as coffin silk.

We braced ourselves all we could, lest we drown in tears and mourning blood. We had many months to steel our souls, harden our hearts and dam our tears, as you lay dying.

That frozen summer of your departure: Bob was 24, Jean 22, Bill 12, Helen 10, I was 8, and Phil only 6. Pity the children. Pray for the little ones.

As I reflect back, my resident scientist stands up to lecture: he starts to fill the board, and I grimly settle in. There is, he says, a wagon full of research on children who lose a parent early on. They, we, are marked with a soul stigmata: like warriors home from battle, we suffer from repressed and confused memories, depression, anger, paranoia, shame, various addictions, scary dreams, and a host of other challenges.

The scientist in me is happy to tell me that memories are stored in our hippocampus, near the mid part of our brain, noting with a smile this is also the place where old neurons come to die. A charnel ground of final repose. And with a bigger smile he notes our inner library is also a nursery, a place where baby neurons are birthed to greet the day. He likes the notion of a cradle and charnel ground all in one.

This, I think, is a lecture that can go on and on, like a runaway bus on a freeway of words headed south. I fan my courage, finally asking him to hush.

I've lived long enough, listened enough, read and learned enough to know that we humans have compassionate hearts. This truth is at the heart of Buddhist teachings, along with that other unwelcome truth about suffering. The ants, the busy bees, the leaping dolphins: maybe they can forget and move on. But not us. We pride ourselves on our big brains—the same brains where we bury our pain, until the day of resurrection. Buried pain bends us as it will, breaks our families, ignites our wars.

Our mother who art in heaven: your many thoughts as you lay dying, your wee ones running all about. Your death, you knew, would scar us so; you surely worried much about how we'd navigate the delights and traps of life. You wove, methinks, imagined futures, dreams about and for us, interwoven with your prayers and loving wishes that we be safe, and trust the Lord. As you were leaving, you committed us to God.

Awake in the time of stars, my mind slipping through time and space, I've pretended I am you, bedridden in the south bedroom with death coming on, my body racked with pain. I lie rigid, flat on my back, barely breathing. I know my time is short. I'm launching prayers for my own healing, for respite from pain. Even more, over and over, I launch soulful prayers for the fruit of my womb, for my children. If you, oh God, protect my babies, I can handle this pain. These my soul prayers, launched from deep within.

And I, Albert, keep the faith: I know your prayers have carried me across the years. I know you've been with me, in my cells and heart. As I pen these words I hear a Leonard Cohen song merging with my words:

> *There are children in the morning*
> *And they are leaning out for love*
> *And they will lean that way forever...*

LEONARD COHEN, *Suzanne*

Like most children deprived by the early death of a parent, I have only a few, smudged memories of Mother. Thankfully, other family members have shared their recollections, and from these I wring all the sweetness I can. The adults who helped care for Mother have told me that she'd ask for one of her little ones to sleep with her during her nights of pain. She snuggled with me, and we breathed together? Such memories, if I ever had them at all, are gone. I can imagine Mother holding me, but it seems I'm making this up in current time.

Two of Mother's letters have traveled with me across the decades.

The first letter from Mother was sent to Bob, who was twenty-three at that time. The letter is dated January 12, 1945. She tells him that she is lonesome since he joined the air force. She notes it is not quite as cold as it was, and, *one notices the twilight a little longer.* She writes about the interest that our neighbor, Harold Francis, takes in our family and feels we don't respond in full. Then: *I did not go to church in Eden last Sunday, as there was no one to stay with the youngsters. . . I have Billy and Helen to make ready for school.*

Another letter is dated October 31, 1946, written to her second born, Jean, who was then twenty-one. She notes that this is her first letter since her operation, and reports: *Dr took out 12 stiches, and more to come out on Friday, tomorrow. . . I may come home on Sat. I miss good food, and long for Mrs. Larwood, or someone to make a good meal.* Then this: *I could cry when I think of the poor youngsters at home. Helen wrote and told me she had no one to comb her hair.*

She notes that Grandpa and Aunt Maggie were in to visit on Saturday, and no one since. She had learned there were 115 operations in October, many for tonsils. She closes by saying that she is tired of writing and will try to do better next time.

And a brief passage from a letter of May 18, 1947 from her pastor, Reverend Jim Ratcliffe, responding to her letter: *My dear friend in Christ. . . Sorry to learn you are not so well and that you fear the end draws closer. . . .* This followed by lines of encouragement where he assures her she'll meet Jesus and loved ones after death. He signs the letter, *A brother in Christ, Jim Ratcliffe.*

Our Dad kept a diary of that year, beginning on New Year's 1947. He must have known this was the year. He chronicles the trajectory of his wife toward her place in mother earth. His love, his wife and helpmate, was dying, but life went on with unrelenting chores and fickle weather. From his few dozen entries of that year I quote the few that refer to his wife and our mother, the first entry four months before her death.

Mar 12, 1947: Fair and calm A.M. Did chores then got load of straw east of barn, P.M. Dene and Abby went to Norgate with Toboggan. I heard President Truman's address re U.S. policing Greece and Turkey. Billy shot owl.

Mother's full name was Uldene, and Dad called her Dene. She was diagnosed with cancer in March of 1946. I'm happy to see that she was still active. *Abby,* was my childhood name for several years. Our toboggan: homemade, rough wood, wide enough to seat two children side by side, with sides up to our knees, a rounded front and maybe eight feet long, dragged about by one horse.

I like to imagine Mother and I snuggled in the toboggan, wrapped in the hairy rug from a bear shot and skinned by her dad, and our grandpa. Mother and I snuggled in a bear rug! The image warms me. The fact that Dad calls me *Abby* in this context, seems soft and feminine, and helps me think Mother and I were close.

Among my box of old pictures, one shows Mother and me, side by side, in a horse drawn buggy, when I was six or seven. She has a stylish hat on, and we are headed west together on a trip that will be far too short, our horse and destiny chaffing at the bit.

March 13, 47: Thursday. Zero. Wind got up at 9 am. Children went to school. Stormy in pm. Albert and Philip brought home news that Margaret Wallace would come here tomorrow. Audrey James here with Helen.

As Mother's illness progressed we had more and more visitors, coming to help and support us. The James family lived two miles north of us.

After March 13, more empty pages, until April 7 1947: *left for wpg at 9;45 mr and mrs A.D. Russell came with us. Dinner at Minnedosa. Called at Jean Wilmotes. Had lunch. Marg and May with us to wpg. Arrived at 7:30 at Windsor hotel.*

Trips to Winnipeg (Wpg) were rare and I assume this was a doctor's visit for Mother. This is confirmed by the next entry.

April 8 1947 : up at 7am went around town. Dene out to Ingersol street. We went to hospital about 4:30 then back to hotel. Supper at embassy grill. Frank out at Strascona.

April 9: Saw Dr Dingle. Said Dene should see Dr Evans re operation. Dene and I had dinner at Eatons. Left with Frank W. for home at 4 pm. Supper in Neepawa.

Frank W. was Uncle Frank Wallace, husband to my mother's sister, Margaret.

April 19: Sat. snow on ground. Les took us to St Rose. Dr. Gendreau said I was normal. Home at 5:30. Roads fair. To add to our family troubles, Dad was now having a health problem, and again this was veiled in secrecy. Dr. Gendreau's office was in St.Rose, thirty miles north. He was believed to be a miracle worker by many in our area, and prejudice against the French was forgotten in his case.

On April 20, Dad notes that Jean went with Uncle Frank and Aunt Margaret to the little log church in the town of Riding Mountain, some fourteen miles south. I'm surprised that Uncle Frank would go to any church preaching *the full gospel* with its furnace of fear. He was a sensible business man, not someone I could see on his knees, surrounded by the scary circus of the full gospel mission. Due to Mother's illness, family members were praying and going to church more often.

On April 23 I'm happy to see Mother's name again, when Dad notes we *little ones* helped with housework.

Dad's moving finger writes on:

April 26: He notes a few more inches of snow have arrived. Uncle Les drives us to Brandon, ninety miles southwest—the biggest small city around. *Dene sees Dr. Evans at five pm, and Dad and Helen go to the Strand theatre to see the movie, Fifteen years Before the Mast. They stopped at the Brandon Hotel.* His usual neat handwriting is blurred, and I can't be sure the number is *fifteen*. (The actual movie is *Two Years Before the Mast*, based on a book of that title).

Prairie silence rules again in empty pages, until May 25: *bright but cold, and we went to St Rose with Bob, Aunt Jessie and Uncle Bob Todd. Harold stayed with boys. Dene some better. Home at supper time.*

I can see our family huddled in the old, cold car headed north to see Dr. Gendreau. Aunt Jessie and Uncle Bob were Mother's siblings, and Bob her eldest son. They bump, bump along on the gravel road, avoiding potholes, praying we won't have a flat tire.

On May 26, again he is doing chores, including planting potatoes and other vegetables. The next day it is very cold and snowing. In a prior passage he noted he had planted wheat early, and was seeding it again on May 28. The seeds may have frozen in the ground and this may have been a re-planting.

More empty pages, until June 22 when visitors from Neepawa, as well as Mrs. Glover, come to see Dene.

With spare words he works and writes toward the fateful day. Even with all the years behind me, I also want to choke my words down. Here in my study, as my fingers move across the keyboard, I feel my chest compressing with sadness. I want to stop the clock, to cancel out all the lines, to stop turning pages of Father's diary. Who has piety, wit or tears enough to cancel out the coming darkness? I escape into cheap therapy, and run off again to Costco to do some random cart banging.

On June 21, 1947, he reports rain all day, and Bob and Art Thorpe do odd jobs while he fixes the fence near Howard Glover's. Bill has gone to stay with Uncle Les. Art Thorpe was a brother in Christ, and a frequent visitor.

June 22: Rain on and off all day and night. People here from Neepawa to see Dene, also Mrs Glover. Jean Wilmott here with Jessie. Bob and Art went to church at Riding Mountain.

The void in my memories is filling in as I read our father's words. I'm re-creating a vanished past. Loved ones are coming, praying, fearing the worst, saying their farewells to Mother.

June 23: still raining off and on. I fixed pig pen in barn. Bob and Art finished granary and Art left for home. Creek very high.

On June 25th: *Dene is sitting up in a chair,* and Aunt Jessie, her sister is with us.

The weeping skies give way to glorious sun on June 26: Dad reports it is bright in the morning; the pensive rain has retreated to the hills. Mr. and Mrs. McKenzie visit and help with garden work. Dad fetches potatoes from Mr. Francis. The next day more chores, including cleaning the barn. Les and Bruce come to get Aunt Jessie. We walk with Dad to get the mail at 4:30. And then what would normally be good news, *Children home at noon having finished school.* The end of school was exciting, and we loved the wild summers of play with berries coming on. Looking back, I imagine us playing with a savage intensity, hoping to forget the dark silent clouds within.

June 25: Again Dad notes *Dene sitting up in chair,* and that Aunt Jessie returned to help.

Before the long, rigid prostration of body, I imagine Mother sitting like a queen in her chair, and as I write I see her there, gaunt but regal.

The moving finger, the flowing ink, the striking clock: like dark cloaked winter chill, time rushes forward as it will.

June 27: Sat. Started to rain about 7:30 Bob went to get Jean at her school. Dene very weak.

The mourning skies are back. A convent of black clouds crowns our hills, and hooded nuns glide cross our land with baptismal waters. Soon the creek is overflowing, her waters leaving their bed ahead of Mother. Nothing can be done; the creek weeps away across the land. The flood cannot be stayed.

Cessation. Silence and stillness. No more of Father's moving finger till the day of death, The baby birds no longer sing.

July 9th. I've grown to like the blank pages and wish the rest were blank, wish all the rest were washed and canceled out. July 9th was Dad's birthday and Mother's day of ascension. The history of our family pivots, raven-like, round this solitary page. Then finally, this, in muddled ink as though his pen is weeping:

> *Poor Dene unconscious most of the time. She recognized me at 5 a.m. Getting very weak and tired at 4:50 p.m. Very sad. Margaret and I went to H. Glover's to phone Franklin and Aunt Sarah.*

There it is. Our father: his love of words nearly fails him. His moving finger has written and all our grief, our fears and wit can't wash out or change a word of it. In sunny California my fingers hit the keys. I take a breath. On a summer afternoon his beloved opened her eyes one last time before slumbering away forever. Now we must let the little ones know.

❧

I too kept a diary for 1947, imitating my father as well as I could. I also must have known this was the year. I peek shyly at my words. I see my child-self, little Abby, working my pen like my father, recording events of the day. Awe, reverence, sadness, curiosity pile up in me as I follow my words back in time and space.

I make a promising start in my diary, as many of us do, making entries for the first four days of January. Like my father I note the weather and talk about the chores we do. Then, empty, silent pages until July, when Mother dies. Blank pages, like my memories of that time. The pages cry for words, yet I hear, I read nothing. As we say, silence sometimes speaks louder than words: my heart, our brave hearts, had stopped, our blood thick with grief.

Falling snow, then spring arrives with her thunderstorms, and robins hop about. Summer cannot be stayed. July rolls around, her days parading like cows returning home to barn, all in line—one, two, three, four, five, six, seven.

Mother was dying. We had no words, for we were dying in our own way. We had lost our voices. Our unspoken creed: say not a word. Use our arms for work, not for hugging, and our hands for milking, not for touching. *Work hard and the time will go. Keep our noses to the grindstone. No sleeping in, and remember to whistle while you work. Many hands make light labor.*

Milk the cows, feed the pigs, milk the cows, feed the pigs.

Farm routines kept us going, those long days when it seemed that the Lord had retreated to His far heaven, and like us, fallen silent. I milk the cows and say my silent prayer: *Jesus, Jesus heal Mother, come and save us. Jesus we love you, we love you.* Unspoken words, echoing within over and over. Our beloved Bobby was saved from war, *so Lord why can't you make Mother's cancer go away?*

I turn the pages again, like prayer beads, mindlessly thinking someone will step forth and say something, maybe offer a hug. Only frozen reverie. Who is this eight-year-old boy with a dying mother in the back bedroom? Who is he? What terrors and prayers flood his soul? Does he want to die, and fly off with his mother to heaven? My pen skates obsessively on the surface of all that burdens me.

Then on July eighth the excruciating silence is broken, not by me, the little boy with the frozen soul, but by our father, who has mysteriously chosen to record these holy days of passage in the diary of his eight-year-old son. The diary of us.

Father! Thank you! You wanted us to know a little more. You honor me, honor us by sharing more of your heart. And can you also understand how hard it is for me to read your words, and how I want to wash these pages from our life and halt the crying pen?

My eyes can't avoid the words. I brace against the door. Resolute time, not courage carries me forward.

Written in my childhood diary, here are Dad's fateful words, describing Mother's final hours:

July 8, Tuesday. Jean's birthday. Had breakfast and prepared for going to McCreary to get medicine for Dene. She was bright in morn. Margaret Wallace went as far as Jessie's with kiddies and I. Les and boys away to fair at Dauphin.

Harold Francis here painting barn. Home for dinner. Gave Dene hypo. She was very poorly in evening and Harold Francis went to get Dr. Watkins. Could not locate him as he had gone to Fred Elliott's. He came at 10:45 p.m. Dene was unconscious part of time. Jessie and Maggie Wiggins and I stayed with her most of the night. She recognized me at five a.m. on Wednesday morn. Alice and Clinton Prior had come on evening bus and Bob and Billy slept in little tent. They went to Neepawa on bus in morning; Jean going with them and returning on 1:20 bus.

The hypodermic needles with morphine might stay the pain, but not the clock. All of our prayers, hard work, hopes, and longings, wash out not a line.

July nine, Wednesday: Dene very sick and did not seem to recognize any of us.

Suffered a great deal. Gave hypo in morning. Very weak and moaning, poor girl. Jessie and I with her most of the day. She got much worse around 3:30 and finally died at 4:50 p.m. We were very sad to see her suffer so but felt she was now relieved of pain and had gone home to God. Margaret Wallace and I went to Howard Glover's and phoned to Whyte's funeral home at Neepawa and to Mark Todd and Franklin Wallace. I phoned Annie Rinn at Angusville.

Mother's chains have fallen off. She has flown the farm, *gone home to God.*

As sad as I am to read my father's words, I'm thankful he shared more of his heart, his sadness, his relief that Mother had finally abandoned her painful body. Because we did not talk about Mother's illness or death, I could not know how others felt. The silence in our family with its death of words. We buried our emotions and thoughts of those terrible hours—hours that had become months, then this sudden ending, these final breaths.

Now through a timeworn tunnel, I peer back: blunted, muddled memories slog round in me: I'm emerging from the little tent in the front yard, and someone runs up and tells me: *MOTHER IS DEAD.* The sun is lowering in the west across a field of barley, and my world has stopped. I'd seen dead animals and I knew what death meant. Dead animals never came back. We hauled our dead animals to the field, and the wolves ate them.

Another possible memory: I'm playing at the creek, with Helen and Phil, and someone runs up with a white face and tells us *MOTHER IS DEAD.*

Mother dies in late afternoon, and that night Phil and I tremble together in our upstairs bed. It is a sticky, hot July night. A bull is roaring in the east pasture. Either Aunt Jessie or Margaret comes up to fan us with a piece of paper. There is little talk, no one touching or holding us. Cold, sepulchral silence. The flies buzz like mad hornets. I bury myself in the sheet, shielding myself from them, from the night, wanting to disappear into sleep and not wake up.

Then I hear the pounding. I pull the sheets over me, wanting to be deaf. Downstairs, the pounding. I know what they are doing. They are building a box for Mother. I imagine the working men, the sharpness of nails. The pounding goes on and on. A box for our dead mother.

The morning after she dies, standing on the porch, I hear a car coming down the north road. Then it emerges from the trees. It is black and longer than any car I've ever seen. Finally it stops by our front porch, and two men in black suits get out. Like the car, my memory stops.

On July 10 Dad pens this: *G. Beairsto took me to Neepawa to see re. grave. Mr. A Newall had been up night before. Norgate sports day. Very warm.*

A memory snippet of this day remains: I stand on the front porch, shielding my eyes against the afternoon sun, watching people in the Glover's field half a mile to the west, happy voices floating to our farm. They are playing ball, racing about, having fun at the annual sports day. I'm angry and jealous. How can they do this? How can anyone have fun when Mother is dead? Don't they know? Don't they care? If I was there I'd win all the races and jump the highest bar, and here I stand, heavy with grief.

My eight-year-old mind, knowing we must bury Mother. Wait. Words unuttered: *Why do we have to bury Mother? Is there not something else we can do?* All my choked down questions, with no answers.

Another beaten-down uncertain memory: just awake, I come downstairs and see the blue box, sitting on a pedestal in our living room. It has fancy silver handles. I know this is Mother's box. Our housekeeper, Sister Rachel, insists Phil and I look at our dead mother. I shiver with terror and shrink away behind Sister Rachael's legs. She insists and leads us toward the awful blue box. Mother is all white and looks terrible. She's dead alright, really dead.

My brother Phil remembers Rachael insisting we kiss Mother's forehead, but I don't know, I just don't know. Who wants to think about kissing a dead mother?

Our father's moving finger writes, but it's not the same finger, for his love has died:

July 11: Warm. Billy Rinn and Annie came and the Witmoths about 12 noon. Mr J. Radcliffe and others from Neepawa. Quite a large funeral.

Elusive memories of clouds of dust as cars arrive. People crowd into our living room, and I'm really scared, scared to look at their faces, for they might see my broken heart. Don't touch or hold me, for I'll fall apart. I'll drown in your arms. Flowers everywhere, with suffocating smells. We sing sad songs and someone talks about Mother. Can she hear us? I'm numb, lost, scared.

Somehow Mother and her box are placed in the long black car. Then I'm in a car, in a long line of cars, following the long black car carrying Mother, down the dusty road to Neepawa. On the north side of town we pass the creamery, and the tall chimney of the salt mine with its long shadow. Finally, through some spruce trees, into the place of standing stones. There is a pile of dirt, and Mother's box is lowered into the earth. Flowers hide the awful black dirt.

We go to the Chinese restaurant for lunch, and I feel the first hint, the promise of ongoing life. I'm hungry and excited. I have a new pair of grey, gabardine pants and am proud of them. I rub my hands on my thighs feeling the silky fabric. For a few breaths, thoughts of Mother fly away.

Mother is dead. Mother is dead. We, I, have to accept this. She is gone forever. Jesus might return, but Mother won't. Even though I want to stop living, the hours carry us forward. Another frozen thought: I want to be buried with her, to share her box, her silence. But farm life goes on, demands our time. We can't leave the cows in pain with udders full of milk. Like others who grieve, we are going through the motions, acting normal, burying shattered souls behind stoic faces.

Dad's fingers move and write again:

July 12: Frank and Margaret Wallace stayed and went home P.M. Also Mark Todd and wife. We were very lonesome.

Like Mother, Dad falls silent, but he comes to life again:

Aug 2: Choring, A.M. Bob and kiddies and also Geo Glover went to McCreary to T.B.chest xray. Got load of hay in. Billy helping me.

Aug 3: Sunday Went to Parson's. Alma and Kate home. Came home at 5 P.M. Missed church. Sorry. Claude Cameron had gone to Clear Lake with Howard Glovers.

Rains, I pray to you! Pour down from your hardened skies. Wash our days away, speed up the time. Amidst the flatness of prairie, we continue through the valley of sorrows.

CHAPTER 7

Animals: Birth, Life and Death on the Farm

But ask now the beasts and they shall teach thee; and the fowls of the air and they shall tell thee. Or speak to the earth and it shall teach thee...

JOB 12: 7, 8

Hast thou given the horse strength, hast thou clothed his neck with thunder?

JOB 39: 19

LIFE GIVES US *both open and closed doors, and each helps us change directions. Pregnant with life, damp with rain, we journeyed one night hoping to find shelter, and were told there was no room at the inn. A great door closed on us. How different all would be had* **that door** *opened. Each of us knows what it is like to be banished to the barns of life. There, close to the pulse of mother earth, we feel humbled, stabilized, grounded. We give up pretense, find our guiding star, and rebirth ourselves.* me

♉

Our common images of farm animals, based in part on the warm, fuzzy pictures in childhood stories, are a bit romanticized. I confess to being a romantic, however having spent nearly two decades with farm animals, I've come face to face with the occasional, brutal reality of animal behavior, and it is not pretty. As human animals we have our moments, and this is true for the *lower* animals too. They can be downright ornery and worse. An animal that has been gentle and loving for months, can suddenly *lose its mind* and cause injury, even death. Newspapers like to report such stories, as if to remind us that we alone are predictably tame.

And while I'm at it, I register one more digression: we humans spend much energy pretending we're not animals, yet we are collectively the most destructive animals on our planet, and are destroying many other species. Some believe we are creating the sixth extinction. It may be that our notion of being far above the animal kingdom leads to our surprise when a so-called inferior critter lowers its horns or takes a bite out of us.

With our big brains we spin fantastic stories, one of which is that we really, truly are not animals at all. Proudly we point to our libraries, our computers, our cars and tall buildings thinking other animals are lower, even stupid compared to us. However, as we wake up our large brains and learn more about the alleged dumb critters all around us, we begin to see astounding signs of intelligence in the bees, termites, birds, sea creatures and so forth. Termites, for example, design and build mounds that in relationship to their size, are thousands of times higher than our skyscrapers. And they are all organically air conditioned too. Bees have queens as distinguished as our own, with more servants at their disposal. We've learned that bees talk with each other in their own ways, and have a keen understanding of social class, labor unions, workers, drones and all the rest. Like us, bees are political creatures, and when two queens appear, they take sides, engage in crowd sourcing to organize a rebellion, then drop out of the union by swarming into the sky.

My latest and favorite example of animal intelligence comes from an incident in an Australian aquarium where a young dolphin, nose pressed against the glass, watched a person staring back while smoking a cigarette. The baby dolphin swam quickly to its mother, mouthed some milk, then returned and blew the milk into the water! Such an action requires layers of reasoning, some quite abstract.

It is important for farmers to study their animals, to have a sense of their personalities and have some idea about what might cause an eruption of fury.

Farmers are good scientists in this way. Our barnyard was our lab and linear accelerator all in one. We had more than enough collisions of four legged particles, especially in spring when the animals were released from our barns. The animals would *go nuclear,* and Phil and I harnessed some of that atomic energy when we strapped our sleds behind a young calf. Just before we reached the speed of light, we'd bail out. Hockey was dangerous enough, but this was light years beyond ballistic pucks and the flashing blades of skates.

Watching Old Bess, our best milking cow, we learned much about pecking orders, social ranking, power and privilege, honor and dishonor. Watching her I started to see the common behaviors between cows and humans—our famous big brains notwithstanding. Bess with her lovely, mournful cow eyes. Oh, my. She belonged in one of those children's books, with the manicured grass and red barns. Until she gave you a swift kick because you were not milking her the way she wanted.

Sometimes she wouldn't let her milk down, and we had to sweet talk her, and pat her back. How human is this, I ask you? Do we not daily seek approval, liking and love? And do we not withhold the milk of kindness from each other? No doubt about it, we like to be buttered up.

Farmers in our area, including us, kept a variety of animals, and most months, in our front row seats, we witnessed matings, births and deaths. We fed and entertained chickens, turkeys, sheep, cows, horses and pigs. The Sam Glover farm, to the west of us, had a similar zoo and also kept some geese, and would occasionally give us a fat one for the holiday season. When we walked into their yard, a wave of explosive energy would sweep across the geese as they gaggled around us, moving their necks like snakes along the ground, then rising up with mighty wings. I was terrified of them and more than once was bitten by a gander. The ones that bit us would be the first ones marked for the next feast.

My prescription for hubris is this: if the big city has led you to think too highly of yourself, if you are signing too many documents and tax forms, buy a small farm and put your hands into the dirt. Along with other animals, farmers know they are smaller than the seasons, less important than the cycles of birth, life and death. Standing in a field of barley or cleaning a barn is different from strolling Park Avenue. Farms have no discount coupons. Shopping lust vanishes when a bull turns his head to you and ponders the possibilities. If he paws the earth just once, you better run for cover. The smell of plowed earth pierces our soul more deeply than a whiff of Chanel #5. Rub some wheat in your hands, my friend, and tell me how it feels compared to a ten dollar bill.

For the first seventeen years of my life I had both feet on the farm. Then I became a city dweller, starting with my move to Winnipeg, with many cities since. I so prefer city life, thank you. And yes, because of this I find it easy to fan the illusion that, as pecking orders go, I am a superior animal to other critters, including small dirt farmers. For several decades, many called me Professor or Dr. McLeod, but not once did I hear anyone call my father Farmer McLeod.

Farmer Irwin McLeod. Our father, who art in heaven, since May of 1969. He was barely five feet tall, as if by design, proportionate to our few acres. He'd struggle to fathom the size of our giant California farms, and blanch to see how much we pay for an occasional meal out.

The last time I saw him was in January of 1969, when he Greyhounded the long roads to visit us in California, during my first year as a young, heady professor. I proudly drove him up to see our giant Sequoia trees. All he knew were the cold-stunted trees of the Manitoba prairies, and he could not, would not, believe that any tree could be Sequoia sized, even when the official sign said it was thirty feet in diameter. He stood in the snow, staring at the tree, scratching his head, mulling things over, finally deciding it might be as big as five feet, but no more. I wanted him to drop his illusions, to stretch his mind, and see the size of the tree and perhaps my stature in life. I read the sign out loud to him, and finally paced the distance in the snow, having him line up with one side of the trunk and me with the other. I counted snowy steps out loud as I paced and chewed on dark, sonful thoughts. In desperation, standing thirty feet away from him, I finally got him to admit the tree might be seven feet in diameter. Fathers and sons. I was exasperated and little Sequoia seeds watered my eyes.

If Farmer McLeod could only see our vast farms in California, with thousands of acres splayed so far out one can sense the curve of mother earth. The tractors and special equipment that have banished the animals are nearly as big as barns. Thousands of acres of lazy cantaloupes and tomatoes holidaying in the sun, watered and fertilized to strict scientific protocols. Mark, a friend of ours and a west side farmer, put in drip hose a few years ago. Eleven thousand miles of drip hose. As he said, it was enough to run from San Francisco to New York, nearly four times over. My father stirs in his grave.

On our prairie farm, as with other small farms over the centuries, our animals were part of our family. Like other farmers we had names for our cows, horses, cats, dogs, and even some of our sheep. Pigs, chickens, turkeys and geese were faceless and anonymous. Our animals kept us in vibrant relationship with the cycles of birth, suffering and death, and with weather cycles. Because of the severe winters we went into lockdown mode in late October or early November, ushering our critters, large and small, into the barns. Winter's coming. Gotta run for cover, take shelter, hunker down.

Occasionally, with cows, we were midwives in the delicate, magical and primal process of birthing. Hands on, without surgical gloves, we'd pull on the bloody legs of a calf struggling to join our barnyard fray. Birthing meant the promise of life would continue, with the guarantee of milk and food. Our babies would grow, and we mourned them when they died, and when we loaded them into the truck for market. Those that we slaughtered for food left traces of blood in the land and in our hearts.

Like other scientists, we liked to make predictions. With pregnant animals, the person who guessed the closest date was lauded as a prophet of sorts. If the precise date was guessed ahead of time, we'd start the myth making: *That Helen! She can tell you exactly when the cows will birth! She's just like her grandma; can see the future a mile away. How can she tell?*

Over the weeks we'd scrutinize a pregnant cow or pig, sometimes running our hands along their bellies, and even look them in the eye hoping to get inside information about when they'd *drop* their babies. I wondered if this was how Helen knew. Was there some glint in their eye that gave the time away? *Helen! Please tell us how you knew!*

Farmer McLeod was a farmer, not a prophet, yet he too had a remarkable ability to sense when our old sows would birth. He'd make sure to have her alone in a stall, and would do repair on the wooden rails as a kind of proc-lamation of the miracle about to occur. Granted that animals *have smarts,* it was obvious that sows were not top of the class. Sows would occasionally flop down atop a baby and crush it. To help prevent the death of the babies, Dad built lumber overhangs a few inches high, under which the little ones could scoot to avoid the crushing weight of a negligent mother.

When it was close to a due date, at sunup, we kids would fly to the barn early to check things out. If the birth happened at night, the next morning we'd find as many as sixteen pink little rooters, scrambling to find a free teat. Darwin might have enriched his theories had he watched our little pigs, struggling for survival.

We'd take a first excited look at the babies, and streak back to the house yelling the news about the new babies: *THERE ARE SIXTEEN BABIES!! SIXTEEN!!* Then we'd rush back to the barn.

Pounding hearts and goose bumps all over. We kids were mesmerized as we turned our moon-eyes on the little piglets popping out the rear end of the mother, well coated with slime and blood. If we had to wait more than a few minutes for another to be born, disappointment would claim us, only to be replaced by exciting cries when other babies showed shy faces.

Within minutes the little critters would roll and shudder, then start working their legs, beginning a life of rooting and snorting. Food first: the eternal quest for the milk of life. They always knew what to do, and mommy pig would open her legs, exposing her great belly to the world. All over again, the mad scramble of a new litter, each baby addicted to the elixir of life.

If one of the pigs was a runt and could not fight its way to milk, we'd get a baby bottle and feed it by hand until it was strong enough to compete with its brothers and sisters. As the pigs grew we helped feed them slop—a mixture of ground grain and milk. Slopping pigs: a sure way to detox a city brain, and cure the Fifth Avenue blues.

And of course in the midst of birth, death is not always forgetful, not always as reverential of new life as we are. With dark eyes, hiding in the shad-ows of barns, death jealously watches the coming of life. After a sow rolled over and crushed a baby, we'd dutifully, sadly, tenderly scoop up the broken promise, and bury it in the woods east of the barn. Sometimes we'd make a simple cross of wood and pray to Jesus. As we got older we were more apt to toss the dead ones in the manure pile, where they'd go with the rest of the load to the field as fertilizer. In a few hours the coyotes and wolves would again haunt our fields, always ready for a free snack.

After watching the birth of calves and piglets, then feeding them, we were solemnly silent when the truck arrived to take them to market. We'd chat with the driver, and if one of us turned away with tears, the driver might concoct a story to help us think they were not going to be killed. When we slaughtered our own hog we'd pick the most ornery one, to make the killing easier.

Loading pigs into the truck was a tricky business, for they often had other ideas, and would escape from the barn and take off for the creek or the woods, with us in pursuit. As kids and teenagers, we honed our football and hockey skills by chasing and tackling errant pigs, and on good days would announce the chase, pretending we were broadcasting across Canada. Eventually, from a farm magazine, we discovered a neat trick for loading pigs. It was too easy, too good to be true. Taking a pail of delicious grain, we'd slowly approach a pig, then once it started nibbling, we'd pop the pail over its head. The pig would shift into reverse gear, hoping to get the pail off its head, and if we nudged and steered his back quarters properly, he'd back up the ramp into the truck. Brilliant. For us this was a great scientific discovery, and amidst lots of guffaws and laughter we shared the news with our neighbors.

In nursery rhymes, pigs are famous for their tails; our pigs were noted for their pails. Watching them grunt and back up with the pail on their heads proved to the entire barnyard, that we humans—notwithstanding anything else I've said—were smart and pigs were stupid. Impailed pigs. Butt first into the world. Funny, stupid pigs. If we were bored we'd go to the barn, and planting a pail on a pig, steer it around the barn yard, creating as much mischief as we could. In reverse gear pigs move at a snail pace, yet we were amused when they bumped into barns or the back legs of a cow that liked to kick.

One time we got a pig drunk, not at a bar, but in his stall. This was long before we tasted the magic brew, but we'd seen adults stagger about and knew the potential. Mother, our sisters and different housekeepers carried on the tradition of preserving fruits and vegetables in glass mason jars. These were stored in our basement, on shelves several tiers high, and after a few years some would ferment, even popping their tops. Standing in the shadows one day, peering up at the jars, yet another idea birthed in our pregnant neurons. A few jars of rhubarb had scary, intriguing froth on the top, and in the dim light it seemed to actually glow. We'd heard that beer was fermented, and a sudden epiphany broke lose: we'd get a pig drunk.

I plead innocence here, for along with many of our fun experiments this was not *our* idea; rather it came from some rogue part of our brain that really was *not us*, and quite beyond our control. Now, with my scientific knowledge, I see that such ideas were part of our genetic inheritance, odd bits of twisted DNA from eccentric ancestors. Grandpa Todd? Who knew, who cared?

We blur-legged it to the barn with gurgling quarts of fermented rhubarb, dumped the lot in the pig trough, and sat down in a scientific way to observe the results. Before long the pig started grunting in a bizarre way. As his squeals hit higher notes, we started falling about, joking that he was warming up for an opera performance. Then he proceeded to turn round and round, as though he was looking for a long lost tail. Was the darn pig going to join a dance troupe after all? Phil and I were drunk with laughter.

Funniest of all, the pig tried to climb the chute up to the second level where it slept. It somehow made it the few feet to the top, then proceeded to repeat its circle dance, then fell off the chute on the way down. We were hysterical, and kept up a running commentary, teasing the pig with various comments: *Hey, funny pig, stand on your back legs! Hey Pig! See if you can jump out of your pen...sing to us, oh pig!* Stuff like that.

This was one of the most successful of our many laboratory projects, and no one was hurt, not even the pig. After the staggering and snorting, the pig fell asleep, not even waking himself up with his snoring. By late afternoon he was back to normal. All good.

It took us longer to sober up. We'd be playing soccer or tag, or sitting in class, and that darn pig would snuffle alive in our reverie, and we'd giggle as the drunken pig danced and sang in our heads. *That darn, stupid pig! I tell you it was the funniest thing I've ever seen. If you could only have been there!* Our drunken pig tale joined the other mythic stories from our feral childhood, eagerly repeated to anyone showing the slightest interest. These decades later he staggers about in my head as I write this.

⁊

Our Grandpa McLeod (1848-1924) was not only a great hunter and trapper, he was also a lover of bees. He gave away and also bartered honey, along with wild meat and skins.

Bee-wise, I heard my father say that Grandpa had as many as fifty or more hives at a time, each stacked three and four high.

Our father (1890-1969) carried on the tradition of bee keeping, though on a smaller scale. He also kept them in our front yard, perhaps because he loved them so much and liked strolling among them coming and going to the barn. Dad whistled when happy, and walking around and tending his bees was his delight. His whistled notes and the humming of the bees was music to our ears, as we tacked around them with our milk pails. After the long Canadian sunsets, with the bees all snug in their boxes, we could safely walk among them, our fears of their sharp stingers lulled to sleep.

City choirs and drunken pigs have their own wonderful music, but the soft slumber of bees after a busy day of flying, is exquisite. We'd crawl up to a hive, gently putting our ears on the box, and be lulled into dream land by the sonata of bees. I'd imagine myself as a bee, scrunched in with family, wiggling and buzzing about, feasting on honey.

Bill, Helen, Phil and I, and any little visitors who came to play were routinely stung by the bees, especially when we played at the creek. Big people may have been stung as much, but they did not scream or cry, so we could not be sure. They wore shoes to protect their feet from stings, thistles and more.

The bees loved the creek as much as we did, and would creep close to the water and tank up. While the bees knelt and drank reverentially, we'd be frisking about playing water tag, throwing sticks and stones and other kid stuff, our bare feet often landing on the back of a bee. As younger kids we'd scramble to the house, screaming as we ran. As we got older, we'd still hurt, but would deal with the stings ourselves. With the steady hands of childhood, using our fingernails, our teeth and a needle, along with mouth sucking, we'd remove *the darn stingers*.

Dad would occasionally ask one of us to go with him as he worked with his bees, and we'd put on adult-sized white gloves, shirt and head netting and help him out. I was always quite afraid of this, for I'd been stung enough times to respect the formidable weaponry of bees. We used a smoker to help settle the bees down so they'd not be upset by our meddling hands. All the bee keepers we knew used smokers. The belief was that smoke would lead the bees to think a fire was underway and they'd better grab some honey and head for the hills, and being so occupied they'd ignore the burglary in progress.

Our bee smoker consisted of a can perhaps half a gallon in size, and attached to this was a small bellows made of either canvas or leather. From our yard, we'd gather small wood chips and twigs and put a handful in the bottom of the smoker, using a match to light the fire. Once a small fire started we could add more wood chips, being careful to have them not too dry or wet to create the proper amount of smoke. When we had the right balance of fire and smoke, we'd pump the bellows and force the smoke out the small funnel at the top hoping this elixir would send the bees to dream land.

In idle moments I wondered what the bees might really think about the smoke, and I puzzled about this off and on. I'd sit and stare into space, pretending I was a bee inhaling smoke, letting myself relax, letting go of my fears and worries. It worked, for I'd fall into a dreamy state, forgetting all about the theft of honey.

Bees are intelligent, hardworking and magical. When they riot and swarm they are a force of nature, a buzzing cloud of anger and confusion. Dad believed that when a hive had two queens *the ladies would get jealous and fight* and the rest of the bees would take sides, and one group would angrily flee the queendom. Rather than killing each other as male warriors might do, one queen was wise enough to flee her sweet palace, and fly away to start all over and get back to making honey.

When I heard these stories I thought of the ancient queens and kings I'd read about, how they loved power and demanded respect, and had wars and all. I could see bees were like us. I could hear them whispering, plotting in the dark hallways of their honeycombs. I figured it was much like the games of cowboys and Indians we played, sneaking about and planning attacks.

In all of nature, a swarm of bees is unforgettably unique. A small and furious knot of bees clustered in the air looks like a miniature tornado. Honey making and long flights all forgotten, they take to the air with shouted demands, proclaiming that something has torn loose in the cosmos. The first hint of a swarm was the droning sound. Because I was in love with planes, I'd hope it was an approaching P-51 Mustang fighter and streak out the kitchen door to scan the sky.

After the first swarm-shock, our screams gone silent, we'd gather in the yard, awed at the wonder and power of nature. After coming to our senses, we'd run into the house, grab some pots and pans, then race under the swarm while making a terrible racket as we pounded our pots together. If the bees could swarm, we could too, and we hoped to out-swarm them.

Fresh from the city, viewing such mayhem, you'd know we were batty from too much inbreeding, and drive quickly away. *Did you see that one kid's eyes..? Really scary....! They're stark raving mad.* You might have been talking about me.

Farm wise, along with chicks, we hatched theories for most everything. The mad running about, the yelling and pounding pots and pans was not random or chaotic and had nothing to do with kissing cousins. We'd read that if we made enough sound the bees could not hear each other and would helplessly, perhaps humbly fall back into their hives. As the swarm spiraled higher, and their sounds of fury increased, we pounded harder and harder on our pots. Indeed, as we reached higher decibel levels, knowing we were holy rollers, you could mistake our actions as a fiery revival meeting. Such a holy racket we made.

I had a favorite piece of roofing tin I stashed away for bee swarms, and I was confident the thunderous sound it made would quiet any swarm. As I created thunder I'd also pray, under my breath, that our father's bees would not leave the farm: *Oh Jesus, Oh Jesus, don't let our bees fly away! Oh, Jesus please calm them down. We need the honey, Lord, we need the honey.*

If Sister Rachael, our housekeeper and leader of our ragged group of holy rollers, was present, in a voice as thunderous as my tin sheet, she'd demand the devil come out of the bees in the name of Jesus, and a breath later order the bees back to their hives, again *in the name of Jesus*. There was nothing meek and mild about Sister Rachael. She knew little about asking, and preferred making commands and giving orders to kids and bees alike. In one breath she'd order both the devil and her Lord to follow her commands. She was the high queen of our domain. Around her it was wise to stand back, and not even think of rebellion.

Bee swarms ignite mind swarms. I wondered what the bees thought of us. Just as we had theories about them, I figured they had a theory about us. In my wild-child mind, I imagined the swarm collapsing to earth, not from our noise or Sister Rachael's demands, but from laughter. I could see they gloated in winning the great swarming sound battle.

Our buzzing, and frenzied dancing never worked. The willful bees were more committed to their beliefs, their destiny, than we were. They knew nothing of Jesus or the devil. They had a plan and were sticking to it. As their tribal dance gathered force, their cloud would begin moving westward. They were no longer tame bees. They were wild and free, following some secret impulse of delight. They had heard the call, and were headed west for new adventures, fleeing our yard and away from our warm basement where we stored them when Mr. North Wind came howling.

Around the world the imagination of childhood soars as it will. Standing under that rebellious cloud, I become a bee: as I wing west toward the hills, with my tiny brown eyes, I spy our farm and far below, miniature people waving to us. I spread my wings toward the blissful quiet of the gentle hills. My buzzing turns into voices: *Now I can make honey the way I want, doing what I most love. Now I've found my true calling, my real home.*

I imagine our new home as a fallen tree secreted in the dark woods, the snow covering and warming us in winter as we thrum away. I see too, a small mouse, making her home just under our nest, so she can share our warmth. In my bee's mind, all this and more I can see.

Mainly, I was sad when the bees winged west to the hills. We loved them and loved their honey. I also felt happy for the bees, as I celebrated their freedom, for by age ten I had dreams of flying away, dreams birthed under spacious prairie skies. What would it be like, I wondered, to go west? I was hearing my own life dimly calling, calling.

These urban days, when I'm with our grandchild, Somerset, and we see a bee at our fountain, I'm happy to point out that it is a tame bee, as I note the brown and black stripes around its tummy. We also share a magical ritual of standing under a blossoming tree, and closing our eyes so we can more keenly hear the buzzing bees savoring nectar.

We called our bees *tame bees* and I was not sure why, for they seemed perfectly wild to me. They winged all over the country and stung us at will. They had no bridles like our horses. Other wild bees, swept in on summer wings: wasps, hornets and bumble bees.

We kids liked the bumble bees, and made a game of tracking them to their nests so we might plunder their special honey. It was not easy to track them across the fields after they left a flower. With our keen eyes, we'd race about chasing them. They were as fast as my favorite plane, the P-51 Mustang, and I felt as slow as a wounded bomber. I'd be at full throttle as I watched them disappear into the blue. To help track them we'd spread out across the field in the direction we thought they might go, then yell the word ahead as we spotted them.

When we found a bumble bee nest, Dad would drop everything, for he loved their secret honey too. Bumble bees make their homes in the ground. If the ground was soft enough after a rain, he'd plunge his gnarled hands into their nest, pulling them out, dripping with honey and bees. When the ground was hard, we'd get a shovel to dig out the honey.

The bees would bumble angrily as Dad continued uprooting their home, scooping the honey into a bowl. A few stings were not worth thinking about, considering how we loved that honey. We kids would stand at a safe distance, ready to pounce on the honey as soon as Dad stepped away from the nest.

Bumble bee honey was a special treat. Dad might quote one of his favorite Bible verses as we rolled the honey in our mouths: *Stolen waters are sweet, and bread eaten in secret is pleasant*. Eating the honey as we walked, we'd head home and finish it with tea and bread.

༄

The first April thaw day, when temperatures soared into the mid-thirties, provided one of our greatest adventures. Icicles would start to drip, and late in the morning under dazzling sun we'd release the cows, horses, pigs and chickens into the yard. After months of imprisonment in the barn, our animals were like time bombs, and the first breath out of the barn, they'd explode, prancing, kicking, roaring and running about.

As we got a bit older we realized all the exuberant animal energy wasn't doing us any good, so we devised a plan to use it for fun. We selected an adolescent steer for our experiment, strapping a horse harness on it with our sled tied behind. It seemed like a really good idea at the time. Two or three of us piled on the sled, while someone else flung open the barn door, and stood well back, adopting the curious look of a scientist.

We kids often acted like wild animals, but our wildness was nothing when the harnessed calf ricocheted into the wild blue. The explosive energy was beyond calculation. Because we had no bit or bridle, the launch was beyond the control of man and beast, and heaven help those who got in the way.

The calf ripped around at a terrifying speed, only to suddenly stop and kick snow in the air, spinning and leaping about, then returning to supersonic, nostril-flaring flight. With excitement and terror, fueled with pure adrenaline, we clung to our sled, our voices screaming like rocket engines at full power. After a few flights around the yard, the calf realized it might strip us off if it roared into the woods north of our barn. It was a brilliant move, and we had to throw our arms up for protection, as branches lashed across us. The calf shook off one of us between two narrow trees, and the rest of us bailed when it headed close to a barbed wire fence.

Our path around the yard was marked with mitts, scarves, and snow boots stripped loose at warp speed. The adults watching our circus stunt were down in the snow, convulsed with laughter. We all agreed if calves could laugh, our calf was laughing.

In truth, I believe we were actually the first to break the sound barrier, even though some fighter pilots later claimed credit. Unlike jet pilots, we had only two feet of air under us, and faces full of flying snow. We saw no need for helmets or ejection seats. Without benefit of engineers or blueprints, we'd created a rocket-powered sled.

Not to slight Werner Von Braun and his rocket experts—I'm sure they were smart enough fellas—but they limited their possibilities by focusing only on inert machines. Had they taken one look into the boiling eyes of a young steer confined for weeks in a barn, they'd have seen the possibility of a moonshot. The rocket scientists were also handicapped by small office cubicles. Our imaginations stretched from the hills to Lake Manitoba, and were high as prairie sky.

Given the success of our first launch, in the interest of science, we repeated our demon project several times over the years. Hockey was mad enough, but our rocket sled experiments were pure insanity. More than in hockey, we ended up with scratches, bumps and bruises, and sometimes a bit of blood would mark our skittering tracks in the snow. This particular madness became a rite of spring.

Another fun game involved little pigs and was the brain child of Grandpa Todd. He was our mother's father, and had retired to live in McCreary, eight miles north—the same town where we had our religious street meetings when Sister Rachael brought down holy fire.

We saw Grandpa Todd several times a year, usually when he visited our farm. Eight miles, in winter and in the muddy roads of summer, was a good distance by horse and buggy, or horse and sleigh. Our old car was often broken down and gas was expensive, so he'd drive into our yard with his buggy and horse. We were always excited to have visitors, and Grandpa Todd was especially welcome, for he was full of mischief. We'd put his horse in the barn and feed it, then get ready for some fun.

Like most life, Grandpa Todd hibernated during winter, and his visits would begin in April or May as the sun rose higher in the sky. I loved the smell of his pipe, as he smoked in our kitchen and outside on the veranda. He had a sparkle in his eye and a loud laugh, and when he was really tickled he'd slap his hand on his right knee. One day as we ran about with the little pigs, an idea sprung easily in his mind. He called us over and told us he'd pay us a nickel for every little pig we caught by the tail.

Bill, Helen, Phil and I had strong speedy legs and so did the pink little runts. Working as a team, we would eventually corner one and grab the tail, even picking the pig up as proof we had it. The pig would be squealing and we'd be laughing, and grandpa Todd would nearly fall off his chair, as tears of laughter ran down his cheeks. His sense of fun ripples down the decades in the genes of many of us.

We had a clutch of sheep for a few years and only one stands out in memory—a female who had nearly died in a couple of blizzards. She had one ear partially frozen off and we called her *Hardship.* She was especially loved by our older sister Jean.

Shearing sheep was also special and like the other rituals, we planned this a week or so ahead. Regular chores were boring, and any new activity was welcomed.

Like all humans and other critters, sheep put on false faces and engage in deceptive advertising. They work the angles to their advantage. They look rather large and heavy, but if you pick one up it is surprisingly light, much like a balloon. Light they might be, but when rams are having a bad day, they are properly called *battering rams,* and we'd take the long way to the barn to avoid nasty encounters.

Some memories are best forgotten, and this is true for the time a ram attacked me when I was finding my first, wobbly legs. I heard the story when I was seven or eight. A ram decided to use me for battering practice. He pinned me against the barn, and was honing his terrible skills on me, slamming me, backing up and repeating the process. Hearing my cries, my older brother Bob rushed to the rescue, throwing the ram against the barn to *give him a taste of his own medicine.* Some of my family thought the ram might have killed me had Bob not heard my screams. I heard too that Bob wanted to kill the ram.

It is ironic that my astrological sign is Aries, the ram, and my training in Jungian theory leads me to see the ram attack as symbolic of something, perhaps the ways in which I am my own obstacle, and *batter* myself. The other connection I make with the ram is this: I love watching TV nature shows, and am especially taken by the horrific fights male animals have, as they lock horns and try to kill each other. I sometimes think this may go back to my buried memories of the attack I suffered.

On shearing day, we'd herd our sheep into a pen, then snatch them up one at a time; and with one person holding them, we'd cut off their wool with hand shears. A shorn sheep is a pathetic creature; compared to a sheep in full wool evening dress, they look like a different species. Naked sheep have shame just like we do, and elicit compassion. They lower their heads, they slink about with confusion and embarrassment as though they've fallen out of Eden. They shiver and shake, contemplating their new sense of self. Their transformation is on the order of what we prayed for during altar calls, wanting our load of sins shorn away so we could be lighter. Jesus we knew as our shepherd and we were his sheep, and sometimes my faith was more wooly pretense than the real thing.

After shearing a dozen or more sheep we'd end up with large burlap bags of wool, stomped down by our feet. A few bags full would be half as big as our car, but no matter: we'd tie them to the front of our car, making sure the driver could see around it, and head south to Neepawa to sell it.

By late April as the first baby grasses poked out, our animals were free to graze the fields. After a winter of dry feed, the cow's stomachs would revolt and diarrhea was common. A few cows would *get the bloat* and their bellies would swell with gas. Milking a cow with diarrhea was tricky, for as tightly as we tied their tails, like a snake they'd find a way to get loose and bite us in the face.

When a cow went down with bloat, we'd walk to the store and phone the vet in Neepawa. He'd hustle up as soon as he could, and from his black bag of mysterious instruments, would select a hollow, sharp nosed needle, about eight inches long and the width of a human finger. I shuddered every time I saw that needle. Using his hand on the prostrate cow, he'd measure to the precise spot on her belly, then with a swift movement plunge the needle through her tough hide, right into her stomach.

A volcano of gas and green stuff would erupt from the needle, hissing into the air halfway across the barn. After many trips he instructed Dad how to do the nasty business. Dad instructed us in this art, so that if he was not around we could do it. Eventually the dreaded day came round. Dad was gone for a few days, and one of our cows fell to the barn floor with a bloated belly.

Helen, Phil and I were petrified to use the needle, knowing if we hit the wrong spot our cow could bleed to death, so we avoided the task as long as we could. We'd go to the house for a while and read, hoping the cow would be better when we went back to the barn. Anything to avoid using the waiting weapon. We tried various prayers, staring into her pleading eyes, and laying on hands: *Jesus, Jesus, in your name we ask you to heal our cow. Jesus heal her right now, in your name.* We'd seen this work with people and figured it might work with our beloved cow. A few hours passed, as we prayed and paced back and forth to the house, hoping for a miracle.

Finally, her painful moaning led us to the fateful decision. We retrieved the terrible needle from its dark place on top of a beam, and fell to our knees beside the cow, uttering more prayers as we did so. With shaky hands we measured from her hip bone, down along her belly, to what we hoped was the perfect spot: *there, there, that's it; five fingers down and three fingers to the side. That's the spot. Keep your finger on that spot. Okay, just to be sure, let's measure one more time.*

We spit on the needle, then one of us raised it on high, and with coiled muscle flashed it down, down into her hide. We stood clear as the smelly gas shot out, thanking Jesus that we had hit the right spot, and no blood was coming out. Shaken, we stood and watched our cow thrashing her legs around. Her moans subsided and we patted her and comforted her with our words, as her belly shrank down. Then, more prayers before we went to bed, with hopes she'd be standing up again in the morning.

Was it Phil who used the needle, or was it I? I'm happy to not remember who it was, and to forget too, if our cow survived. I know that we lost one or two cows with the bloat, but am uncertain which ones.

When cows or horses died in the barn we'd get our trusty John Deere, wrap a logging chain around the hind legs and drag it into the east field. Digging a grave by hand was hard work, and impossible in winter time. We had no power shovel on our tractor, so we never buried them. The wolves and coyotes, and sometimes a fox, would come round to feast on our dead animals, and the excitement of this would soften our grieving.

As the wild animals feasted on our animals, Phil and I might grab our .22 rifles, and crawl across the field, staying low behind snowdrifts and weeds, to see how close we could get to Mr. Coyote. We'd pretend again, as we often did, that we were Wetzel and Jonathan, our two favorite hunters, from books by Zane Gray. Happily, we never shot the wolves or coyotes, and carried our rifles only in case they turned on us.

Our father was small in stature, and had little formal education, but this did not prevent him from having dreams bigger than our 160 acres. The wide open prairies call forth a natural expansion of mind, heart and soul, and I suspect that like our dad, many farmers had big and equally secret dreams. Dreams, fantasies, emotions, deep questions were not shared with others, so I can only speculate.

One of our father's big dreams was to develop a herd of prize-winning cattle that would be the envy of our area—if not the province—and bring people around to admire them, as well as providing company. We were little people on a little farm, and hoarded dreams for more. His dream of having a blue-ribbon herd culminated in two exploits: acquiring a prize calf when Phil and I were in the 4-H club, and also getting a prize bull to upgrade our line of cattle. Like many dreams, ours had mixed results, badly mixed, I might note.

In our early teens we belonged to the 4-H club. A new provincial agriculture advisor named Mr. Bates was assigned to the Neepawa office and he actively recruited kids to join the club, and we rushed to sign up. We always had a garden, but the year we grew one for the 4-H club we added some different vegetables. We learned to align our rows in the proper direction to the sun, to increase growth, and to use proper fertilizers. Our 4-H garden project was too tame and orderly and we stopped after the first year, choosing to raise calves instead. With one calf we had more excitement than we bargained for.

We spent hours grooming and feeding our special animals, often purchased from a neighbor's herd. Part of the project was to teach them to be obedient to various commands for the show day, and we'd march them around the yard with a collar, instructing them to stop and go by touching their legs with a cane cut from the woods. Enough chucks under the chin and they'd soon be holding their heads up with pride.

Show days were in McCreary or Kelwood, and if a calf was good enough we'd then show it in Neepawa. We took pride in parading our calves about as people clapped their hands, and it was especially exciting to win a ribbon. All along we knew the fate of our pets, yet could never be ready for the sadness when it was sent to market. We'd give our calves one last hug, whisper something in its ear, then release it to the auction ring where it no longer belonged to us. We'd be broken hearted, but were practiced at swallowing our tears and pretending it didn't matter. This seemed necessary as part of farm life, even when our mother died.

One year our father, flush with extra cash from a good crop, decided it was time to get a calf that would bring pride to our family. We drove thirty miles north to the farm of our famous Dr. Gendrieu. He was not only heralded as *the best doctor in the province,* he also had a farm with neat barns and a herd of purebred Angus cattle.

We were excited about helping Dad realize his dream by caring for a prize calf. My excitement was chilled because St. Rose was infested with Catholics. As a fundamentalist God-fearing Christian, believing in the true God, we were repeatedly warned about the false beliefs and terrible deeds of the Catholics. Priests were either seen as funny or as evil conspirators. Nuns were just as scary and there were more of them: when they walked the streets their weird black and white robes swirled about in the north winds. They did not fool us. We knew they soaked their babies in lye and buried them in the woods. They were possessed by the devil and much to be feared. Because Dr. Gendrieu was a miracle worker, we never thought about his religion. After some thought, I concluded his cows might be catholic, but our calf would never choose that false religion.

Dr. Gendrieu and his halo. I too, worshipped him, apart from one terrifying moment when I had my tonsils removed at the age of eight. Petrified with fear, I lay on the operating table draped in a white sheet, and a blinding light in my eyes. Out of the light a ghostly figure appeared, holding a large ball of white cotton reeking of ether. Before I could scream or put up my arms, the cotton smothered my face and I was out.

After the bumpy ride north, we passed through the pearly gates of Dr. Gendrieu's farm, and the farm manager walked us around, discussing the virtues of this and that calf. We felt them with our hands, chatting with them, standing close then backing away a bit, affecting an expertise beyond our ken. Soon one calf claimed our attention: he had stout legs and was lower to the ground, with more beef in his rump, and a fine head. He gave us a friendly look, and we decided he was our future provincial champion. Turns out we had misread his look, and he was conning us.

The calf was beautiful indeed, with fine hair and good posture, and we proudly took him home in our trailer. Soon enough we saw he *had a hair in his bum.* His enchanting black eyes would flash about in a fearful way, and in the first weeks we realized he was as wild as the prairies that had birthed him. He was pure north wind: wild, whimsical, destructive and cold. Did he carry the evil Catholic bug?

Not wanting to live in despair at the hardships that beset us, we often took an optimistic view of things, and despite the disturbing psychotic signs, we felt we could train our bad seed. *We'll tame him with kind words, lots of brushing and good food! We'll charm our calf with love and prayers.* It seemed reasonable at the time: Jesus had saved us and changed us from evil to good kids, so of course we could save our calf.

Along with extra brushing and so forth, we had prayer circles, even laying on of hands. The calf seemed to mightily dislike our prayers; his eyes would dart about, and his nostrils steamed in a peculiar and disturbing way. Was he possessed of the devil? This was an easy thought for me to have and it turned out to be true. This was a demon-possessed animal, black like old Satan himself. Not necessarily Catholic, just black. Nothing seemed to soften him, and as the weeks passed, his temperament got worse. Yea, verily the old devil was waxing strong within him.

When we led him out for halter training it took both Phil and I, and sometimes Helen, to control him, and usually after a short period we'd be tired and discouraged and force him back into the barn. Kid power and calf power are not equal. Especially when the calf is satanic. We joked that he might be part wolf. On sunny, winter days we might throw a harness on a calf, and rocket about the yard, but not with our Angus devil. We were wild, yes, and didn't do careful risk assessments prior to most adventures, but this calf had our respect from the get-go. There was no way we'd try to ride behind him.

Farm life. Random weather, weird, wild happenings, surprising projects and shattered dreams. One day our calf disappeared. This was a mixed thing, for we were relieved to be rid of him and his insanity, and on the other hand were sad to lose the money we'd get for his wretched meat. Our wild one could not resist the call of the wide open prairies and he had flat taken off.

We thought he'd come home after a few days—certainly not apologetically, but at least back home. After a few days, when he did not return for his prized food and grooming, while at the post office we'd ask our neighbors if they'd seen our calf. As the days passed, the black ghost seemed like a bad memory, and we thought we'd lost the dough we paid for him.

Then a reported sighting, much like we might have with a moose or bear. A neighbor walked over to tell us someone had seen *a black calf, looking lean and acting mean,* roaming the bush, in the foothills of the Riding Mountains. We launched a hunting expedition to capture him. We drove to the hills with our car and the trailer, carrying yards of rope, and lots of hope. I had mixed feelings. We had an expression, one I still sometimes hear, about *going native,* and we used this phrase when we talked about our calf. *He had gone native.*

It took several of us to corner the loony beast, and miles of hope and rope. Once home, we locked him in our most secure stall, and called the trucker to come take him to the slaughter house. I was happy to have this calf turned into meat, and Phil and I hoped someday we'd enjoy him as a hot dog, with mustard. We joked that if the hot dog jumped from our hands, we'd know where it came from.

Often we had a herd of fifteen to twenty cows, with four to eight milkers. Because we milked by hand, and had only two hands each, we could milk only so many cows. We rarely had a bull, for we knew the power of a stubborn or angry bull would only add to the other challenges we faced. Bulls were dangerous and we knew several farmers who had been gored.

A few of our neighbors usually had a bull around, and when a cow went into heat we would lead her across the field, usually to Howard Glover's farm south of us. As a youngster, I would watch this ritual with a cautious curiosity; however, when my hormones mugged me, my interest curve went off the charts. My father must have sensed this, or perhaps he simply decided I was old enough to survive the process of controlling the cow and not be traumatized by the mating process.

The coming-of-age day finally arrived when he asked me to take a cow for breeding. We threw a rope around her neck and I headed south, excited to witness the high drama first hand. The old cow knew something was up and was eager to take a walk.

The scene unfolded like a perfect Hollywood script: as I rounded the barn into the Glover's yard, there were thirty or more cows munching away, and one bored bull lost in the herd. The cow and I were only a few feet into the yard when the air started to simmer, and the ground to quiver. The indifferent bull lifted his head inquisitively at first, then as he caught the drift, he flared his nostrils, started snorting and pawing the earth, while his eyes shot laser beams at us. My first reaction was to flee to the barn fearing an angry charge, and in the next minute, I realized he didn't even notice me. Our cow was the center of his universe.

His consuming lust was fearsome. I was as mesmerized by him as he was by our cow.

After his first snort of the new, rare air, and his pawing the ground, he aimed himself in our direction, his trot growing faster as he brushed the other boring cows aside. Most cows seemed to know what was up and quickly moved aside as the kamikaze bull rushed toward us.

Once the bull was upon us he pawed the earth a bit more, then screwed up his face as he smelled the cow: his nostrils pulsed and flared, his mouth frothed and his face wrinkled into a vortex as he pushed his lips out to suck in the intoxicating smell of our cow.

This explosive romance needed no extra perfume, and the bull made his own music with his snorting and his ravenous sucking of air. I stood astonished as I watched this latest miracle of farm life. The final act of consummation was electrical: the pawing, sniffing and snorting done, the bull leaped onto the cow, performing the desperate deed that drove him. He'd do this for a few more times, then spent and content would turn and walk away, bored all over again.

Our neighbor's bull, like our cattle, was an ordinary farm animal, lacking pedigree. One of Dad's cherished dreams over the years was to get a prize bull. Just as Dad's visions could be sky-high and airy, this is a story about a little bull with ideas too big for his britches, and a bull who nearly killed himself mightily striving for his ultimate goal.

Again, after a good harvest season Dad had some cash hidden away, and knew it was time to finally buy a prize bull. One April morning, we climbed in the Chevy and headed south to the famous Brandon Fair. This was an unusual and exciting event. We rarely went to the Brandon fair as it was nearly a hundred miles away, and due to the road conditions, the rattletrap cars we drove and possible April blizzards, a successful trip was not guaranteed. We'd walk around our dusty car and kick the tires really hard, pull out the oil stick, say our silent prayers and climb aboard.

We'd leave someone to do the chores, and drive south for two or three days of well-earned relief from farm routines. Our father had a friend who'd put us up for a few dollars in a small room, breakfast included.

We spent hours looking at exhibits, meeting interesting people, eating different food and having an all-around good time. The most exciting event of the fair was the horse jumping contest, held in a closed-in arena, each evening. With many in the province, we had a favorite horse named Bouncing Buster. That horse could jump a country mile.

With Dad, we checked out the bulls that were coming up for auction, patting their rumps and casting calculating eyes at the owners. Finally it was auction time, with a few dozen bulls up for sale.

I recall how proud I was as my father continued bidding up the price on the year-old Hereford bull he had selected as the best of the lot. Our father, not much over five feet, who lost repeated battles to storms, contrary animals and other large forces, was now a power player in this bidding war, and all eyes focused on him as he waved his arm smartly in the air. Our father, the poor dirt farmer, had taken over the room and I, my face flushed with pride, grew a foot taller as the bidding roared around us. Arms going up and down, the auctioneer's musical voice lulled us into a trance state, teasing us to commit or drop out.

The competition was keen, and I cringed as the price went over a thousand dollars, while the cries of the auctioneer swept us up on a roller-coaster ride: *I have twelve hundred, I need thirteen, yes! Yes, over there, fifteen….do I hear sixteen…Yes!…sixteen, sixteen, and now seventeen, seventeen.* The auctioneer was on a roll and so were we. My pride was turning to fear. Could we really pay this much for one bull?

My face is flushed and I feel sweat running down my back. *I have two thousand dollars, I need twenty-one, twenty-one,…who'll give me twenty-one for this prize animal…..twenty-one, twenty-one….do I hear twenty-one?* His eyes pierced the darkest corners of the crowd like an evangelist seeking a sinner. *Anyone? Are you all done, all done at two thousand? Is this your final bid for this beauty? Look at him! He's a pure bred, a fine one. He's worth much more, much more…..twenty-one anywhere, anywhere…? SOLD! SOLD! FOR TWO THOUSAND DOLLARS!!*

Our Dad's arm is the last one up, as the gavel smashes down. I can't believe it. I'm trembling. We've bought a prize bull for what seems like millions of dollars. We rarely won anything, and here we were, the McLeod family from Norgate, the proud owners of a beautiful red and white bull. After my rush of fear, I'm left only with pride. This bull will make us rich, and people will come from all over to see our fine herd of purebred cattle. We were no longer ordinary dirt farmers. We were the owners of a bull so fine, he and the calves he'd sire would turn heads everywhere. Finally we'd be famous.

As we left the auction we had an admiring audience rich in compliments: *oh, you got a fine one…the best. Yes, that's right. We live in Norgate. Really good soil there…..* The word was already going forth. Our bull was our ticket to fame, no doubt about it.

Along with neighbors who'd heard the news, we stood in our barnyard, admiring our beautiful, prize animal. As sweet as he was to look at, our minds and talk ran ahead in time: we could see the herd of perfect calves milling about in our fields, along with the money we'd make, as buyers would travel from afar to come and see The McLeod Farm. We'd ride our father's dream and our bull to fame and fortune.

The official papers that came with our bull were themselves a source of wonder and pride, for they traced his royal ancestors back many generations, and bore several ink signatures and a red wax stamp to guarantee the truth of everything. Looking at our bull you could tell he was a fine one, but if you had any doubts we could wave our documents and end all questions. Besides, he had sweet eyes and a gentle disposition that fit his breeding.

Our noble, much pedigreed bull had a special stall and food, and daily brushing, and we'd lead him around the yard to train him for future showings, all of which would add to our family pride. Things looked rosy, and already neighbors who lived close by would drop in to see our prize bull. I'd stand around and glow, crossing my legs like a real man, as I leaned against the barn.

Then, when he was barely past his first birthday, something in our barn yard did not feel quite right. Like the first and gentle winds of a coming storm, something unspoken, barely felt, was brewing in our farmyard. Our worst spring storms often followed a warm day, with gentle breezes, and our hopes would soar that finally winter was over. Next day Mr. North Wind would throw us back into January, and bury us in snow. Now a similar feeling of disquiet, of wondering, crept around and into us.

We went about our regular chores, as though an endless spring was at hand. I harbored secret suspicions, too awful, even traitorous, to say aloud, and wrestled with these at night. I looked as keenly as I could into the faces of other family members, wondering if they were thinking the unthinkable as I was. I watched their faces for telltale signs, as they looked at our bull. There was an elephant, rather a bull in the farmyard, and we refused to see and name it.

Eventually someone had the courage to float out a soft opinion, more of a passing question over lunch. *Maybe our bull is not growing as fast as he should, eh?* The question fell like the apple in Eden, and now everything was different, now we could feel the shaking of the apple tree, the slow darkening. God was about to walk into his garden, and we were ready to hide our faces.

Our questions soon turned to statements, and shaped our talk as we stood scratching our heads and staring at our bull. We had fits of denial and excuses. Perhaps we were not feeding him enough, so we upped his food intake. We added special things to his food. After a few months reality was rearing its horns, and we called in the vet. Our vet seemed equally reluctant to speak the awful words, and wanted time to think about it and wait awhile. When he returned a month later he dropped the bomb we expected. Our bull was a runt. A true, real, darn runt. He was a bad apple, an apple that had fallen from the tree of life smack into our barnyard.

Not a regular full bull, but a runt. *Yup, he's a runt. Just a runt.* We had to say it aloud a few times to grasp the terrible truth of it. Just as we had to beat down our most grandiose dreams, perhaps the bull, sensing all bets were on him, decided he simply couldn't live up to his promise and pedigree and flat gave up.

It was a costly tragedy and we were down in the dumps. We'd walk around our runt, talking to him, hoping we might inspire him. Rub his belly, stroke his face, search his eyes and talk with him. Over and over we did our rituals. Sister Rachael, God's fireball, had left by this time and the rest of us weren't fiery enough to lay hands on the bull and shock him with the fear of God. I prayed fervently, silently for him, and I know Helen and Phil did too.

What made it worse was he had full-sized hormones, raging as strong as any bull, and one day, when the stars were aligned right and a cow had come into heat, our runt knew it was time to do what he was born to do. It was his day of infamy. He trotted over to the cow, eager and full of promise, making great courting moves—huffing, pawing the dirt, flaring his nostrils, snorting and wheezing. Great moves all.

Brief courting done, he reared up to do his fateful deed, and immediately realized he was not up to the task. We stood in the barn yard with him, part of his team, hoping against hope, yet secretly despairing. His mounting technique was doomed from the start.

If you can imagine me competing in the pole vault at the Olympics you get the picture.

Here was a runt who didn't know it. He had not taken notice of his short legs. His pride and ego were vast, he thought he was a gold medal guy, but couldn't get a leg up on that cow.

After a couple of failures, he backed up to gain more speed and height as a pole-vaulter might, churning the dirt with his feet, making a desperate charge, leaping into the air. Incredulously we watched, wanting to look away, yet entranced by our newest circus act. Impelled by pure desire, he reared up at the cow, doing a perfect backwards somersault in a cloud of dust. His crash echoed between our barns and across the fields, and in the dust lay our broken dreams.

We must not forget the cow, the other, quieter part of our barnyard spectacle. While the show was in progress, the patient cow looked kindly bemused, and eventually I sensed pity in her curious eyes as she looked around at her suitor. Like us, I think she had hope, more desperate than ours.

And not to forget the human animal spectators: stunned by this primal animal behavior, once our hopes were dashed, as the debacle moved into the final act, like the bull, we fell backwards with laughter. We had fretted so much about our runt, and now all we had left was a prairie full of guffaws, jokes and puns. Other dreams had died on our farm, but none with such an operatic roar, and the hilarious ending of this one made it all seem quite perfect: *The bull is a runt, yes, but darn, does he have gumption. He's such an eager little fellow. There's a bull who knows what he wants, and tries his best to get it. He's really something, that bull.*

We had come full circle, accepting the funny reality of runt-ness.

Our circus was not just one act. Our little bull with his vaulting ambitions repeated this performance with many cows over the coming months, all with the same spectacular falls. Just as with humans and all animals, his hormones made him dumb, and inclined to overestimate his powers.

We were impressed he never broke his back with all his falls. *He was one tough bull! We could say that about him. And he never gave up! What a bull!* After we put our shame to rest, our story spread around like spring pollen, and neighbors would occasionally drift by for a ringside seat.

And of course, we wanted to help him out. We had various discussions of building a mating platform for the bull, and like many plans this one lacked traction. We increased his portions of special grain and supplements till the cows were so jealous they'd not look at us. Somewhere in the quiet recesses of his brain, he decided he was big enough, and stopped growing.

As humans, many of us are convinced we are truly superior to all other creatures; however, new evidence tells us all animals are uniquely intelligent. So while it was hard for our father to watch his dream die, it must have been harder still for our little bull. He was born and driven to mate and his feverish dream fell flat. Like us, he'd get up, dust off his dreams and make another charge: *Look at that guy! There's a guy who knows what he wants and goes after it.*

I peered at the bull, and it seemed he shared our emotions—the hopes and dreams, the embarrassment, the hopelessness and sense of defeat. As I watched his eyes I could only hope he was not shamed by our belly laughs.

Our prize circus act eventually became tiresome and a thing of pity. In his third year we shipped him off to market for the same price per pound as any beef animal. I recall watching the truck drive away with our runt aboard, feeling concern and compassion for our father, wanting to hold his hand, but I was a big boy and knew big boys didn't do that.

With our neighbors we usually had one or two dogs, used for herding as well as scaring away coyotes, wolves, foxes and other predators. Farm dogs were not house pets, and remained outside, sleeping where they would. In cold weather they'd sleep in the barn with the rest of the animals. On cold nights, the body heat from our animals kept the barn warmer than our house.

Due perhaps to isolation, most dogs were paranoid and in attack mode when anyone walked into their home territory. Also, unlike their owners and Canadians generally, they didn't have hockey as an outlet for aggression.

Most of us, myself included, bore scars from dog bites. Dog fights were frequent, and usually happened when we took our dogs with us to the store or post office. These days I watch strange dogs in various places around town and they all seem so quietly in love with each other, and it remains pleasantly surprising to me. Watching two or three dogs engaged in a death battle is not fun to watch. They are nearly impossible to separate, and the risks of a bite are quite real.

As much as we liked, loved and needed our animals, at times we could also be violently cruel with stubborn animals, dogs included. Based on what I saw, few of us had fun with our dogs. We were attached to them, and they were beside us much of the time, but fun and petting were infrequent. We loved them in our own winter way.

My saddest memories of dogs relates to those we had to get rid of because they had started biting or killing cows and chickens. They might start with the fun of chasing chickens, but as their wolf natures arose, this could turn into nipping, then killing.

Like humans, though not at such a dangerous scale, primal animal instincts slumber just beneath our domesticated surface. The thin veneer of civilization, as Freud called it.

The belief I heard many times from adults was that once a dog tasted the blood of an animal, it would never stop. Several of our dogs could not resist the taste of chicken, spring lamb and the blood from cows that never learned to kick smartly enough to fend off the attacks. The pigs were protected by their tough hides, and the quick pirouettes they'd perform when pestered by a dog practicing hunting skills.

We were faced with the tough reality of what to do with a dog that discovered the primal taste of blood. Hoping to keep the dog, we kids would begin with the belief that our dog would not bite other animals, and we'd blame it on a coyote, fox or a stray dog. As closely as we could, we'd watch our dog to learn the truth—usually the sad truth. Most dogs seem to know something about guilt and shame, and would not draw blood when someone was watching. We used our cowboy and Indian spying and skulking skills to watch them unawares, and that was the fun part. The sad part was facing the reality that we might find them nipping our chickens, turkeys or cows.

There were no easy options when our dogs became killers. One way to solve the problem was to abandon our dog on the road when we made a trip to Neepawa, thirty miles south. A few miles north of town we'd open the door, force the dog out, and speed away. With forlorn eyes we'd watch the discarded dog racing after us, finally tiring and standing looking at us as we drove away in a light snowfall. We were all sad, but in the face of tough reality, tears were not welcome, and we'd fall into deep silence, each of us alone with our frozen grief.

Shooting our dogs was the most painful option of all, and this duty fell on our father. He had witnessed the death of many wild animals while hunting and those we killed for meat on our farm. We could tell by his grim reaper face, how hard it was for him to shoot a dog. He steeled himself for this terrible deed. His mouth and eyes would turn fearsome, and he'd avoid eye contact with us on the fateful morning when he tricked the dog into going into the bush. After the killing he'd be sure to work faster and harder doing chores. He may have cried in the barn, but I never saw his tears.

Because shooting a dog was so terrible, he'd prepare himself and us with short talks on how it was necessary and inevitable. His logic was compelling, but still left us with questioning hearts: *Maybe Glover's can use another dog, and can keep him tied up? Maybe we can just drop him off on the road, like we've done before? Maybe we can feed him more meat so he won't bite our chickens?* As we knew they would, our plea bargains felt on deaf ears. Too much of farm life demanded we blunt our ears, close our eyes, harden our hearts and freeze our tears.

Every morning I'd fear the day of execution was at hand, and it always came too soon.

Dad might skip his breakfast, sipping only a bit of black tea, as we went cold. *Pleasing* all done, we'd sit around the table in silence, as Dad stepped quickly to our gun rack at the foot of the stairs. He'd select an execution rifle, usually our grandpa's hunting rifle, the 45-75 Winchester, for it had devastating killing power. We'd hear the scary, hard metal sounds of him loading the rifle. *He's putting in three slugs, no, four...why does he need so many bullets ... oh Jesus, help us.*

With the rifle under his arm, he walked grimly across the yard, face drawn like a soldier ready to engage in bloody battle. Beside him our bounding dog, eagerly innocent to take a walk, unaware of the executioner beside him.

Those long moments, waiting, waiting, heads down, paralyzed over our kitchen table. As the prairie silence deepened, each of us would send arrow prayers to Jesus, listening for the thunderous eruption from the tranquil woods. Our prayers, our gulping tea, our closed eyes, one ear open to hear what we didn't want to hear. We could not stop the wind, we could not stop the clock.

And then the death knell, the shot from the woods. And then another shot: *Maybe the dog got away? Maybe he ran for his life? Oh, Jesus, Oh Jesus, save us, save us. Would Dad shoot himself after he shot the dog? Could he do this? Jesus, Jesus, save us please.*

And our tremulous peeking out the north kitchen window: *there he comes, there comes Dad. He had to do it; Dad had to do it. . .* Hunchbacked, walking slowly to the barn, unable to face us, seeking comfort with his animals. *Good! He's left the rifle in the woods. . . .it's such a terrible rifle. . .let's get rid of that darn rifle. . .* We could not talk about or share our grief, for it was frozen over like the creek in winter.

The most tragic dog-killing story of all happened after I left the farm in 1956. I've heard the story from two or three in our family. After being shot once or twice, this time the dog did not die in the woods, and dragged himself back home. Desperate, Dad picked up the .22 rifle and started shooting at it again and may have hit it, however, it was able to slink back into the trees along the creek. Within a day the dog returned, confused by the incomprehensible breaking of the bonds of love, desperate to restore the lost paradise of family. This time it was greeted by a fusillade of lead, guaranteed to end its life.

Then the stark winter morning that terrorized us with sound and fear. A strange dog had torn flesh from one of our cows, and the wound became infected and the cow died. Dad growled around, planning vengeance. One morning over breakfast, someone looked out and spied that dog snooping around. Dad leaped from the table, grabbed the Winchester, slammed a cartridge in, and turned around just in time to see the dog jogging close to our east porch. Standing in the kitchen, he opened the door and fired. Our kitchen exploded, shattering us with a sound louder than any thunderstorm. Too late, our hands flew to cover our ears. Cups were dancing on the cupboard shelves.

The snow just outside our door had turned crimson red. The dog's head was gone. Phil and I put on our snow boots and mittens, and dragged the body into the woods, along the path to the outhouse. Our ears had been deafened by the shot, and we had to yell to be understood. *This darn dog will never kill any more of our cows, that's for sure! Dad really nailed him good...look at him! He has no head!* We used bravado to cover our broken hearts. We were skilled at that.

Like our cows, our horses were especially important and loved. Dad used them to work the land, and they faithfully pulled plows, harrows, rakes and the seeder used for planting crops. If we were cutting trees to clear more land, we used our horses to pull the stumps, and to haul the wood to the house.

At harvest time our workhorses pulled the binder that cut the grain, and hauled wagons full of sheaves to the threshing machine. The grain that came from the thresher was hauled by wagon to the United Grain elevator at Norgate. When the roads were too muddy for walking and for cars, we'd use the large wagon or our one-horse buggy as transportation.

In winter our horses were used to pull different loads on large four-runner sleighs. The rear runners were always in a straight line, but the front ones swiveled, enabling the sleigh to turn. When blizzards tore across the land, our Dad would hook up one horse to our homemade toboggan to take us to school. The toboggan was ten or so feet long, with walls about two feet high, and we'd climb in and snuggle under a stinky and heavy bear robe, from a bear killed decades before by our Grandpa McLeod. The toboggan was just the right width for two of us to wedge together, sitting against the back for support. Our bums would be chilled, for the cold would creep through the few inches of straw on the floor.

Our cows, horses and dogs were hard working family members and like us, were named. We took care to make sure they were watered, fed and stabled properly. At least three of our horses came to violent ends.

A couple of the violent thunderstorms that shivered the land killed two of our horses, each within a hundred yards of our home. Thunderstorms were common and we slept through most of them, but when lightning strikes close, the thunder that follows makes an especially sharp crack. The strike that hit the horse south of our home woke me up and sent me crying to Mom and Dad's bedroom. Come morning, we were alarmed to find one of our faithful working horses dead on its side, with burn holes in its shoulder and on its feet where the electricity had gone into the ground. A year or so later another horse was hit, and we found him dead on his side, east of the red barn, with similar burn marks.

Animals would sometimes stray into the woods or to the neighbor's and we might not see them for a few days. Usually they'd come home on their own, or with the help of a neighbor. So when one of our horses did not show up for feeding, we were not concerned the first few days. After the third and fourth day we started casually looking, as we went to bring the cows in, or walked to get the mail at the post office. Phil and I found the horse as we walked the cow path, through the woods west of our farm.

As we rounded a small turn where the path was only a few feet from the creek, nearly hidden by underbrush, we were frightened to see the head of a dead horse staring at us with white eyes. A ghost! Alarmed, we fled along the cow path, summoned our courage, then slowly moved back toward the scary creature. As the horse peered at us and we peered back, we saw that it was indeed our lost friend. Somehow he'd leaped or fallen off the path and ended in the muddy stream bed, sinking to his belly, his feet trapped in the mud. We could imagine his struggle for life, as he worked his powerful legs in the mud digging himself deeper until only his head and top shoulders were above water.

We ran back to the house, bubbling words as we told our story. With others, we rushed back to the death scene, spouting our speculations about how the horse ended in the creek. The next day we pulled the horse out with our John Deere tractor. He was so heavy and so stuck in the mud we had to use low gear, and different pulling angles to free him. We dragged him to the field just north of the creek, where he provided a two-week banquet for the coyotes and wolves.

Like other small farmers around the world, we were cash poor. When we went to McCreary, eight miles north, we'd follow our Dad into the bank, trying to hear as much as we could as he talked to the manager. How much money did he have? We never knew, for that was also a secret, along with much else reserved only for big people.

Our garden and animals provided us with most of our food, including milk, eggs and meat. Once a week or so we'd pick up a few items at the grocery store: sugar, salt, canned soup, cheese, maybe some apples or oranges. Some folks made bread regularly, but we did not, and we'd buy bread at the store.

Our garden was planted in late May, with hopes an early June snow would not come. Radishes, carrots, onions, potatoes, beets, peas, beans and corn grew in ragged rows. In a warm year, by mid-July we'd start picking things, and by the end of September made sure to have the garden picked clean before the first snow flurries. We canned fruits and vegetables, preserving them in glass mason jars for winter meals. These were stacked on a rack in our basement where they were less likely to freeze. Jack Frost was nimble and quick and could sneak into the tightest, darkest places, including our basement.

We slaughtered chickens, turkeys and pigs for meat. We didn't like the taste of mutton so our sheep were generally safe. Dad told us stories about his generation when deer and elk meat were common, and occasionally a bear was shot by our great hunter, Grandpa McLeod.

Because of the lack of refrigeration, animals were slaughtered communally every week or so, and the meat divided among several families. The neighborhood slaughter house was located in the woods at the west end of our farm. Farmers would take turns donating a beef animal, and those skilled in butchering would cut up the animal, placing pieces of meat in little cubicles for pick up.

The communal slaughter house stopped being used shortly before I was born, however the building was still standing and several of us kids would visit it routinely on our way home from school. In part, we liked it because it was spooky, and we made up scary stories about the dead animals. We knew many animals had been killed there and we could imagine the grisly scenes of slaughter, and sense the ghosts of animals departed. The flies and bugs liked meat too, and were first in line.

The slaughter house had a concrete floor, with a hole in the center, where the blood drained away. Above the drain was a thick rope wound around a pulley near the peak of the roof. The rope had a hook used to pull the dead animal up, so that it would bleed properly before being cut up.

Once or twice a year we butchered hogs, but did not use the slaughter house. Helen, Phil and I would hide fearfully behind the barn, curiously peeking around the corner when Dad killed the hog. At age 12 or 13 I underwent another rite of passage, when I was asked to kill one of our pigs for meat. I wanted to be a grown-up, yet I trembled as I prepared for the terrible task. By that age I'd shot hundreds of rabbits, some birds and squirrels, but shooting a pig was different. I will spare myself and the reader from the gory details, for it now seems like an act of barbarism.

After killing the hog we'd hang it up to bleed, then pour boiling hot water over it to burn off the hair. After the hot water burned the hair, we'd take knives to scrape the skin free of the remaining hair, then Dad, and often a neighbor helping out, would cut the pig into pieces.

Standing in front of a hanging hog, alive only moments before, filled me with fearful wonder. Where did the pig go, I wondered? I'd look at the bleeding body and still be missing the pig and its sounds and movements. Each pig had a different character to some degree, and I wondered where all that went when we killed it.

Like Jack Frost and the north wind, the old devil was everywhere. With each butchered pig, our father would point to the teeth marks of the devil on the inner hind leg. Pearly white teeth marks all in a row, right where old Satan bit the pig in Biblical times. I'd stare at those marks with reverence, transported back thousands of years with images of Jesus and the devil dancing in my brain. Dad explained that the tooth marks dated back to the day Jesus cast the devil out of a man at Gadarene. Some pigs were rooting close by and the devil, always seeking a hiding host, entered them by biting them on the leg. The possessed pigs fled into a lake and drowned.

∞

For many years after leaving the farm, I felt little warmth toward animals in general, especially pet dogs. I was perplexed that people could love their dogs so dearly. I met folks who let their dogs sleep in their bedrooms! How could this be?

My heart had softened some when Shasta, our German Shepard, died in 1987. After weeks of barely being able to walk, the time came to take her to the vet to end her life. I'd finally learned to love a dog, and rather than expressing my grief openly, I raced away for my morning run, leaving Ruthie and Todd to take Shasta to the vet, then to bury her in our yard. As I raced through the almond orchard I was sobbing, thinking of the terrible deaths of our farm dogs. I ran as fast as I could, hoping to outrun my grief.

After Shasta died, a black lab named Shadow joined our family. Todd picked her from a litter of puppies, and this time, most of my fears gone, I opened my heart and let her in.

Pet lovers around the world believe there is a secret understanding, a bond of love and knowing, between themselves and their pets, and this was the case with Shadow. Shortly after my encounter with Tibetan Buddhism in May of 1993, Shadow also began meditating. She would roll on her back, cross her front paws, and remain motionless in a trance state for several minutes. We were delightfully mystified and honored her quiet times. Occasionally, to see how serious she was about her Buddhist practice, we'd call her name; other than wag her tail she'd remain in her meditative posture. With the other splash of pictures on our refrigerator, we still have one of our beloved Shadow, prostrate on our rug, deep in meditation.

When Shadow could no longer walk, Todd and I dug her grave in our backyard, crying as we did so. Then Rick, our good friend and vet from next door, came to administer the drug that would carry her into the spirit world. Todd kept hugging her, fed her lots of raw meat and chocolate, and assured her of his undying love, promising she'd be alright. Her eyes were big and open. She seemed to know she was leaving us. We trembled and cried as her soul drained away and her eyes stilled. We put a baseball cap on her head, then later Todd had a statue made of her, to mark her grave.

෴

I must say one more thing about lightning.

Because thunder and lightning storms burned such deep memories in my soul, I've read various articles on lightning over the years. The collective impact of the millions of strikes on our planet is still not fully understood. The fact that the skies can generate enough electricity to create a lightning bolt remains a puzzle to science. I imagine Zeus, hurtling thunder bolts to earth and smiling as he plays with us. Recently, scientists have been surprised to learn that lightning generates gamma waves at high altitudes, and these can travel halfway round the world.

Some lightning strikes are better than others. While the bolts that killed our horses were bad ones, I want to acknowledge a strike of grace that delivered over a million volts of grace into my life.

In the fall of 1962 a storm blew into Houston, Texas, and hit the home of Reverend C.N. Rice and his wife Samona, blowing out their TV and causing a fire in one bedroom. Rev. Rice and his wife decided if they got the insurance money, they'd use it to take their daughter, Samona Ruth, to visit Evangel College, in Springfield, Missouri. The money came in time, and in February of 1963 they made the trip to Evangel College.

I was sitting in the chapel the morning they walked in and when I saw Ruthie, her beauty was a lightning bolt that set my heart on fire. The effects of that strike continue to radiate in our lives and those of our children and grandchildren.

CHAPTER 8

⟡

The Art and Science of Milking

⟡

IN THE BEGINNING was milk. Next to clean prairie air, milk was the thing, the life blood for us, our pigs and cats. Milking cows was a high ritual, and beginning before age ten, we went forth as supplicants in dark winter mornings, toting milk pails, creating dancing shadows with our lanterns. Summer suns rose before us, and we filed to the barn in radiant light, seeking the holy grail of milk. Our barn was often warmer than our home, and was a sanctuary from the cold. All the animals pitched in to keep the barn warm, and our cows wanted us to have their warm milk.

Cows' teats are a covert world, well hidden from most of us. After hundreds of hours on three-legged stools, and exposure to dozens of cows, I think of myself as a reigning, titular expert on teats. A veritable Ph.D. in udders and teats. Not that it does me any good these days. (Interested readers can go online to see my telling Ted Teat Talk....)

Just the color of teats is fascinating, ranging from pink and brown to whitish. Some have little brown spots on them, some have tougher skin than others. All of them have a similar musky animal smell. Here as everywhere, Mother Nature delights in variety. Most cows will have one teat shorter than the others by a country mile. Some udders carry a useless dummy teat that hangs at the bottom of the ladder of evolution—an aggregation of tissue that started out with a big idea then lost focus. Given our whimsy, we'd occasionally try to coax a dummy teat into giving us a spot of milk. All fun. It never worked, and the cow would look quizzically round at us. Cows and their big, innocent eyes. They can fool you. Let down your guard and they can cow you.

In 1949, even after we got *the power,* all 110 volts, we never thought once of electric milking machines. The infinite prairies encouraged our imaginations to stretch mightily, yet the idea of using milking machines lay beyond the horizon of possibility.

By age ten to twelve, the kids in our area bore the stigmata of overly large hands and forearms. I look at pictures of our Dad, when he was in his seventies, with his Neanderthal hands hanging nearly to the ground. In top farming shape, he weighed in at about 130 pounds, and I figure his hands were half of him.

The charm of milking fascinated us long before our fingers were strong enough to coax the milk down. Like other kids, we were in a rush to grow up and help out. From watching our dad and older brothers, we learned there were two ways of milking: the common way, using the whole hand to squeeze and simultaneously pull down on the teat. The other way of milking was to slap some axle grease on the teat and strip it using only thumb and forefinger. Axle grease makes the wheels go round, makes the milk come down. Milking this way demands strong fingers, and my brother Bob was adept at this, but I could never do it. It was magical to watch his thumb and finger work together, creating a snapping like Dad tuning his violin. We could tell he was in the barn by the chords he struck.

Milking was a team sport, and we did it together. We'd head to the barn with our pails—and bobbing lanterns in winter time—armed and ready for the liquid gold.

You might think hand milking is something you could pick up in one semester of college, right? Wrong. Like many things that seem simple on the surface, there are nuances, tricks and complexities involved. If you saw me sitting with my clumpy boots on a teetering stool, you'd think, *Heck, I could do that.* No way. Not by a country mile. The teat-feat requires exquisite timing, to say nothing of balancing on a homemade three-legged stool held together with a bit of tired wire. The cows seemed to know our stools were precarious, and they showed exquisite timing; finally balanced on our stools, hands on and ready to go, and the first kick would strike like a snake, right on target, sending us flying.

Let us reason together and ponder this: we might watch a cello player and think it would be easy to do. All you have to do is hold the thing and move the bow across the strings, right? Milking cows is equally deceptive. Instead of holding a cello between our legs, we held a milk pail. Yes, there is one difference here: a good cello might cost thousands of dollars, while a well-used milk pail is worth pennies—Canadian pennies at that. Yet comparing milking with cello playing is instructive.

Not to discourage those of you now keenly interested in milking. Still, I warn you again, there is a real knack to milking, apart from the fine hand and finger coordination. Let's talk pails. We begin with the milk pail placed properly between our knees, lined up properly below the udder. The knee pressure at first is light, and must increase as the pail becomes heavier with milk, and in this way milking is actually harder than the cello where knee pressure is not of concern. Eventually the pail is too heavy to hold and is placed on the barn floor. If you are with me here you might note that cello players begin with their instrument on the floor, and have it rather easy this way. The timing of when to set the pail down, then doing so without spilling a drop is an art in itself.

Cello players also have it easy, for they sit on solid, crafted chairs. I look at their chairs with awe. Whoa! Look at that chair. Four legs, heavy, solid oak. That is a real chair! Earthquake proof. No danger of tipping and falling onto a stinky barn floor. Our stools were homegrown, fabricated from small tree limbs, with each limb embedded in the round piece of wood at the top. Nails and screws were not needed, for the tree branches were turned tightly into holes in the seat. Nothing complicated. When stool legs became arthritic, we used bailing wire and hockey tape to keep them upright. I ask you: have you ever seen a cellist's chair held together this way? And they have insurance!!!

Not to belittle cello playing, for I'm sure it requires a certain knack, but now we come to the sound part. The sound of the first jets of milk hitting the bottom of a metal pail ring clearly in my ears, all the way from Manitoba to sunny California, unfrozen by prairie cold, undimmed by the anvil of time.

Imagine a cellist hitting a high note to begin a grand symphony, and you have some idea of the sound of milk piercing the air as it hits the bottom of a pail. The notes repeat in rapid sequence for a minute or two; the symphony builds and softens as warm milk modulates the sound into the lower ranges. Cows really are as stupid as they look, but they know the notes, and if you hit the bottom of the pail in the wrong spot guaranteed they'll take to kicking. Have you ever heard of a conductor kicking a cellist over a wrong note? Of course not. The cellist, of course, has the loving support of an entire orchestra; we had only mewing cats, the snorting of a pig or two and Bob snapping his fingers three cows down the line.

Like all symphonies, the music of milking requires the attentive cooperation of many players: the barn is the acoustic chamber, the cow agrees to stand still and give up her milk, the stool must hold his place, the pail with upraised arms, and the milker with honed fingers, poised just so.

As I write this I'm finally appreciating the nuanced skills demanded by the art of milking. Back in the day, we took it all for granted: pull up a stool, plunk down and go to work. Seeing the art and science of milking as I now do, I'm feeling quite feisty and hereby propose a milk-off competition. This is an actual, official proposal and not to be laughed at.

My proposal is barnyard simple: I invite a talented cello player—insisting it be one of the mesmerizing, elegant ladies I've seen in various symphony concerts—to come to our barn Friday evening next week. Being respectful again, I propose too that she not wear heels.

She'll carefully, happily bring her precious cello, and I'll PLAY IT while she tries her hand at milking Ole Betsy, our most gentle cow. She in turn can pick a difficult Beethoven piece for me to play. I'll stack the deck further in her favor, by nursing the sweetest possible cello sounds to help Betsy let down her milk, so our lovely cellist can strike the proper notes at the bottom of the pail.

For our judging panel I propose an unbiased and independent panel of farmers—milkers, all with a keen eye for the requisite skills involved. No money involved. Just for the fun of it. Our contest has no expiration date.

Long before modern corporations were adding vitamins to milk, we had our own way of fortifying milk, all totally organic. We were decades ahead of the curve, more skilled than the great Gretzky with his gift of knowing where the puck would be a few seconds ahead.

Again, there was nothing complicated about our fortification process. No big assembly lines or paychecks, or stuff like that. Nobody was lawyered up or thinking lawsuits. Before milking we'd usually take a small bucket of properly fortified creek water, using an old rag to haphazardly wash the cow's udders. Often as not we'd not fuss with the washing part, choosing to pull up the stool, butt down and milk.

Many things were added to enrich our milk, none of them questioned, for it was just part of life. Ever curious, I recall casually watching as hair and dandruff and unmentionable animal stuff would fall into the milk. Interesting bits of straw, like the first snow of September, continuously fell through the cracks in the loft floor, settling on us and in the milk.

We had occasional questions about our milk additives, but it despaired of any easy solution. We'd never heard of government regulations or inspectors. Milking was milking, breathing was breathing and we saw no reason to change things. We dragged ourselves to the barn, pulled up a stool, grabbed a teat and started the concert. Barnyard simple.

I caution all readers at this point to skip the following paragraph if your urban sensibilities are highly tuned, remembering that I am a survivor, and in excellent health. I cut to the bottom line: Part of our milk fortification program consisted of fresh cow manure. Guaranteed totally organic and farm grown by widely roaming animals. For better or worse I saw it all, I drank it all in. The additives were as inevitable as blizzards, and like the snow, all this stuff drifted down into our milk pails.

Here I sound another advisory to skittish readers: the worst time for dealing with cow manure was spring time, for when the cows were furloughed from the barn to eat the first May grasses, their digestive systems would riot, and loose stools (think the D word) plagued the land. In spring time we'd usually wash our cows before milking. This, of course, was not an either/or thing; the cows were cleaner after we washed them, but if you looked closely you'd wonder if they'd been washed at all.

We know that dog tails have a life of their own. Less widely known is the truth of cow's tails, for they are entirely ungovernable, and especially so when layered with brown stuff that was green grass only an hour ago. As best we could, we'd tie their tails with binder cord, wrapping, wrapping, knotting, knotting, and lash the whole mess to the stall. This helped but was never fully satisfactory, for her tail could readily slather free. Cow tails are a separate department and act freely on their own. Ole Betsy, anxious to please, faked an apologetic look when her tail broke free. In the worst case, without warning, the tail would exact revenge on us with a few snake lashes across our face, and we'd go howling to the creek (fortifying the water for those downstream).

It is quite impossible to describe the sheer sensuality, the fragrances that come with barn facials. You feel cowed, flabbergasted, gobsmacked. I've never had a spa treatment, so I'm guessing that spa facials are more gentle and of better fragrance than the organic cow-tail treatments. Every man to his own, I say.

Our milk fortification was further enriched when a cow slammed her rear leg into the milk pail. Cows. Bless 'em and their big innocent eyes. Usually they'd stand quietly chewing their cuds as we relieved them of the pressure in their udders; however, any cow at any time might suddenly kick or replant a leg smack in the middle of our pail. With the persistent kickers we'd take a rope, wind it round their legs many times and anchor them to the stall, a laborious process also with paradoxical outcomes.

When the inevitable happened and a cow planted her rear leg in our milk pail, we'd put a hockey shoulder into her while pulling up on her leg, and with verbal encouragements—some of which might be heard clear to town—hoped to change her grounding. Then we'd dump the milk in the cat's dish and go back to milking. The closest water was down at the creek, and our job was to milk not wash pails. No one complained, certainly not the cats.

In addition to the ingredients already noted, our milk was further enriched with flies, mosquitoes and ever present wasps and bees that enjoyed farm life, also free range and certifiably organic. Bee wings stayed on top and gave us precise targets, spinning about as milk hit the outer edges, adding fun to the complexity of our milk.

The journey of milk is a long one, beginning with the sun ninety-three million miles away, then the grass it lures out of hiding, along with the miles of fine ducting within the cow, and then a hundred yards more from the barn to our house, where we might use a cheese cloth to strain most of the visible materials from the milk, then dump the *clean* milk into the large metal bowl atop the cream separator. Like our clothes, the cheese cloth was rarely washed, and when hanging to dry it was fantastic fly bait. When used, the cheese cloth added a gourmet delicacy to the taste of our milk.

The cream separator was another flavor enhancer. It was about four feet high and operated by rapidly turning a crank, which spun metal disks that magically separated the milk from the cream. We'd crank, and milk would come out one spout, cream from another. Simple enough. Just like an atom smasher, except different.

We heard the discs were supposed to be cleaned every day, and that sounded right. Like many fine theories this one was hard to actually practice, for the discs, layered with vintage cream, were tricky to clean and we had better things to do. Our milk enrichment program was totally complete from grass to the final drinking. I'm proud to say we had no added colorings, no sweeteners, nothing artificial at all in our milk.

As a city slicker, you might think that given all the work and skills involved in milking, we'd drink most of it, and you'd be wrong again. Would you want to drink most of the milk? Most of it was mixed with grain to provide slop for the pigs, with some for the chickens, cats and dogs. Occasionally we made butter in an old ceramic, waist high container, using a wooden plunger, moving it up and down, up and down until we had butter. So boring.

Eventually we modernized to a gallon glass container with a crank handle. A modern butter maker! That roused us out of our boredom for a day or two. Then it was just more round and round with the crank. Round and round. I need not point out to the millions of butter makers out there, that some cream will solidify quickly, and other cream is like a bad hockey team and can take a terrible beating and not butter up. We had different tricks, sometimes adding a bit of lemon juice. We believed too, that thunderstorms curdled milk, which soured it for drinking but helped in making butter. Good theories all.

When we had enough milk cows we'd make a few dollars selling milk. Our milk would be poured into tall metal containers with large handles on either side. Each container had a heavy lid, hammered on with a piece of wood. Either a truck would come to our farm to pick up the liquid delicacy, or other times we'd take it to the railway station a mile away. Every month or so, we'd go to Neepawa to shop, and we'd throw a can of milk in the trunk of the car to deliver it directly to the creamery.

Neepawa, like the sun, was light years away, and we were always excited to go there to see all the people, cars and shops. If we could get our car started we'd head south, first to Kelwood, and amidst a cloud of dust, hit the gravel highway to Riding Mountain, past the little log church, and finally the city on the hill, Neepawa! Sometimes our old cars would give out, and we'd not make it. If we did make it all the way, the deep potholes in the road guaranteed the milk would get as much shaking as it did before it left the cow.

Now here's something else. They actually had professional milk tasters at the Neepawa creamery. Along with dozens of other farmers, we'd unload our five gallon can of fine, pure milk, drag it into the tasting room, where a man would ladle a bit in his mouth, and swirl it around, making weird faces and sounds. The final stunning ritual was the way he'd spit the mouthful into a hole a few yards away. Purging it like chewing tobacco. I always imagined this hole drained straight to hell.

The milk tasters commanded my highest interest, and their courage astounded me; I watched with scientific curiosity and disgust. That anyone could taste milk for a living was incomprehensible. Along with our brave soldiers, I felt they should have their own medals and memorial cairns. I knew enough about milk to be nervous. Sure, I could trust the purity of our own milk, but all those other farmers? What might be in their milk? I'd accidentally tasted countless samples of sour milk that had sat too long on our shelf. Projectile spitting is a real thing: I'd launch the raunchy stuff a mile further than the creamery tester ever could, with an expletive that must have made the cows smile. I knew too, that some milk was bitter from certain weeds eaten by the cows. Pig weed for example. Sometimes milk had blood in it for reasons I never wanted to know. And here was a man who tasted all kinds of milk, no questions asked. We all stood around gawking as though this was normal, waiting for the taster to issue his decree about the quality of our milk.

And here is another mysterious fact: I never saw any milk turned away. I kept thinking there must be a can or two that was beyond the human pale, fit only for pigs. Not once did I see any farmer humiliated by having his milk banned from the creamery. Taste a bit, forcefully expel it, make a few notes in a book, and send the can into the creamery. That was the ritual.

As if milking was not fun enough by itself, when Phil and I were lined up across the aisle from each other, we'd have milk wars, with hot jets of milk streaming across the barn. We had one cat that would fling himself repeatedly into the air to try and intercept the milk. Milk contrails and leaping cats make for interesting theatre. I was pleased with how far we could shoot the stuff. Again, much practice and skill were required to put milk into orbit. The trick was to pump the teat several times without letting any milk out, to *load it* as one might a shotgun, then once loaded, to give a staccato squeeze to launch it into space. Like the insatiable cats, we'd be soaked. Our clothes were not washed regularly, and surely smelled of manure, sweat and sour milk, but we were the last to know.

I must say more about milking and cats. Cats hate to get wet, but they are total addicts when it comes to warm milk. Cats are smarter than we like to think. They'd hear the clanking of our milk pails, and when we opened the barn door they'd come running. Cats are known for their independence, and farm cats for their obsessive dependence on milk. They were skittish about our fortified milk, preferring pure milk, without the fortification from the pail, the cream separator and all the rest. They liked it sent direct, airmail, right into their mouths.

They'd sit up in praying postures and often we'd tease them, talking nonsense, making them wait. *Hey, pretty kitty, what you looking for, eh?* or, *Hey, Phil, look ! This kitty has its front paws folded like it's praying...oh, sweet kitty, that's right, bow down, bow down...you pray now sweet kitty...* Watching a cat squirm and pray as it waited for warm milk made our milking go faster. After we got the rhythm going and milk flowing, we'd start firing away. Our aim was not as accurate as our hockey shots, and the cats received a free milk shower. They'd be drenched, yet continue to sit with their mouths open crying for more. After it was over they'd spend hours grooming, putting on their Sunday best for the next outpouring.

Our universe was the barnyard: like gods, we sat on high, rickety stools, baptizing our genuflecting cats with holy milk. There was no need for acolytes, choirs, priests or pastors. We were it and our cats worshiped us. One taste of our religion and they never missed a day of church.

Yet, given our active imaginations, showering cats would sometimes bore us. Again we'd improvise other fun things. A horse's butt was always fair game and a wandering pig even better. Hitting them in the ear earned high points. Pigs really are stupid. They have no reverence. Had they watched the cats, they would have learned to sit, salute and get mouthfuls of sweet milk.

We had millions of flies, all impossible to hit, but one night Phil claimed to have dropped one in flight by aiming ahead of it. I was insulted that he might think he was a better shot than me, and I protested his claim too loudly. He dropped his pail and charged at me, and we tussled each other to the messy floor. I convinced Phil to let me up by making the hollow promise I'd never squirt him again. The flies went back to buzzing, the cats to prayer, and we to our milking.

Early on, I'd sit at the foot of the stairs between our kitchen and living room, drinking a glass of milk, with bread and jam. It was one of those things we do as children, and not so much as adults, letting our bodies lead us into a place of comfort and security without thinking about it.

Because I'm rarely sick, my family thinks I have a robust immune system due to the daily exposure to unlimited microorganisms in childhood. I fancy they're onto something.

On days when I'm aware of thinking too highly of myself, ready perhaps to enunciate an absolute truth for my less enlightened family and friends, one silent, corrective mantra consists of words like this: *I'm just a farm boy going out to milk the cows...* When I say this, I see myself walking from our house to the barn. If I linger with the image, as I enter the barn, I feel a rush of warm air and the full frontal assault of a hundred smells. This memory and the truth of it, help me put my plow back into the soil, grounding me, leveling out the natural tendency of the human ego toward inflation.

I stopped drinking milk in my thirties, due to what I was reading about the negative impact of dairy products. At the unconscious level it may have been my memories of the murky milk from farm days that motivated me more than the research evidence. Like the rest of us, I tell myself stories, fabricate beliefs and so forth, as consciously as I can, knowing as I do so that there are always factors that are beyond awareness, especially our childhood dispositions combined with our genetic impulses.

As I've noted earlier, most of what we ate was raised on our farm. On the rare occasions when Dad went shopping for additional food items, he was faithful to his Scotch lineage, bringing home only a few cans of Campbell's tomato soup, a bit of cheese and perhaps a few oranges or apples. His sparse shopping was a joke in our family, and over the years I've worked at being more generous with my money, including shopping. For the past decade and more, I've done most of our grocery shopping. As I load up the cart I occasionally think of my father's parsimonious shopping habits, and decide to toss in some more items. I smile and float a prayer to my dad, loving him for who he was, letting my judgments go.

Costco is my favorite store. When I put on my farmer's mind I see things simply and clearly, realizing that history pivots around two critical events: B.C. and A.C.—Before Costco and After Costco. It's all clear to me: before Costco we were lost souls, drifting here and there, uncertain where to shop, torn between many masters. Costco saved us, and as one of the great cathedrals of capitalism gave us purpose and direction. When I line up for free food samples I have memories of taking communion. Like the Lord Himself, Costco forgives everything. If we don't like something, just take it back, no apologies needed. My occasional forays into improv theatre help fuel my imagination, and occasionally I have an odd image of my wife putting me in the cart and trying to return me. In my head I play out the conversation Ruthie has with the woman at the front desk: *I got him right off the shelf before you were born, young woman, and he didn't work out the way I wanted... so here he is...*

A bumper sticker I'd like to see: There is such a thing as a free lunch: Costco.

Elsewhere I've mentioned that Esalen Institute, since my first visit there in spring of 1993, has been a vital spiritual home for me. In one group, in the late 1990's with my good friend, Kenny Hallstone, we took turns sharing happy childhood memories with our group. I shared my story of sitting at the bottom of our stairs in our farm home, drinking milk, and eating bread and jam. The leader of the group asked me to close my eyes and actively imagine being my child again, noticing body sensations, emotions and smells and other details.

Soft music played in the background, and as I dropped into a more focused awareness of those happy hours of bread and jam, it seemed I was actually a child, back on the farm. I could smell and taste the bread, and feel my small feet on the floor.

After several moments I was invited me to open my eyes. I was shocked to see a piece of bread with jam on a plate in front of me. I was so startled that I wondered for a moment if my return to childhood had materialized the bread and jam. I laughed with surprise, then broke into tears of gratitude, as I realized our co-leader, Joel, had sprinted to the lodge and back with the bread and jam. I have a file of magical Esalen experiences and this is one of my favorites.

CHAPTER 9

The Broken Promise

If I take the wings of the morning and dwell in the uttermost parts
of the sea, even there thy hand shall lead me, and thy right hand
shall hold me.

PSALM 139: 9, 10

.....They that have climbed the white mists of the morning:
They that have soared, before the world's awake....
How they thundered up the clouds to glory,
Or fallen to an English field stained red.....

JOHN G. MAGEE, JR. PER ARDUA

ALONG WITH THE millions of other families, World War II invaded our lives; the goose- stepping Nazis, thankfully, could not bridge across the Atlantic, yet they still had life and death consequences for families around the world, including our isolated area.

Bob, our eldest brother, signed up to serve in the Royal Canadian Air Force in 1942, when he was nineteen and I was three. Alvin Jackson, from the Jackson family north of us, also joined the RCAF about the same time. Many other young men and some women from our area signed up to join the fight, and some families lost more than one son.

I have memory snippets from age four and five, of our family talking anxiously about Alvin. We were all reminded to pray for him as much as we could, and I faithfully, fearfully did this. Then one day we were stunned to learn that Alvin had been killed the night of August 26, 1944 when his bomber crashed. Darkness and fear, as cold as any north wind, claimed us, and we spent more time on our knees.

By age five I knew who Hitler was, and I hated him. Based on the tricks I'd learned from playing cowboys and Indians, I hatched plans to kill him, enlisting help from my wee brother, Phil. Phil was usually ready to fight and play war games and even after I told him we could be killed, he was ready to fly across the ocean and go after the bad man who had killed Alvin and might kill Bob. We practiced with our cap guns, and brandished our swords against the barn.

From a letter dated September 28, 1944, sent to our sister Jean, Bob shares his fears about flying, and about war, as he completed final navigation training in England. He writes that his fear is so constant and deep it is like hell. On many flights at night and in bad weather he is convinced they'll never return to earth, and as a navigator he felt great responsibility to guide his ship home. He despises himself for his fears, blaming himself for his lack of faith in Jesus, and tells his sister not to write, as he feels unworthy of a letter from her. His comments, like those of our sister Jean (below), reveal the shame, anxiety and fears that were imprinted by our hellfire religion.

His fear may have had a precognitive element, for shortly after writing his letter, Lew Brewer, the pilot of his crew, asked Bob to take a break and not fly with the rest of the crew on the night of October 11, 1944, so another navigator could gain more hours of night flying. This was the first flight Bob missed.

It was a fateful night: his crew, in a new Wellington Bomber, departed the base at Kinloss, Scotland, disappeared into the darkness, and were never found. Bob was shattered by the news, and given the fears he already had, asked to be released from the RCAF. From the copy of his military file, I learn that the hearing board reviewing his case gave him an honorable discharge.

As I write about this horrific event, my heart weaves a movie as clear as any Hollywood might create: I'm a child and I see the new Wellington Bomber leave the airstrip at Kinloss, and as it passes over, I wave, sending them off with a cheer. Even in the night, I see the glimmer of light from the shiny bomber, and hear the smooth thrust of the new engines, as four propellers shred the damp air. Tonight Hitler will die and I laugh at the thought. Then, magically, I'm flying with them and we soar over sea, the waters dancing with reflected star light. When we enter the clouds the plane begins drifting, then starts to fall, to fall toward the night sea, and the pilot and navigator are yelling, trying to stop the fall, and then the impact of metal on water and all is black.

My adult reflections lead me to think the name Kinloss might refer to an ancient battle where many died. In any case, the name fits Bob's crew and the families who lost their sons, and here to honor them, I note the names that Bob remembers: Lew Brewer, Dennis Sharmon, Fred Lilywhite, and the flight instructor, Mr. Lucas. Bob does not recall the name of the navigator and one other crew member and notes in a letter that they were all Royal Air Force and not RCAF. Because they were RAF, they don't show up in the massive book listing all RCAF casualties, *They Shall Not Grow Old*, sent as a gift by Bob to family members.

My sister Helen also has a letter dated Oct 26, 1944 from Mother addressed to: Robert McLeod J41677, RCAF, Overseas, England. Mother refers to Bob's news of two weeks earlier when he had shared his grief over losing his friends and flying crew, and Mother tells him how hard she prayed for those lost, and how she hoped a few might be found alive in the water. She supports his decision to leave the force, even if it means giving up his commission.

The news from home to Bobby in far off England notes that threshing season ended on Oct. 14 and Dad finally was able to disc the fields. Mother apologizes for not writing for three weeks, and says she has to sneak writing time in between all the chores and minding the children. She reports that Albert is sleeping and has a swollen cheek from a tough day cutting teeth. The house flies are terrible, and she is bothered by how careless she's been about praying and writing.

She tells her son she has much pride in how well she's learned to drive the car since he and Jean left, remarking that George Glover told her she drove better than Dad. She describes how she and Jean are extracting honey in the kitchen, and that it is *just another experiment of my precious intemperate rule.* This last statement puzzles me, for it is so out of tone with the rest of the letter, and I've never heard that Mother was intemperate.

In a letter to me dated Oct 25, 1985, my sister Jean writes about her relationship with Alvin. The letter reveals something about her relationship with Alvin and more about her relationship with Christ and the profound way religion colored her life.

As context for the letter I note she accepted the Lord as her savior in 1942, and for the rest of her life was a fearsomely faithful, ardent Christian. Her letter is a goldmine of insights into her spiritual belief system.

She writes as follows: *Your letter (and the pictures) brought back some sad memories of Alvin's youthful death at only 20 years of age!! Alvin was such a nice fine fellow, very shy and humble and unpretentious etc,—a very faithful, good boy, so solid and dependable with few words, and a great big generous heart of gold (as far as the human heart goes). I often wondered about (and sincerely hoped for) his conversion to God before his sudden death! We heard that his plane was blown up, and Alvin being a rear gunner in the plane was unable to escape (as there was no time to parachute out etc)! Let us hope that dear Alvin's spirit was quickened into true Living Faith in Christ Jesus before his body came to its end here on earth! Even so Lord Jesus!*

Just after my conversion in August 1942, I went home for a few days en route to my first teaching job at Merridale (near Roblin). For some mysterious reason (quite a quandary to me) Alvin had somewhat of a shine on me! The first time he approached me to take me out (before I left home in July, 42) I was in the field rounding up the milking cows in early eve! Poor, dear, painfully shy Alvin came creeping across the fence looking so very guilty, with his head hanging down to hesitatingly request my "highly esteemed"(by him) presence at some simple outing. Actually my heart was not along, but, because he had such a nice car, I pretended to give my presence with pleasure! How corrupt and dishonest is human nature! So after my change of heart which was truly a miracle of God's grace and love and mercy—for I had been such a rebel toward Him— my conscience had been keenly quickened and awakened! I recalled my hypocritical attitude toward dear Alvin (and several others) and I determined to make amends as the Lord led and enabled me to do so!

Dear Bob thought I should not go out again with Alvin (after this great change of heart) but I did so lovingly, desiring to give him my testimony of God's Salvation and transformation from death into Life (the beginning of the growth from a babe in Christ into the full stature of His divine Nature). So I did go out for one last drive in Alvin's car....that fall Alvin went into the air force! We never met again as far as I remember!! After hearing of Alvin's shocking death (about 2 weeks or so after he was reported missing) my conscience was so relieved, to know I had witnessed to dear Alvin's heart and how fervently and earnestly I hoped that he had also called upon the Lord to be saved, before his sudden departure from his body!

Bob arrived home in early spring of 1945, paying a surprise visit to Jean where she was teaching in another part of the province, prior to returning to our farm at Norgate. No one had heard from him in a few weeks, and one day walking home from her teaching job, Jean a spied a lone figure coming toward her on the snowy road. At first she thought that the person walked like Bob, and she assumed it was only wishful thinking. Then as they approached she saw indeed it was him and ran and gave him a hug of joy. This reunion scene seems so archetypal of the soldier returning safely home, and I imagine millions of reunions similar to this occurring over the centuries.

Bob returned to our home with new life energy, happy to have survived the war. Like the rest of us he was frugal and had saved most of his money, and immediately bought Mother a new stove, put new linoleum on the kitchen floor, and best of all, installed electricity in our home, a feat I still consider a work of near genius.

To create electricity he purchased twenty-four large glass-enclosed batteries, and installed a windmill on the roof of the house to charge the batteries. He also had a small gas motor to charge them if the wind failed for more than a few days. We children would stand for long minutes in the basement, watching the glass batteries bubbling away as they charged, and marveling at the wizardry of our RCAF brother.

Having electricity meant we had joined the civilized world! We could flip a switch and lights would come on, both in the house and the barn. We were happy to put aside our old coal oil lamps, with their putrid smell and dim flickering light.

Bob also spent the unearthly amount of $19.95 for a purple ballpoint pen, the first in our area. Like his life itself, and the other things he was doing, this too was magical. It never needed ink! We'd write away with it and it would go on and on. He let us take it to school one day and we were the center of attention. We were excited to put our inkwells away, until one day the magic ran out.

To continue his generosity, Bob bought a train ticket for Mother and Helen to travel west through the Rockies to see relatives in Vancouver. They returned to our farm as excited world travelers, with stories that filled me with wonder and a box that said it contained Vancouver sunshine. I too, wanted to go west of the Riding Mountains and see the Rockies, and if I was lucky I'd go all the way to Vancouver where flowers bloomed in March.

Now I felt pride in our family. A new day had dawned! Bobbie was home from across the sea, and he had seen many things. He had a fancy uniform, with an especially striking officer's cap, and he let us wear it for war games. We had lights and a magical pen. We were a modern family, we were going somewhere, and now more than ever, I enjoyed inviting friends over.

In 1977 my wife and I took our first trip to Europe, with our children Heather and Todd, aged eight and six. Life, once again, gave me an experience of synchronicity with regard to my brother Bob and his time in the RCAF. Without any planning on my part, as my family and I were driving in northern Scotland, headed to the spiritually-based Findhorn community, I was delightfully shocked to drive by the air force base at Kinloss. I at first could not believe the sign I was reading, for I knew this was one of the places where he'd trained.

We stopped the car, got out and peered across the fields at the few, drab buildings near the runways. I felt a nostalgic warmth as images of Bobby possessed my mind. I could see him walking from building to building, and having tea with friends, then see them all rushing to their bombers as the alarms sounded.

During that trip we stopped at a few military cemeteries on the chance we might find Alvin Jackson's grave, but we were not favored with any serendipitous discovery. I felt oddly haunted as I thought of Alvin and how his loss had impacted me.

In 1992 as I recalled the dreaded war years, I wrote my remembrances of Alvin's death and the safe return of Bobbie to our family. I present the story here, and add some comments at the end. As I wrote this story, I felt as though the vaults of childhood memories opened in a rare way, and I had some strong emotions, ranging from grief and sadness, to excitement and wonder. I sent this story to Bob and his eight children, as well as a few others. Here, then, the story.

⅌

When a young man falls from the night sky in a metal womb, we are easily moved to tears. It matters not if we are five years old, as I was then, or if we are middle-aged, as I am now. Neither does it matter what his color, creed or nationality: when we open our hearts to receive his fall, they naturally break, for at some time we've all loved a young man and so we mourn his passing. As much as anything, this is what it means to be human: to have big, broken hearts.

For every young man carries half the human promise; they are the seeds of our future and in fleeting moments when we look into their eyes we can see the face of a grand baby.

I was five the night Royal Canadian Air Force rear gunner Alvin Jackson, aged 20, surrendered his promise in a German pasture. I know now that he fell the night of August 26, 1944, but of course did not know it then, so can only imagine that I slept innocently through Alvin's night. I may have had unusual dreams, for already at that tender time I was a comrade-in-arms, an imaginary flier of vast skies, brothered to all fliers. With other five-year-olds I pieced my world together with dreams, intuitions and fiery imagination.

I'm uncertain when I first heard the report. I assume our neighbor walked the half-mile to our farm with more news from the front. The Jackson family lived closer to the post office so they would often have news ahead of us.

Nothing Norgate, our town. An insignificant town in time, yet something, everything, to us, serving as our connection to the outside world. The town had a post office, which was really a home with a small room attached into which the trickle of mail would come, and a grain elevator, a one-room school house where I spent the first eight years of my education with kids ages 5 through 17, a slouching grocery store with an antique gas pump, a hopeful church. That was it. Surrounded by all that prairie, all that sky. Insignificant, vast, frozen, flat, boring. Had any of the residents been mathematically inclined they would have discovered the concept of zero prior to its discovery in the middle-east. It seems now that the place might have been built for spite—to prove lastingly to humans, they were, as measured against the all, mere nothings, and that any dreams sprung to life in that tundra were born only to sour folks against all dreams.

If you steamed through here on the four-o'clock headed north to McCreary, peering out your train window, you'd be incredulous at the excitement among the natives caused by nothing more than a bit of mail, or if it was a high day, a package with new socks, perhaps, from the T. Eaton Company in far off, much-rumored Winnipeg, *The Peg.* Hah! We all believed it existed. The true believers even talked of visiting there, but it was endless talk and rarely grew wheels.

From the warmth of your chamber, you'd cast unbelieving eyes back to your magazine, knowing in your worldly mind that the loins of men and the wombs of women here would never bear fruit other than milk maids and plow boys. You'd be anxious for the train to smoke on down the line, knowing that from this place nothing noble could come. And you'd be wrong. Dead wrong, as we say. Especially if you'd seen Bobby and Alvin there at the station, or me with my wild child's eyes and the little jig I'd do when the train would start up with a great roar, flattening my pennies. I'd live and die in those moments. The pennies would be hot if I picked them up too early. Bobby, my big brother, and Alvin were as experimental and wild-eyed as me, although fifteen years older. Along with me, when the train rolled north they must surely have had a secret hunger to move on, move on, for this was the song the wheels sang.

So, of course it is wrong, just as dead wrong to call our town Nothing Norgate, for it was nothing less than Everything, it was all we knew; it was the center of our universe and we loved the town and all its people. There we lived our lives and buried our dead.

Because this is a true story, you might want to find a map and look for the place. I'm excited to see if this place of beginnings still gets penciled in when officials decide which places are official. I can tell you this: if it shows up on your map, get a new one, for yours is out of date. The town no longer physically exists. In the late 60s the all-powerful Canadian National Railway (CNR) tore up the rail lines as if in a rage to undo its decision to ever run through Norgate, pathetic Norgate. The brave schoolhouse was hauled away one frigid morning, to the town where the high school was located. The little store, abandoned, collapsed on itself when it could no longer resist the flirtations of gravity. The post office was closed after many of the families had moved—some like myself to The Peg. Mainly the young people got the hell out, as you can see, for good reasons. The long winters and the restless north wind were reasons enough to go. I left at 17.

The church had vanished prior to the time of my last return. I'd guess it was moved like the school, but certain residents—myself included—allude to a possible rapture, half believing it was swept up to heaven. They were not folks without imagination, as I've said.

Into the unfathomable, magnificent prairie skies roared the first air-machines, not long before I was born. Neither the country nor its people were ever the same. Eyes that until now were riveted to earth turned skyward; spirits that had been hostage to gravity now took imaginary flight. Imagine, if you will, sepulchral winter skies untrammeled since Eden-time and then let yourself hear the sound of the first airplane shredding this space. Feel twelve opposing pistons hammering against each other at 2600 rpm's, each insisting on tearing free from the crankshaft, each piston with a lion's throat, each screaming for more fuel and air. The long sleep of the prairies was over; terror and inspiration followed the onslaught.

Abed and bug-eyed in the pristine, I'd first hear their far off thrumming, never sure if it might be rain or a car on the country road. Interminably, the sound would mount and when I thought the sound was as demanding as it could be, it would get louder, then louder still. As the angry lions crossed over our home, my body would involuntarily arch upwards, forming a rainbow that was a wish for more planes to come. I did not know until later which craft were commercial, which for combat; all of them seemed at war with the liquid silence God had poured across our earth. At every passing our house and land would shiver and when September carrots grew curly in the ground I knew why. Summer thunder was the only other sound like this, and for both I held my breath opening wondrous eyes upward. I became a supplicant: these airplanes were gods, rending my skies, burning memories deep in my heart. If their path was right I could see out my east window their winking lights. That was a Christmas feeling.

I was an observant child and by age four had learned a bit about military ritual. When the sky mashers stormed over, from my bed I'd offer a secret salute, holding my arm in proper position for breathless moments. This was how I became a little pilot and joined the ranks of those early captains of the sky. I still have a first grade text in which various airplanes are drawn, put there by my obedient right hand, the hand that really had no choice but to draw and salute. The planes I drew were military, mainly fighters, each carrying the marking of the Royal Canadian Air Force—the best darn air force in the world! Most of my sketches showed machine guns blazing and had speed streaks flashing off the wings. In the cockpits I had little pilots with brown helmets and big noses, irreverently called McLeod noses because they run in our family.

It's hard to believe, but Alvin and Bobby may have been more captivated by flight than I was. Thinking back, I'll bet they trembled in the night, carving their own salutes and dying to be among clouds and stars, to sail the blue, to make the shivers rather than be hammered by them. Unlike wee Albert, as I was called, they were strong enough to act on their dreams. They had hormones. Serious talk must have started around 1940 or '41 as the war grew in Europe. The war gave a solid reason for flying and parents were persuaded to let sons sign up. Becoming an airman could no longer be dismissed as rebellion or craziness.

Bob and Alvin signed up. They ached for more than talk and stretched strong arms towards the tumult of clouds and war. I have a vague memory of missing Bob. Later I learned he had gone to the induction center, and for basic training to Brandon—a real town of a few thousand people—100 or so miles southwest of our farm.

While Alvin and Bob's departure was tough on everyone, it must have been most traumatic for our mothers. Mothers are the first casualties of war, their spirits being wounded even in the anticipation of a son's departure. Mothers: I see their last, desperate wave and feel their tears as the train pulls away, their firstborns, their great hopes torn away by this awful metal monster. Pulled to war amidst the smoke and steam, they wave their prayerful hankies. It must have been for all those mothers, horrible. All that strong muscle vital for farm work, shipped by rail as animals to market.

Abroad, as whiskered infants over trenches fly, mothers at home, from broken hearts, in empty bedrooms die. The saber singing for the soul of doomed youth, scars all the loves left at home, makes cruel joke of prayers, lays all low. As a father with a lovely son, I can see now how this is true.

Postcards! They started arriving from Brandon, then from foggy London. The Jacksons, the McLeods, the Campbells, the Finnemores, the Shintons, all the families tracking the movement of special sons, from the training schools to across the sea. Cards were shared back and forth, news relayed several weeks after the fact. I can still see the cards with my hawkish, child's eye: strange, arched buildings, colorful flower gardens, lush London parks, strolling people with umbrellas, and trees five times as thick as on our frozen plains. Most intriguing were the kings and palaces; kings in sharp colored military uniforms covered with medals. They were brave, I knew. Small fingers, mine, touched and turned each card with loving fascination; each time I rolled a card a new vista emerged. I longed to go where Bobby had gone, to fly far away on a magic carpet. More than anything I missed him. My gentle fingers told me that.

Simply put, it is difficult to go on with this story for I've already cried in the telling and in the knowing how it ends. Bobby came home from WWII and Alvin did not. I struggle for answers as to why some are called and others not. I hear different speculations: God keeps a ledger; He loves some more than others and the really loved ones are called home early; it's the luck of the draw. I'm savvy to the notion of reincarnation. For me, at five and today, none of the explanations are compassionate or grand enough to do justice to the saber song that brought our Alvin down.

Some of Bobby's postcards carried talk of life back in Norgate, of picking up where things had left off, of milking cows in winter cold and waiting for the four-o'clock to roll in. Everyday things. There was a growing sense of expectation. Then came the visitor from the Jackson's with the bombshell and the secretive, low voiced talk around me. Alvin had perished. The story I pieced together with painstaking intuition based on overheard conversations was that two bombers had bumped into each other in the night and that he was trapped in his rear gunner's turret, and the big birds had fallen to earth, broken, crushed, dead. And, because I was good with rhymes, I knew the ending: *all the king's horses and all the king's men could not put Alvin together again.* And, quick to ask, *Oh, Mommy, will Bobby come home, will Bobby come home?*

There was so much secrecy about it all. Or perhaps I have repressed the memories that also made of me a casualty. There was a void in talk, a void of people, a hole in our lives. Our part of the prairies felt so blue. As planes crossed our uncertain skies, Phil and I started sending them messages. One windy morning we were tossing pigeon feathers into the air, and as the wind swept round the southern end of our barn, the feathers were lofted toward the clouds. We decided that these feathers carried messages from us to the men in the planes, and that for sure Bobby and Alvin would get our words.

The messages I sent were of hope and cheer. Each feather released was a prayer to Bobby, Bobby, Alvin, Alvin. Magic and laughter infused our play and I believed we were helping win the war. Five-year-old magic. It was all I had in those lonely times. I expected to be bombed any day, and I knew that if a German or Japanese plane flew over, our feathers could be deadly missiles. That knowing gave me comfort. I could protect our family. After all, I was five and had a big brother who needed help. If he could soar into the heavens by plane, I could launch feathers. And I knew, even though he had all the roar, that my craft had the advantage of lightness and silence. I could sail up and under the Red Baron, stinging him like my daddy's bees, silently in the belly: *Aha! Ahahahahahahahahah:* the sound of my machine gun with spit flying. After my bullets riddled him, I'd see his startled face with moon-white eyes, just before he rolled into a death spiral. Bobby could use all the help he could get. *Ahahahahahah: Take that! Take that! You devil Red Baron. Darn you, darn you.*

Our prayers were helping and the excitement about Bobby's return was building. I think I always believed he'd come back. I needed to be terrified by his monster games again, to hear him rush up from the dark basement as Phil and I crept agonizingly down infinite stairs to find him, our eyes peering into the black maw behind the furnace. The basement was blacker than a German night, more silent than flung feathers, still we could not help but creep closer. Empty silence. Nothing there but the dark void. Perhaps he'd gone out to work after all, for there was no movement, no sound—only our two small hearts tearing holes in frozen lungs.

His timing was perfect. On the razor's edge, just when we'd almost given up and I was putting a tentative thumb in my mouth, then, only then, the Basement Monster would spring from the dark. Full of life and muscle, he'd rush up at us and our legs would turn into slashing propellers; a blur of childish terror, we'd fly up the stairs as we blasted full bore into the kitchen, two lightning left turns, then a screaming dive under Mom's bed. Home! He could not slide under the bed at 400 mph, slam up against the wall and be ecstatic. We had him on that one. A few times I wet my pants. I'd seen dogs do that, but never people. So until now, I never told.

Bobby would come home. My heart kept the faith, my legs were my creed. I needed the terror of the Basement Monster so I could forget the war and the fall of Alvin from the sky.

And so I began my nightly vigils. It was hard to pull out of the clouds of sleep, which at five was almost like a death dive itself. My excitement about Bobby's return was enough to roust me and get me into the kitchen. I sometimes slept there for a few hours. I don't recall an alarm clock or anyone waking me, so this part is a mystery. The kitchen had its own war going, with the dying embers of wood, stabbing light into the dark, beating it back so that Bobby could walk into a field of light. I'd add fresh wood and get things ready. Bobby, Bobby, where are you? Oh, Jesus, let Bobby come home soon.

I feared seeing Bobby's ghost, or maybe Alvin's, and sometimes would avert my eyes when the shadows danced a certain way. With an expectant heart, I stood, faithfully poised as a night watchman, waiting, peering about for clues of Bobby's return.

Holy nights all. I say this deliberately and carefully after a life of living. Holy nights they were. Now I see my dawn patrols were a crucible of faith, awe, wonder and longing, in which my sense of self, of God, was formed. Our kitchen was the void of pre-creation, my reverent heart the garden ripe into which Adam would appear to walk among us.

And then one night he was home! Just like that, he burst upon my vision. Bare-footing into the kitchen, the first thing I saw was his jacket hanging over a chair, then my eyes spied the gold buttons, solid gold buttons, radiating shafts of fire. My eyes flew to his fancy cap with golden wings... ahhhhh, the sound of my breath falling like an apple from my mouth. This jacket, this cap, was Bobby's and he was home! Another shivery step forward and I grasped the glistening peak of his cap, inspecting it with careful fingers, until it glowed in my hands. Then, ever so gently, as a priest handles the wafer, I lift up and lower Bobby's cap on my head. It covers my eyes, my ears, but I don't care, for I'm three feet taller. I wear my brother's crown, the one that scared the pants off Hitler. I suck in my breath and carve a perfect salute, touching the peak of the cap. Bobby is my brother, and now I'm a comrade to all the hunters who wing across the skies.

Boldly, I slip my arms into his kingly jacket with its buttons of fire, caressing them, feeling the silky fabric that falls right to my feet. To the rhythm of dancing fire light I do my little jig, round and round, forward and back until I'm dizzy. Lost in the rapture of cap and coat I celebrate the sacrament of skies, whispering undying vows to Bobby and my sky comrades, pledging to die for the RCAF if needed. Tut, ho! I snap to and hear the sharp crack of my military boots.

What I knew was this: Bobby and I were RCAF officers and had just returned from dangerous missions overseas. We could share little for our deeds were top secret, others so bloody they'd sicken you, but one thing we could tell you—we'd killed the darn Red Baron.

It had happened in an odd way. We'd gone on a mission seeking a kill, found only empty skies and headed home. As we crossed into home territory my trained eyes saw the smallest glint of sun from something at ten-o-clock high. Friend or foe? Bobby, my navigator, plotted a path that carried us toward the object, and as we barreled closer we were shocked to discover the famous red plane in all its glory. He was lazing along, not a worry in the world. Could he have fallen asleep? Was he taking a smoke? Or was he playing fox, thinking we were French? I was insulted by his red colors knowing he flew them to taunt us.

I flipped off my safety and fired a warning shot under his snout. Indeed Mr. Red Smarty Pants was being cute. He had powered down and sucked us in, and now he went into a full power loop to bring himself in behind us, a trick he used to kill many of our boys. The red fox was smacking his lips, but he'd committed a fatal error in thinking we were French and not prairie dogs. The sun could not have followed him more closely as we arched up and over, tucked behind him in the wake of his prop, as I racked him with terrible bursts from my machine gun. Just as imagined, we saw the whites of his eyes as his plane began its death spiral earthward, smoke pouring from the tail. His arms jerked upward as he tried to escape his burning cockpit, but it was all over. He'd never mess with prairie dogs again.

We could tell you, thank God, right now, that his soul was rotting in hell. I spat hatefully on the kitchen floor. I couldn't say it out loud, but I could think it: that bastard Hitler. That terrible bastard.

Sadly, what we could not know or tell was that in Mommy's womb, the place from which her just returned day-star had sprung, different war clouds were forming. Her grieving for Bobby had taken root in her body. Hitler had bombed a bunch of countries and now his troops had marched into Mommy's tummy. Because I loved her so, I tried every way to save her, with my prayers, with magic, singing my Sunday school songs over and over, launching prayer feathers toward the heavens, doing my little dances. My machine gun was of no use, for Mummy's enemy was faceless, and had no target, and I had nearly lost my voice. With its comrades, my trigger finger made a fist, angry at life and my helplessness. I was not much of a soldier in this war. Nothing worked. She would die from cancer in less than two years.

༈

May 30, 1985. Country roads. Breathless roads that rise and fall, in the now benevolent southern part of Germany, following streams, cradling trees and farms like infants. Soft breasted hills cuddle oak forests, and under it all I can imagine the heartbeat of mother earth. Perfect storybook villages surprise at every turn. Castles atop the hills, glimpsed from afar, are postcard size.

Family McLeod—Ruthie, and our two teenagers, Heather and Todd—spent the night in a private zimmer, breakfast included. I recall it was a two-story home that had flower boxes, and a window through which we could see across a large meadow, clear to a town celebrated by a church steeple looking like hands folded in prayer. My eyes had followed the indicated trajectory up to clouds and sky. I could count only three clouds, the rest were springing sun and delirious blue. A great day for flying.

I have a picture, for the record, of this meadow and church but it doesn't do justice to the sky. Cameras cannot hold the feeling of sky. The picture also shows standard, four-legged, big-headed, two-eared, soft-eyed cattle grazing, and I barely see them, but there they are, still chewing (always chewing), prototypical brown bovines. Don't let them fool you. Milk is milk and cows are cows. They could be rooted in any field, anywhere. Born to chew. Exciting! I grew up with them, learned to hand milk them at age ten and had, well, interesting encounters with them when they refused to go into the barn, or would not let down their milk. Or when they kicked me and put their foot in the milk bucket. They constantly tried, but could never fool me with their great innocent eyes. I knew they were guilty, yet they continued to flash those damn, gentle eyes, charming and distracting me. Frustrating, dumb cows. That's why I forgot them until I looked again at my photo. If I ever found one cow looking properly guilty, I'd hug her and take her home.

I'd like to tell you that we had strong black coffee that stung in our mouths and sent us roaring into the morning, but we didn't. In many stories, dark coffee has an exaggerated role, hanging like a veil between night and day, defining the parameters between one state of consciousness and another. In those stories the cool people drink strong coffee and survive. We had tea, made mild with cream that was, I remember thinking, only pasture yesterday. That thought startled me more than black coffee. Process. Life is process.

And cows. Nothing is static. Our BMW is eager to race, to feel the curving, country roads.

Aboard, we had three frayed maps a-jumble, and were yammering about where to go, what to see, shortcuts vs. the longer scenic routes. We were making quite a racket even without a coffee boost. Todd, 14, wanted to head off to a lake where he could windsurf. The rest of us were pleased to let him know this would desecrate Europe and encouraged him to look for castles, or at least to try and understand the weird road signs. That would be helpful and educational and somehow leave Europe untarnished; as surely as cows were chewing, we were putting the McLeod family stamp on the morning. Absorb it all, value it, process and analyze it from all possible angles, wrest deep meaning from it, tie in a bit of philosophy and maybe write something about it. Even if it is only a road sign that means nothing more than to slow down. Truthfully. Even signs like that, after we were done with them, contained interesting hypotheses about psychology, philosophy and life in general. And of course none of us could read German. There is no need to romanticize coffee in this story for we were jugular enough without it.

To be driven by all these McLeod imperatives and, at the same time to drive the BMW, was a challenge. The jerking car and my eager son both reminded me that I was being cowed by the stick shift. Our inclinations about where to go were as diverse as the roads on our maps. Of course no one even thought about going back the way we came. That would be unthinkable. It's a McLeod law: you never go backwards. I was stressed before we slid into this first curve.

We averaged out all the conflicting ideas and headed in a ten-o-clock direction. We drove for perhaps an hour, weaving intricate theories, before yielding to practical interests, wheeling into an antique shop where, curiously, we almost bought a chair at a bargain price. Our enthusiasm was almost unstoppable, until among our four voices one late and faint logical note was heard, raising a troubling question about how we might get the thing home on the plane. We had no difficulty with the sensible notion of tying it on the car roof. That would be a natural. Drunk on morning air, an image was hatching in my brain: a 747 jumbo jet with a chair strapped to the top! If it were to ever happen our jet would be the first. We abandoned all hope for the chair and were grooving round those corners once again. Sun-spilled mornings, gypsy-loose in Europe. There is nothing like it. Each corner has something new, something old.

More curves and trees, then we flashed by a military cemetery with stone posts. I wanted to stop but was in full flight mode. Ahh: memories of Bobby and the war float to mind, while our hot car eats the road. Then I thought of Alvin and asked my family if I could do a look-see. After getting their permission, I checked my mirror and palmed the Beamer into a crunching one-eighty.

As I drove back I recalled that in 1977, our first time in Europe, we'd found a couple of military cemeteries and had walked into them. I had dutifully checked the log books to see if Alvin was listed and had decided there were likely dozens or hundreds of similar places, and my chance of finding Alvin was a wispy childhood fantasy.

I had never heard where he was buried, nor did I believe that anyone from Norgate really knew. It was even possible that his body had been shipped back to Canada. In one of the cemeteries, while Ruthie and I wept, the children had played hide and seek among the gravestones, yelling and rolling around. I was offended by their exuberance, which seemed disrespectful, then had an image of all the fallen come to life, almost children themselves; saw them laugh and join the dance beneath the larks that bravely singing flew. My Nikkormat recorded the moment: the children dressed strangely in red, a blur against rows of dark stones.

My urge to wheel around was not strong or compelling. I just wanted to take a look, on the chance, on the chance. We all know such moments and there is usually nothing portentous about them. The exception is the rare time when we touch our child's hunger, stepping through the door like Alice, we start down a path and the moment draws us into itself.

All was innocent and then the moment ripened: I park the car at the gate and step out. The silence is softer than usual, descending like a parachute around us. Now the morning has an edge, an untouchable sense of something, something. Our family banter has softened, slowed. I'm scared and shy to mention that I want to check for Alvin, for my quest feels so improbable, so ancient, personal and silly.

As we pass through the gate, I read the inscription on one post: Durnbach War Cemetery 1939–1945. We've passed the point of no return, through the gate, moving trancelike toward the shelter that houses the logbook.

My hands, now on automatic, find the formal, navy blue book and open the cover. I am holding back, wanting to resist the cascade of history. I stutter past the anonymous first names, eventually finding the *J's* while bracing against the coming rapture. My postcard finger slides down, slides down to the first Jackson name. Sadly, lots of Jackson's are buried here, but surely not our Alvin. My eyes surrender to the page, and dreamily I scan up and down, the names of hometowns and countries flashing chaotically by: England, Somerset, Australia, Sydney, Canada, Montreal, Manchester. Major cities and little towns from around the world thrown together. Then the words that seize my soul: Norgate, Manitoba, Canada. And in reverie, who else could know this place, and how and why is it printed here? I brace against the grave weight of forty years of memories, scarcely able to look for the first name, yet my eyes insist. There, there, there it is: *Alvin Jackson,* the words like worn prayer beads spilling through my mind. I need to read it again, to verify against all odds. Then with a creaking voice, I ask Ruthie to read it. Our son Todd, and Heather our daughter, cloister around, peering to see if the name might wink off the page. Again, to measure the truth of it, like a school boy I move my finger under each word, reading aloud:

Jackson, Pilot offr. (Air Aimer) Alvin Roy, J92355, RCAF 419 sqdn.
26th August, 1944. Age 20. Son of Roy A.R. Jackson and Louise V. Jackson of Norgate, Manitoba, Canada.

All my dreams, all these years, wondering, imagining, and now this. My brother flier sleeps here, bowered deep in this foreign land.

I don't have time. Time has me. Nor do I have life, life has me. Pretense and reflection are replaced by quiet knowing and automatic movement. We find the map, record proper row and column, and move dreamily among rows of stone to end our search.

I am walking, walking, a fire growing in my belly as memories warm to life. Now, in front of me is the stone that marks the place, the fracture point of dreams. Alvin, my magical flier is here. I absorb the words:

Pilot Officer, A. R. Jackson,
Air Gunner
Royal Canadian Air Force
26th August, 1944. Age 20

Deep in our hearts a memory is kept
Of one we loved and will never forget.

Deep in our hearts a memory is kept. I feel pain in my chest as I feel the memories, and my lungs feel strangely small as I squeeze the words. My heart is breaking. I loved him, I love him, I love Alvin, I love you Alvin. I am only five, I am Bobby McLeod's brother, wee Albert, come from Norgate all the way here. Do you remember me? And then time sweeps me up and back.

Unexpectedly it is nighttime, clear and dead calm: silent night, holy night. From this place I can see and hear forever. Above is the dome of stars. Then I hear the rattle, soft at first like distant prairie thunder and my body starts to arch as the sound comes on, comes on. My childhood is calling; it is a sound I cannot forget and in the land and along my back I feel the ancient shiver, see the migration of bombers, hear slamming pistons in the night. Excitedly, I realize what is happening: tonight, the Royal Canadian Air Force is flying! Launched from southern England, the finest fliers in the world swarm now as avenging angels of death, bound for targets in the heartland of Germany. Their shadows fill the sky! Hitler will pay, tonight he'll pay!! In the planes men in flight suits are talking, reading maps and listening to radio crackle. Now I see Alvin sitting in his nest at the rear of one of the bombers, warm hands on cold metal, playing with his machine gun then back to counting stars. I join the apocalyptic steeds on their mad gallop eastward, my small hands on top of Alvin's, forming a team of the meanest tail gunners in the world. He does not know it, but I am there with my keen eyes, my hunting skills, watching, ready to help, alert for danger.

And then: Wait! Wait! I am frightened, something is wrong; our sound has changed. The engines which have been singing of rage and justice sing a new note. The song of the bombers has changed to a song of mourning. I see two bombers bump, hear the banshee cry of propellers biting into metal, see the bombers break, see them break. We are falling. Men yelling. Fire. See the fire! Plane upside down. Plane falling, the sky breaking. Screaming, scream-ing. Oh, no. Alvin is stuck. Alvin does not fly. Alvin falls. Help! Help! Alvin is falling. Alvin is crying, crying, his head bumping metal and glass. Poor Alvin. Mommy! Mommy! Help Alvin, please help Alvin. Alvin is falling, falling. Mommy will save Alvin. Alvin's ball turns and turns. Mommy, help! Alvin stop! Stop! Stop! Stop! Alvin and Albert cry. The ball hits hard and breaks on grass and flowers. Alvin is asleep. Alvin sleeps. It is night and Alvin sleeps.

My throat pains and my lungs hurt as terrible memories race back. I am sobbing. I feel Mommy's hand on my shoulder, then realize it is Ruthie. Then I see Heather and Todd. My eyes are clearing as I come back. Our family sits in a circle on Alvin's grave, each in our own worlds, paying homage. I'm back in my body, happily back to present time. I look around.

The cemetery is beautiful at the end of May with summer coming on. We are surrounded by flowers, shattered dreams and broken promises. Here the good earth lies open to the great sky, the earth that with open arms received Alvin and all the others, secreting in her bosom all their promise against some future day. In the murmur of trees bordering this foreign soil I hear the cries of a generation unborn. Beyond the trees gentle cattle graze. They look like they've been here forever. I wonder if any of them with startled eyes saw our bomber fall. Alvin is surrounded by his crew mates, and I'm thankful he is not alone. Alvin and Albert, plow-boys, penny-lovers, gallant fliers, together as men at last. As painful as it is, I'm thankful, amazed I found this place.

For ourselves and the Jackson family back home we take pictures: from two o'clock, from twelve o'clock, from out of the sun I shoot, click, click, click with my Nikkormat, from north, south, east and west, various poses.

We may not be back. When I shoot from out of the sun I hear Alvin laugh; he is no fool, he is RCAF and knows all the tricks. It was not a Nazi who gunned him down, it was blind fate.

The morning and my family want back on the road. We start to pack out. My soul launches a comforting Psalm from the past: *If I take the wings of the morning and dwell in the uttermost parts of the world, even there Thou are with me...* From prairie snow fields to German greens, with morning wings he came. Once more with reverence I whisper his name. Alvin, we do love you and will not forget. And may you fly forever.

After returning from our trip, I was excited to send photos of Alvin's grave to his family in Canada, thinking they had likely never traveled to Europe. A few weeks later a letter of thanks arrived from the Jacksons thanking me for the photos, along with twenty dollars to cover mailing expenses. I was grateful that we'd found Alvin's grave, and that his family could finally see where he was interred.

Grieving the death of a loved one is an endearing and universal trait among humans and other animals. I'm especially touched when I watch nature films of elephants who return to nuzzle the bones of loved ones. With us, they also want to remember, they need to grieve and say their goodbyes as suits them. When I see photos of people standing on a beach, peering out to sea to where loved ones disappeared after a plane crash, I am sad and uplifted by our profound longings to revere and remember. We leave flowers, light candles and launch our prayers for those now gone, and heal ourselves in the doing. We hope too, that we are remembered, when that day we might think will never come, comes finally for us.

I felt this way about finding the grave of our heroic Alvin. Kneeling, crying at his grave with my family helped me complete my childhood grief and honor him as a soldier and native son.

In the therapeutic trade we encourage open, truthful writing, supporting people in pouring out the depths of their hearts onto paper, as one way of healing scars. Writing my Alvin and Bob story was this kind of writing, and I sobbed several times in the writing. In fact, there are still parts of it that lead me to tears as I read it, and I can't bear to read it out loud to others. The act of voicing deep emotions to others asks of us a courage we may not have. There are rooms in ourselves with sealed doors, behind which lurk profound emotions, and some of these doors refuse to open despite our deepest imprecations. At some point we are wise to kneel before such doors and honor all that lies hidden there.

As I've noted, my Broken Promise story was written in 1992. Now, in the spring of 2014, as I read it again, I'm struck by a couple of things. When I list the logbook *home towns and countries* of those in the cemetery, the first two I list are England and Somerset. As I wrote my story I could not be certain of the actual names and the order they were in, and now believe that indeed I had stepped into a serendipitous moment, a curvature in time, at the Durnbach Cemetery. As I've written, it truly felt that way at the time, though not absolutely so. Here is the forward moment:

In 2001 Heather married a wonderful young man, Elliott, from England, and their daughter was born in October, 2003. They named her Somerset. (I call her Lady Somerset.) The fact I added the name *Somerset* in my inventory seems most surprising to me.

There is now robust scientific evidence that our brains/minds can, and do, go backwards and forwards in time, and I encourage readers to read the research (which I believe is at the cutting edge of a paradigm shift in science). From what I read in physics, there appears to be no reason why time can't run backwards, and in the heart of the atom, time and space break the rules we know in everyday life. Atoms, molecules and cells, including brain neurons, are full of information, much of it past information written into our DNA. As we watch children grow and ourselves age, it's clear the future architecture of our very selves was there all along, triggered constantly by our environment—especially the first few years of life. Our brains have surprising abilities and it is likely that in odd moments touch into the spooky time frame within the atom, decode it, yielding—wanted or not—a transcendent experience.

Synchronicity, as defined by Carl Jung, the Swiss psychiatrist, is the experience of having two odd events fall together in time, impacting us with surprising meaning and curiosity.

I've taken a lively interest in his writings over the past several decades, and his belief in the far reaching scope of our unconscious minds. He thought, as I do, that our conscious awareness, our egos, see only a fraction of all there is. With Jung, I take delight in the mystery of life, and the way nature veils herself—and in odd moments of synchronicity how she unveils herself.

Over the years I've written down my experiences of synchronicity, and have a file an inch or more thick. Finding Alvin's grave, on a *random* morning, on a *random* road in southern Germany is one of my most precious experiences.

I smile as I write this next paragraph: The Red Baron was, of course, a gifted warrior from the First World War, and his airplane underscores this fact. But I was oblivious to this when I wrote my story, for I was so immersed in my inner child, my childhood imagination, I was unconscious of this time juxtaposition, and only many years later was I startled and embarrassed to discover this.

Finally, another note of an awareness emerging years after the fact. In my broken promise story, after I write about Mother's death, I move to describing the countryside of Germany with feminine allusions and metaphors—even with the specific reference to mother earth. I don't recall being conscious of this when I wrote my story twenty-two years ago. Now I believe I had entered my childhood world to an extent I could not consciously know. I see bits and pieces of this in other things I write. Again, this seems to me to be evidence of the vital undercurrent of our unconscious minds, including childhood memories, and how they impact us.

CHAPTER 10

∞

Airborn: Our Magnificent Harvard Plane

∞

BOB, *BOBBY* ARRIVED home in 1945 from across the sea following his time as a navigator in the Royal Canadian Air Force. He was thankful and happy to have both feet back on our farm and to breathe again the sweet prairie air. Many from our area had perished in the war, and he celebrated his rebirth, his new freedom, with a flurry of creative activity.

From his letters and his conversations after he returned, we knew that he was a fearful flier, obsessed with making sure he plotted the right course for his crew and devoted to getting them home safely. On the one night he did not fly with them, his crew, along with their new bomber, were lost in the North Sea. He was devastated and could no longer fly, so he received an early honorable discharge.

Back home on the prairie, his world, his dreams were no longer fenced-in by our little acreage, for his soul had taken flight across the sea into the uncharted blue. He had flown into the starry night and sun-splashed skies, and could never belong to the farm in quite the same way.

One night, when I was six, he walked back into our lives, and I awoke to find his officer's uniform hanging from a chair, brass buttons aglow in the firelight of our kitchen stove. That was a rebirth for me too. Our family and neighbors had launched innumerable prayers for him and others, and now he was home, asleep in his upstairs bedroom.

Bobby kept his faith, never partied, and saved all his money. He bought a new wood cookstove for Mother; it was white with a glistening chrome finish that bounced fire beams on the walls. Next was a new green and yellow John

Deere tractor, with heavy rubber tires and thick cleats. From him, we were learning what it meant to take flight, rising above the primitive dependence on horses. Our hard scrabble life took wings. Finally, we were a family to be reckoned with. He talked about the power of the engines in the bombers he flew, and we were feeling that power; we hitched up our pants a notch, and our prairie horizons were bigger than ever.

Our first ride on the Johnny was pure ecstasy. I climbed aboard with an armful of brothers and sisters, and around the barnyard we went, with Bob as pilot and navigator. Our dear Johnny had a two cylinder engine, and made a pom, pom, pom sound as we chuffed through some weeds and over a few small logs. I knew our green machine could power through snow banks and muddy roads. Our proud workhorses watched with mournful eyes. Finally, we headed across the west field, toward the Glover's farm, ostrich arms aflutter, waving and yelling. *Look at us! Bobby is home and we have a brand new tractor, the best tractor in the world.*

The prairies were palpitating with new energy, and soon Bobby had wired our home for electricity, powered by a wind propeller he installed atop one of our sheds. The wires from the propeller ran across our yard, around the tree that held our swing, then into the basement of our house. He bought a set of large batteries, with clear glass cases, each about a foot tall, placing them on wooden shelves in our basement where they wouldn't freeze.

Because Mr. North wind occasionally took a day of rest, he devised a backup system to charge the batteries. This consisted of a gas engine with an exhaust pipe running through the basement wall, and up through the sod to vent outside our house. In a few months, we had leaped from the dark ages into the modern world.

Bill, Helen, Phil and I were fascinated as we stood in the basement watching the batteries bubble away as they charged. Busy, big bubbles that I feared might explode, but Bobby assured us it was all safe. When the motor was running, we could barely hear each other talk in the house, and the roar in the basement rattled dishes. All our animals were nervous at the strange goings-on, but finally grew accustomed to our whirring propeller, our fancy Johnny, and the noisy, smelly engine.

Bobby had an ever bigger dream. He'd flown into the big blue, over Canada, Scotland and England, and wanted to take wing again. He'd ridden behind enough pilots, charting courses, staring at the back of their heads. He talked feverishly about the various planes in which he had flown, describing the features of each one. He not only wanted to fly a plane on his own, he wanted to own one, and as a man of the world, he knew how to harness his dreams.

The war to end all wars was over, and the RCAF was selling bombers and fighters for a small roll of bills. One early morn, he left home with our four-wheeled trailer and a couple of friends. Phil and I could sense more electricity in the air, unsure what it meant, doubting that anything could surpass the magic we'd already witnessed from Bobby's hands. Late that afternoon he rolled into our yard with a bright yellow airplane on the trailer. We screamed and danced about as we circled our new yellow bird. This was more exciting than a circus, and made us as dizzy as a merry-go-round.

As he patted the craft, he made various loud-voiced pronouncements about his latest magical feat. *Gather round, children! This is a Harvard airplane. It flies at 200 miles per hour! It can climb above the clouds and do rolls and dive. Its engine is a hundred times stronger than our new tractor! I'm going to fly it! And you can fly with me!*

These were the high, wild days. We had our feet on the ground, but nothing more, for our heads were in the sky. Over and over we'd heard about the second coming of the Lord in clouds of glory, and now could see that we would fly up to meet Him, up beyond the sound of meadowlarks, winging into the heavenly northern lights to greet our Savior.

How we loved Bobby, our brother, our navigator, world traveler, inventor, magician, and soon to be pilot. A new stove, electric lights, a new tractor, and now we were free to fly away, to escape the cold gravity of prairie, to peer down from dizzy heights. These were days of delirium and runaway, flyaway dreams.

Our friends came to visit more frequently in order to fly with us. The hours we spent in the plane were surpassed only by the hours of imaginary flights. I'd think of our yellow bird when milking, as I sat in school and awoke in the morning. As I rode my bike, I'd put my arms out and pretend I was over

London. I forgot about Jesus—until bedtime prayers, when I'd ask forgiveness for putting him in second place.

Deeply indexed, filed imperviously in the library of memories, is this number: 3378. That was the number of our Harvard, in large black letters against the sunflower yellow. 3378. I called out that number on our radio, as I talked to traffic control towers around the world. *London! Can you hear me? This is Albert, in 3378. I'm coming in for a landing! Yes, I'm landing in the fog! I'm Bobby McLeod's brother, coming in. I'm 3378, over and out. 3378, Roger, over and out.*

After refueling in London, I took off for Germany, wanting to drop a bomb on the evil Hitler. I knew he'd started the war, knew he had killed our neighbor, Alvin Jackson. I'd darn well kill him. *Darn him. I'd drop a bomb right on his head!*

Phil and I flew day and night missions over Germany, with many kills, all of them fiery and bloody. For night flights we mounted a flashlight on the wing, taking turns as pilot and navigator, one in front, the other behind. We donned the leather flying helmet that Bobby wore, along with his wool-lined mitts for higher altitudes. We also took turns wearing his demonic black gas mask, with the hose running to a canister belted to our waist. With our monstrous glass eyes we knew we could make the Nazi's run. *Hold steady, hold steady. Okay, we're over Hitler! Bombs away, bombs away! We nailed him good. We nailed him!* We made a sharp turn and headed for home, yelling victory cries.

I've said too much already. Like other veterans, I don't talk about the terrible things that happen in wartime. *Gotta spare the women and children from the bloody stories.*

During our dog fights behind German lines we made loud engine sounds, enhanced with the louder, rat-a-tat-tat fire of machine guns. No one, not even the pesky Red Baron, could survive the way we dove and climbed and the accuracy of our guns. Rope-swinging in the barn and playing hockey were risky enough, and now we had risen to the level of true killers. The coming of our Harvard plane made us into real men and eager pilots.

We didn't have to make engine sounds the first few minutes of flight, for Bobby showed us how to use the large crank to make the engine rumble.

The engine would turn over easily, for it had no spark plugs, and all we had to do was leap to the wing, put the crank in the hole and grind away for a minute or two. After we removed the crank and dove into our seats, the engine would continue roaring and rotating, and we were free to fire our guns ever more wildly. Our parachutes were jackets and pillows, properly folded under us. Just in case. With our skills and courage it was unlikely we'd ever be shot down, but Hitler and his soldiers had killed Alvin, so we were careful.

And of course we had to pee. The RCAF had thought of this too. Under each seat was a cone shaped rubber pee cup, with a hose which ran out the bottom of our plane. Perfect. On long dangerous missions we used the cups. Over and over, we used the cups. It was so much fun we peed into them even on short flights, thinking the pee would vaporize into the air. In a short while our Harvard smelled as bad as our outhouse, but we were familiar with animal smells and this could not distract us from our missions. We had taken our vows as killer pilots and nothing could stop us.

Thankfully Bobby's dream of flying never got off the ground, try as he might.

He was desperate to fly our Harvard, and his dream led him to order a parachute, His dream, like all dreams, had some reality stirred in, and in other ways was full of air, as wispy as clouds.

After weeks of impatience, the parachute finally arrived by train, at the Norgate station. We carefully unpacked the layers of white nylon with its dozens of cords. Our first thoughts were to test it by jumping from the barn. We'd engaged in the common farmyard project of lobbing various items from the loft, and had a feel for how gravity worked. Some neighbor kids had tossed cats from various heights, and reported they always landed on their feet. We were nimble enough, but not sure if we were quick as cats. Even after much goading, no one wanted to do a barn leap with our new parachute. We knew we'd find another way to have fun with it.

The parachute was not the only thing Bobby needed to ride the skies. The government figured there would be men with crazy dreams of flying, so our Harvard was sold without a propeller. Once the parachute arrived, Bobby felt safe enough to order a prop. It came in a long box, and was so heavy it took several men to offload it from the rail car.

We hauled the prop home with our trailer and tractor, using hammers to open the box. Then the revelation: a massive, curved, perfectly formed prop, with yellow insignias on both sides, and a large gearbox in the center. We ran our hands over the beautiful, sculpted steel, feeling excitement in our fingers and fire in our imaginations. I could see it tearing into the air at blur speed, pulling the Harvard up, then leading it down into a spiral dive. *Hitler, now for sure you better take cover!*

Many dreams have a fracture point, a death spiral, where they shatter on the earth. The prop may have marked the end of Bobby's dream of flight. The weight of the propeller alone told us something of the power the engine must have to rotate it, leading us to appreciate the dangers involved. We calculated how many men and ladders it would take to lift it up to the nose of the plane. Making sure it was properly bolted on was another challenge. We had no manuals, except for the dream images burning in our brains. Bobby wanted to fly, and we caught his vision. Then, over the weeks, as we went about our chores, this dream, like others, died before harvest time.

Happily, the Air Force and big city guys who owned planes were able to mount the blue, and we quickly realized that even a grounded plane had plenty of magic. Flying machines of various size and hue began circling around, dropping down for a look. Our Harvard Hawk, all nestled down, was ruffling her yellow feathers, sending mating calls on high. The other planes heard her cries, and as they circled about, we'd run out flapping our arms, pointing to a field where they could land.

The P-51 mustangs, with their speed, noise and power, were the most amazing of all.

They only came round a few times a year, but when they did, the ground and my soul would shiver. In winter months their sound was deafening, and the pilot might do a few rolls as he climbed aloft with sun glinting from his wings.

Our magnificent, mythic Harvard was blessed to miss the war and to host us as little fliers, yet was doomed to the capricious nature of farm life.

We started feasting on our yellow bird, using parts of the plane to fix broken farm equipment, improvising as farmers do. A leg here, a leg there, but spare the neck. When my hockey stick broke I used a Harvard bone for the upper half of the handle, and when I fell on the ice it would peal like a church bell across the land.

We used the cup shaped engine cowlings to make a fort, impregnable to bad cowboys and Indians. One day I sat alone in our fort with the rain pounding down, and an emerging wondrous sense of my separate life, a life I could steer through uncharted skies.

The wings, with their colorful Air Force markings, were removed and used as a roof for the dining room at our children's summer camp, next to our log church. Prior to mealtimes, as part of our blessing, we'd sing the old hymn, *Under His wings, Under His wings; we'll safely abide forever...* With bowed head I'd sit there, thankful to Jesus, and imagine myself flying our yellow plane.

Bobby used one of the gas tanks from the plane to make a small boat. This required a few hours of serious deconstruction, for the tanks were in the wings. The tanks were made of steel and aluminum, about four feet square, not as large as the Titanic, but more durable.

He cannibalized another piece of metal, forming a dangerous-looking propeller, using yet another part for a driveline which he attached to a small engine. For a week or more the boat project created another ripple of barnyard excitement. We had wild images of Bob and the rest of us in his boat, zooming about the lake in the same way I'd seen other families do in magazine pictures. Early one morning after milking and slopping the pigs, we loaded the speed boat onto the wagon, chained it to the bumper of our Chevy, then headed east on the dusty road to Lake Manitoba.

Once at the lake we eagerly carried our boat to the water, and the engine roared to life the first time Bobby jerked the cord. This trial was solo, for we younger ones were afraid of the wicked speeds he'd surely reach. We stood back a safe distance from the shore as he lowered his mighty propeller into the water. The propeller spun furiously in the lake, throwing water cloud-high, and creating an impressive amount of foam, while we yelled encouragement.

Neither the roaring engine, nor our yells could get that boat going, and another frothy project drowned there in the cold waters of Lake Manitoba.

We spent the rest of the morning swimming in the choppy lake, ate our lunch and headed home to milk the cows.

ℱ

What happened to the resolute bones of our Harvard? I left the farm in 1956, and by that time not much was left of the plane. When I returned for our father's funeral in May, 1969, I recall seeing a few yellow parts of the plane by the barn, but the engine and skeleton had disappeared. The north wind that howls across the prairies is strong, yes, but not potent enough to carry away the heavy Harvard engine, or the propeller abandoned in our barn. Family members and neighbors have surely picked some bones. Where the carcass went remains a mystery. I like to think that someone grafted parts of our craft to another plane, and that she flies again.

Because of Bobby's flying experience and the stories he shared, many Clan McLeod family members fell in long-lasting love with planes. My interest can be seen when at age twelve, I wrote a letter to my sister Helen, and I was already making estimates about speed: *there have been four planes flying around here today. One was a big twin-engine seaplane and was it ever low. The other two were fighter planes and they were traveling about 350 miles an hour. They saw us school children out playing, I guess, so they did a lot of stunts. They turned halfway around in midair.*

As prairie dwellers, we were always aware of the great dome of sky around us and entranced by the cloud formations, northern lights and dazzling weather. Now we had another reason to look upward, as more and more planes shattered the silence of our skies. During school hours, while our teacher worked with the kids in the higher grades, I'd soar away in my imagination, sketching airplanes, most of them bearing the Harvard number 3378, and most of them with guns a-blazing. I have a couple of old school notebooks in which my crude planes still engage in ferocious dogfights with Hitler and his evil pilots.

Of much local interest was the bomber that crashed in the Riding Mountains near the end of the war. Some of the crew were killed, but a few were able to walk out and get help. In the late 1940's, Bobby launched an expedition to find this plane, spending many days with a few friends hiking into the area without success. About this time, a local man earned his pilot's license and after a few hours of circling, they found the crash site, lobbing long red ribbons from the plane to mark the spot. When they hiked into the thick bush the next day, they could not find the ribbons or the plane.

Then came one of the most exciting airplane days on the farm—the day of the streaming B-36 bombers.

It was a May morning, not long after the arrival of our first crows, when one of us heard the low rumbling sounds of a plane. We raced to the field west of our house, to see a giant bomber slowly approaching from the south. This was bigger than any bomber we'd ever seen, so big it scared us. We jumped up and down, crazed with excitement, as we pointed skyward. Then, from pictures we'd seen, we recognized the giant. *It's a B-36! A B-36! Look, it has six engines.*

We were hypnotized, as we watched the huge craft surge through the cloudless sky toward us, the engines pounding louder and louder, until finally it was overhead as we danced in the field. Like a great thunderhead, its powerful engines filled the sky with noise.

Sadly, slowly its vast shadow passed over us as it winged away, heading for some secret base in the north country. My heart strings were stretching upward following the shrinking bomber, and then more magic: from behind us came a new sound. As I turned to see where it was coming from, I spotted another B-36, roaring, churning its way toward us as it followed its brother northward. Our excitement again rose upward in greeting, and as we watched this second bomber, far behind it was a speck in the sky that we knew was yet another. To see one such plane was more than enough, and then we realized we could see three.

We were having our own private air show of this new and rare bomber that I'd read about in some magazine. As the second B-36 cast its shadow over the prairie, we watched as the third followed the hole in the sky made by the ones ahead, and then, unbelievably, we saw a fourth speck further south. For the next couple of hours we witnessed the greatest air show on earth, as twenty or more of these great birds migrated north. Where had they come from? Where were they going? They were part of the mystery of childhood, of life itself, for which there were no answers. I loved it all.

Our parachute sat neglected for many months, then an idea blew in one day when the north wind was singing his song: we could fly it like a kite. We wanted an audience, and we packed our chute over to Bob's farm, hoping to attract drivers from the highway. We contrived a long rope with strands of binder twine, anchoring one end around our tractor, with the other end attached to the cords of the chute. We held the parachute open to the wind, and it flew upward, blossoming like a large flower over the prairie.

Soon curious visitors from the highway drove in to see what was happening. We were happy to let them know that there had been no plane crash, that all our boys were safe.

In the next year the parachute was cut into pieces, and our sister Helen and others made some nifty white silk dress shirts. These were the only silk shirts we'd ever seen. They too, fell short of perfection, and fell apart because the silk could not hold the thread. Our parachute died like our Harvard, whimsically dismantled in our bubble of time. We were left with piles of parachute arteries and veins, used as ropes for everyday purposes.

The best use for the strong nylon cords was the high trapeze Phil and I made in the loft of our barn. This was a two-day project, requiring several ladders upon which we struggled to the pinnacle of our loft, the home of our pigeons. We laced the cords, round and round, to the large beam at the top.

We dreamt of being high wire performers in a traveling circus and spent hundreds of hours during our adolescent years swinging to touch our feet to the slope of the east roof, then pushing off and twisting in midair, touching the west slope. Over and over we'd swing, sometimes with the rain drumming on the roof.

In our early teens we tried to use Bobby's bug-eyed gas mask for diving underwater. Our friends, Nels and Bill Arvidson, had a dugout full of water and a small boat. We made the mask hose longer by adding an old bicycle tube. Three of us would get in the boat, then push the fool with the mask overboard, so he could explore the deep for sea monsters. Our first attempts were filled with spluttering and gasping, as the bike tube collapsed with the water pressure, and our gallant diver could not get air. We tried various fixes, with repeated dives, but nothing worked, and after a few days we moved on to other projects. The many sea critters in that dugout wait to be discovered.

In the background to all our fun and love of our Harvard, there has been a question about her breeding line and pedigree, and a couple of times it has been suggested she was not really a Harvard but a Yale. Wanting to be as exact as possible I've done some web research, learning that many models of both the Harvard and Yale were built. The picture I came away with is that the two planes were quite similar. One bit of information was especially exciting: one of the former airplanes bore the serial number of 3383, a truly close brother to number 3378. I imagine the same workers who built 3378 also built 3383, perhaps the same day or week.

Our Harvard created lasting, emotionally charged imprints in my heart, and these can spring alive again in odd moments of conversations, or when I read a poem or see a movie. One of the most dramatic movie scenes I've witnessed comes near the end of the movie, *Empire of the Sun*. Jim, the young boy who has survived imprisonment in an enemy POW camp, sees the first P-51 mustang fighters fly over as the prison camp is being liberated, with bombs falling all about. He runs up a guard tower, screaming and waving to the pilots: *P-51's!! The Cadillac of the skies!* repeating the phrase several times, as he flings his arms and jumps about. He is delirious with excitement, so wildly animated it seems he will explode like the bombs falling around him. One of his prison mates, a grown man, is worried about Jim's chaotic emotions and runs up and embraces him. Jim's soul cracks open and repressed memories and words gush out, as he cries about how he can't remember what his parents look like, and then, like a ripe apple, a memory falls into place: he remembers being with his mother in her bedroom.

So much of my life is captured in the few moments of that scene: the separation due to Mother's death when I was eight, my longing for the tenderness and touch of an adult, and my love of planes, especially the P-51 mustang, the Cadillac of the skies.

As I'm writing this, I decide to view the movie clip one more time, thinking I've matured beyond the tears I've had watching it in the past. Once again, watching Jim, my soul splits open, and I weep as I watch his mournful confessions, and surrender to the embrace of love.

I've read that Spielberg, the director of the movie, saw this film as one of his most profound works, for it captured the feelings he had as he separated from his parents in his middle teens.

When I left the farm, I took all of me along, and this included my love of skies and planes. Memories of the vast and vibrant prairie skies haunt me still, along with long, long thoughts of Bobby, our hero of the skies, and his desire to be a pilot.

In retrospect, it seems to me I had to learn to fly, so in 1976 I decided to take flying lessons. Even though I was terrified of heights, I thought if I learned to fly I might overcome my terror.

Again, a door opened in my life: this one was actually two doors down the hall from my office at the university. Paul Logsdon, the head of our ROTC program, offered to give me free ground and theory lessons if I wanted to sit in his class with other students. By this time we were friends, and he decided to also give me flying lessons in a Cessna 150.

My first lessons were white knuckle affairs, with high anxiety and a few full panic attacks. It took me longer than most students, but I eventually earned my license. I only flew for a few years due to my nervousness and the cost of flying. My favorite experiences were the solo flights over the Sierra foothills just east of us, when I'd sail up to a mile or more, then pull the power off and glide back to earth. With the motor on idle, I enjoyed the silence, the sound of the wind and the beauty of our mountains.

Like all pilots I have stories to tell, some better than others, some best never told. My favorite escapade was the landing I made on an isolated country street, fittingly named Kittyhawk. Our friends, Pete and Laura Herzog, lived at the end of the street, with only a few other homes around, and a few safely spaced power poles. At that stage of our lives Pete and I were merry pranksters, so it was natural we'd think of this. I picked the anniversary date of the Wright Brother's first flight at Kittyhawk, and decided that was the day for our adventure.

As I write, I imagine I'm back in my pilot's seat. We drive to the country airport, jump in our Cessna and fly south to his home, taking some pictures at low altitude. I work up my courage to do our street landing. On my first approach, as I near the ground, a truck appears at the end of the street. Wanting to avoid a messy collision, I put on full power, and we wave to the trucker as we spiral aloft.

I do a go-around, then shoot what I thought was a perfect landing, especially since I'd never landed on a narrow street before. On the ground we take a couple of quick pictures, I spin the Cessna around, and we fly out of there.

The sheriff is waiting for us at the airport. Four people, with average vision and paranoid tendencies, have noted the letters on our plane, and phoned in alarms. The airport authorities put me on alert for possible suspension of my license, and demand a report from me. I write that as a nervous, beginning pilot I noticed oil pouring from my engine, and needed to do an emergency landing. What I did not say was that this plane often had a drizzle of oil running over the front cowling. Once again, I was touched by grace, and my reckless impulse was forgiven.

As a memory of those impulsive days, I have a photo in my office, of me standing by the Cessna, with a street sign behind the wing. The sign shows the intersection of Kittyhawk and Rialto.

Family loves, stories, and traditions are passed down through the generations, and my son and various nephews carry the love of planes and flying. My nephew, Paul, and a pilot friend, liked to swoop down to crop duster levels and buzz hapless farmers at work in their fields.

In 2008 our son, Todd, an avid writer, published a wonderful story, where the main character returns to our farm and restores the Harvard to flight condition. (Todd has written more than forty novels, and my favorite is his story about the Harvard.) As part of his research in writing the book, he contacted a group of dedicated pilots and Harvard lovers in Ontario, and made arrangements to go there and take a flight. I've watched his YouTube video of that flight several times with envy and excitement.

Finally, a couple of observations, that reflect the odd turns in life. The Harvard connections: Our daughter graduated from Harvard University, and our son lived on Harvard Street for several years.

And a laudatory note of gratitude to the late Paul Logsdon, my flight instructor. He spent hundreds of hours flying over and photographing the ancient Native American cultural sites in the southwestern U.S.A. In addition to the photographs, from his lofty Cessna perch, he discovered some new sites. His photos and research are published in a lovely book entitled: *Ancient Land, Ancestral Places*. Thank you Paul and family, for your important legacy.

Me Starting Out

Me, headed to California

Bill, Me, Helen

Helen, Phil, Me

Bill, Helen, Dad

Phil, Helen, Me, Bill

Bill, Helen, Me, Phil

Helen, Me

Helen, Me and sheep wool on front of car.

Bill, Helen, Keith Jackson

Me, Helen, Bill

Phil, Helen, Me (on tricycle), Grandpa Todd (on bike), Dad (far left)

Our farm.

Front Left: Helen, Me, Phil (far right).

Helen, Cousin Bruce, Phil, Me, Bill, Uncle Bob (in uniform).

Phil, Me, Mother, Dad

Mother, Me

Front Row: Helen, Phil,
Me, Bob (in uniform).

Me, Helen, Phil

Bill, Helen, Me

Cousin Jimmy, Helen, Me, Phil,
Dad, Aunt Margaret, Mother

Phil, Me, Helen, Jean

Back Row: Mr. Shyiak, Me (back row, second from right), Phil (seated on my left).

Dad

Dad and Bees

Me Holding Baby Duck

Me, Helen, Phil

Me, Phil

Norgate School

Our Beloved Harvard Trainer

Moving Day

In the town of McCreary, we held street meetings by the tree on the right.

Bringing Firewood Home

Me, Mr. Moreau, Phil

Phil and I hunting.

Snowplow

Ruthie at Alvin's Grave (Durnbach Cemetery)

CHAPTER 11

—— ૐ ——

Cherished Objects I've Carried

We have not even to risk the adventure alone
for the heroes of all time have gone before us.
The labyrinth is thoroughly known....
We have only to follow the thread of the hero path.
And where we had thought to find an abomination
We shall find a God....we shall come to the center
of our own existence.
And where we had thought to be alone
We shall be with all the world.

JOSEPH CAMPBELL

ૐ

BRAIN SCIENTISTS BELIEVE we form memories based on the chemical-hormonal-electrical properties of our brain. Based on what I've read it seems likely that the electromagnetic (EM) pulses in our brain are most directly involved in recording memories, and to the degree this is true, the memory part of our brain resembles our computers.

The brain — whether that of the butterfly or bumblebee — is more complex than any computer, and unlike computers, its chemical-hormonal factors also play a role simultaneously with the EM that permeates all cells. Again, the core word here is complexity: we can choose to record memories, as when preparing for a test; however, most memories happen to us and are not consciously chosen for storage. We are sometimes surprised at what we remember and why we recall one thing and not another.

We've all had the experience of memories fading or being completely lost, and that is reason enough to keep journals and various records, and why some of us pack around cherished objects from childhood, as I do.

As I've written about my childhood, I've surprised myself with the number of cherished objects we have in our present home, most in my office. Just as memories can slumber on the edge of consciousness, so can the objects that surround us. I've spent many hundreds of hours in my home office over twenty years, and while I'm sometimes aware of the objects described below, mainly they are invisible and taken for granted, like my days of childhood. I like to think they have comforted me nonetheless, just as a favorite blanket comforts a sleeping child.

Each of us invests objects with meaning, with symbolic power, and this is especially true for family heirlooms and other precious items. As Joseph Campbell says: *Life is without meaning. You bring meaning to it. The meaning of life is whatever you ascribe it to be.*

With others, I believe objects, like people, can carry an energy that impacts us. This is has been my experience as I've run my intimacy-seeking fingers over childhood talismans, staring at them and sometimes closing my eyes, hoping to better sense the energy they carry. Like our bodies and brains, every object is composed of atoms, and thus is a field of pulsating electromagnetic energy.

As I've renewed my friendship with each object, I've made new discoveries, stimulated old memories, and come to appreciate how each of these objects has symbolic value and meaning. Each item is a thread to my past, connecting me to my early family; each expands and enlivens my heart, mind and soul. For these reasons I experience them as sacred, and a few arouse a sense of the holy, of something larger than self, stirring the universal emotions of gratitude, reverence, awe and mystery. From what I know, when we slow down and drop into ourselves, our feelings of the sacred easily arise, and can surprise us with their intensity.

The past few years, as I began cherishing these objects more, I've placed them on a small altar in my office. The altar itself is made of old Appalachian oak and is about two feet high and wide, a gift from my wife's parents, and has two matching book cases. The idea of creating a home altar came from my readings in Buddhism and some of the workshops I've taken at Esalen Institute in Big Sur, California.

I begin with examining the loved objects on my altar, and as I do so, I enter into a special relationship with each one, and in moments I wonder, with a smile, if this attitude is more in them than me. Do they want to be touched as much as I want to touch them?

As I explore each item, I don't think of it as *mine*. Rather, I see it as belonging to our family and to those who come after me, and thus I often refer to them as *ours*. In a larger sense, we own objects only in the most fleeting way, for many things we claim as our own were here before we were and will be here after we are gone. I think of the Buddhist story our son, Todd, likes to tell about the man who died and someone asked, what did he leave? And the response was *everything!* As of this writing I plan to leave everything too. Well, almost everything.

The oldest family item on my altar is our Grandpa McLeod's powder horn. My father shared stories about how he earned part of his living hunting and trapping in the hills of our revered Riding Mountains that bare small shoulders west of our farm.

The powder horn is about seven inches long, pear shaped, made of metal and covered with black leather. The small part of the horn, the neck, is metal and has a small lever used to open a pencil size closure from which the powder was poured into the rifle chamber prior to firing.

My Grandpa McLeod died before I was born; however, as I handle the horn I see him amidst the trees on the trail ahead of me, hastily pouring powder as he prepares to shoot an elk. His hands are bigger, stronger and more weathered than my academic hands that leave suggestive trails across my keyboard. I wonder if my hands move around the horn in the same way as his, hoping they do, surrendering my movement to what I imagine was his, in the way a pianist would play a song as it was played hundreds of years earlier.

I seize my magnifying glass, hoping to find his initials or other personal marking, wanting to connect more deeply with him, finding nothing. Nor are there markings on the metal part to indicate when the horn was made. The stitching holding the leather cover around the metal container consists of crude, grey colored string, and I imagine my father or grandfather threading these stitches after the original ones gave out.

Next I open the spout, sniffing it in hopes of smelling gun powder, and the vaguest aroma rises to greet me. Is it my grandpa who whispers the next impulse to my soul? I turn the horn upside down and tap it gently on a piece of paper, and am excited to have a couple of grains of powder fall out. I don't want to tap the horn again, choosing to leave the remaining grains of powder for future generations to discover. Warm images float into awareness and I imagine one of our grandchildren reading this, and picking up the horn to inspect it as I've just done. I pick up the few grains that fell out and drop them into the horn again. This horn was vital to his life, for it helped feed his family. Over and over he filled it; then came the day he could not know, the day he last filled it.

Another object of endearment on my altar is my father's inkwell, which may have been passed down to him. It is slightly more than an inch wide and not quite two inches high, and has a metal lid that opens, revealing a blackened glass container for the ink.

Again I take out my magnifying glass, hoping to pierce the veil of time and space. The only marking I can find is on the lid, and as I turn it round and round it looks either like a little angel, or else three stars in the sky radiating beams into the cosmos. I remove the little glass container, still caked with ink. Seeking more soul connection to our family, I smell my way back through time. As I hold the delicate glass to my nose, I'm excited to detect a whiff of lemon, as imprisoned molecules leap up like freed birds along the trail of memory.

Then, this image: I'm a child again, in our chilly living room, watching my father crouched over his desk, moving his pen back and forth from his inkwell to the page, the scratching sounds reminding me of baby birds. As I write, I imagine him filling his pen for the last time, closing the lid on thousands of unwritten words, each filled with longing, each important to him, each seeking the light and wanting to be remembered.

As I put my grandpa's powder horn and father's inkwell back on my altar, I make sure they are touching, smiling at the intimacy I've created, wondering if they know.

My altar also bears a lone porcelain bookend that sat on the top of our piano, and like our family itself, this sibling piece has traveled cross-country. It is about five inches tall, and shaped like an open book with a small girl in a skirt, sitting in the book. She sits with crossed legs, reading a book, reading, reading all these years. She may have inspired me and my life of reading.

The oddest thing about this statue is that its head is missing, and as far as I remember, it never had a head, and this puzzled me not in the least. It is clear the child is reading and her missing head does not change this one iota. I see her with a cherub face and classic blond hair with a ribbon. Perhaps someday, in a pawn shop, I'll find her sister, and I can record that experience in my thick file on synchronicity.

As I ponder the symbolic meaning of the missing head and my interest in it, I wonder if it reflected back to me the way *I lost my head* and my memories of Mother. I think too, the missing head may reflect my passionate search to find the meanings under our conscious life, to fathom the unconscious workings of our brains.

My quest in life has been more about heart, soul and emotions than thinking, and it may be that I knew this as a little guy, and thus did not mind the missing head of the bookend. The longest journey in the west is from the head to the heart, someone has said, and for our bookend the journey is even shorter, for she has no head to fret or confuse her.

Part of my altar collection is a round crest that says: *Murray's Garage, Neepawa.* It is made of pressed metal, is five inches wide and seven inches tall, and was bolted to the top of the license plate of the first new car my father ever bought, our pride, the sparkling blue 1948 Chevy. The center of the metal plate has a cornucopian horn with a grape cluster resting in its mouth. The metal plate once had two legs for mounting it to the license plate, and like the head of the reading child, one of the legs is missing. Farm life! One can easily lose a leg, if not careful, and even a head.

Murray's garage—thirty miles south in the big town of Neepawa—was an impressive place, with a large show room of new cars, along with many stalls for repairs. Tire repairs that took us an hour or more, they could do in a few minutes. More important than the garage itself, the town of Neepawa has a special place in our family history. Back in the day, it had a population that may have been as large as a thousand, all well-chilled, free range souls. I was born in the Neepawa Hospital, and I think most of my sisters and brothers were too. Our mother, father and brother Bill rest in the cemetery on the north side of town.

The '48 Chevy was the only new car we ever owned, and we filled with pride and popped shirt buttons when we drove to town. I've thought over the years that Dad's purchase of our Chevy may have been part of his birthing into his new life after losing his wife the year before.

Our sparkling Chevy: dark blue with silver trim, very modern and streamlined, unlike the older, box style cars. I was so proud that our father could afford such a magnificent machine, and we loved driving around and displaying it to everyone. I felt we'd finally made it big. We were a family to be reckoned with. Because our roads were dirt and gravel, it was often dusty, but every now and then we'd park it by the edge of the creek and renew her luster with soap and water.

Nothing leads me to be more conscious of our farm than the two paintings we have in our home, one in my office and one in our family room. A few times a week, my eyes are claimed by them, and I have a moment of sweet nostalgia. Each is about two by three feet in size and with their vivid colors, hard to miss.

The paintings were done by an artist friend, Lavone Sterling, from photographs, and both are meticulously detailed, even to the rust that runs from one of the drain spouts. My wife, Ruthie, gave me these paintings for my fiftieth birthday, and kept the secret till the last minute. We were celebrating with family and friends at an outdoor picnic area, and she had an easel covered with a sheet. I suspected it was a portrait of the two of us. When the time came and I pulled the sheet away and saw our farm home, I was flooded with memories, and held her and cried at her sweetness and her love for me and my family.

Most every day I look at either the painting in our family room or the one in my office, sometimes letting my eyes linger on them, and a river of reverie flows through me. Both paintings show our farm home from the north side, with summer trees in full leaf on the west and east. I imagine our grandpa and father, constructing our home in 1908 and 1909. The painting in my office shows me in my early thirties standing in the front yard with a thin body and thick black hair. In my jeans and t-shirt I fancy I look like James Dean, who was my hero back then. Where, I wonder, did my black hair go, and why didn't I save at least a few strands of it?

On top of one of the five book cases in my office stands our old kitchen clock. The hands have been stuck for the past several years at ten to nine. It is a clock that survived decades of cold winters and strikes no more, shocked and undone perhaps by the heat of our great San Joaquin valley, (where from May through October temperatures routinely are above ninety degrees, and when we have a *hot* spell in summer the highs can range from 100 to 110 degrees Fahrenheit.) I've nearly thawed out after forty some years here, but it seems the gears of our family clock have wilted quite away.

I can see my father now, standing on his oak chair, reaching up to wind the clock, and after the coiled spring made a proper and painful note, he'd give the brass colored pendulum a nudge with one of his oversized fingers, and once again we'd hear the familiar talking in the background that marked the irrepressible march of time across the prairies.

As I write this, I take the clock down, not to wind it, but to investigate what secrets it might hold. On the faded white face, I read that it was made by the New Haven Clock company, in New Haven, Conn. The clock is nearly two feet tall and about 15 inches wide and is made of wood. I'm guessing it is oak or maple, and it has swirling designs with carved flowers at the top. The glass door that opens for winding is embossed with a gold design that looks like the gate to Buckingham Palace. This is a proud, royal clock, silenced like kings and queens of old, yet in my mind it still strikes the hours, as faithful as Big Ben, pacing our family as we moved from house to field.

Pasted on the back of the clock is a 3-inch by 3-inch paper, with instructions in faded ink. It is not so much paper as congealed time, crisp, cracked and shredded along the edges. I can't read most of it, so I take our magnifying glass and can make out some of the words: *Five day merchant's time. Striking.*

Below that, with some words missing, are instructions about lowering and raising the pendulum to get the thing at the right tempo, and a brief note about moving the hands forward. I scan over the front and back hoping to find a date, and the magnifying glass reveals nothing.

Now more curious, I head downstairs to get a screw driver, to see if the metal gears might share a secret. I feel like I'm tunneling into time as I use the small screw driver to remove the two screws holding the metal face to the wooden frame. Then I encounter a familiar problem: try as I will, the small pin holding the two hands to the face will not budge, and I can't inspect the mechanism. The stubborn pin on our clock has helped me recreate a common farm experience involving the recalcitrance of mechanical objects that would not conform to our desired ends. Routinely we had breakdowns in equipment, and after considerable work removing nuts and bolts to get to the heart of the problem, we'd discover an implacable barrier that laughed at our logic and the power of farm muscle. On such occasions we forgot about the Lord and used cuss words, and might even throw a hammer at the machine.

Also among the small trove of things carried from our farm, is an oval metal access panel, yellow in color, the size of a small dinner plate, and cannibalized from our beloved Harvard airplane. The plane was purchased by our sky-soaring brother, Bob, after he returned from the war to end all wars—*the big one across the pond* as we sometimes called it. Like the other objects I'm describing, as I handle it, thousands of saluting memories take me back to the scary missions we kids flew over Germany, searching for the evil Hitler so we could drop a bomb on his head.

From 1955, and my summer in the Canadian army as a sixteen-year-old, I have a copper colored badge with two crossed rifles, three tiny maple leaves and a crown on top, bearing the inscription *Canadian Infantry Corps*, and below that, *Acer*. Because of our early hunting days, my brothers and most of the kids I knew were excellent shots, and I earned the ranking of *ace* during target shooting with the old Lee Enfield .303 army rifle. My sergeant suggested I think of entering the sniper corps, and over the next few years the thought casually rattled around in my head.

On my altar there is also a yellow curling badge with blue printed letters: *Manitoba School Bonspiel Dec 26-28, 1956.* In the middle of the badge, in hand-written black ink is this: *A. McLeod Miles Mac*, referring to Miles Macdonell High School, where I spent my final year of high school. For those not familiar with curling, this is the funny game you may have seen on T.V. where people are frenetically sweeping brooms in front of a large round rock that slowly winds its way along a lane of ice. A bonspiel is a tournament, a competition between curlers. I was an average curler, but when my brother Phil was in his thirties, he perfected his curling craft and led a couple of teams to national playoffs.

I have three other sacred objects on my altar, made by my son Todd when he was a little guy: one is a Christian cross carved from a bar of white soap, with a hole in the top for a chain. Another is a cross about a foot tall, made by nailing two pieces of thin wood together, which Todd then wrapped with tin foil and embellished with red plastic jewels. On the back Todd put his name, and the writing suggests he was perhaps five or six when he made this. This cross is the first sacred object I took to place on an altar at Esalen.

The third small art piece is made from wood, and bears an image of a Canada goose, drawn in ink. As I handle these I am touched at his early love for me and the intuitive insights he had into two core pieces of my heart: the role of the Christian cross and of Canada, my native land.

My father was a regular reader. When he was finally done with tilling the fields, milking the cows and other chores, after a quick dinner he'd pick up something to read.

His favorite weekly was *The Family Herald* along with *The Reader's Digest*. The local, bi-weekly newspaper that covered news for towns nearby was always of interest, but was quickly read due to the fact it was only 6 or 8 pages.

In addition, we had a few hundred books in our home, most hand-me-downs of obscure origin and in various stages of decay, housed in the bookcase at the top of the stairs. The last time I was at the farm in 2003 with our son Todd and friend Kenny, there were still several dozen books well rested—or frozen—in the bookcase, some covered with mold and spider webs, some with torn binders from partying mice.

In the few visits I've made to the farm since our father died in May of 1969, I usually come away with a few books, and other objects that call to me. On the last visit, one book I carried away was one that caused Todd, Kenny, and I to laugh when we looked at it. It is a small red edition of Shakespeare's *The Tempest*, and I look at it as I write this. On the front in crude handwriting is this: *In case of fire throw this in!* exclamation point and all. I'd guess this bit of humor was put there by my brother Bill, who like many of us, struggled with schoolwork. Because we were a family of hand-me-downs, including shoes, clothes and books, this book has two names on the inside cover: the name of my sister Jean, in her lovely hand writing, the other, Bill's name, written in a way that shouts his protest against formal education.

On the side of the book, where the pages come together, he posted another reader's alert: *POISON do not take eternally*, Of course I suspect he meant *internally* but the shift of words adds delight for me, while also drawing attention to the challenge we faced with words early on. I think even devout Shakespeare lovers might find it boring to read the bard eternally.

At in the back of the book, in Bill's awkward writing, is a list of his grade-nine classmates, fifteen in all, making up the entire 1949 class at Kelwood High. I remember most of his classmates, for they were familiar to me either from meeting them as we shopped in Kelwood or visited the little grocery store or post office at Norgate. The name of George Harrison leaps out at me, and I smile as I think he may have moved to England and learned to play the guitar.

I go through the book looking for underlines, or notes in the margins that might indicate a spark ignited in the mind of the reader, an *aha!* moment. On page 33 one passage is noted, with the word *memorize* next to it, beautiful lines that I may have read.

On page 65 is another passage, marked *memorize*, tied to one of the central themes at hand:

These our actors,
As I foretold you, were all spirits and
Are melted into air, into thin air;
And like the baseless fabric of this vision,

215

The cloud-capp'd towers, the gorgeous palaces,
The solemn Temples, the great globe itself,
Yea, all which it inherit, shall dissolve,
And, like this insubstantial pageant faded
Leave not a rack behind. We are such stuff
As dreams are made of, and our little life
Is rounded with a sleep....

WILLIAM SHAKESPEARE, THE TEMPEST. THOMAS NELSON &
SONS, LONDON AND EDINBURGH. 1941.

Helen, Phil and I were infatuated by a couple of Zane Grey books, entitled, *The Last Trail*, and *The Spirit of the Border*, and talked longingly about various incidents in those books. Twenty years ago I felt an ache in my heart to re-read these books and ordered copies of them. As I read through them memories of several incidents and scenes were re-etched in my mind, and I felt the same emotions I did when I was a kid.

The stories focus on the settlers who lived in the Ohio valley, the western border of the USA in the late 1700's and early 1800's, and their battles with the elements and the native peoples. The Indians, of course, are portrayed as wild savages intent on killing the invading Europeans, while the white folk are decent, moral Christians with only the best intentions. The stark portrayal of good guys and bad guys caught our fancy at that age, and Phil and I spent many exciting hours pretending we were the powerful border scout, Wetzel, the skilled Indian killer and hero who leaped to life from the pages. We'd alternate roles as Wetzel, while the other would play a pesky Indian, and the woods would fill with the whooping of Indians on the war path, then the sounds of Wetzel's long rifle as he shot the Indians. There in the leafy shadows of our woods, we died many deaths as half-crazed Indians, and after we had closed our eyes, Wetzel would stride up with smoking rifle, standing with one boot on the dead Indian.

As Zane Grey described it, Wetzel had a special rifle with a unique sound when fired—a sound that *scared the living dickens out of the Indians,* for they knew Wetzel loved to kill, and never missed a shot even from a great distance. Wetzel could smell and track an Indian for days, even when he tried to hide his trail in stream beds or on long stretches of rock. Wetzel was a hero and played fair; leaping from the woods with raised hatchet, he'd give a mighty yell before his ferocious attack. We loved something else about him too: he was known as the *death wind* by the Indians, for he made a soft ghostly sound that blended with the wind, as a way of spooking them when they camped at night. Phil and I were as decent as Wetzel, and perfected his sound to give fair warning to those about to die. And like many other memories, this one is in me still, for when I walk through the woods I try to see how softly I can tread, how gently I can weave around and under branches, just like Wetzel. I am a ghost in the forest, and if you look my way you'll never see me.

Among my stack of twenty-odd farm books is *The Canadian Speller, Book One, Prairie Provinces* especially torn, stained and aromatic. On the front page is my sister Jean's name, then my name, Albert McLeod, in her handwriting on the next page. (I was called Albert or Ab until around age 17, when I began calling myself *Al*.) The book was for grade two, and has simple words, showing how they are used in sentences, such as *I can tell you a story,* and *I like to go to sleep in the dark,* and chillingly realistic, *the west wind was cold.* The book has handwritten notes on a few pages, and as I leaf through it, I have images of my brothers and sisters touching the pages with their fingers, as they labored with word and spelling tasks. Across the decades, they arise in my memory as we cluster around our wood stove in winter.

There is an enigmatic question, awkwardly written on page 73, and I write this as it appears, *what is the 3 biggest keys you can't feel in your pocket.* I come up empty on solutions for the riddle. On page 88 is a Christmas stamp, dated 1947, with a picture of two oxen pulling a large sled loaded with Christmas trees, and I swear I have a memory of this stamp and of pasting it in the book. As I leaf through the book I discover the same stamp on pages 91 and 95.

The book is 134 pages in length, and by the time we reached the last chapter we were learning words including the following: development, politics, equipment, temperature, genius, undoubtedly and orchestra. The pages at the very end have several drawings that look like my own, done during one of those long, boring hours in the classroom. One of the pencil sketches shows a cowboy boot with a big spur, and a five-pointed star next to it. Also there are crude pencil sketches of rifles and pistols, with smoke and fire coming out the end of the barrels, and all are oddly familiar, drawn by my hand when it was wrinkle free.

In the bookcase next to *the speller,* is a book titled, *The Biography of a Grizzly,* by Ernest Thompson Seton, circa 1900. Inside is the name of the previous owner of the book, Lilian Winthrop, Kelwood, Man, 1927, age 14. I'm guessing this book migrated to our home through the hands of one of my older brothers or sisters. And a curiosity: a few of the pages are missing, and someone has written the words from those pages on a blank sheet and glued them into the book. Again, a tumble of images as I try to fill in the blanks in history, seeing young people talking, working with pen and ink and filling in these pages, perhaps for a sibling or someone else to read.

From a file of memorabilia, I also have a little pamphlet two by three inches in size, with only a few pages, and on the front page *Thoughts from the Writings of M. Louise Haskins.* Inside the front page, this: *To Albert McLeod, from Ed and Jean, Feb 15/49.* I have a clear memory of my older sister Jean and her husband giving me this gift, and I loved the poem and memorized it, then, of course, forgot it over the years. However, the words follow footsteps in my memory as I read them now. As I do so, I am moved by the simple wisdom of the poem, the depth of insights, and the truths it contains for the lives of all of us. The first stanza calls us with these words:

And I said to the man who stood at the gate of the year:
Give me a light that I may tread safely into the unknown.
And he replied: Go out into the darkness and put your hand in the hand of God
That shall be to you better than light, and safer than a known way.

As I go over these words, I see that in my own way my steps seem to have been ordered, graced and guided by a higher wisdom, a loving life force many of us think of when we use the word *God*—or all the other words we've used for the divine across the eons. I've had my share of suffering, my challenges, yet, in retrospect, I now see these as an important part of my journey, as difficult as they were.

There are several other books that I fondly remember from childhood, all of which have hitchhiked away from our farm home. One was the story of Uncle Tom's cabin, another a story of the sinking of the Titanic, written only a few years after it sank, replete with haunting pictures of that great vessel. Another was a black book, a favorite of our father's, about hunting big game in Africa, and this one, too, had pictures of the courageous hunters with their dead trophies.

We also had a book on Revelations, the last book of the Bible, with scary pictures of many-headed dragons and other surreal creatures from St. John's great vision. It may be that my interest in visions, including St. John's, (and the book I'm writing on that), can be traced in part to the deep imprints left by the book.

Among the most sacred items I've carried from the farm is an old stone, probably shaped by the hands of a member of the Cree, Assiniboine or Ojibwa peoples. It can be variously called a stone ax head, or hammer stone. It belongs not to me or my family, but to the ages. The stone itself is millions of years old, and was lovingly, carefully shaped into its oval form, with an indented band around it. (There are many pictures of this type of stone on the internet.)

It is a dark grey color and sleeps comfortably in my hand. A small piece has been shattered off one end, perhaps by our dad's disc or plow, or the cold hand of father time. The stone has a groove around the center where a leather strap could attach it to a handle, thus making a primitive hammer for pounding and hunting, or for a weapon of war. The leather strap would be wet when stretched around the stone, and as the leather dried it would tighten, ensuring a lasting connection between the wooden handle and stone.

As I cradle our stone, I have an image of the person who might have carved it, sometimes seeing a woman, other times a man, sitting in focused meditation chipping and sculpting. This is one reason the stone is sacred to me. I like to call this stone *our* stone, meaning it belongs first to mother earth, thus all of us, and then to the one who sculpted it. Seeing the stone in this way helps me feel connected to the history of our planet, and to all humanity.

Over the years I've developed an appreciation for the people who lived in South, Central and North America before the Europeans arrived and changed the flow of history. My interest has focused primarily around the Oglala Sioux, who were part of a larger group who lived on the Midwestern plains. Because of my reverence for them, I've read about and participated in shamanic groups, including a dozen or so sweat lodge ceremonies at Esalen Institute—a place I call my spiritual home.

Our stone is sacred too, because our father found it as he worked our fields, and carried it back to our house, creating a reverential interest in all of us. Over the years he turned up a few other stones like it, along with arrow heads and small pouches of pemmican.

Like everything, we can invest whatever meanings we want onto objects, weaving images and stories as we will. Beyond what I've shared, our stone has another level of sacred meaning, this more recent and tied to current reality, for it has been handled in a sacred way by a few hundred people I've known and loved during the weekend retreats I led for over twenty-five years.

My weekend retreats provided a chance for my students, family members, friends and others to slow down from everyday life and spend a weekend exploring their lives through the use of special exercises, meditative silence and sharing deep experiences and dreams. Usually ten or twenty of us would gather on Friday evening, in a rustic mountain or ocean place, ending our time at Sunday noon. These were passionately sacred times and left us with sweet memories.

In the early 1980's I adopted the practice used by some indigenous people, using a *talking stick* to pass around the circle in a sacred manner. We followed these simple rules: you can either talk or pass the stick in silence to the person next to you. If you chose to talk while holding the stick, speak as deeply as you can from your heart and the rest of us promise to reverentially listen with our *third ears* without questions or comments. This ritual led to deep sharing and listening, and helped us drop into our hearts and souls.

In spring of 1983 when Ruthie, Heather, Todd and I visited our farm, our sacred stone caught my attention, and I immediately knew I wanted to use it instead of a talking stick in my workshops. Expressed the way some indigenous people might say it, the stone called to me in muted voice that it wanted to be used in a sacred way. Seen this way, it saw me coming; it reached out to me first and cried for my hand to pick it up. I heard its cry and carried it home to California, excited to tap its secret powers in my workshops.

As part of the context here, I note that in the early 1980's a student had given me the book *Black Elk Speaks*, by John Neihardt. Again, even though I had not expressed interest in native people, she somehow knew I needed that book and it needed me.

The story of Black Elk, his life and great vision stunned my soul, and as one of our ending rituals for our workshops, I'd read the first lines of his prayer at the end of the book, then pass the book around the circle inviting others to read additional sentences. The book would find its way around the circle with most of us reading parts of the prayer.

And thus it was, our sacred stone came to be touched by dozens of us gathered in our sacred circle. On Friday night, I'd introduce the stone to everyone, sharing its history. I'd go over the simple rules on how to use it in our group, then pass it to a person next to me. What followed was sacred, magical, tender and heart-rending. In keeping with what many first nation people believe, the stone seemed to bring a special energy to each of us. Over the years I watched in awe as people held it, stroking and cuddling it like a baby, sometimes with tears, at other times laughing or talking from deep soul places. Others would hold the stone in silence for a minute or two, sometimes to their hearts, then perhaps kiss it and pass it on.

This sacred ritual stirred up a range of feelings, and always there was amazement at the magic of what emerged as people fondled the stone. It seemed to me that most of us were so focused on wanting to speak our passionate truths, we were not fully conscious of the wedding dance of stone and hands, the stroking and caressing. I thought of making a video of this process, but decided this would profane our sacred moments. As I write this, I know these memories are recorded in my blood.

For all these reasons *our* stone slumbers under our bed, and when I think of it, I not only see the faces of some who nurtured it, I also imagine, in the shamanic traditions of indigenous cultures, that ancient wisdom and protective love emanates from it.

Finally, I want to mention a book that also colored my life entitled *The Valley of the Silent Men*, by James Oliver Curwood, published in 1920. I remove it from my bookcase as I write this. As I look at it, I can feel a ripple of excitement in my blood as I recall how it stirred up the most romantic feelings, and the urge to launch forth into challenging adventures.

As with our other farm books, this one is musty, has no backbone, and time has browned the pages. With gentle finger tips I tease the pages open.

On the inside cover, scrawled in large, uneven letters, is the name *Keith Jackson*, followed by *Norgate, 1944, Manitoba*. Somehow this book ended up at our house, and I view this as one of those odd things, a kind of synchronicity, that happen with all of us, some of which change the direction of our lives. Keith was the younger brother of Alvin who was killed in the RCAF bomber, covered in my chapter *The Broken Promise*.

As I leaf through it I discover a label from a wine bottle, bearing the name *Sammezzano*, which was the name of an 800-year-old castle where we stayed in 1977 during our first trip to Europe. The fact this label rests between pages 88 and 89, is perhaps testimony to the love of adventure I've had, part of which may trace to the book itself.

The book is set in the far north of Canada, beginning a few hundred miles north of Edmonton in the area of Lake Athabasca; then the story moves further north to the Great Slave Lake, Yellowknife and finally the mighty Mackenzie River that carries her frigid waters north into the Beaufort Sea.

The tale is a clear example of a class of stories with the central theme of a hero's journey; such stories exist in all cultures across the centuries. The tale takes place in the late 1800's, when that country was still unexplored and without roads and railways. The hero of the book, James Kent, is a Mounty, a member of the Royal Canadian Mounted Police. As a young boy, the Mounties were my heroes and the book drew me in for this reason alone. Kent falls in love with a mysterious woman, Marette Radisson, from even farther north, and she alludes to her distant and secretive home in the Valley of the Silent Men.

Kent has been falsely accused of a crime, and manages to escape from the prison where he is being held for trial, fleeing with his love in a small boat. As they float north to her home in the distant wilds, their boat breaks apart in some rapids and they are separated in the water. Kent spends weeks looking for her along the river, concluding finally, she has drowned. He spends the winter grieving and living in the woods near the spot where she disappeared, and finally as the spring thaw comes on, he begins his quest to find her far off home in the mysterious Valley of Silent Men.

Recalling a few clues she shared about her home in the Valley of Silent Men, he treks north, canoeing along the Mackenzie River. After months of struggles, including traveling across a sulfur desert that nearly kills him, a mountain range begins to appear on the horizon. As he gets closer to the mountains, he sees three of them are shaped like human heads, each peering down into a silent valley. I end my summary of the story here to protect the ending from anyone who might read the book.

Years after Ruthie and I were married, I thought of this book, pulled it from the shelf, and was struck by a few parallels to my own life. Like James Kent, my Mounty hero, I too, fell in love immediately, and like him, I journeyed to a far place (Houston, Texas) to find my love. I too, had my struggles, though unlike those of Kent, mine involved the struggles of my inner life, my fears of love and the challenges of most relationships. I had no conscious thoughts of imitating the life and love of James Kent, yet I can see that the seed planted by his story may have been one factor that unconsciously altered my life.

The vitality of the hero's journey was central in the work of the great mythologist, Joseph Campbell. In addition to the example found in *The Valley of the Silent Men,* another clear case shows up in one of my favorite movies, *Close Encounters of the Third Kind.* The hero in that movie is obsessed with sculpting a clay mountain with a unique shape, and he doesn't know why. Others think he is quite crazy, and he doubts his own sanity, until finally a conscious recognition breaks free and he is clear about his mission. He continues his hero's journey, facing obstacles as he travels to his mountain, where he discovers a profound secret, his *Holy Grail.*

Each of us is on a hero's journey, a search for deeper meaning, for the secret of life.

This quest is mainly unconscious, and it leads us into interesting situations with challenges and delights. I now see that my love and pursuit of Ruthie, my wife, has many elements of such a journey.

CHAPTER 12

❦

Our Father's Diary: Everyday Life on the Farm

Let not ambition mock their useful toil,
Their homely joys, and destiny obscure;
Nor Grandeur hear with a disdainful smile,
The short and simple annals of the poor.

The boast of heraldry, the pomp of power,
And all that beauty, all that wealth e'er gave,
Awaits alike the inevitable hour,
The paths of glory lead but to the grave.

THOMAS GRAY, (1716-1771): *ELEGY WRITTEN IN A COUNTRY CHURCHYARD*

❦

OUR DAD VALUED the written word and enjoyed quoting lines of poetry, launching them as we slung hay, cleaned the barns or walked to the post office. Some of his most loved lines, quoted above, came from Gray's Elegy. He had only a grade school education, but this did not blunt his love of reading and of poetry.

He knew his place in the order of things. He was a small dirt farmer and didn't pretend otherwise. His clothes and giant hands announced him for who he was. His was a life of *...homely joys, and destiny obscure...* and he accepted the fact that he lived *...the short and simple annals of the poor.*

225

He was diminutive in size, but his humility made up for it. He was low to the ground and could only look up—to nearly everyone. In the company of others, he'd stand with his hands behind him, or folded over in front with a hint of supplication. He was shy, and when he spoke it was with a thin, Irish tenor voice.

Perhaps because of his lowly viewpoint, he elevated famous people the more, speaking their names with awe. Many were masters of words: Robbie Burns, Churchill, Sir Walter Scott and Thomas Gray were names that flowed from his lips without provocation. On winter nights, as he sat reading, his feet toasting in the oven, he'd read aloud a phrase he liked, inviting us to listen, to catch the beauty of the words.

Beyond his love of language, he enjoyed music. Caruso and Jenny Lind were lauded as the greatest singers of all time. Dad also played the violin at family gatherings. He loved the old hymns, and when he played, tears might baptize his weather worn cheek. Apart from hymns, *Turkey in the Straw* was perhaps his favorite violin piece. An Irish tenor who sang *Danny Boy* at the McCreary musical gatherings brought Dad to tears, and I'd be weepy as he talked about this man with the gifted voice. I have yet to recover.

Other farmers might, like cream, rise to the top of Dad's list of heroes. Charlie Oak was a local hero. Charlie lived east of us and was admired for his ability to memorize long poems. One of Charlie's favorites was the poem by Robert Service, *The Cremation of Sam McGee*, and at community gatherings he'd mesmerize us by quoting the poem with proper cadence, never missing a beat. After he served up the last line we would start to breathe again.

Our father kept a diary for part of his life. While most of his entries note the happenings of everyday farm life, in a few places he also refers to Mother, her illness and then her death on July 9, 1947. Here I select parts of his diary that capture his farming routines, leaving his words about Mother for another chapter. His description of daily life strikes an anvil note to Gray's Elegy, imprinting the mundane reality of his barnyard life that was ....*to fortune and fame unknown....*

My resident academician notes that I don't have permission to quote him. My heart believes he'd be delighted if he knew I was recording his words for posterity with the hope of rescuing his life from complete obscurity. I'm sure he'd want to read all this, and laugh and weep at times, savoring my words, perhaps in the dead of winter, with his feet warming in the oven, to the timpani of burning wood.

His diary has a ragged cover and torn spine. I hold my breath as I open it, hoping it remains intact, fearing his memories might fall out. His diary, like his body at the time he wrote, shows the burden of time. Happily, the seeds of his life sewn into the pages seem as fresh as when he planted them.

The brown-covered book announces itself as *A Five Year Diary*. Inside the cover are these words from the printer: *This is my personal Diary,* followed by three lines for someone to enter a name. My father filled in these lines with blue ink from his fountain pen: *March 10th/47 Irwin McLeod, Norgate, Man.* (*Man* stands for Manitoba.)

The next page contains the name of the publisher, the Bert Manufacturing Company, in Irvington-on-Hudson, New York. The page also contains words of encouragement for those wanting to record their memories:

Memory is elusive—capture it. The mind is a wonderful machine. It needs but be just refreshed and incidents can again be revived in their former clarity. A line each day, whether it be of the weather or of more important substances, will in time to come, bring back those vague memories, worth remembering, to almost actual reality.

From the first pages on, it is clear he took the prompt about weather most faithfully. Farmers and weather are one, and most of his entries begin with weather notations.

I carefully leaf the pages in my hands, opening and touching his life, sensing into secrets he may not have shared at the kitchen table or as we worked the fields.

Despite his large fingers, his hand writing is neater than mine. As with most farmers, his body was overworked. His arms were oversized for his small frame, from years with the axe, fork and shovel, and his hands were oversized for his arms. The daily labors, combined with unremitting winters, spoke to his devotion to the land. He was a man of few words, spending most of his time in the barns and fields. During the evenings, after chores were done, he'd have his head in a newspaper—our weekly Family Herald, perhaps a book, or the Reader's Digest.

I open the pages and peer furtively into the sacred enclave of my father's life—a life that started July 9, 1890, and ended on May 21, 1969. My fingers ply the pages, and the musk of book draws me into the past.

As I've noted elsewhere, we were well practiced in shielding our hearts and souls from ourselves and from each other. Our talk skated on the surface of things. His generation was hardworking and tough-minded, not easily given to sentimental expression of emotions. As I read his words, I long to hear more than the brief descriptions of daily behaviors. Imagined and desired conversations ring in my head:

Dad! You were a shy man, with few words, and now I want to talk with you. Almost aloud, I say, Dad! This is wee Albert! Please talk to me.

I want to know who you were, and the cries and songs of your heart. Yes, you were a farmer, but you had the soul, the heart of humans everywhere. What did you think of when you walked those long furrows? When the cannons of fierce summer storms cornered and quartered us, awake at night, did you think of God, as I did? Did you celebrate and quiver in the heat of battle, scared, but praying for more to see if the hills might wash down? When you watched the hail wipe out your wheat were you, like me, angry at the Lord? I'd like to know, Dad, what did you most love and fear about life, and what most caused your soul to soar? In the thousands of hours we shared, what utterances in you never blossomed, never felt the warmth of spring?

I know that like other farmers, you had little time for inward looking. Your eyes went to the horizons of the fields you worked. You wondered if you could cut one more row before dark, then the horses to water. Your desperate quests were to find lost cows, to get the crop in before winter, and to make sure our animals were fed, the barns cleaned. Busy all day, at sunset, you'd finally pause, lift your left arm to brow, shielding your eyes against the dying sun.

I, your son, who fled the farm at seventeen, turn all eyes inward, taking careful inventory of the layers, the nuanced emotions of my inner fields. The furrows I plow stretch achingly to the unreachable horizons of soul; the wheat and chaff that run through my hands cannot in barns be kept. I'm hoping to make up for all we did not say, back in the day. Words, words and more words run through me. I want to capture all those silence-soaked, unspoken hours.

Yes, from you, from others, I often want to hear more of heart and soul, yet, as a kind of proclamation, I want to also honor you and all you shared. You spoke, you wrote all you could. Your skills were not with pen and ink; your life was written into the sod. Vast prairie skies and shattering Canadian sunsets were your highest revelations, a bushel of wheat your testament. Your voice is gone, and we have only your written words, and I feel gratitude for what you did share.

Because your words are prairie-bare, each invites me to imagine much. I tip-toe along your inky trail, stalking your words, ears wide open to the cry of birds and the enigmatic sounds of forest. My gratitude for your words quiets my cries for more. Your words, like all words, hide and reveal much, and I'm happy to have you here, happy to fill in the spaces between words, the places where I lose your trail.

I'm five, and watching you again as you sit at your desk in the living room. You've returned from the fields, and before milking time, your fountain pen scratches the pages as the late afternoon sun slouches through our living room window. I stand silently, smiling at the baby-bird squeaks of your pen. Your weather-cracked hands move back and forth between inkwell and page. Like a toy soldier I stand guard, hushed by the sun and your hungry pen. I don't understand what you're up to, yet am fascinated. Are you feeding the little birds that clamor on your page?

At your desk, you have stilled: the milking, the barn cleaning, walking the fields come to rest here. This stillness, this silence puzzles me. More than in the busy hours, here I feel my son-ship with you, and the connection we hold during our silent, sun-warmed hours.

Unfettered childhood eyes. I stare at your pen as it greets the page. I imagine the mother bird feeding her babies. Before long you turn the page, and mother flies away, returning with more food. Back and forth, back and forth with little chirpings.

Across the decades since that 1969 May day—May Day! May Day!—when you left your worn out body, I'm eager to tell you I have your magic inkwell in my office. I pick it up, cradling it in my hand, hoping the unfinished words you did not write might come to life, but all the ink is gone. Only the blue stain remains, along with a metallic smell. You fed the birds all you could.

Just as I hope family members will read the words I now write, so you must have hoped that someone would eventually read about and remember your life. As I take in your words, will my hope of knowing more of you, ripen here? Our father who art in heaven: the time has come, and I reverentially open another page. With open heart and soft eyes I follow the furrows of your thoughts and notice I'm barely breathing. Are there secrets here I fear to discover? In these pages will there be some late harvest of surprise?

Dad, I want to continue the conversations we never had: you were a regular reader but very sporadic in recording events in your diary. Most of what you note is about routine events, including the weather—the preoccupation of farmers everywhere. Weather, weather everywhere. More than any person, more than the Lord Himself, the weather is the central character in all you write. The weather is the villain and the saint, both loved and hated. In the end the weather lives on.

I want to know. I wonder, for example why your trail of ink begins in the spring of 1947. Was this because you knew the end was near? Did you guess, did you fear your helpmate, friend, lover and wife, would be off to heaven after her long, silent days of suffering in the south bedroom? Did you record these dark days so we'd remember? So we might know what the unforgiving hours were like for you? Those dark days of frozen darkness as Mother suffered, and just as silently we suffered with her. The words you, we, could not form with lips, bleed out in sparse words in your diary.

In the past, I've read and re-read your stark entries on Mother's death, desperately searching for missing puzzle pieces, wanting to pull back the curtain of secrecy that cloistered her final days.

I'm your curious Albert, still wondering after all these years, hoping to fill the vacuum in my soul. Forgive me, bear with me please.

You relished the big words of famous people, and liked to quote lines from Thomas Gray's poem, *Elegy Written in a Country Church Yard.... Full many a flower is born to blush unseen, to waste its sweetness on the desert air...* That was you. You with your few cows and acres and all that work, pathetic and proud in turn. Like the flower in the poem, you knew you were *unheralded and unseen.* Shorn of pretense, your diary captures the simplicity of the life you were given.

Another of your heroes was *Winnie,* Winston Churchill, the grand and pompous English bulldog. When you mouthed his words, you'd stand more erect, pulling your shoulders up and back. Your Irish tenor was no match for the drum roll of his voice, as you swelled your chest, filling his words as well as you could: *....We shall fight on the seas and oceans.....we shall defend our island....we shall fight on the beaches....we shall fight in the fields and streets....we shall never surrender.* We, your little ones, along with cows and horses, listened reverentially as your House of Lords.

℘

Dad's diary gives us direct, unadorned insights into the daily life of one small farmer, a pinpoint in time and place, and more generally, lends insight to the life of farmers around the world, past and present.

Like most of us who make sincere new-year pledges, forgetting them come February, our father was sporadic with his diary writing. There are places where he writes faithfully for a few weeks, then the prairie wind shifts his mood, and vacant pages look back all empty-eyed.

I begin with his notations for 1948, starting in November when he is struggling with a personal medical issue, which, like much else in our family, remained unnamed and ostracized from conversation.

All temperature notations are in Fahrenheit, so 32 degrees is freezing. A frequent midwinter temperature was 20 F. degrees below zero, which is minus 29 degrees Celsius. Cold.

Nov 24, 1948: Bob took me to the bus at 1P.M. and I went to St Rose. Hospital full up. Came home with Gordon Franke. Weather mild but snowing here. Dr Gendreau's office full up.

Dr. Gendreau was lauded in our area as a miracle worker and Dad had great faith in him. Our family was extremely private about our bodies and emotions, and understandably, Dad does not want to put a name on the symptoms he's having. Shame, silence and secrecy covered us like winter snow.

Nov 25: they phoned from hospital they had bed for me so Bob took me up in evening. Got me ready for operation but was coughing in morning so Dr. would not operate. Slept all day.

Dad's handwriting for this entry is smudgy, and may reflect his struggles with his illness.

Nov 26: Friday. Slept all day and Jean and Ed called also Doris M. but did not hear them. Seemed to be awfully tired and remembered nothing.

As I read his words my childhood terror arises: Mother died and now Dad is sick with a secret illness. Does he have cancer too, and will he also leave us? He was a wiry, working machine, rarely ill, and for him to disappear into the hospital opened another dark pit of fear in me. I don't recall any conversations about what might be going on, or what to expect.

Nov 27: Saturday. Dr Gendreau operated but I knew nothing until afternoon until I heard nurse talking to me, bless her. Asked me if I had my operation. I finally roused up.

Nov 28: Sunday. Feeling very good but weak. Had some soup and light pudding. They moved us from 26 to 23 and took Mr. Clarke up to 31. Mr. Tucker called on Mr Belious.

Nov 29: Monday. Feeling very good and eating more solid food. Nurses very good to us, and Mr. Belious always saying something funny. Mr. and Mrs Beairsto called with ice cream and apple juice.

He must have felt honored to have the Beairsto's visit, for they were among the most prestigious farmers in the Norgate area. They lived in an imposing two story white house, and their yard and land were immaculately groomed. They had smart, clean tractors, parked in order. Fittingly they also lived above us in terms of elevation, for their home was in the hills on the north side of Highway 19 that led to our famous Clear Lake. They drove late model Oldsmobile cars. I wanted to be rich like them so I could buy a green Olds like the one they floated around in. Their car ran as silently as a ghost, quite unlike the noisy cars we forced along the roads on wobbly wheels. Mr. and Mrs. Beairsto were faithful members of the United Church, rarely missing a meeting unless they were traveling—to places I imagined as quite exotic. Mrs. Beairsto played the organ in church, and I held her in high honor for that alone. She was a high fashion dresser and wore dazzling jewelry.

Nov 30: Tuesday. Feeling fine and enjoyed all meals. Also the smile of our dear nurse, Miss C_____. Owen Hanson of McCreary called, also Norman Shineton and Mrs. Hudcliffe.

Because he does not give the full name of the nurse, I suspect he was shy about his fondness for her. Given that his wife had died the previous year, he must have been lonely for feminine warmth and her smiles may have meant all the more.

Dec 1: Wednesday. Weather still mild. Our roommate, Jeremy Comartin operated on for appendicitis and tonsils. Very sick and struggling. His father in to see him. Bob and others up in evening.

I may have been one of the *others* visiting him, for I have a memory of one trip to the hospital.

Dec 3: Friday. All doing well and Mr Comartin up. Jean and Ed came in afternoon, and brought nice grapes and oranges. Nurse D.C. brought chocolate bars.

Revelations! Now the nurse has as a first initial! And she brings chocolates! The relationship is progressing and my heart warms at his words. After Bob, Jean was the second born in our family, and Ed her husband. I'm curious as to where Ed and Jean bought the grapes, for they were rarely available. As I read this now, I'm betting the grapes came from the great central valley of California where my family and I now live.

Dec 4: Sat. Storming and colder. Nice and cosy in hospital. Not many visitors.

Dec 5: Sunday. Still storming and hospital very quiet. Mr. Comartin had stitches taken out.

Dec 6: Monday. Clearing and cold. Feeling fine and had dinner, then stitches taken out. Dr. said I could go home now. Moved around some in afternoon.

Dec 7: Had breakfast as usual 8 A.M. Clear and not so cold. Dressed about ten A.M and shaved. Went upstairs and saw Elmer Glover and H. Cliffe, also Miss C____E, bless her. Said goodbye and came home on bus P.M.

The last letter of the nurse's name is nearly unveiled! As I think of her I feel gratitude that she was so loving with him. A voice in me says, *Thank you, Miss D. C_____E!, whoever you are. I hope you've had a great life.*

His diary falls silent until Dec. 18, with several entries through Dec. 31. In these he notes additional trips to the store and to get mail. On Dec. 20 he mentions our school Christmas concert, which for us younger ones was a highlight of the year. A few days before Christmas, Bob helps kill one of our turkeys for our feast. On the next day Dad goes to the Parsons home to help kill their turkeys, and later that day takes a pig over to the Glover's. In one entry he refers to Ab and Phil walking to Norgate.

Christmas day, 1948. 10 degrees above zero. Merry Xmas. Had worship and singing, then breakfast and gathered to open gifts. All very happy and thankful. Young people went to Sam Glover's in evening.

I recall Dad being thankful for many things, and I imagine at this Christmas his scars from Mother's death (in July, 1947) are healing, and that he feels blessed to be alive after his operation a few weeks earlier. He also notes he gave Bob a copy of the book, *Uncle Tom's Cabin,* ordered from the legendary T. Eaton Company. He reports we had a houseful that day, including our immediate family still at home, along with Sis Rachael, Ed and Jean. Sister Rachael was one of our housekeepers, a sister in the Lord, one of the few in our little clutch of holy rollers. I fancy she'd be glad to hear she was the most God-fearing person on the planet at that time. I know: I came away with wounds, but I survived the fiery vortex, the Golgothic blood of her reign. (Elsewhere in my book, I have an entire chapter on her and that time.)

We kids loved going to the Glover's, and they were kind enough to invite us over several times a year. After Mother's death, neighbors took more time to be sure we were cared for, and the Glover family reached out to us regularly. Doreen, their daughter, and my brother Phil shared January 17 as their birthdays, and often we were at Glover's for dinner that day.

Dec 30, 1948: Mrs Johnson mending clothes for children and also my suit coat. Mr and Mrs S. Glover and children here for supper. Some wind through the night.

Most families, ours included, were hand-me-down families, and routinely mended clothes and inherited shoes from older brothers and sisters. I trace my hammer toes to wearing shoes that were too tight. We darned socks by putting a glass jar inside them to make the stitching easier.

It was rare we had the Glovers over, so this was a special occasion. We went to their home far more than they came to see us, maybe because there were so many of them and Mrs. Glover cooked consistently good meals.

Dad's diary for 1948 closes with this: Dec 31: 12 above in morn, 25 in P.M. Late getting up. Went to S. Glover's with team and pig. Bob cleaned piano A.M.

This was indeed a warm spell. At 25 degrees the icicles that claimed the eaves of house and barn would begin to run. Many of them were three feet or longer, and several inches thick, and could produce a fine stream of water. We'd stand under them, letting the water trickle into our mouths, or catching it in a cup. Icicle water tasted better than creek water. As with many things tied to farming, we had to be mindful, for when giant icicles fell, they turned into spears. For this reason, we gripped them tightly as we stood under them with open mouths, letting their clear water baptize our faces and fill our mouths. Icicle water right from the Arctic. Nothing like it. And of course, a favorite past time was knocking them loose with snowballs.

On a warm day we'd parole the animals from long barn days, and they'd charge into the sunlight, racing across the yard, kicking snow into the air and spinning about. Along with their cavorting, they'd make loud sounds of freedom as they celebrated open space and sunshine. Warm winter days were days of high celebration, and a good time to strap on the skates and fly up the creek or across the pond. The wildest fun was to throw a horse harness on a yearling calf, tethering our sled behind. With one or two of us aboard, when the barn door was open we'd reach speeds of Mach one in a second or two, while the Lord turned His head.

Jan 1, 1949: Mild 20 degrees above. Billy and I took team to Norgate. I got mail and Bill went on to corner and met Aunt Jessie, Les and Bruce. Dinner at 2 pm. Bob took them back to the station at six pm. Got fish at station.

Billy was my older brother (by four years), and Aunt Jessie was my mother's sister, married to Uncle Les, and Bruce was their son. The *station* refers to the CNR (the Canadian National Railroad) railroad stop, consisting of an old boxcar with the wheels removed. This was the repository for incoming and outgoing mail. It was also the waiting room for optimistic travelers who believed blizzards would not delay the train. In the center of the room was a small stove with a pipe out the roof. To stave off the cold, we made the stove fat with wood, and sometimes fed it Alberta coal for a hotter and longer fire.

The fish at the station were frozen hard as rocks and stored in a burlap bag, peddled by a fisherman who would come by every month or so. He piled his fish in the back of his truck where they were guaranteed to stay frozen. When we brought them home we'd bury them in a snow bank, pulling them out as needed. When my father talks about *the team* he is referring to the team of horses we used when the snow was especially deep, or the temperature so cold our car was a frozen ice sculpture.

Jan 2, 1949: mild, 18 above. South wind. Went to church P.M. and children caught second bus to Riding Mountain. Bob and Mrs Johnson and Irwin went to Riding Mountain with Harold in evening. I listened to Calvary Temple, radio sermon on "What think ye of Christ."

The Greyhound bus carried us in all but the worst storms to the little log church in Riding Mountain, where Brother Ed, our sister Jean's husband, was the preacher. They lived in a tiny house next to the church. Mrs. Johnson was our God fearing Sister Rachael, noted above and elsewhere. Harold refers to Harold Francis, a neighbor who was close to our family, and appeared to enjoy the antics of our small religious clan. Calvary Temple refers to the church in Winnipeg that became the home church for Phil and me, after we moved there in the late 1950's.

January 7: Bob went to Kelwood with team and sleigh. Took lumber to be planed. Had to leave it. I went to Norgate, also helped Roy Jackson pump up tire on tractor.

The Jackson family lived half a mile north of us. Pumping up a large tractor tire by hand required strong arms and back, and usually we took turns working the pump. In my chapter on The Broken Promise I relate the story of Alvin Jackson dying in the war.

Sunday, Jan 9, 1949: frosty, 15 below but bright. I went to church P.M. Eleven present. Harold came at 6 pm and he and Bob and Irwin Costen went to church at Riding Mountain.

Bob was the first born in our family (born June 18, 1923.) Irwin Costen occasionally visited us from his home in Sprague, some 250 miles away. He and our house keeper, Sister Rachael, and a diminutive band of brothers and sisters were dedicated believers of both the Sprague Full Gospel Mission and the one in Riding Mountain. Both churches shared many beliefs, along with some sharp differences that led to bitter doctrinal arguments, often splitting churches apart. Each side, of course, had an absolute, unwavering conviction they knew the truth. *If the Bible says it, I believe it* was a phrase often used to pummel infidels who dared to believe differently.

On January tenth he notes we shipped our spotted calf to market. It was hauled to the station by Bob and our team of horses. He notes too, that Irwin Costen left for Sprague by bus.

Jan 11: Milder, ten above, up at seven and milked. Breakfast at eight. Kiddies walked to school. Bob and Mrs. Johnson cleaning upstairs.

Sister Rachel Johnson loved to keep things clean and orderly, and especially so when it came to matters of the heart. Her highest desire was to obliterate sin and sinners from the world. Sin and dirt seemed related. I wryly note that to call her *obsessive* might slight her zest for cleaning. As only one example, her impeccable eyesight could spot a fly turd at fifty yards, and in a few seconds the scat would come under attack. She could cite scriptures to shore up her scrubbed and clean approach to life. Like all gifts her zeal to leave the world a cleaner place had mixed results.

As I read Dad's words, I have warm images of us *kiddies* walking off to school. We learned at a young age to crab into the wind, walking sideways and backwards so our faces were less apt to freeze. As part of our survival training we watched each other's faces, and when a white, frozen spot appeared we'd rub it to get the blood flowing into the skin again.

By 1949 Bob and Sister Rachael, along with help from us younger ones, had repainted and wallpapered much of our home and we felt much pride in our accomplishments. We figured it was about the nicest home around. Unlike the rest of us who drank tea, she loved coffee and along with her burning love of Jesus, this fueled her busy hours.

Monday, Jan 17, 1949: eight below. Phillips Birthday, Letter and card and $1.00 from aunt Margaret at Vancouver. I gave him pair of socks and bar.

Aunt Margaret was Mother's sister, and *bar* refers to a chocolate bar. Farm life was hard on socks, so they were a common gift, usually ordered from the

T. Eaton catalog or purchased at a store in Kelwood. As I noted earlier, we'd darn the holes in our socks as needed.

Jan 19: thirty below. N. wind. I drove kiddies to school. Bob went to Riding Mountain on bus to help Ed saw wood but too cold. Came home on train. Letter from Bob Douglas. I did chores.

Bob Douglas was my mother's brother. He came home with what we called *shell shock* from the trench wars of World War One. He seemed fearful and lonely, and we believed it was due to his war trauma. When it was really cold, Dad would drive us to school in our homemade toboggan, pulled by one horse. The toboggan was about ten feet long and perhaps two feet wide. Helen, Phil and I would snuggle together under a heavy bear rug, from a bear killed by our Grandpa McLeod. The rug had long fur and a thick hide and it took two of us to lift it. It had a musky smell, that seemed to get worse as it warmed from the heat of our bodies.

Jan 20, 1949: 36 below, wind in south. Children walked to school. Bob took out manure. Train three hours late.

At thirty-six below zero, if the wind was blowing it could cut to the bone—or as we might say, it was cold enough to freeze a witch's tit. Bob taking out the manure refers to the animal waste we collected from the cows, horses and pigs, to spread as fertilizer in our fields. With our team of horses we hauled the manure by sleigh or wagon (in summer), dumping it on the field for fertilizer. The inner layers of the manure would be warm and give off the most splendid steam when it hit the ground.

The fact the train was three hours late was not unusual, for often there was deep snow on the tracks, and the freezing temperatures created mechanical problems for all vehicles.

Jan 21: Friday. Cold. Doing chores. Children went to school. Brought mail. Letter from E.B.

I'm not sure who E.B. was. A few times a year Dad had letters from a friend in Cape Town, South Africa, and this letter might have been from him. He had the most beautiful hand writing, and crafted his letters in broad strokes of blue ink.

Jan 22: He notes it was cold, and the train was three hours late again. Also mentioned is a trip he and Phil took by bus to Neepawa, where they bought parkas and long underwear, returning home late on the night bus. Parkas, long woolen underwear and felt boots were basic survival items. We wore heavy rubber boots over our felt boots, and we called these *rubbers*.

Our laundry was done by hand, using water heated in a copper boiler on the stove and a glass and wood scrub board. We'd wait for a sunny day so we could hang our clothes on the outside line. Our long woolen underwear would freeze solid, and after bringing them into the kitchen, one of our fun games was to stand up two pairs, putting them in the position of boxers. After admiring our creative sculpting, we could stand behind and animate them, with one of us announcing the fight.

Jan 24 1949; Twenty below zero. Still very cold north wind. Bob and I did chores. Children at home. I went for mail at 5 pm. Parcel for Helen and Mrs. Johnson.

Jan 25 & 26: The next two days are 25 below and Dad and Bob slog to the Norgate railroad station to get gasoline, but it was not delivered. They also needed sugar and bought a 100 pound sack home on the horse-pulled sleigh. The gasoline arrived the next day by truck, and because of deep snow the truck could not make it to our farm, so the gas was stored at the Jackson's farm, half a mile north.

Jan 27: Thurs. 14 below but calm. I went to Norgate, got mail, saw Percy Parsons. Cutting out water hole P.M. Finally got water where fence crosses creek. Bob and Mrs. Johnson putting paper on walls of cellar way. Dance for Red Cross at school.

In summer and winter we hauled our drinking water in pails from the creek. In winter we'd cut a hole through the ice, and this hole had to be cut fresh each morning as ice would freeze over the hole. As winter progressed and the ice thickened, we had to cut through more and more ice, and the water hole might be three or four feet deep. The hole would be just wide enough to lower our three-gallon pail down to the gurgling water below, and as we pulled it up by a rope, the spilled water would make the ice higher around the hole. Near our hole we had a trough for watering our animals.

Like the weather, the creek had its own mind and would change course under the ice and leave us dry. This led to a crude mining operation, and we'd crawl around on the ice, putting our ear down, listening for the water running below. When we thought we had a good spot we'd begin chopping a new hole, and of course, some were dry holes. When Dad notes he *finally* found water he may have chopped several dry holes to find one good one. Chopping each hole might take half an hour of hard work with an axe.

The school dance for the Red Cross continued the wartime practice of raising money for that organization. As many as forty or fifty folks might show up for such a dance.

Jan 23: Monday. Around eight below. Bob put battery in car and I went to McCreary and got license. Harold Francis went. There was an accident on highway.

Cold batteries are powerless, and when it was very cold a battery might *bust open* and be ruined. We routinely took the battery out of the car and placed it atop the kitchen stove to juice it up. New batteries were expensive, and we might have to sell an animal to get cash to buy one.

Feb 3: Fifteen below. Doing chores. Took a pig to Sam Glover's. Bob doing some painting upstairs.

On February fourth, it warms to only eight below and Dad reports taking Phil and me by bus to the bank in Neepawa where he deposited sixty-six dollars. Going to Neepawa, thirty miles away, was always an exciting event, for it was a town of several hundred people and had various shops, and better still, a Chinese restaurant where we might splurge on a unique lunch. After leaving the café, one of us might pretend to speak Chinese and that too was fun.

Feb 5: 10 below, sunshine. Went to store in afternoon and got groceries and cream can.

The cream can, about four feet tall, was used for shipping our cream to market. It held ten gallons, had two handles on the side, and a lid with a hefty handle that pushed into the top. As I write about it, I can feel the heft of the lid, smell the cream, and hear the ringing sound of the can as we dragged it about.

Feb 6 1949: 12 below zero. Sunshine and N. wind. Heard some wonderful sermons over CJB and Brandon CKX. Bob and Mrs. Johnson and Helen went to catch bus. I went to Sam Glover's.

Dad loved his United Church and attended faithfully. When our housekeeper, Sister Rachael, stormed into our lives in 1947, Dad mounted a gallant resistance to her hellfire and brimstone view of life. Rather than attend the Full Gospel Mission with Sister Rachael and us kids in tow, he went on attending his United Church. When blizzards gripped our land he'd listen to sermons on the radio.

Hiking across the field to the Glover's home was a special treat, for he loved the bacon and eggs Mrs. Sam Glover cooked in her black frying pan. The lard was left in the pan for the next batch. It would make popping sounds when hot, and if the wind was right, we could smell her cooking half a mile away.

His entry for February 7 is a one-word classic: *Cold*. Nothing else needs saying about our prairie winters.

Feb 9: 25 below, bright.

Feb 10: 18 below, wind south, storm in evening. Did chores AM. Went to agricultural meeting at Kelwood, P.M. Walked both ways. Mr Whiteman, agronomist, spoke on "what to grow in 1949." Also Mr Bates spoke.

Walking the five miles and back to Kelwood was common, and when the snow was deep it was a sweaty workout. Dad always had a keen interest in reading about farming and going to various talks.

Feb 11: Mild. No wind. 10 above. Had snowed some. Doing chores and went to Sam Glover's for pig. Church meeting P.M.

Presumably the pig was the one left on Feb. 3, most likely a sow left for breeding. When we had a hog the neighbors might bring their sow to us for breeding.

Feb 12: He notes it was stormy and the snowplow cleared the road to Norgate, and Billy went to Jackson's. Our brother Bill was fourteen in 1949, and increasingly, he spent more time away with friends. I've noted elsewhere he wanted nothing to do with our fanatical *Sister Rachael* religion. We were led to believe his actions were *of the devil* and began ostracizing him from our family. We launched many prayers on his behalf, hoping Jesus might save his blighted soul.

Feb 14: Valentine day. Monday. 8 above. Took over can of water to school and can to Mrs. Dobinsky. Doing chores. Bob papering upstairs. I went to McCreary P.M on bus to renew hospitalization. Home with L. Cripps.

Mr. Lawrence Cripps was the man who ran the United Grain elevator, and in my eyes he was important and successful. The Dobinsky family was part of the wave of immigrants from the Ukraine and Poland. They owned and ran the little dilapidated grocery store. Mr. and Mrs. Dobinksy had two kids, Orest and Nadia. Their home and store was little more than a rundown shack, with the store in the front, two rooms in the back and the standard outdoor toilet. It was one of the first Norgate buildings to give up the ghost to gravity, after the family left for points unknown.

The store was only a thirty-second sprint east of our school, and we'd pop in for candy treats. If we were short of money they'd tell us we could pay next time—an easy thing for us to forget. On a small writing pad or envelope, they'd jot down the amount owing.

Candy was dandy, but the store had something even more tempting. As we became more aware of girls, we boys would be at the store as often as we could, to see Nadia Dobinsky. She liked to flirt with us, and being with her was the best treat of all. To me she was one of the most beautiful girls in school.

Feb 15: 10 above. Billy and Keith played hockey at Kelwood, came home ok. Heifer calf born to black cow. Doing chores AM. Bob and I crushing in afternoon. Bill Shaw here to grind axe. Calf born to spotted heifer late, about midnight.

Crushing refers to grinding up grain, with the tractor-powered crusher. When he notes we got safely home after hockey, his words skate on the surface of things. Surviving a hockey game and a five-mile walk home through snowy roads in one night is not equivalent to climbing Everest, yet each is a potential death zone. If the wind was blowing snow around, it was both cold and scary. Our parents must have felt relief to see us home. We all knew of folks who'd perished in storms, and after hockey, we might be nursing a few wounds that slowed us down.

We had a round grinding stone operated with a crank, and this was used to sharpen various instruments, including plowshares. Neighbors would drop by and use it occasionally.

Feb 16: doing chores AM, cleaned pig pen.

Feb 17: I drove to Norgate with water for school and for Mrs. Dobinsky. Went to agricultural meeting at Kelwood with Mr. Jackson. Mr. D. Foster and Miss Dyke spoke on poultry and food.

Feb 18: Friday. 12 below. Cold north wind. Kiddies went to school ok. I and Bob doing chores AM. Bob went to Riding Mtn on bus. Did not come home.

When blizzards kicked up in mid and late afternoons, it was common to sleep with the person you were visiting. Most of us did not have phones, so we were never sure where another was staying over. It was nothing we thought much about. Dad's words convey the casual attitude we had if someone did not come home during a storm. After age ten or so, most of us were storm-smart and lived to tell our stories.

Feb 19: Bill and I did chores AM. Billy and Keith went to Kelwood PM to play hockey. St Rose won tournament. I went for groceries to Norgate and got mail.

I recall the St. Rose and Laurier team winning many tournaments. Because they were French, we felt they were naturally good players. Our stereotypes of the French were mainly negative, and we had various derogatory names for them, including *Pea-soupers* because they enjoyed pea soup. For whatever historical reasons, English-speaking people disdained pea soup as a peasant dish.

Like most superficial categories, sometimes they had a positive spin, as in our admiration for them as hockey players. Our hockey rinks were all open air, except in larger towns like Neepawa and Brandon. If it was 30 or more below, we'd sometimes spit blood from our throats due to sucking in cold air at high speed. Along with the bruises, cuts and scrapes, such events were part of the taken-for-granted fabric of our lives.

Feb 20: Sunday 15 below. Bright sunshine. Did chores AM and went to church PM. 14 present. Sermon on building bridges. Harold and Mrs. J went to R.M. We heard Mr Todd, from Brandon church.

Reverend Todd of the Brandon Baptist church was one of Dad's heroes. Helen, Phil and I would sit with Dad by the radio and take in the warm, liquid words of Rev. Todd's sermons. Just as when we listened to the Saturday night hockey games from Maple Leaf Gardens in Toronto, we'd have 3-D movies dancing in our heads. I had clear images of the big Brandon church, and eventually we made several trips there for Sunday picnics. The church was older and more fancy than I had imagined. It had a large choir loft and big lights hanging from the ceiling. Most impressive were the massive pipes of the great pipe organ. I'd have goose bumps as I listened to the bass sounds and the high trumpet notes, and had vivid images of wanting to play such an instrument.

The most energizing memory of our few trips to Pastor Todd's church was finding a large cigar butt by the sidewalk. I palmed it in my hand behind my Bible and sneaked it home. A day later, Phil and I walked up along the creek and smoked it, and the secrecy of it nourished my soul as well as Rev. Todd's sermons. After just one puff we felt like real grown-ups. It was so strong we'd be coughing, and could only take one or two hits, then we'd hide it under a special rock by the cow path, making several return visits to our magical potion. I like to think that today I could walk up along that cow path and find our hiding stone. My guess is the worms devoured the last of our sacrament. *Honking*—as we called it—on that cigar was a fine protest against the religion being forced on us. We could not openly rebel as Bill did, but we could honk on our cigar and blow smoke around. The smoke seemed to calm the old devil, helping us feel happier overall.

June 15 1949: Jean came home with Alb and Phil and they left for Portage P.M. on way to Sprague. We were stooking north of bridge.

Sprague was a two-day drive away, in the southeast part of Manitoba, and the home of another caldron of true believers. Like us, they believed they had the final, total and absolute truth of the Bible. Sheaves were bundles of grain, shaped by our McCormick cutting machine, known as a binder. After cutting the grain, the sheaves would be on the ground and we made stooks by standing six or so of them against each other, allowing the wind to blow through and dry them. Mice and other critters thought of them as ideal suburban homes, and moved in immediately. The stooks might stand for a week or more, and on threshing day, when we came along with our horse drawn wagons to load the sheaves, we had great fun chasing the little mice around the field.

Stooking in late spring or early summer was unusual, and done only when prior autumn rains prevented the stooks from drying.

Aug 16 1949: finished cutting field in front of house A.M. Started cutting oats in north east corner in afternoon. Fair crop. Samuel Johnson with us. Very warm.

Samuel Johnson would be about sixteen. He lived in Sprague, and had a crush on our sister Helen, and I think she also loved him.

After August 16, the pages are blank until Oct. 8 when Dad picks up the pen again, making daily entries from Oct. 8 to 19. Below is a sample:

Oct 8 49: Took up potatoes. Also went to McTavishs to get M. Wallace. Frank and Jim came, then boys and I went to Neepawa and got auto insurance. Irwin Costin came home with us.

In addition to special shopping and buying auto insurance in Neepawa, usually we'd visit Mother's grave, taking flowers purchased at the graveyard. If we visited on this date, it may have been too sad for Dad to mention in his diary. Our potato crop was often harvested under heavy skies, with rain that might turn into the first snow of October.

When I see Millet's famous painting (1855) of the Potato Harvest, I go back to the earth-spading days of our own potato harvest. Turning up a potato from its hiding place, and rolling it in your hand, forms a lasting memory.

Oct 14: On this day is a mysterious entry reporting that Helen brings a message for Bob to go to Winnipeg, and he leaves promptly on the 2:30 Greyhound. There are no clues about the nature of this urgent trip. Once again secrecy prevails.

Oct 15: Ed and Jean come in evening and go to meeting in McCreary. Boys and Helen go along.

This refers to one of our street meetings where we delivered the gospel truth—and nothing but the truth—to the benighted sinners in that town. From our jaundiced and judgmental view, the town was swarming with sinners and deluded Catholics and United Church types. They were blessed to finally have us reveal the clear truth of the Holy Bible. Street meetings and prairie lightning storms seemed fiery companions, lashing out simultaneously. Both left you feeling happy to have survived. (For details on our street meetings see my chapter on Sister Rachael.)

Jan 1, 1952: very cold, 25 below. Did chores and Alb and Phil did house work. We put fire on in the garage P.M. then went to Aunt Jessie's for supper. Mr and Mrs Lyons there and children.

This may have been a time between housekeepers, when we took turns cooking meals, often nothing more than a bowl of canned soup, some potatoes, toast and maybe a bit of cheese. It was always special eating with another family. Lighting a fire in the small stove in the garage would thaw our car in a few hours, so that we could start and drive it.

Aunt Jessie, Mother's sister, lived four miles north of us, and she too, would die of cancer in 1953, six years after our mother.

Jan 2: A bit milder, 20 below. Did chores and had dinner. Boys went to Glover's

ço

Our father died on May 21, 1969, after one night of suffering alone in the farm home he and grandpa had built in 1909.

A few months before he had visited our family in California, returning one morning astonished that he could pick a fresh orange in January. That, he said, was the best orange he ever tasted. The last time I saw him was in the Fresno Greyhound bus depot, wearing a forlorn fedora at an odd angle, tapping his fingers together as he often did. He was headed north to Vancouver, then east through the Rockies to his home on the runaway prairie.

Two months before he died he nearly burned his home down. He was doing what we often did together, burning some weeds and bush, just south of the house. This time the fire was too close, and the lower part of the house ignited. He desperately raced back and forth to the creek, carrying pails of water. He had a strong farmer's heart, but he was not a young Olympian. He saved the house, and in the doing so may have sacrificed his heart.

A few months later, home for his funeral, as I stood in the dark basement looking at the charred timbers, the only thing I could figure was that it was not the water—only his prayers could have saved the home. Water does not fly upward. Only prayers do that.

Along with the possible heart damage from racing back and forth to the creek, his stomach had given him problems for over ten years, a condition finally diagnosed as ulcers.

He routinely chewed pills to help him with digestion. On the night of May 20, he lost a lot of blood from bleeding ulcers and was barely able to walk. He struggled to the porch where he clung to a post and waved to our neighbor, Stuart Campbell, who had stopped by. Stuart drove him eight miles to the McCreary hospital, located only a few blocks from the spot where we'd had our come-to-Jesus street meetings some twenty years before.

Farmers, women and men alike, are a tough and independent breed of humans, and need reservoirs of hope and optimism to keep them going for all seasons. These virtues were at work after Dad checked into the hospital. Dad assured everyone he was merely tired, and if he had a few hours of sleep he'd be back to plowing. I'm sure he believed this and convinced the hospital staff it was true, so they let him fall into sleep—a long eternal sleep.

When they checked him again, his spirit was halfway gone, and attempts to bring him back were useless. His pioneer soul soared into the prairie skies—skies that had watched over him, blessed and pestered him with a stunning brew of weather, clinging sunsets and northern lights.

He loved the haunting calls of sandhill cranes as they winged through chartless skies, north at planting time, south when wheat fields came in. He talked of them with wistful reverence. As his soul migrated upward, I like to think he heard them calling once again.

His hands, scarred by seventy-nine hard-scrabble years, now suddenly useless, were hard as marble, and a fitting monument to his life.

We, his sons and daughters and grandchildren who had flown to places far away, returned, and with neighbors, gathered in remembrance. The log cabin that housed our full-gospel days had weathered away, so we clustered in the United Church. The faithful organist, Mrs. Beairsto, had passed a few years before, and a brave, younger lady coaxed final wheezes from the pump organ.

As we had done with Mother in summer of 1947, we made the fateful trip to the Neepawa cemetery where his body was placed next to his love.

When my father rises from the grave of memory, I see him walking to the barn with his milk pails, whistling as he goes. He often whistled, preferring Irish tunes and old hymns. More than his whistling, I hear the passion in his voice, see the tears form in his eyes, when he quoted Gray's Elegy. In remembrance of him, I close with the last verses of Gray's Elegy.

Gray's poem talks of a youth dying young. When he transitioned, our father was seventy-nine; no youth, yet in the long history of our spinning galaxies and the millions of light years of time, we are all children, bequeathed only a breath or two before we wink out.

Here rests his head upon the lap of earth
A youth to fortune and to fame unknown
Fair science frowned not on his humble birth,
And melancholy marked him for her own.

Large was his bounty, and his soul sincere,
Heaven did a recompense as largely send:
He gave to misery all he had, a tear,
He gained from Heaven ('twas all he wished) a friend.

No further seek his merits to disclose,
Or draw his frailties from their dread abode,
(There they alike in trembling hope repose)
The bosom of his father and his God.

CHAPTER 13

— ❧ —

Cars, Tractors, Fire and Ice

❧

FARM MORNINGS: IN winter we were rousted out of bed in the freezing dark, to the sound of a crackling fire in the kitchen stove. Our Dad was the firelighter, up first, stealing sleep from the night, stoking the fire. If the sound and smell of the fire did not wake us, we might hear his footsteps coming up the stairs, and his cry, *Daylight in the swamp*! I often wondered where the phrase came from, but never asked.

In summer, the precocious sun would have us up even earlier. Sometimes we'd have breakfast first, then milk our cows; other times we'd do the barn chores first.

In addition to the many tasks in our barn and barnyard, our help was needed in the fields. Most kids in our area started driving tractors, trucks and cars with an adult present, at age eight or nine. By eleven or twelve we were driving tractors on our own. Given how little we were, and how heavy and powerful the machinery, as I look back I'm puzzled and thankful that we survived. I recall hearing of injuries tied to farm equipment, with more connected to animals that kicked, bucked and ran amok.

The frigid weather gave us constant challenges with all our mechanical equipment. At zero degrees and colder, engine and transmission oils are as thick as porridge, and batteries are flatter than pancakes. The death rattle of a frigid battery is a terrible sound, especially if we were excited about going to town to play hockey or see friends. The low growling sound would last a few seconds, then, as the battery died, depressing silence would reclaim the prairie. And of course, sometimes we'd break the silence: we could not say *damn* but we could say *darn it*, and scream a bit, and pound on the steering wheel in frustration.

It was standard practice to carry battery cables for connecting to another battery, with the hope of jump starting a dead battery. If no one was around to do a jump start, one cure was to bring the battery in and set it atop the stove for a few hours, where it would gurgle its way back to life. I heard tell of exploding batteries that were left too long on a hot stove top.

We had another way to get our cars and tractors started, and this also involved certain risks. We'd scoop ashes from our cook stove into a large cooking pan and place them under the vehicle. This was especially dangerous, for our older machines typically had gas and oil leaks. The odds caught up with us one fiery morning. Our older brother Bob had slid a pan of flaming coals under the tractor housed in the east barn. Luckily he was walking away when the engine exploded, firing metal parts backwards into the yard. Bob was a bit deaf, and a better Christian for a day or so.

Hot coals and batteries are a magical pair. After an hour or so of basking over hot coals, motor oil softens up; then drop a hot battery into its slot, and the engine would be tricked into thinking it was June.

While hot coals took the chill off an engine, the transmission oil would still be sludge, and because of this, I once broke the gear shift mounted on the steering column of our dad's 1948 Chevy. The engine was running, and I was determined to get the thing in gear, when the metal lever snapped in half. We drove in low gear, with our Chevy growling all the way to Kelwood, where we had it welded.

Our problems with icy cars did not end once we had the engine running. The next order of business was to scrape a small viewing slit in the windshield, so we could see where we were headed. We might also scrape a slit in the rear window, so we could see if anyone else was foolish enough to drive behind us. The windows were typically frozen shut. However, with enough struggle we might roll down the driver's window and stick our heads into the chill. The frequent winds and blowing snow meant our eyes would quickly water up, and we'd duck our white faces, with frozen tears, back into the car. Peak and hide, peak and hide, over and over.

Jack Frost brought other challenges. Tires freeze flat on the bottom when a car sits for a few hours, and we'd lurch down the road until the tires remembered their original factory shape. I'd read about the tanks used in wartime, and peering through the slit of our car window while bumping up and down made it easy for me to imagine I was headed across a battlefield into Germany to get the evil Hitler. Sometimes I'd yell to help get my battle juices flowing. Hitler had killed some of our boys, and I wanted to kill him.

Tractors were especially vital to farm work, and each family took pride in them. Like we say, you can take the boy out of the country, but not the country out of the boy. Decades later, when I see a tractor, I want to jump aboard and hit the field. I want to feel all that power under me. There are no twelve-step programs for my addiction, and I'm really not wanting a cure.

My wife and I take delight in my tractor addiction. I'm especially excited by the monster tractors built the past few decades, with their large tires and both front-and-rear-wheel drives. By contrast, our little John Deere AR model, even though at the time we thought it the best darn tractor in the world, seems pathetically small. I want to make the long climb up and into the air conditioned cab of one of the big, new ones and rip up some earth. My urge is halted mid-flight when I recall the hours of dust endured as we worked our farm. Dust! Dust! It saturated our hair, noses, ears and lungs. On the tractor and after the day was done, I'd spit dust into the air, coughing, wiping tears from my eyes. And only our creek for a shower. I'd drive up and down the fields, up and down, up and down, bored and dirty, and think of dinner time.

During my childhood we made the transition from horses to tractors. I don't even have to close my eyes to see my father hitching up his team, going to and coming from the fields. Our animals were almost family members and had first names, with their last names taken for granted. The only team of horses I recall by name were Pat and King, presumably both McLeods.

From the generation before me, we had an old Rumley tractor parked in the darkness of our east barn. It had massive rear wheels, perhaps two feet wide, with large metal cleats, and looked like it could pull the entire barn across the prairie. In addition, I have a few old family photos of the fantastic steam driven tractors. Dad talked about them with awe. The real monsters, the *steamers,* had tireless muscle, especially when pulling out tree stumps. He said they'd never stall or die out, but would go on snorting, never giving up. They drank more water than a team of horses.

Like the town of Norgate, the old Rumley and all his brothers and sisters have disappeared from the land, and I have no idea what graves they occupy. Were they melted down? Were they buried in the earth? Did a neighbor drive ours away one night, and does it stand now, forlorn, in some decaying shed? Like much else, the death and disappearance of hard metal remains a mystery to me.

Half a mile across our west field, toward the purple hills, was the Sam Glover farm. Their family shrank and expanded with the seasons as different relatives came and went, all crowded into a house about half the size of ours. Like the rest of us, they used a wood-burning stove with a pipe going out the slanted roof. Mrs. Glover cooked delicious food on her stove, for a family that ranged from nine to fourteen in size. Attached to the kitchen was a small living room with two small bedrooms on the side, where the women slept. Those rooms haunted me; they were dark and secretive and full of the mysteries of womanhood. Even though I was curious, not once did I pass through or peak through those doors for any length of time.

The Glover's were good neighbors, except for the fact they owned a Case tractor. We had loud, verbal fights with the older Glover boys over our tractors. Our tractors were like family members, and we took much pride in them, defending them as we would a brother or sister. The Glover kids knew their Case tractor was the best in the world. It had four cylinders, an electric starter, and at work in the fields had a sweet purring sound. We knew our green John Deere was the best tractor in the world. Yes, it had only two cylinders, but they were big ones! Our Johnny didn't purr, but it made a resounding pom-pom-pom, like a mighty drum, across the prairie. Under heavy loads the pom-pom sound would slow, and if the pull was heavy enough, drummer Johnny would stall out in favor of prairie silence. We'd have to restart it by turning the large flywheel, a daunting and often discouraging task even with our strong bodies. It was easy to flood the thing with gas, and once the spark plugs were wet we'd have to remove them and dry them off. Then we'd go through the entire process again. Our struggles with our John Deere were secrets well kept from the Glover boys, for we didn't want them to think our precious Johnny had any weakness whatever.

The tractor bragging confrontations were as hot as July lightning, for we were defending our family honor, just as they were. Gordon Glover, a few years older than Phil and me, would hurl out a blistering challenge: *you bring that wimpy Johnny over here and we'll chain it to our tractor and pull the butt end out of it!* This was the shaming taunt that was flung in our faces over and over. *Go get that piece of junk, bring it over and we'll pull the rear end out of it.* Over and over: the bruises, the blows, the shouted chain lashes. We could not use bad swear words, and they had that advantage. When they talked about the rear end of our tractor they used the *A* word, and we were not even supposed to think of that word. They knew this and beat us up with it, along with other curse words.

The younger Glover kids would stay out of it, so Phil and I faced off with older brothers.

Even though we were scrappy little buggers, the older boys were louder, had bigger muscles and words, and had developed scary, lower sounding voices. Phil and I were frequently reduced to shameful tears as our precious tractor was humiliated with derisive shouts, curses and challenges. Our tears would elicit more humiliation. They knew our John Deere was pathetic and powerless, and during the heat of battle I'd also have doubts about it. As I cried, I felt I'd let our family down, that I had not defended us well. Phil and I would drag our tails home across the lonely field, nursing our wounds. A few days later, because Mrs. Glover loved us and made great food, we'd have another yelling match after lunch. For whatever reason, our verbal bouts would happen as we sat in or near their well house, just outside the kitchen.

The other machines central to our lives were cars. I've owned many cars over the years, but the most legendary one was our 1939 Plymouth. It was the first car Phil and I owned, and given our boiling hormones in our late teen years, we used and abused it with mainly happy results. The car was another crucible in which we formed ourselves, testing ourselves repeatedly with the forces of gravity, time and space.

We purchased our dark blue Plymouth from my Miles Mac high school buddy, Joe Korponay. I spent my last year of high school at Miles Mac, living with the Confrey family on Leighton Avenue in East Kildonan, a suburb of Winnipeg. The Confreys had taken refuge for several weeks at our farm during the Red River flood of 1950, and we started visiting them in the city. Phil and I, and our friends, used our Plymouth to travel back and forth to the farm, and to tool around the city.

After tasting the excitement of city life, I could not look back. I needed to escape from the boredom, the hard work and isolation of the farm. Our cold house was reason enough to migrate the 150 miles south to *the Peg*. The Confreys had big hearts; they loved me and perhaps sensed that I needed rescuing from myself, and invited me to live with them.

Joe lived near the Red River, a few hundred meters west of the Confrey home, and occasionally he'd wheel by in his Plymouth to pick me up on the way to school. The roar from the hole in the muffler announced that he was only a few blocks away.

As I write this, I go downstairs and pull out my high school yearbook, making sure I've spelled his name correctly. I peer at his face again, standing my memory up against reality. The face in my memory fits the photo: his slight grin, his Burt Lancaster face with a big jaw. If he had been taller and kept his car, he might have made it to Hollywood.

I look at his picture, am drawn in, and turn more pages, falling back into those days of high innocence. In the picture of our high school soccer team, Joe is two seats away on my left. A total of sixteen baby faces stare back, each full of promise. In addition to a few group photos, we also had tiny, individual ones. Next to Joe's is this, written by a classmate: *Blue plate of room eight. Handsome, dashing Casanova. Interested in all sports—especially tiddly winks. Plans to be a high school teacher.*

I have no idea what *blue plate* refers to, and assume it was a colloquialism of that time.

I knew Joe did not come from *money,* and his old Plymouth was only one indicator of that. Only a few classmates came from well-to-do families, and their parents dropped them off in new cars. They talked differently from most of us, and their clothes were different too. The rest of us were broke most of the time, and when our friend Joe reached rock bottom he offered to sell his car. Phil and I were able to come up with fifty bucks, made from part-time jobs and money our sister Helen had sent. We handed him the large roll of fives and ones and drove away, proud of our first car, excited about all the fun we'd have in it.

This was another big step toward manhood, freedom and full constitutional rights. In my mind I saw us driving out to Winnipeg Beach, or other resort areas, a few times a week. I could see my hair blowing in the wind as I drove about with a pretty young woman. I had little idea of what escapades lay ahead, including a scary encounter with one of Winnipeg's finest, a real city policeman.

Before long, with a sense of irony, we named the car *The Coach,* for it had four doors, and if you looked at it in a certain light, it might have transported important people about. The car was a dark, dress blue, marred with faded spots, rust and dents. It smelled bad and not only did the muffler emit loud rumblings, other troubling sounds would emanate from unknown and soulful places within the car.

Cars and adolescents are not a marriage made in heaven, unless we're talking about drive-in theaters. We all have car stories from our dreamy days of youth. I begin with a common problem we faced. Because we were so cash poor, we'd only put a couple of bucks worth of gas in the car at any time, and running out of gas was a plague. The early warning signs gave us familiar chills; the gas dial would flutter for a few miles, then the six cylinder flathead engine would sneeze a bit, then cough, and finally the car would jerk about, and our rolling adventure would die on the spot.

We'd grab our gallon can from the trunk, and stick out a thumb. If no one picked us up in a few minutes, we'd start to hike in a direction we hoped would lead to a gas station. Occasionally, someone would carry an extra gallon in their trunk and would get us up and running that way. Our age, in contrast to our wrinkled coach, told a quick story, and once in a while someone would buy gas for us.

A complete inventory of the problems with The Coach might be a book in itself, so I'll mention only a few. Because we never had extra cash, we'd fix things only when the car would not start, or if the shakes and wobbles reached critical mass—a distant goal indeed, and one we never seemed to reach.

It had only one tiny, sun-warped wiper for the driver's windshield. Above the windshield was a small toggle button to turn the thing on. This was one of the many things we didn't ask Joe about, nor did he volunteer the information, nor did we care. When we pulled the button to make the wiper work, it would make one jerky pass to the right, then stop. The only way to get the wiper blade to return was to push the switch off. This was not a problem in light rain for we would only use the switch every five minutes or so. Peering through the rain gave much more visibility than the small slits we scratched on the windshield in winter time.

In heavy rain and on long trips, the lazy blade was a problem, and the way we solved it was to have the passenger continuously operate the wiper switch, while another person drove. Every fifteen minutes our arms would be tired from reaching up to the switch and we'd rotate with the driver. I can see us now, with our belching muffler, our wobbly wheel, and our two-man crew working the wiper and steering wheel. I'm guessing many traffic cops who took one look at us wisely decided not to pull us over, for it would take too much time, and they might run out of tickets.

Because our blue jalopy lacked power and didn't have a passing gear, we randomly discovered a way to make her jump like a rabbit. The car had a long, goosenecked gearshift, rising three feet up from the floor. One day, whoever was driving decided to slam that shift from third gear up to second gear without using the clutch. The car leaped forward like a rabbit scared out of hiding. We yelled with delight. In one second, we'd go from thirty miles an hour to warp speed. The clanking sound of gears, and the sudden roar of our engine, told us this was not the wisest thing to do, and for this reason we only used our *passing gear* a few times a week.

More dangerous than our wiper and passing gear, was the collapsing front seat. The metal frame had broken, and the seat would fall backwards, sucking the driver and passenger with it. This was part of the overall circus effect. Our barnyard solution was to prop it up with a piece of two-by-two, braced against the back seat. We'd have days of routine driving (as routine as it could be in our jiggly jalopy) when suddenly the stick would fall, and the front seat would collapse backwards. After the usual screams, we'd be left clutching the steering wheel, springing upward to peer out. After a quick swerve, we'd recover and pull over and replace the stick. One man on the wheel, one man on the wiper, and both of us wondering if the stick would hold.

Even though our stick routinely failed us, one night I discovered it had magical properties. It was a bone-snapping January night, perhaps thirty degrees below zero. I had taken Gail, my girlfriend, to her home out in the country, on Pembina Highway. I had thoughts she might be *the one,* but friends warned me that any woman who'd ride in my car might not make a sensible wife.

The scene unfolds in my mind: I see that Gail is safely into her home and slither away with bald tires barely gripping snow and ice. Soon I notice smoke coming into the car. The Coach had continual problems, so our rule was to keep driving the thing as long as the motor was running with general forward progress. As the smoke thickens, small flames peek out from a hole in the floor. I decide to break our rule and pull over to avoid a possible explosion.

I step into the cold night, and see fire flickering from the side grill. I fling the hood open and step back to check it out. All in a panic, I rip off my prized high school jacket, and snuff out the fire, getting a slight burn on one hand. My jacket is on fire, and I throw it to the ground and stomp it out.

Having faced various problems with our Coach I keep the faith in her recuperative powers, but now fear grips me. After the smoke clears, I calm down and try to start our faithful machine. The battery is still warm, perhaps in part due to the fire, and the engine cranks over and over, but won't start. So this, I think, is how it ends.

I'm many miles from a gas station, with only a few dollars in my pocket. I launch a mighty prayer, a zinger that I hope goes directly to Jesus. Prayer and practical action. I seize the stick that props up the front seat, and stir the burned electrical wires around the engine, hoping against hope that they might magically reconnect themselves. Apart from prayer, I don't know what else to do; this is one of those crazy, intuitive moves I might make during a game of hockey.

As I stir the wires, I fire off another prayer, praying out loud as many of us did, using my own voice to increase my faith. After a few stirs I replace the helpful seat supporter, climb aboard and crank the engine. It starts right up! I am astonished, relieved and grateful. I immediately get my machine rolling down the road lest she stop again. As I head north to the city lights, in full voice, I sing my favorite hymn: *Great Is Thy Faithfulness, Oh God my Father…* I keep singing this, as it seems to be helping us go. Ancient crystal stars in the cold, clear night look on in wonder.

I park the car behind the home where Phil and I lived, at 814 Arlington Street, and am happy to crawl into a warm bed. The next morning we try every which way to start the Coach, including stirring the wires with the stick, but it will not start. We call a mechanic, and he does a serious re-wiring job. I tell him how I got it started the night before, and like many who encountered our car, he simply shakes his head.

Another issue was the severely warped rim on our back wheel, which caused the Coach to shimmy and lurch as we drove about. Helpful citizens would commonly pull up behind us, honking their horns, pointing, yelling, and making hand motions that imitated our drunken wheel. After months of this, one day my curiosity led me to ask Phil to drive away from me, so I could check our wobble. I knelt by the road, putting on my best scientist eyes, observing the wheel as Phil snorted away in the Coach. No doubt about it! The wheel looked like it would collapse on the next rotation. For three years we drove the car that way. Better to spend the money on gas. And we continued to have fun with the natives who pulled up alongside, shouting various warnings.

The wobbly wheel may have contributed to a bizarre incident on the day our car lurched partway off the front chassis. Coming around a curve, there was a sudden, crunching sound, and the steering wheel was nearly frozen in place. We stepped out to survey the latest incident. Our Coach looked really tired, for it had canted down and to the right at a truly odd angle. It was so hard to steer it took two of us to get it to the garage. The mechanic had never seen anything like it, and used various jacks and chains to realign it, before welding it in place.

One day, driving along a country road that had a three-foot pile of gravel made by the grader, Phil decided to drive over the pile. Another hockey move. The car bucked and lurched, but we drove on. Soon we noticed all our gauges were registering extreme ratings, and we decided we better check things. We lifted the hood to find the battery hanging by its cables. It had jumped right out of its container, and as the cables touched the frame, lovely little sparks were dancing about. That was an easy, one-minute-fix. With gloves on we hefted the battery back in place, using some haywire to keep it there. We were certain we'd not have that problem again.

While our imaginations were full, our Plymouth ran on empty. Phil recalls the time he and our buddy, Ray Unger, were driving back to the city and again ran out of gas. They hiked across a field and knocked on a farmer's door. He was not home, so they borrowed a bucket along with a gallon of cheap distillate, left a few dollars, and returned to the car.

The faithful Plymouth barely coughed to life on the cheap gas, and they had to do CPR several times as they wheezed and wobbled their way to the nearest gas station.

When our rambling wreck sucked her last gas fumes, it had to be push-started, as our pathetic and overworked battery was not up to the task. To protect the bumper of the car pushing us, we carried an old tire in our trunk, and would place it between our rear bumper and the front bumper of the Good Samaritan foolish enough to give us a push. The Plymouth liked to get up to 35 or 40 miles per hour before deciding to ignite. Because most Canadians have played hockey, any other risk seems trivial, thus the first driver would usually stop when we waived for help. Oh, the innocence.

While milking cows is a high art form, with somewhat predictable outcomes, push-starting a car is really chancy. Once the tire was in position between the bumpers, the pilot of the Plymouth would start with the car in mid-gear, while pushing down on the clutch to keep the drive wheels from engaging. If the weather was warm, we'd take our chances and do our first clutch-pop at around 25 mph, hoping things might work out.

When we popped our clutch, the rear tires would seize the road and send a bolt of energy to the expectant engine, and in theory, if the spark plugs weren't too dirty, the engine would roar to life. That was the theory and hope. In reality, after sucking another tank dry, our carburetor and fuel line were filled with only the air of despair. This meant the clutch would have to be popped several times, and each time the bucking of our car against the pushing car would yield a significant but localized earthquake. Not only would our car hump backwards, it would also skid sideways when the rear wheels locked up as the tire fell from between the two cars. Worse, the steel bumpers would lock horns and get all dinged up. One glance at our bumper and you knew there was a story there.

Dismounting from our car to reposition a fallen tire was especially embarrassing, for it meant actually looking into the blanched face of the other driver while not cracking up, or prostrating ourselves on the hood of their car and throwing money at them.

If our Good Samaritan had not engaged in malfeasance like this before, after going dangerously bug-eyed with our first clutch popping, they required more pampering than our Plymouth. We never actually had to do CPR, and that was a good thing, for we'd never heard of it back in the day. If we blandished them with the right words and a healthy dose of pathos, usually they'd give it another shot, and this time we'd make sure we hit 35 or more before we popped the clutch. At that speed the bucking and skidding was barely manageable. If our prayers hit their target, the Plymouth would belch a black cloud as the engine sputtered to life. We'd jump out, properly genuflect to our helper, throw our tire in the trunk and roar away in a black cloud of embarrassment, thankful that we'd survived another push-start.

As far as we knew, those who pushed us also survived. After dozens of push-starts, Phil and I figured we'd cured many a Good Samaritan. Over time, we figured that hockey might actually be safer than push-starting a car.

Our beloved Plymouth Coach had yet another nuisance factor that resulted in an exciting and fearful event one freezing night near Christmas time. The front headlights behaved more like flirting eyes, for they winked on and off, and fluttered about in their sockets due to old electrical wiring, rust and other undiagnosed problems. Fluttering headlights are not a good thing. Winter darkness claims the prairies early, starting in mid-afternoon.

As we skittered about on snowy streets, the Winnipeg Police officers walking toward us liked to wave us over for an inspection and a Socratic dialogue about car safety. They were unfailingly cordial: they didn't try to intimidate or lecture us, and treated us as real humans. *It looks like your lights are ready to fall off, eh? Have you had them looked at? How can you see where you are going? Can you promise you'll get them fixed?*

No handcuffs or pepper spray, and we never got a ticket. One look at us and our car elicited compassionate concern and curiosity. We were young innocents, sputtering along the road of life in a rambling wreck, and the police could see this.

One night the Socratic dialogue took a new twist. In winter, the police wore heavy, ankle long, buffalo hide coats, rumored to weigh seventy pounds. As additional buffers, they also wore hairy mittens that went nearly to their elbows, and on their heads, impressive buffalo fur caps. In the falling snow and dusk of late afternoon, tourists mistook them for buffaloes roaming the streets, and even I could mistake them at over fifty yards. The dark bulk of these men could scare you as they trundled about. They didn't carry guns or night sticks, and this furthered the illusion they were stray animals seeking shelter.

These were days of holy innocence: Winnipeg's finest patrolled the streets, on foot, to keep their blood moving and stave off the cold. Other than trudging about, they had little to do. Except when we rattled along with our flirty headlights. This is how they earned their money, and compared to milking cows, easy money it was. Pull someone over, warm the night with a friendly chat, and send them on their way. Not only were they fine, decent men; it was too darn cold to write tickets, and we all understood this. Besides this, removing their heavy buffalo mitts merited overtime.

Then came the night I broke the law. Phil, I and other kids we knew, often bent the rules, but the law was sacred and we never crossed that line. One night after leaving our Friday night youth service at Calvary Temple, through falling snow, I see a massive buffalo approaching from a block away. Wow. This animal darkens the street, and must be a bull buffalo. A moment later I see this buffalo has a headlight, and I realize it is one of our finest on a motorcycle. One of our biggest, and finest.

I skid up to a four-way stop sign, figuring he'll do the usual routine and pull me over for a chat, eh? Even though I've just left prayer meeting, on this night I'm feeling the devil's breath on my neck. Don't ask me why, but that sometimes happened right after an altar call. I don't want to hear another safety talk; don't want a friendly encounter with this buffalo. I'm thinking: if I back up and park just south of the stop sign, he'll drive on. He might be frozen to his machine anyhow, and in any case he'll have the stiff legs of winter, making it hard to dismount and walk. I shift the old Plymouth in reverse gear, and back up twenty or so feet, parking between two other cars. I turn off my engine and lights. Maybe he'll forget and drive away.

The hairy shape on the loud machine parks across the street and fixes me with his white, buffalo eyes. Then, the moment: I stare back at his big eyes, and this time it's not fear but mischief that grips me. The old devil mischief. He shuts off his great machine, and begins his frozen-legged dismount, with radar eyes locked on me. I know what I'm going to do. Why not take the chance once in a lifetime?

This is like a face-off in hockey: first guy to the puck wins. I don't have to think up a plan, for it is born fully formed, birthed in the rocket fuel of pure testosterone. My hands grip the steering wheel just as I'd hold a hockey stick. As the dark shape lurches stiffly toward my car, I have a familiar moment of dead breath, face-off silence. All my forces are gathering up in me. My muscles are primed, and I'm ready for the face-off, ready to race to the goal and slam the puck home.

I wait until his shadow dims the light of my rear window. With a grin, I mutter: *no chat tonight thank you!* As he moves even closer, I gun the Plymouth into the icy street, and with spinning wheels, fishtail around a corner, making several sliding turns down back lanes and ending up in the church parking lot. My escape is perfect. I know that by the time he gets back to his machine and starts it, then turns it around, he'll only remember me as a crazy kid. He'll go home, tell his wife, and laugh about it. End of story.

I've instinctively fled to our church as a place of refuge. I'm shaking with fear. I had never thought of running from a policeman before, and now I've done it. With the fear, waves of guilt wash through me, mixed with gratitude that I've gotten away with my impulsive stunt. I launch a prayer of thanks and repentance: *Jesus thank you, thank you. Jesus forgive me please, forgive me.* I reach for the door handle, eager to run into church and fall at the altar.

Then I hear the terrible noise: pom-pom-pom-pom. It's not possible. My brain registers the sound as our old John Deere tractor, bogging down under heavy load. Then I see the big buffalo, blocking the sky, steam puffing from his nostrils. He shuts down his Harley and steps, this time smartly, to my car, his furry shadow freezing me in place. The testosterone drains from my soul, leaving only fear. I go into full surrender mode, open my door and step into a night that is colder, darker than ever. This will not be an educational talk.

He's at least two feet taller than me, and much broader in the beam. The wind from his brilliant pursuit has created tears, now frozen to his cheeks and beard. This is not Socrates. This is not your everyday buffalo. This is a real cop—a really big cop, on full alert and with a big Harley. I'm looking up at the face of the law and it doesn't look good. His first words: *thought I couldn't catch you, eh?* I stammer a yes, and without being asked hand over my driver's license. I'm full of penance, ready for the cuffs.

Then, to my relief, he reverts to the dialogue form we both know so well. He asks who I am, and why did I run? He wonders why I've parked in the church lot. My innocence bubbles forth: *I've never, ever run from a policeman before! Honest! I'm a Christian and go to this church, the famous Calvary Temple, and just left the Friday night prayer meeting. Can I take you in and introduce you to Pastor Barber? Pastor Barber has a radio program, and maybe you've heard him? He's a great pastor.*

My confession stops there, as I await his next question. He's curious about my car, and checks the drowsy headlights, the erratic brake light, while pointing out the illegalities of other things. He asks me to fire up the motor and notes the coughing sound made by the holes in the muffler. He opens the hood to check my engine, and seems surprised to find it intact. He's shaking his head more and more. He kicks the tires, I think more to rid himself of anger, possibly disgust and pity.

Now his curiosity leads him back to me. He wants to know where I bought my car, and almost with a salute, I tell him that Phil and I each paid twenty-five dollars for it, from our friend Joe Korpornay at Miles Mac High School in East Kildonan. I'm in full confession mode and don't want to hide a thing. I feel the night warming, I sense a relapse on his part, to the familiar Socratic form.

You paid fifty dollars for this car?! You know what you ought to do, eh? Be smart and sell your half to your brother! Hope is stirring in my heart. Then more car talk. In an official, fatherly voice, he informs me that he could decorate my car with so many tickets *it would look like a Christmas tree, eh. Please sell it to your brother.*

And then another hopeful sign: he shakes his head. The night warms with kindness and fatherly concern. Praise the Lord for answered prayers. He shakes his head some more, then, right from heaven, a chuckle. Ah, the beauty of it. Obviously, the car is a hopeless case, and he figures me a good kid.

As quickly as he has stepped toward my car, he turns away, wishing me a good evening. He humps his Harley once and pom-pom-poms into the dark. I'm holding my breath as his sound fades away. Autumn is gone, but I'm a leaf in the wind, trembling with fear. I'm happily alone, standing in the silent snow. I cry with relief and gratitude.

ود

One of the slides that rolls up on my computer every few weeks shows me standing by the Old Plymouth, in a white sports coat. I recall that Donna, the girl I almost married in the late 1950's, took this picture, and the orange tints remind me it was near sunset. The license plate number is 72 A 3, in yellow on a black background with a buffalo on the lower left corner.

In spring of 1983 our family returned to the farm. Heather was 15, and Todd 13. I wanted them to know more about my roots, and to see the old place. I was excited to show them the barns, my secret hiding places, and to tour the home my grandfather and father had built in 1909.

The tractors had disappeared, with only odd parts scattered about.

I was especially happy to discover the old '39 Plymouth, looking quite forlorn, parked where I had left it after its final run, in the fall of 1959. It was nearly hidden by tall weeds, and spiders and mice had claimed it. We found an old tube of lipstick in the glove compartment, and I remembered it was the color used by Donna. When my family had wandered away from the car, I shyly pulled back a tear in the upholstery on the drivers' side, and found a note I'd written to Donna. It was a note of lamentation and remorse, written when we broke up in the summer of 1959. I felt a rush of loving memories and gratitude for our young love, and the hours we'd spent in the Plymouth.

Finally, I express my gratitude to all the Winnipeg Policemen, who had fleeting and often funny encounters with us in our rolling wreck. I'm especially thankful for the kindness and wisdom of the policeman who chased me down that freezing night long ago. My wife has expressed her love and thankfulness too, for how sweet he was toward me. Had he wanted to enforce the letter of the law, I might have ended up in jail for a few days, and my life could have gone off in another direction. Two paths crossed in the snow, and his act of kindness made all the difference. I'm sending a copy of my book to the Winnipeg Police Department, hoping a few of the young officers might read my story, and remember again, that leniency and kindness is sometimes the best policy.

My nephew, Paul, returned to the farm in spring of 2015, and tells me the old Plymouth has vanished along with nearly everything else. If someone plans to restore it, when they find my love note to Donna, I hope they smile and think of a love they once had.

CHAPTER 14

⸙

The Games We Played

⸙

THE FORMAL GAMES gave us hours of fun, yet the games we made up were as much, or more fun. Formal games had frozen rules made up by old-timers, and our minds, stretched by prairie horizons, needed to create new games with our own, homegrown rules. Our games were created on the go, and we made up and changed the rules as we went along, always improvising to keep us on the edge. We were lucky to not be distracted by TV, telephones or any of the newer city gadgets. We had time on our hands, and we used it successfully with various games and scientific projects.

One of the things we loved was to launch ourselves into the towering skies, both in actuality and vicariously, with arrows and kites.

The highest place on the prairies was the fire tower atop the small hills west of us. When trees dried out in late summer and fall, a forest ranger would be posted to the tower to watch for fires. The fire tower, which we usually called the lookout, was on the road to Clear Lake, and we would go there a few times in summer. The lookout tower was a point of much excitement, for it expanded our vistas, letting our eyes sweep across the prairies. As small children we were afraid to climb very high, and we'd peer up at our older siblings hanging in the sky above us. They'd encourage and tease us to climb a few more steps.

The first time I made it to the top, fear and excitement shook my bones, and as my eyes pierced across the shimmering distance, I could see a line of eastern blue that was Lake Manitoba. From the top we'd yell out familiar landmarks to each other: *There's Norgate!* and closer, just on our left, *Look! It's*

Bald Hill. And there! See where I'm pointing! Our red barn and white house! From here our farm buildings looked like the tiny clay models we made in school, and our everyday lives seemed trivial. I imagined us as ants moving from house to barn, toting thimbles full of milk.

To gain another perspective on things, we also liked to climb to the loft of our barn and the roof of our house. Prairie trees, stunted by cold winters, were too small for serious climbing. We had helicopters too: from the loft we'd fling feathers, straw and paper planes into the wind, watching them spin about. Happily, we never tossed a cat from our loft door, but I knew friends who did, and they confirmed that, yes, they always landed on all fours.

The western peak of our home became a regular roost for our brother Bob. He was unafraid of heights, and this may have helped inspire him to become a navigator with the RCAF. In the long summer evenings after the chores were done, he'd climb to his roost, taking the red accordion with him. He'd sit with one leg on each side of the peak of the roof, his back against the brick chimney, playing and singing hymns, saluting the drowsy sun. His Irish tenor voice and the notes from the accordion floated like pollen across the fields, all the way to the Glover's, who told us they too, were soothed by his music, and felt it gave the cows more milk.

With his prominent McLeod nose, Bob reminded me of a hawk perched atop the roof. From his precarious nest, one of his favorite songs drifts across the years and miles, and echoes in my mind: *Beyond the sunset, oh glorious morning, Beyond the sunset when day is done....* It seemed to me that the whole barnyard hushed to his music, and the cows ceased their lowing.

From Bob we learned we could use our imaginations to probe the skies, while keeping our feet on the ground. As airplanes began crossing our heavens, Bob would paint a picture of what it was like to look down from a plane and see clear to Lake Manitoba. I could imagine what it was like to have the sweeping eyes of a pilot from on high.

After dark winters, spring skies would fill with migrating birds, and our kites became part of the flying celebration. Like most of our other toys, they were handcrafted. In the garage or granary we'd collect small strips of wood, forming them into a diamond shape, lashing them together with strings and screws, then covering the frame with newspapers. On the back side of the kite, we'd have a tight string connecting the short sides of the diamond shape, so that the front part of the kite had a bow shape, enabling it to ride the wind. The length of the tail was critical: a kite with a long tail would be too stable and no fun, while a kite with a short tail might dip and dive too much. We'd take twine from the harvest binder, and every two or three feet, wind it around a piece of newspaper to form a tail ten to twenty feet long. We'd adjust the tail length so that the kite would dive and swoop enough, but not too much. If we wanted a stable ride in the wind, we'd make the tail longer.

If it was a rare quiet day, and Mr. North Wind was hiding behind the barn, we'd tease him to come out: *we know your hiding place; we know your hiding place, so come out and show your face, come out and show your face.* The chants of childhood were magical, and soon he'd be puffing away, ready to frolic with us.

The first flight was especially exciting, for we never knew if our craft would fly. Once launched, we could make the kite dive by running with it, or snapping the cord in various ways. Often, after the initial excitement wore off, we'd grab our .22 rifles and fire away at the kite, pretending we were the Red Baron, firing as he had done, making the chat-chat-chat sound of his machine gun as we blazed away. When we pulled our sky-bird back to earth we'd count the small holes in the kite. I recall only one time when someone fired a shot that snapped the wooden cross beam causing the kite to crash to earth amidst much applause. A true Red Baron moment.

Our runaway imaginations were easily bored with the familiar, and we were constantly tinkering with things to see what might happen if we changed this or that. One day we decided to build a gigantic B-29 bomber kite, something big enough to darken the sun. We spent many hours working on our B-29 kite, stitching paper together with straight pins, needle and thread. Helen's sewing skills were vital in constructing our giant bird. After several hours, we had a kite that reached as far as a six-year-old could throw a snowball. Given our fever to fly, we could barely sleep the night we'd completed our project.

As expected, the next morning brought a stiff prairie blow, and we rushed into the west field to fill the sky with our bomber. It took two of us to hold it into the wind, and it felt like it might pull us into the sky as it flapped and shuddered. This kite wanted to fly to the moon! It made a sucking, tornado sound as we released it, boring a hole into the sky with its tail snapping behind it, zooming straight up. Seconds later it exploded as though hit by enemy cannons. The sound of breaking wood and tearing paper was fantastic, and caused us to leap and scream as we ran for cover. We considered it one of our greatest experiments ever, and often spun stories about our mighty B-29 kite that had died in a blaze of glory.

Most of our games were wild, high voltage affairs, but nothing was as purely electrifying as our times with our shocker machine. The shocker was made of attractive oak wood, about the size of a shoe box. The beauty of the wood suggested the box was an innocent thing, perhaps for ladies perfume or hair brushes. The wood was a clever disguise for the mischief contained within the box itself, for when the lid was opened it looked suspiciously like a bomb; it housed a black coil, some wires, and a lever mounted on a gauge. In a real sense it was a bomb—with a slow, enduring explosion that shattered routine days with shrieks and laughter.

Our family had inherited the shocker box from nameless folks who had wisely disappeared from our lives, perhaps because of the box itself. The story I heard was that it had been created by a devilish genius as a cure for arthritis—and anything else that ailed you. The shocker was a form of snake oil, all coiled up, filled with a double venom that came from two insulated cords tied to the evil-hearted machine. On the end of each cord was a silver handle that you immediately wanted to put in your hand, for it was obvious it was made for holding. If your hands were sweating, you knew the metal handles would be cooling, even relaxing. And you'd be wrong, nearly dead wrong.

When hooked to a battery—the bigger the better—the handles would deliver a charge of electricity designed to zap the arthritis, the lethargy, boredom and any fuzzy thoughts right out of you. You could regulate the desired dosage by moving the lever along the black dial. The color black was surely chosen to warn triflers of the inherent danger of the machine.

Prior to meeting this machine, you might have fancied you knew what it meant to be excited and alive; however, one moment with this demon machine would properly inform you of the nature of true excitement, and ignite a new fire in you. Even cranked halfway up, the electrical jolt would focus your mind like a laser, and all your troubles would vanish in one holy moment. If you had arthritis—or any other malady—you'd instantly forget it, as the pain of the shocker devastated your cells. Likewise, any semblance of normal consciousness of self would disappear into thin air; this was remedial itself, and lent a new perspective to life.

When cranked near the upper limits, the fabric of time was rent, and the past and future no longer existed—this too, was healing in an off-kilter way. The machine was tailor made for farm kids and hockey players. Some uninformed adults thought the shocker was actually dangerous, and we made sure to tell them it was not even close to being an electric chair. This news did not seem to comfort them.

While the shocker was made as a cure for arthritis, and perhaps to roust the dead, we never used it that way. We were kids and entirely free of arthritis, thank you, and thoughts of death far away. We used the machine for pure, diabolical fun. When rope-swinging in the barn, snowball fights, hockey and baseball were not enough, we'd head upstairs to Bob's room and open the magical box.

We know that electricity happens between people, and perhaps this is why we liked to use the shocker when neighbor kids came over. Usually we'd have a small group of us holding hands, standing in a trembling circle around the spirited shocker. The two kids at the ends of the circle would each grab one of the lovely silver hand grips, and another person would be picked to move the lever across the evil black dial.

Out of respect for all concerned, whoever was operating the dosage lever would usually start with a low voltage, the same way we might start a joke by downplaying it a bit. The low curative dose would immediately create some giggles, and for first timers, a sense of relief that it was not nearly as bad as the McLeod kids said it was. *Heck! The McLeod kids always exaggerate!*

However, as the healing balm was more deeply applied, the giggles would subside and anxious shimmers would ripple through us, like sheet lightning in summer time. You could hear it in our voices; see it in the way our eyes started to bug out. As more juice was released, our arms would begin to stiffen as though early arthritis had gripped us, and as the anointing increased, our arm muscles would begin to dance, then go rigid.

As the amps revved up, we were no longer in charge of our bodies, as the shakes, shivers and stiffness took over. In those moments, as long as we held on, we were forced to surrender, to let go, Hallelujah! letting the spirit have its way with us.

As we felt our marrow melting down, inevitably, one of us would let out a terrible scream, yank our hands free and spasm on the floor. This would be followed by laughter and taunts of being a sissy, as the truly sadistic ones clasped hands for another round.

Inevitably, in the first second of a round, one of us would slam the lever to maximum death-to-all-of-you! position, and the chain would explode as we fell around, holding our heads and stomachs. While this was dramatic, it did not have the healing effect of a gently administered round.

Bob, our older brother and high-flying RCAF navigator, had a delightful fiendish love for the shocker and took it with him when he moved to his farm in Sprague. He and his wife, Donna, ended up with a marvelous barnyard of kids, and Bob happily introduced them to the shocker early on. I've suspected he used it to inspire them from crawling to walking—a jolt to get them up and going, as it were.

His sons, Paul and Mark, and his daughter Beth, have shared their stories of the hours of shocker mayhem they had. Beth recalls her arms going straight out from her sides, and fearing they might depart her body, was wise enough to fall down in the spirit of things. Mark likes to tell the story of how they'd put coins in a basin of water, and attempt to pull the coins out of the electrified water. Mark and Paul, and maybe others, learned a way to actually do this, prior to rigor mortis. Here I can say no more, for this deft hand trick is a closely guarded secret. The CIA has secrets, and so does clan McLeod.

Perhaps the highest, scientific, wake-the-dead experiment was done by Paul: holding the shocker wire with a piece of insulating material, he'd touch the bare wire to his tongue, sending forth a small lightning bolt. He duly noted that his sense of taste would not be right for a few days. Continuing with his experiments, he was also able to ignite a spark from his ear, but this did not alter his hearing in any way, and that proved a curious matter to him.

From their letters to me, I've learned their mother, even though she loved them much, routinely hid the shocker. Why she'd do this is a curious matter, and remains an open question. It may have been a wise thing after all, for all of her brood have lived to be adults. She also realized she could use the shocker as a potent bribe. In one of her last letters, prior to her death in 1992, she reveals that she could get Bob to watch the kids if she brought it out of hiding. And of course, he'd use the machine to kick-start them toward adulthood so he didn't have to babysit so long.

I'm happy to report that Bob and Donna's family are all in good health, physical-wise, and Paul no longer speaks with a forked tongue.

Our electric fence was nearly as much fun as the shocker. The blue box that contained the coil, attached to a car battery, put out a strong jolt and kept the cows from breaking out. The box emitted a low humming sound, so we knew when it was up and running. We usually tested the amount of current with a dry stick or straw, and if that was mild, we'd wet the straw and test again. If it seemed safe, we'd then touch one finger to the hot wire and see what happened. Eventually we might put our whole hand on the wire, and if there were several of us, we'd hold hands as we did with the shocker.

If the jolt was not strong enough, all we had to do was get something wet to stand on, most often a bucket of water poured on the ground. As part of our scientific experimentation, when we stood on the wet ground, things would get interesting. If we took off our shoes, things would be even more interesting. Meantime, the astonished cows would stop their chewing and stare at us with their big brown eyes. They knew better than to mess with that fence.

By age five or six, we and our friends were playing cowboy and Indian games, learned from the older kids and the books we read. We had a collection of weapons that included homemade wooden rifles and pistols that would fire rubber bands. Our weapon of choice was the cap-gun revolver, and we were constantly seeking newer models, hoping to find one that fired consistently and didn't waste a lot of unfired caps. The caps came in red round rolls which were placed on a spool inside the gun, then threaded through the firing pin. Some guns delivered a barrage of rapid shots, others would miss and rarely fire; we died a thousand deaths over the years from guns that did not fire, and a crazed sheriff or cow thief would drill us full of holes.

The pungent smell of the gunpowder and the smoke that flowed from our guns made our wars seem quite real, and as we chased around, we'd leave a trail of wasted cap rolls behind us.

As with most games played by kids around the world, we agreed to take different roles from day to day; on some days we were cowboys, on other days Indians. Hopalong Cassidy, Roy Rogers, Gene Autry and Wyatt Earp were favorites, and usually won their wars with the bank robbers and Indians. As Indians, we had homemade bows and arrows, along with rubber hunting knives that we could throw with some accuracy. We practiced our knife-throwing skills with real hunting knives, hurtling them at the side of the barn or a fence post, and each time one stuck into the wood we'd give a loud Indian whoop.

I read somewhere about the Blackfeet Indians, and loved their name and the images I had of them, and for a few weeks I was a Blackfoot Brave, with a special straw cave I created in our barn loft. I took a nail, and on the wall by my cave, scratched the words, *Blackfoot Indian Cave.*

At age eleven through fifteen, Helen, Phil and I were in love with a few of the Zane Grey books, and for Phil and me, the two most loved ones were *The Spirit of the Border* and *The Last Trail*, written in the early 1900's. Jonathan and Wetzel were the two heroes that captivated us. In the books they were called border scouts, for they patrolled the boundaries of the early white settlements, chasing white traitors and Indians.

Jonathon and Wetzel were tall and strong, and possessed many skills that let them track and sneak up on the bad guys, shooting them or killing them with their knives. Wetzel had a special rifle with an extra-long barrel, and once you heard it, you'd never forget the terrifying sound it made, nor could you forget the deadly accuracy of his weapon.

Jonathon was the more civilized of the two, and lived part of the time in the fort with his family. Wetzel was a loner and lived most of the time in the dark woods, loving nothing more than tracking and killing Indians.

At night, as he sneaked up on them around the campfire, he'd make the sound of a sighing wind, and when they heard the sound of *death wind* they'd flee into the forest.

I loved being Wetzel more than any character. After the first few seconds of pretending to be Wetzel, I became him, squirming snakelike on my tummy through the woods, not moving a fern or branch, then making my death wind sound just prior to killing. As Wetzel, I was part of the forest, the earth, and could appear and disappear at will. You'd swear you saw a shadow move behind a tree, and on second glance you'd see nothing at all. I was the ghost of the woods and loved every minute of it. Deep in the woods I had a secret cave, with an entrance you would never suspect. With my special long rifle my shot was always on target. Once I had a bear or bad guy in my sights, he was a goner.

༄

One of our most fun experiments grew out of the intrigue Phil and I had with the lift in the United Grain Elevator at the train station. We'd watch Mr. Cripps, the man who ran the elevator, walk into the shadows where the lift was, plant his feet securely, and disappear into the mysterious caverns above. After his magical ascent upward, we'd see a stack of metal bars coming down, and we realized these were the weights that pulled him upwards. We were not only farmers; like all children, we were budding scientists, always ready to contrive experiments that suited our fancy; and so it was, we decided to build our own lift.

The maple tree just a few yards south of our home was picked as the platform where we'd conduct another great experiment. Our garage was full of cast off parts, and we easily found a metal rod about two feet long and an inch in diameter, and with it, a solid iron pulley through which the rod would fit. We climbed ten or twelve feet into our tree, found a place where two branches formed a *Y*, and hammered in some nails to hold our rod and pulley in place.

We built a lift box from lumber left over from dismantled pig corrals, and were finally ready to teach gravity a lesson. On the first few attempts, we took turns trying to pull each other up. Then one of us would climb the tree, and while holding the rope, fling off into space, hoping to pull the other one up. This required precise timing and taxed our strength, and never worked well. We realized we needed to build another box to hold some rocks as counter ballast, like the metal weights we'd seen at the grain elevator.

We filled our box with rocks, and at this point realized we'd have to lug them up into the tree so they could fall and pull us up. It was a struggle for two of us to get the heavy box up near the pulley, and then to secure the load on a tree limb. Phil volunteered for the first ride and balanced himself on the lift, and I proceeded to shove the box of rocks off the tree. Phil shot up like a rocket, barely missing the box of rocks. He stopped when his head hit the pulley, and I grabbed him and helped him hold on.

Repeated attempts to make our lift more civilized and gentle met with a round of failures. The box of stones would slam against us as we passed them at altitude. The solution for this was to find a couple of long boards, anchoring them in the earth and up by the pulley to keep the stones from hitting us. We were beginning to see that gravity was winning the battle.

We wanted our lift to be automatic, like the one in the United Grain Elevator, so that all we had to do is walk out, climb on our platform and ride into the skies. We tried to figure a way to hold the box of rocks at the top of the lift by anchoring our lift to the ground with large spikes driven into the heart of the prairies. Our logic and scientific bent took a beating on this one, and we never did find a solution. In a week or so, our obsession was gone and we dismantled our project. The next time I saw Mr. Cripps glide upward on his lift at the elevator, I had even more appreciation for how quiet and smooth it was.

As I think back on our fantastic project, as with many things we did, I'm impressed we emerged unscathed except for the usual bruises and scratches. The iron bar, the pulley, the box of rocks…had any of them fallen on us we might have missed a day of milking.

Finally, I'm proud to say that Phil and I, with our close friends, Nels and Bill Arvidson and a few others, became Boy Scouts. Our pastor, Rev. McLeod, (no relation to us) decided to form a troop, and just as our brother Bob had joined the RCAF, we signed up. We learned tracking skills, how to tie knots, and different ways we could help people with our skills. We were so proud of our uniforms, especially our hats, for they matched the hats worn by our heroic Mounties. This, of course, gave us another idea.

One night, we decided to pretend we were Mounties. We stood at the north edge of town with flashlights, waving cars over on official business. Making our voices as husky and manly as we could, we asked for names, and asked some questions: *I assume you're a safe driver, eh? Could you turn your lights on and off for me please? I see you're headed north, eh?* Like the Mounties, we were respectful and polite, and the adults returned the favor. Not one protest, not one question. Decent Canadians everyone. Like their fellows, they'd released all their rancor and protest during hockey games. If any of the drivers were humoring us, they never let on.

While our cowboy and Indian wars were imaginary, our great egg fights were real and in your face. Many years we had fifteen or more hens, and they supplied all the eggs we needed. They were in the barn at night and in winter, and outside in good weather. Their soft clucking sounds as they scratched around the yard slowed my sense of time, and reassured me that no coyotes or foxes were around. Watching the little chickens hatch was always a wonder. After we got electricity, we'd put a heat lamp in their pen and they'd cluster under the round shield that radiated the heat downward. They looked so rosy in the red light from the heat lamp, and better still, they fit perfectly in our little hands and felt warm and fuzzy when we put them next to our cheeks.

Every few weeks we'd kill one of the chickens for food, plucking its feathers, singeing off the down over the fire in the kitchen stove. The smell of burning chicken down is one of the most distinctive of all smells, and along with other memories, some of that smell radiates into my office as I write this. And yes, we usually used an axe to cut their heads off. Only a few times do I recall anyone actually wringing their necks—an act that seemed more cruel than axing them.

In summer our faithful hens built secret nests in the woods around our home, and the eggs from those nests provided us with hours of madness. Like most of our fun activities, we did not have any regular times to look for eggs, usually finding their nests accidentally, perhaps when walking to the fields or while playing a game. After a few weeks without egg fights, each discovered nest was a treasure with as many as thirty large, pregnant pearls awaiting us, and knowing what was to come, we grasped them with trembling hands. The eggs seemed to leap into our hands, knowing they would shortly take flight as speeding missiles. Our favorite rotten eggs were those that rattled when we shook them: *Wow. This one is really ripe and rotten. Someone is going to stink to heaven when they get hit with this one.* On good days we might have a hundred or more for our raging barn wars. Neighbor kids were fellow warriors and we'd divide into teams, with our east barn as the battle field. One team would have the loft, the other the ground floor. It was easier to fire downward from the loft, but the ground floor provided cows and horses for cover, and they usually suffered collateral damage.

By age eight or nine we all had slingshot arms from throwing rocks, baseballs and other loose things including frozen horse pucky and dead gophers. Anything that could be thrown was thrown, including slices of bread at mealtime. I loved the feel of a rotten egg in my hand, the way it was balanced, a bit lighter than a regular egg, resting there a moment before I rocketed it at my brother or a friend. Our reckless game demanded a certain delicacy in how we held and fired the eggs. Gripped too tightly, they could break in our hands and it was hard to wipe all the slime off, which meant the next egg on the firing line would be a bit slippery and off target.

It was thrilling to see an egg explode like tear gas on a Nazi or thief, for both the smell and color were fantastic. Getting hit was also exciting and a badge of honor, and if we didn't have enough wounds, we might move more slowly hoping to get hit. Sharpshooter strikes to the face were the most rewarding: much spitting, sputtering and shrieking would follow, then a mad dash where we'd plunge our face into the creek. With icy cheeks we'd dramatically rehearse the hit amidst shrieks and wild hand gestures.

The eggs that missed, fired by the ground troops below, would streak clear up to the roof of the barn, leaving a dripping, yellow signature on the wood. In the midst of winter I liked to climb into the loft, to gaze at the egg marks and think of summer time.

The small creek that ran through our farm was a source of hours of fun—along with some pain and scary times. The creek gathered her waters from the gentle hills only a few miles west of us. During winter months the creek hibernated, gurgling away under feet of snow and ice. We cut holes in the ice, sometimes up to three feet thick, and pulled up drinking water with a rope and pail. By mid April the creek would start to melt and soon the ice would be gone.

Our summers were nearly as small as the creek, beginning only in June and through mid-September. Our bees and other animals enjoyed the creek along with us.

We started our game of racing sticks in the creek when I was eight or nine, and like most of our games, this one was classically simple, usually played when other kids were visiting. We'd each pick a stick from near the creek, sometimes a loose one already on the ground, at other times we'd break a small branch off a tree. We experimented with different sizes, most under a foot long, using both dry and green ones. Once we had picked a likely looking stick, we'd tame it by talking to it, grooming it and giving it a name. Once it was ready to race, we'd go to our starting line, releasing our *horses* into the stream, racing beside them, yelling encouragement and directions and scaring the bees away. The bees that did not scare and fly away, met death under our scrambling feet.

We'd each name our stick, and one of the most common names used was the name of a famous Canadian race horse of that era, Canadiana. Horses that won regularly became famous in our creek lore, and we'd all strive to find a horse-stick that would beat it. I recall one stick that had a long record of wins, and I think it was Phil's horse. It was about four inches long and had an *L* shape, and would spin around as it floated along; this seemed to keep it from catching on weeds and stalling out. For a while we were all using similar shaped horses to try and beat him.

We'd take turns announcing our races for the radio audience that stretched across Canada. We experimented with different voices, some louder than others, sometimes with a British accent or with a feminine voice. I could see the radio audience of millions as we broadcast our races, and in my mind our races were as famous as Foster Hewitt's iconic, Saturday night broadcasts of hockey night across Canada.

Given my quirky sense of humor and my low boredom threshold, it didn't take many racing days for me to want to spice things up, and I readily thought of a way to do this by choosing weird names for my horses. One of the funny names I used was *Third Horse,* designed to bamboozle the announcer by forcing him to try to make sense to the radio audience of scenarios such as this: *and by golly ladies and gentlemen the Third Horse is first,* or, the *Third Horse is racing last.*

At first, this madcap-naming caught on and we were all doing it, laughing and racing along the creek. We contrived many confusing names, including: *Riderless Horse, the Winner,* and, *Dead Last, Dead Heat,* and, *I Can't See Who.* Sometimes we'd each run two horses at once, and this could result in the announcer trying to unscramble something like this: *...and The Winner is running last, and round the club house turn Dead Last is leading by a length, and Dead Heat is second, and now I Can't See Who, is moving into the lead, and The Race Is Over has fallen behind.* I'd dance about, watching the announcer all tongue-tied and laughing at the madness of it, and the confusion we must be causing among our radio audience. It was totally bonkers and I loved it. And of course, eventually our odd names became tiresome, and we created new ways to amuse ourselves. Our quirks by the creek had run its course.

As I write this, I'm chuckling as I think of those days, and my scrambled neurons are lighting up with other paradoxical names for horses. I sometimes embarrass myself with my antics, even though at times I act all grown-up.

The creek also gave us a place for wading and swimming. Except after a large rain, it was usually only a foot or so deep, so come July (with soaring temperatures of seventy-five degrees) we'd build a dam using prairie sod, stones and sticks to make a swimming hole a few feet deep. We had beaver dams around and tried to imitate their creations. Neighbor kids would come over to play in the chilly wetness.

Whatever the game, teasing and cruel jokes were part of our play, and my most vivid memories of the swimming hole are of the terrifying times when the older boys would grab those of us who were smaller, holding us under water 'til we were sure we'd drown. It was a terrifying ritual, and today I continue to be panicky in water.

Another favorite water game was *submarine.* I was eleven when Phil and I, and David Confrey, the city kid, invented this summer fun. This surprisingly quiet game was played in a galvanized, oval shaped horse-watering trough next to our north porch. It was about four feet deep and eight feet long. After May, when the thunderstorms blasted old man winter, our horse trough would be overflowing with water from the rain gutter.

The origins of our game of submarines is lost in mystery, however it gave us hours of creative excitement. Playing submarines was entirely different from the wild, reckless and noisy games that claimed our time, for it required patience, and focused silence.

Like other games, it was prairie-boy simple: we'd each find a jar with a lid, fill it partially with water, then plunge our arms into the chilly water, reaching to the bottom of the horse trough and releasing our submarines from the bottom. This game had a fascinating twist: last was first. The submarine that surfaced last was the winner. In our other games we competed fiercely to be fastest and strongest, and now slow and easy did the trick.

We experimented with many bottles and jars, some two quarts in size, others small perfume bottles stolen from Helen. At the start of every game our jars would pop up too quickly, and between each race we'd adjust the mixture of water and air. After several rounds, our subs would hang out at the bottom and we'd watch with delight as they slowly moved upwards. Sometimes, when the balance between air and water was truly delicate, as a sub floated lazily to the top it would hesitate, turn around and drift back down amidst our groans of disappointment. We figured that subs that nearly surfaced and went back down were taking on water as they arose, and this led to experimentation with how best to seal a jar. Before long we were using an eye dropper, and sometimes half a drop of water could make the difference in rise time. When someone ran off to the bathroom, we'd make sure to pour some water out of his jar so we could beat him in the next race.

Our dad, indeed the skies and prairies, the cows and birds, must have been relieved and shocked to see us so calm and quiet. Without any study of Buddhism, without any reading of the dharma, without any meditation training, we had transformed into masters of focused silence and awareness. As homegrown Buddhists we had discovered a surprising equanimity.

Like any aspect of life, games often develop mythical-iconic elements beyond conscious logical explanations, and this was true for many of the games I've recalled here. As I write about our submarine game, the quiet focus of peering into the water, the feeling of a cold wet sleeve, are alive in me. I especially recall our favorite submarine, a precious little bottle that would loiter near the bottom for so long we were never quite sure if it was moving at all. We'd hang over our horse trough, mesmerized, peering into the shimmering darkness, and sometimes after long minutes, reaching a careful hand into the water to see if our sub was still alive. Sometimes a gentle finger movement would start it on the long journey upwards, toward the light. That, I like to think, is the journey many of us are on.

Besides us kids, the prairie had other wild life, large and small, and equally cheeky and unconscious. During the warm months, gophers acted as though they owned the land, emerging from hibernation when May came round. They infested our fields, feasting on our crops and creating dangerous holes in our fields and schoolyard. Adults encouraged us to kill them, and we let our extravagant imaginations create sadistic ways to do so.

Phil and I had a sure-fire cure. We'd grab our .22 rifles and spend hours lying in the dust, rifles primed, waiting for a gopher to stick his head up so we could drill it. As with rabbits, we found that when they ran, they'd stop and stand tall if we whistled, and then we could nail them with a quick shot. It was always fun trying to hit them on the run, and occasionally we'd bag one; that would be cause for celebration.

Drowning the wily critters was more fun, and during recess and lunch-time at school we had a gang of gopher stalkers. We'd pour buckets of water down their holes and eventually a wet gopher would pop out and make a run for another hole; with whoops and hollers we'd give chase with baseball bats and sticks. This was great sport and didn't seem cruel to us, for we frequently witnessed birth and death in the farmyard, and until we were a bit older, this was simply an unquestioned part of life. Killing gophers was, in fact, a noble cause, for we were defending our crops, and Dad was proud when we gave him the number of kills for a day.

As we did with other games, we continued improvising our mad game of killing gophers, and one way was by putting a string or wire snare around the gopher hole. Then, several feet from the hole, we'd flatten ourselves silently into the sod, holding our trembling wire. When Mr. Gopher popped his head out, if we were quick enough we could catch him by the head. Then we could lead him around, and with proper tugs on the string, have him do circus tricks. Other times, we'd put on leather gloves, tie a string around the gopher for a harness, and have him pull sticks and stones, giving him the same commands we did our horses.

A more dangerous game involved our neighbors, the Glovers. They liked to tell stories about strange dancing lights on the prairies called will-o'-the wisps, and we were spooked by their stories. I listened with wide ears, for I was enraptured by such mysterious lights and had vivid images of what they looked like. Each time they told their stories my curiosity grew, and I was desperate to see a will-o'-the-wisp.

As I grew older, logic and skepticism reared their heads. I began to wonder if the dancing lights—along with ghosts and other shimmery critters—were created by overactive imaginations. I well knew that I had emerged unscathed from nights when I was certain a ghost was in my room. Helen and Phil also had doubts about the illusive dancing lights, and together we hatched a scheme to create our own will-o'-the-wisp and spook the Glover's.

After days of planning and thinking about the risks involved, including being shot at, one summer night we walked to the far end of our west field where the Glovers could see us from their north kitchen window. We separated ourselves by a few hundred yards, and one of us proceeded to turn on a flashlight and start running loopy circles while bobbing the light up and down. After a short minute, the first person would turn off her light and immediately a light would ignite a few hundred yards away as one of us turned on another flashlight and also ran around in circles, again waving the light up and down. This fun process was repeated the third time, and the light would ever so mysteriously jump across the field to where it had first appeared. We were having the time of our lives with this impish game, and it was difficult to swallow our sounds of delight and remain silent like proper will-o'-the-wisps.

Running about with the flashlights was not only great fun, it was terrifying, for I knew and practiced the hunter's code of that time: to shoot any non-human thing that moved. And that was precisely what we were doing as we flew about the plowed field with our dancing lights. Our project was a failure because the Glovers seemed oblivious to our presence: there were no shouts, no dogs barking and happily no shots fired. My fevered imagination created another possibility: they saw us and cowered in a back room, too spooked to grab any of their arsenal of rifles. I was much relieved as we walked home under the blessed, star-pregnant heavens.

Next day at school we floated out some questions to the Glover kids about will-o'-the-wisps, and confirmed the fact there had been no recent sightings.

Like other children, we created our own secret worlds, where we could find and define ourselves as different and separate from the adults around us. Phil and I constructed a secret sleeping area on the wooden structure that supported the porch. We started our project by crawling out the upstairs bedroom window, where we spent a few hours cutting a little trapdoor in the porch roof. We designed it to be big enough for us to crawl through, but too small for adults. Once through this door, we exited onto the wooden beams that supported the porch roof, fashioning a small sleeping platform eight or so feet above the ground below. We used straw from the barn for bedding, and on warmer nights we'd sleep there. My favorite time to sleep there was during a warm rain, for the sound of raindrops hitting the roof a few inches above us would lull me into the sweetest sleep.

The attic of our house was another secret area, not often visited and thus more special. It was easy to get to by a ladder from an upstairs bedroom. The attic had no light, and had tiny alcoves off the main roof, barely big enough for us to crawl into, and these were scary and secretive hiding places. The attic was spooky, for it was dark and rarely visited, and had some old photos of deceased grandparents with fixed eyes staring back at us. The men had long white beards and the women wore strange, black dresses, and they slept in elaborate frames. I was sure their spirits lived in the attic, and some nights these fears kept me awake.

Our attic also had some faded brown pictures of soldiers in the trenches during World War One. The cardboard pictures were curious, for they were twins, with the same soldiers appearing twice, once on the left side and once on the right side. When the pictures were placed in the wooden viewer that came with them, we could see the soldiers, their weapons and trenches in 3-D. We were mesmerized by what we saw as we slid the pictures back and forth on the ruler-like slide, getting them focused just right. The soldiers peered back at us, as real as life, with their whiskers and eyes coming to life, and it seemed they wanted to talk with us. I felt like I was in the war with them, waiting for orders to go over the trenches. I knew I could help them kill the bad Germans.

After long bitter winters, by mid-May spring would be popping out, helping our imaginations flower. And so it was that one spring Phil and I decided to make maple syrup. We rarely had pancakes, but when we did, we flooded our plates with yummy syrup. We heard older folks talk about tapping trees to steal the precious elixir, and we decided to give it a go.

This was the year when spring was not just an external thing, for the first glimmers of adolescent hormones were running in my veins, and perhaps the mysterious, vague impulses of early puberty lead me to think of maple syrup.

As with most of our projects, this was a self-initiated scheme with little input from adults or books. We trusted ourselves to launch into various creative endeavors, and assumed the great syrup project would be like any of the other experiments that sprang to mind, with a real possibility of success. We were optimistic scientists and set to work.

The small buds were happy to help us, and began showing their faces in the middle of May. We figured the sap would be running. From the barns we gathered some pails, along with our old carpenter's auger, a hammer and some three-inch nails and headed into the woods east of our house. The severe winters guaranteed none of our maple trees were more than six inches in diameter, but we assumed they were large enough and would be delighted to share their sap.

With much excitement we picked our first lucky tree, and using our auger with a one inch bit, started our first hole at waist level. The curled pieces of wood that followed our bit into the open air had a delicious wood smell, and we knew right off we'd have tons of syrup, and could even share and maybe hawk some to our neighbors. After drilling in a couple of inches, we expected sap to gush out like the exploding oil wells we'd seen in pictures. We were disappointed and realized it would take time for the flow. Using pieces of tin, we devised small metal spouts to put in the holes to catch whatever juice the tree might share. After driving a nail into the tree above a hole, we hung one of our pails to catch the flow of syrup.

We repeated this process with several trees, and all the while we could taste and smell what we knew would be the first and finest maple syrup ever produced in the Norgate area. There was one tree I especially liked, located just east of our outdoor toilet. It was larger than most and seemed to promise much, and I knew it would give us a full pail of syrup over night.

Early the next morning, chores forgotten, we sped from tree to tree yelling out to each other what we were seeing. Some pails had an inch of sap in them, others had none. On a few trees the sap ran down the trunk, missing our pails, and adjustments were made so this would not happen again. We were concerned that the sap was thin and colorless, and had a terrible sharp taste. Dad assured us that after it was boiled, it would thicken into true maple syrup. We charged ahead with our project.

After a few days, as we dumped our collecting pails into a larger bucket, we had enough to commence boiling, and this turned out to be even more fun than the sap collection. Someone told us it would take several hours of boiling, and because the kitchen stove was used for cooking meals, we decided to use the discarded stove by the garage. We wanted to declare our independence by boiling our syrup outdoors, and hopefully getting some attention for our bold venture.

Phil and I dusted the snow off the old stove, and proceeded to put some old stovepipes together. We'd heard that the higher the stovepipes, the more air would be sucked up, yielding a hotter fire, and so it was: our part of the prairies witnessed the first two-story stovepipe. Building a two-story stovepipe is not an easy thing, and this became a fun morning project on its own. We talked of Jack and the Beanstalk as we wired pipes together.

To hold the first skyscraper in place, we climbed to the peak of our garage and into several trees, securing wires to keep things in place. Finally we had it all tethered to withstand the onslaughts of errant crows, low-flying Canada Geese and Mr. North Wind.

We figured our pipes were almost as high as the Norgate United Grain Elevator, and hoped the neighbors would be properly impressed with our project. When they spied the smoke bellowing from our pipes, they'd know the McLeod boys were coming of age, and cooking up something special. If they were unsure what we were up to, we'd be happy to tell them. I could hear imagined conversations: *Those McLeod boys! That's the tallest stovepipe I've ever seen in these parts, and I bet they'll get some good maple syrup.*

With the pipes properly secured, we built a mighty fire that we believed would break all records. We found the driest wood, and continually forced more and more into the burn box, adding a bit of Alberta coal for extra heat. To generate more heat we decided to also burn wood in the lower box of the stove, meant only for catching ashes. The top of the stove glowed red as we added more wood.

The copper boiler with our sap danced a jig on the stove, shaking and making noises, like a hellfire holy-roller preacher. We stayed busy hauling wood from behind the house, and stirring our concoction, hoping it would quickly thicken so we could enjoy the fine syrup. We not only had heat, we had smoke pouring across our yard, drifting into our east field, and we were mightily pleased.

That spring a bridge was out, and the Howard Glover family drove through our farm on their way to town. I recall them slowing and going bug-eyed as they drove through in their green and white Chevy. *We'll bring you a gallon of syrup tomorrow!*

As with other projects, our great syrup endeavor had mixed outcomes. We were disappointed when after a few days of our hottest fires, the sap would not thicken into the golden elixir we wanted. We did lots of tasting and wishing, but the sap betrayed us. Dad figured our maples were not the same breed as those in Ontario and Vermont, and with our severe winters the trees had thin sap. We knew about antifreeze for our cars and this made sense. After a few days we gave up and dismantled the stovepipes, pondering the possibilities for next spring. Meantime we were eager for any other ideas and projects that caught our fancy.

Like other grand experiments that did not give us the results we wanted, we had lots of excitement in the doing and did not dwell on our disappointments. We were gifted with oversized imaginations that stretched to the prairie horizons, and often our reach exceeded our grasp; however, our cloud-high excitement and sense of adventure meant it was mainly fun and done with few regrets.

ଙ୭

Samona Ruth (Ruthie) my wife, has been charmed by my story about racing stick horses at the creek. Over the years we've played this game several times, including in the little stream that flowed by our honeymoon cabin in Estes Park, in August of 1965.

As a follow-up on the shocker machine, I've learned it was passed down to one of my nieces, and that her kids posted a video of them on the internet, as they fooled with it. There are rumors that the shocker acted as an immediate diuretic for one of them.

Unlike myself, we have a few members of our larger clan, who are, er, well, a bit zany and quirky, and my therapeutic insights suggest the shocker as probable cause. The other eccentricities that prevail in Clan McLeod are obviously due to frostbite of the brain and hockey.

The internet also reveals that shocker machines are still being sold, and a few of the older ones look much like the one we had. It's a very odd thing. People spend hundreds, even thousands of dollars on golf, fast cars, bungee jumping, leaping from airplanes and such, none of which come close to the fun and salvific effects of a genuine shocker machine.

The shocker machines on the web are advertised as quack medical devices. If only they knew. I toy with the idea of selling shocker machines, full-time. My ad might read like this:

Bored? Depressed? Feeling blue? Tired of who you are? Missing church? Now you can light up your life, have a new and electric personality, and a profound religious experience all at once. Not in weeks or days. Now. Death to your old, tired self in seconds. Our machine cures all. Constipated? Get things moving again! Canadians have kept this device a closely guarded secret for years. Now you too can juice up your life while captivating loved ones and making new and interesting friends.

Warning: this machine might kill you before it cures you. If this happens, call 911.

Additional shocker research reveals that Disneyland and other amusement parks once had shocker machines, but these are long gone. Our world has indeed come to a sad state of affairs.

When I write about our shocker, I realize I've grown far too tame. I miss those rocket-fueled days and am ready for another go at it, and am actually thinking of ordering one so that our family can continue the mad tradition.

As noted, we often changed, on the fly, the rules of games we played. The past many years, when our family plays board games, I've gained a well-earned reputation for proposing rule changes after only a few rounds. I naturally have profound insights as to how the game could be more fun, and so forth. Sometimes I secretly change the rules on my own—some would call it cheating—impishly making sure my family soon catches on. They tease me about this and consider it all part of the fun. I look for twelve-step programs and can't find one.

Lest any readers gain the wrong impression about the dangers inherent in the games we played, I offer a reference point to help temper undue concern. In 2013 I met a fellow Canuck who grew up on a small farm in Saskatchewan. In response to a few stories I shared, he recounted that he was fond of shooting tin cans off his younger brother's head. With a .22 rifle. With wonderment in his voice he noted too that he had a stern mother who insisted he not do that, even though he and his brother obviously got a kick out of it. Like many things Canadian, I trace his eccentricities to frost bite and playing hockey.

CHAPTER 15

❦

Intentional, Mischievous Bikes

❦

We, our bikes and genes, were passed down through many generations. Rather than evolving with each generation, as we thought we did, our bikes devolved, battered by weather, youthful risk-taking, dirt and gravel roads with potholes and the general mayhem of farm life. They were Neanderthal-low on the evolutionary chain: no bells or whistles, no mirrors, no lights, no fancy ribbons, no color, no kick stands, no weird tires, no suspension systems. They were not twenty-speed, not ten, not even five-speed. They had one gear and that was it. The speed depended on the power and intention of the rider, wedded to whatever schemes the bike had in mind.

Yes, most bikes came equipped with fenders, but on my most abused bike, I removed them in the interest of taking basic to a new level. The bike was a faded red, and I, with my love of word play, named it Red Skeleton, after the famous comedian of that era. I thought the name was quite clever, and others liked it, and the bike became famous in its own way.

Because we had no chain guards, our pant legs often got caught, and if this happened at high speed we could be yanked to the ground. Grease-spotted and torn pant legs were in fashion. To free a pant leg from the chain could take several minutes, requiring us to pick up the bike, then crank the wheel backwards, pulling all the time on the pant leg trying to get it free.

It is well known that genes, bikes and evolution form a complex troika of sorts and demand a short Al Talk, which I happily hereby deliver. Let the cameras roll: evolutionary theory insists there is no intention in or behind the universe. Yet, we find that our most minute actions have intention, and purposeful goals behind them, like ghosts in a machine, er, like a bike, actually. It is my intention to finish this sentence, and I hope, yours to read it. Down to our marrow, we are saturated with intentions. If you'd ever milked one of our ornery cows you'd well know about evil intentions. They'd get that plotting look in their eyes, and then an explosive kick would follow. Our intention was to jump back to safety, often too late.

None of this is a digression, not even a regression, for when we look deeply we see that everything is connected, nothing is entirely separate or cut off from anything else. Bikes have their own wills and desires. Intention is loose on our planet, and we find it from the smallest microbes to the largest animals. I ask you: if intention was not there from the get-go, from whence then does it arise? My inner scientist, red-faced, turns away.

Science happily tells us the universe just happened. BINGO! No universe, no time and space, sheer nothingness, and then all this. Because science is male dominant, we have to work in a big explosion of sorts, and so we say our grand cosmos didn't just happen; it exploded with a horrific bang. Enough to make us shudder, and because we don't like explosions, to drive us back into the arms of God, making us true believers once again. The myriad stories of the Divine Ones, with their thousand names and masks, are easy to believe compared to the big bang.

Axiom one: scientists who embrace the preposterous notion of a universe without intention have never ridden an old, battered, hand-me-down bike on cow paths and farm roads.

I take a breath and state the truth boldly, suspending my fear of blow-back. Bikes have their own intentions and purposes. There. That's the truth, so help me God. Secreted in the atoms of frames, gears and wheels of bicycles, there is purpose and intention.

Let's start at the very beginning, a very good place to start: simply look-ing at a bike tells us it is meant to roll, to move. One can feel this intention just by peering closely at a bike. *Yes. The darn thing looks like it wants to roll forward.*

As with people, the wills and purposes of bikes are often at odds with our personal intentions. Farm kids know this as surely as science believes in the big bang. For example, our bikes would often act like ancient, spring-loaded trebuchets, launching us into space like dumb rocks. Without any planning on our part, we ended up in creeks, ditches and mud holes, because that's what bikes like to do.

As a testimony to my general open-mindedness, I can see that scientists who ride fancy new bikes on city streets, being in civilized control of all known variables, might think that bikes are merely dead mechanical things with no intentions.

Back in the day, before science banished intention out of existence, we knew that not only bikes, but cows, horses, birds and every darn critter planned and schemed things out. To offer another example: our bikes had no kickstands, so we'd stand them against walls and trees—whatever was handy. We'd turn our backs, and before we reached the barn door, they'd have fallen asleep on the ground. Of course they were tired, for we rode them hard, yet it would seem a standing bike should remain standing—all other things being equal.

Why, I ask you, sensible reader, did our bike tires go flat at the most infuriating times? We'd ride out to get the cows for days, or pump the mile to the post office on hard tires full of bracing prairie air. On boring, everyday rides our tires would be fine. Then, eager to fly into town for a hockey game, and one, even both tires would be completely oxygen deprived. Smiling handle bars could not hide their malicious intentions, their sarcastic humor. I'd try to stare them down, and they'd stare back, daring me.

We spent nearly as much time patching tires as actually riding. By ages seven or eight, after watching adults patch tires, we could do it on our own. Removing the tire was the hardest part, and required the use of screw drivers and other levers, along with strong hands and secret timing. Often, the tire would be ready to pop off, then it would decide to snap back into place. Intentionally. Maliciously. When we finally got the tire off, we'd immerse the tube in our horse-watering tank, look for the bubbles and find the leak. Then we'd swab some vile smelling glue on it, and quickly slap a round rubber patch over it. Then more levers and grunting to get the tire back on. If it was a rear tire, we had to remove the greasy chain, then put it back on after our repair job. Often the chain would act ornery, and refuse to stay on, pouting perhaps, because we'd not handled it with care. With all the patches, our tubes reminded me of colorful quilts. As an old patch lost its grip on things, a new leak might appear after only a few miles of rough riding.

Bikes proved a helpful transition to engine-fired vehicles, giving us an appreciation for the nuances of balance, gravity, time, space and motion. By age eleven or twelve most of us were driving tractors, hauling plows, discs and harrows up and down the fields. Around the same age, we were sitting in the laps of adults, learning to drive cars and trucks, graduating to solo flights a year or two later. Bikes, despite their willful acts of mischief, served us well. Horses were more capricious than bikes, and after being thrown many times, I quit riding.

Scooters, mopeds, skateboards and the newer modes of transportation either were not invented yet, or were confined to city life. I recall only one motorcycle in our farm years, this owned by Stuart Campbell, a hormone-saturated lad, in his late teens. He was the proud owner of an old Indian machine, and the source of much talk and wonder. We could hear him and his Indian coming from a mile or more away, with a cloud of dust behind him. He'd roar by in a flash, gunning and changing gears, gravel flying. The prairie silence was palpable after his passing.

Wanting to be like Stuart, I had a fake machine-powered bike for ten minutes. One day, our older brother, Bob, gave me a worn out lawn mower engine. I placed it in the basket on the front of my bike, and as I did so another scheme blossomed in my mind. As I rode home, just before I reached the Glover's farm, I stopped and started that fun loving engine. With the engine running, I pumped my bike as fast as I could, and rode by their house without pedaling, hoping they'd think I had a power bike. I waved and rode smartly by, wanting them to be impressed with Albert and his new machine.

To create the sense of motor power, we also used pieces of cardboard and magazine covers, fixing them to our fenders and frames with clothespins and wire. Some neighbor kids used playing cards and they worked the best, but as holy as we were, the queen of spades, the king of hearts and the whole gang were of the devil, and Lord knows we already had enough devil in us.

To make an engine noise, our bits of cardboard had to engage the spokes at just the right depth, then when the wheels turned, the spokes would flutter against the cards, magically creating the sound of a distant bomber, or perhaps a truck or tractor. I liked the B-25 bomber noise, and preferred heavy cardboard. The more cards, the more noise. Yet, like everything, it had a down side, for when we used excess cards it was tiring to ride our bikes. The cards added another problem, in the form of broken and loose spokes. Repairing spokes, like tires, was a recurring problem, due to innumerable potholes and hard rock encounters.

To further increase our sense of being genuine adults with powered vehicles, we'd also tie burlap bags behind our bikes, creating a cloud of dust as we zoomed about. If you didn't hear us coming with our flapping cards, you'd for sure be intrigued by our dust cloud rising over the prairie. When we roared by, you'd be awestruck by our combination of machine and manliness, dust and noise. Little we may have been, but our imaginations reached to the top of Jack's beanstalk, all the way to the sky.

We played many games with our bikes, racing being the most obvious one, along with hide and seek. It rained often on the prairies, so we always had mud to spin in, and during recess we'd have contests at school to see who could ride furthest through the mud holes. It was rare for anyone to get a new tire, but when one was purchased, it came by rail, from the T. Eaton Company, source of all good things. A wave of excitement flowed through us as we took turns testing the new tire in mud. If it spun out, we appreciated our old tires the more. If it had great traction, we suffered greed.

One of our wildest games was the game of chicken, though back then, at the start of history, that term had yet to be invented. Two of us would ride madly towards each other, gladiator style, taking our chances, usually swerving away at the last second. When we both stayed true to course, we'd crash, falling into the dust or mud, a melee of blood, bikes and bruises, much like hockey itself, as the schoolyard broke into applause. The most common damage to the bikes was twisted handle bars and warped front wheels. Handle bar repair was a simple matter: one kid would hold the front wheel between his legs, while another forced the handle bars into alignment.

Twisted wheels were tricky, and often could not be bent straight, even with repeated jumping up and down on them. Because of this, our tires rubbed against the frames. The singing of a warped wheel meant bells were not required. Wheels that were really bent rubbed the frame so much it made the bike hard to ride, and we'd use all our ingenuity trying to fix that problem, sometimes with success.

We never heard of, or saw a bicycle built for two, so when we wanted to carry a passenger, one kid would be on the crossbar. Nor had we seen a girl's bike before, thus all our bikes had crossbars. Crossbar riding ignites the natural mischief inherent in bikes, and various mishaps happened when we rode double.

One day, I had a younger kid on my crossbar and was moving at a reckless rate, wanting to show off my general manliness, balancing on the border between death and life. With my tires spewing the usual gravel, I was banking around a corner at Mach one, toward the post office, when I had an encounter with an irony. Prairies are known for wide open, empty spaces, but on this day a car loomed up in front of us, just behind the hedge that blocked my view. I made a reflexive hockey move, and went smack dab into the stop sign at the end of the hedge. Ironically, it was the only stop sign in the whole country. I was finally learning the meaning of stop. My little friend shredded the air with screams, tears, curses and a vow never to ride with me again, and I was inclined to believe him. We were enmeshed in the hedge, the twisted bike frame and a resolute stop sign, made more red by one bloody nose.

The lives of children around the world are improvised in the holy now, for that is the only time frame we have. Like our bikes, improvisation has an intrinsically random character, and that is a hallmark of farming. Planning, logic and cause and effect were strangers, living as they did across the great divide of adulthood, frantically beckoning us to come on over, to grow up, to get serious and anxious about things. Now, having seen the folly of excessive planning, organizing and being preoccupied with cause and effect stuff, I've welcomed some random improvisation into my life. It's not only fun, it's cheaper, for I've thrown away bottles of tranquilizers.

Since March of 1993, I've taken many seminars at Esalen Institute, overlooking the pulsing Pacific Ocean—the *big eye of the west* as some poet called it. With other playful souls, I've exposed a few of my sub-personalities in several improve theatre workshops. The first rule of this theatrical insanity is this: once on stage you cannot say no to any character or line that is randomly given you by another player. When you take the stage, you never know what is going to happen, what character you might end up improvising on the spot. As an example of the odd twists taken on this stage-of-fools, I can report than on two occasions, for a few glorious moments, I ended up playing no less a character than God Himself. I must also report, shyly, that I liked it.

As I look back on the weathery, whippersnapper days of childhood and early adolescence, I see that much of our play was really like improvised theatre. We made up games and rules for games, and the rules would change as we went along. We never knew what might happen next, and we were ready to take what came along, to say yes to what the moment offered. Our bikes were wonderful stage partners, always ready to play along.

Our little time was prior to the era of flying bikes, the time before Evil Knievel and his escapades, and all the amazing feats of the bike leapers and flippers of today. I like to think Phil and I were the first leapers of our era, and again, not by design.

After we started Kelwood High School, five miles away, we rode our bikes south across the Howard Glover farm, to catch the school van. The van was a basic wooden box, capable of holding a dozen or so scholars, with sitting benches along both sides. In winter the van sat on sleigh runners, and the other few days of spring and fall it was moved onto a chassis with four wheels. Cold days demanded heat, and a small stove sat in the center of the van. When the stove was fully stoked, it would glow red, and smoke would pour out the stovepipe. As we puffed along our route, you might mistake us for a little lost train.

The van was a two-horsepower vehicle: two bored horses that could walk the route with their eyes closed. Irv Gower owned the horses and drove the van, and he too, could go the distance while nodding off. Irv lived somewhere in the far east, out where civilization ended and fearful rumors began. No one really knew where he lived. He'd appear out of the snow with his van and horses and we never thought more about it.

Phil and I were often late to catch the van, usually due to a kicking cow at milking time. Opening the wire gate at the end of our lane also slowed us down. One day another intentional light went on in our heads: *Hey, why don't we make a ramp over that fence!* As usual, we never drew up blueprints, or thought much ahead as we devised a wooden ramp.

With minimal head-scratching, we picked two posts that were close together, just off the edge of our trail. It was easy to hammer a two-by-four across the two posts, and then, with scraps of lumber, build a ramp on each side. Our first ride went well, with only a small glitch. If we rode a bit too fast, the lower part of the front fender would resent this, snag the top of the ramp, and toss us off. Otherwise it was all good. We proudly invited Helen and Dad to come and admire our latest, practical project.

As we say, the best laid plans of bikes and men do often go astray. The next morning, we were running tight and saw Mr. Gower and his horses slouching toward their waiting spot. We grabbed our lunch pails and leaped onto our feverish bikes, eager to test our ramp. My young hockey legs powered me swiftly down the lane. My front tire sang as it touched the ramp, and then I was airborne. For one brief, shining moment I joined the world where meadowlarks play, free, free at last from gravity and the other restraints of life. Suspended there, my vocal chords entered the fray, at first the cry of freedom, and then the scream of a hawk in a death dive.

I had one moment of darkness; when I opened my eyes, mother earth had opened her arms in welcome. Our faces were mashed together. I had a mouthful of dirt, and I was rolling around on her with nowhere else to go. My trusty right leg was on fire. To save my pride, I stood up smartly, noticing that Phil had wisely braked just before takeoff. Laughter erupted from us as we honored another experiment gone awry. The front forks of my bike had turned to spaghetti. I jumped on Phil's crossbar and we rushed to meet the van. My pain and bruises lasted for a few days. We took our bike to Kelwood for welding and overhaul. Our ramp story spread, energized our schoolyard for a few days, then disappeared into the mists of time, replaced by other daredevil stories.

Once or twice a year, we'd ride our bikes into the hills west of us, heading up Highway 19 toward Clear Lake. Going up the hills tested our strength, and our turnaround point was the fire lookout tower about ten miles into the hills. We'd pack a lunch and leave early and eagerly for the adventures ahead, which might include seeing elk, deer and perhaps a bear. Bears were especially energizing, for we'd heard stories about them chasing and eating people. We knew mama bears with cubs were especially prone to anger, and our escape plan, if we were confronted by one, was to head downhill as fast as we could. If the bear chased us all the way home, we hoped to lure it near our bull, and let the bull go after it. Or maybe the bear would eat our ornery cow.

I have a clear recollection of one such ride. The sky was clear, Dad volunteered to do all the milking, and we headed west on the gravel road. Passing the Beairsto farm was an important milepost, for they lived in a lovely white home that looked like the pictures I'd seen of southern plantations. They had newer farm equipment parked in rows, and black, carefully tilled soil. We were hoping to see them in their new Oldsmobile, and when we didn't, we figured they were off on another trip to places unknown.

Five miles west of our farm, we rode through the impressive, decorative entrance to the Riding Mountain National Park, with its varnished logs high above us. They were connected on either side to a small office, occupied by the forest ranger who checked things over and collected tickets. He knew our dad, wanted to know how our crops were doing, and reminded us not to break any speed limits.

The gate reminded us that we'd left civilization and were entering a no man's land, the home of animals wilder, stronger and faster than we were. We didn't have our rifles, yet felt ready to take on all comers. We were hockey players, habituated to surprising moves, and knew how fast we could ride downhill. We were sweating as we pumped up the hills, stopping every few minutes for water and rest.

Imagining climbing the fire tower empowered us to keep going. When we arrived, we barely rested, then started to climb the vertical, metal ladder that reached into the scary blue. Each time we visited, we climbed higher, and on this day we were old and brave enough to make it to the very top. I trembled as I opened the small, wooden trapdoor at the top of the ladder, pushing it aside and crawling through. Even though Phil was two years younger, as I watched his face he seemed to have less fear than I, and followed me into the tower.

We were on top of the world, up where Bobby flew his bombers, up near where God lived. Along the eastern horizon, we could see the blue of Lake Manitoba, and I was frightened that I was high enough to see so far. We spotted our red barns, and white home and other landmarks. Soon it was time to face our fears of backing down the steep ladder. We slid through the trapdoor, putting it back in place while holding the ladder with only one hand, then snaillike, crawled carefully back to earth.

The ride downhill was free, and on this day, we again started to race, to test our limits, especially on the curves. We had only rear-wheel brakes, and in the loose gravel we rode on the edge of disaster. At times Phil was ahead, but as the older brother I couldn't allow this, so I passed him, only to have him get me on the next corner. On my favorite sharp corner, I got the jump on him and surged ahead into the silence of the hills. Quickly I realized that I was very much alone, and Phil was somewhere in the hills above. I had images of bears grabbing him and started back up the mountain.

Then I heard him screaming, and my fears changed to terrified panic. I imagined a mama bear tearing at him, saw him bashing it with his fists and pitching rocks at it. I surged upward on my bike, just as he appeared around a corner and flashed by me, white-faced, gravel shooting from his tires. From his scrambled yelling, I deciphered the words, *My chain broke! My chain broke!* He was a speeding ghost, vanished downhill, headed hell-bent-for-leather to the flat land, the comfort of prairie. There were no chasing bears, only his screams as his runaway bike streaked homeward.

I leapt on my bike, hoping to catch him, wanting to save him by zipping up behind and grabbing his shirt and using my brakes to slow him down. As I leaned around the first curve, I realized that I was risking my own life, and couldn't match his hellish speed. I could no longer hear his screams, and around each corner expected to find him mangled in a ditch.

Riding as fast as I could, I was praying to Jesus, over and over, fearfully sobbing as I skidded my way downwards, blaming myself for not being able to save him.

As I rounded the last corner, near the gate, I saw him sitting by the road with an odd grin on his dusty face—the grin of someone who has looked into the face of death and won. Gratitude infused me, and I gave it voice: *Thank you Jesus. Thank you Jesus*

Sitting in the ditch, he told me that after his chain broke, he started walking his bike downhill. Like me, he was fearful of bears and scrambled aboard his bike, using his shoe to push against and brake the front wheel. The bike and the downward rush were too great, and his foot tired. *And I let her run, I let her go.* With his new life before him, he happily described how he'd managed to navigate the turns and stay upright.

Using the small rope we packed, we tied our bikes together, and riding behind him I was able to use my brakes down the last hills. When the hills gave way, we took turns towing each other the rest of the way. Our barnyard, our home had never felt more sweet.

CHAPTER 16

School Days, School Days

School days, school days,
Dear Old Golden Rule days
Reading and 'riting and 'rithmetic
Taught to the tune of a hickory stick
You were my queen in calico
I was your bashful barefoot beau
And you wrote on my slate, "I love you so,"
When we were a couple of kids.

WILL COBB AND GUS EDWARDS 1907

OUR FATHER ENJOYED singing the old *School Days, School Days* song quoted above. He had a sweet voice, pitched at the high end of Irish tenor. As we worked, he would often toss out a line of poetry or sing a bit of a song.

As a small dirt farmer, he knew where he stood, and did not stand, in the order of things.

The Lord, in His grand strategy, had sized Dad to his little plot of land. He was shy to the bone, and rarely let his voice out with any volume, being mindful to not take up too much space, not to crowd or infringe on anyone. I may have heard him shout a few times at an errant cow or horse, but that's it.

He liked to whistle as he worked, especially with a swinging milk pail in cadence with his tune. At other times he'd hum like his bees. When he sang, like his violin playing, the sound was thinly muted, floating into space softly and tenderly, just like the lines from a favorite hymn: *softly and tenderly Jesus is calling, calling for you and for me.*

Perhaps as compensation, I'd sing at maximum volume when there was no one around to hear me; if Dad was fearful of his voice, I could make up for it. One day, returning alone from a rabbit hunt a few miles east of our farm, I filled the prairie skies with the song, *Once I Had A Secret Love.* It takes massive volume to fill a big sky, but I was doing it, and with passion, for I was fifteen and in love for the first time. The snow-covered prairie and the big sky knew I was in love, but I couldn't share my soul fire with my family. The rabbits, I fancy, were merely frightened by the sound of high-pitched thunder out of season.

(These days, windows doubly snugged shut, I become Pavarotti in my car. Luckily my car came equipped with a chorus of thousands. At times I am so swept up in it, I fling my arms from the steering wheel as I hear the audience applauding. It's really not funny. It's dangerous.)

Our dad was seventeen when the *School Days* song was written, in 1907. I was always so nostalgic when he sang the song, and it seemed he was too. I imagined him in a small schoolroom and hoped that perhaps he had loved a girl in calico.

I want to know, want to ask and say: *Dad, did you have such an early love? And what was her name? And did she really wear calico? And whatever became of her? Do you still think of her? Maybe she still thinks of you!* My heart longings, my curiosity, never ripened into words, for such matters could not be talked about.

I hear him now, as he feeds his cows, singing of his girl in calico, his voice trailing off like the dying notes of a Highland Piper out of breath.

Just as I loved the sweetness of calico love, I cringed when I thought of children being hit with a hickory stick. I could hear the sound, hear the cries and whimpers, as a big person stuck a defenseless child.

Dad! Did you and your friends get hit a lot? How hard would they hit you, and how much did it hurt? Did you want to hit and scream back? How did you ever survive those tough times?

What I could not think or say: *I want to know you, Dad! I want to hear that golden harvest of words from your soul, about how you felt, what all these things meant to you.*

Let's fill a granary with words!

୫

Like our parents, we attended a one-room school house, a mile from our home, shorter when we cut across the fields in winter and when they were dry enough for walking.

Stark and alone on the flat windswept prairie, unprotected by trees, stood our little school, defiant in the face of the blizzards and thunderstorms that ruled the land.

Some hopeful person had planted a windscreen of small trees, but like most Manitoba trees they remained shriveled, afraid to grow and take their chances. The last time my son and I visited our farm and town in 2003, the trees, like the whole town itself, had lost the battle with Mr. North Wind, leaving only ghostly memories. Mr. North Wind? I'd rather think that when I left, the town died.

A stone's throw east of our school was the old, slouching grocery store, its legs long given out. It was owned by the Dubinsky family who lived in a couple of rooms in the rear, with the standard outhouse in back—ten miles back in wintertime.

The Dubinsky family was part of the wave of Ukrainian immigrants that fled to Canada after the world wars. Our elders were fearful they were all communists, but the Dubinsky family kept a well stocked store and extended credit without complaints about late payments. As kids, we were not concerned about communists. Besides, our new storekeepers gave us candy, and they had a beautiful daughter named Nadia. Indeed, Nadia was so lovely she aroused a new kind of fear in me.

Two stone throws east of the store were the church, the post office, the railroad tracks and grain elevator. That was Norgate in her glory days, before the decline into old age, when no amount of makeup could save her.

I'm not big on numbers, but I have a passing interest in demography, so here we go: the population of Norgate consisted of one school teacher, who was a fitful resident for nine months or less. Then the Dubinsky family of four—who may or may not have been communists—and the Sul family of two, who dwelt in a small home with a cubicle room for the post office. The pastor commuted from McCreary, eight miles north, and cannot count as a resident. Mr. Cripps who ran the elevator for most of my growing-up years, lived a few miles west, but we knew he napped in his office, so he fits as perhaps a quarter full-time resident of the town.

So there it is: the total population of Norgate averaged somewhere between seven and a-quarter and eight and three-quarters people, depending on how we run the numbers. And I'm being generous here. Depending on blizzards and all, around four in the afternoon, when the mail roared in, carried by a huffing-puffing steam engine, we could witness a horse traffic jam of perhaps twenty people, with thirty or so horses. Throw fifteen or more barking dogs into the mix, and we have a typical Fifth Avenue crowd. Except dressed differently.

Our classic one-room school house was actually a bit more than that. In addition to the classroom there were two cloakrooms—one for the girls and one for the boys—where we hung our heavy winter parkas and stashed our snow boots. In the basement at the foot of the stairs, were two toilets, each with a large bucket that might be emptied a few times a year.

On a good day, when we were all present, fifteen to twenty of us sat in neat rows, little kids at the back. We usually had a few eighth graders, some repeating the class for the second and third time because of missed classes due to harvesting and other farm duties.

As a wee tyke I'd sit in the back, trying to comprehend what the teacher was writing on the blackboard for the seventh and eighth graders. Once my lessons were done, I filled the hours by sketching war planes with smoke coming from their guns, each with the prominent circles of the Royal Canadian Air Force. Most of my planes had the number 3378 on them, for that was the number on our Harvard plane, purchased by Bob, after he returned from the war.

I have a prized photo of our class, all properly seated, taken by an itinerant photographer when I was eight or nine. My sister Helen and my brother Phil are in the picture. With our fourteen classmates, we gaze innocently into the camera, peering into our secret futures.

Sadly, for one of us, the future collapsed a year later when Leonard Finnimore, at only fifteen, died from a heart condition. He peers at the camera like the rest of us, each of us trusting time, trusting life. I'm fourteen and cry shy tears at his funeral, then more, as I stand shaking in the snow, watching the hearse drive west toward the hills to his final home in winter's cold sod. I wonder if he'll be buried near our mother.

On the north side of our school were two outdoor toilets used during the tentative spring and fall seasons. Immediately east of the school was the diminutive cabin where our teacher lived. It had a couple of little windows and a black stovepipe peeping like a periscope from the roof. As a child, it seemed to me teachers had many eyes and I wondered if they could watch us through that pipe. At times it seemed to turn to peer at us, but it may have been the wind playing with it. Like the school, the pathetic cabin had no running water, no bath or shower, and the teacher used the school toilets.

Understandably, most teachers stayed a year or less: the prison cell of cabin, the pittance of salary, the unruly big boys and the embalming cold were, each by itself, reason enough to escape somewhere else, anywhere else,

Along the east boundary of our schoolyard and just west of the grocery store was a decrepit barn for sheltering the horses that carried or pulled many of us to school. As cars became more common, the barn served as another fort, or igloo, and as a place for rafter swinging, and hide and go seek.

The cruel hands of winter wrung the life out of everything. In the mornings, our inkwells and fountain pens would routinely be frozen and unusable. If only moderately frozen, we'd clasp them and blow hot breath on them, nursing the ink back to liquid form. When this failed, we'd rest them on the heater vent in the floor—where they might fall into the void below.

Located in the basement was an iron furnace, encased in bricks that streamed the heat up to the floor vent. During the long winters, we burned many cords of wood, and occasionally coal—Alberta coal. Older boys, in seventh and eighth grades, stoked the fire two at a time, and I could hardly wait until I was old enough to do this. One of them could raise a hand at any time, and just walk right out of class to check the furnace. I liked to take a bathroom break when the older boys tended the fire. I'd take a quick peak down the stairs and see them standing with their feet crossed like real men, and perhaps puffing away on an early cigarette.

In early mornings, the classroom was barely warmer than outdoors, and until the room warmed we'd leave our parkas and felt boots on. One teacher had the brilliant idea of having us form a circle and run around the classroom, passing over the warm air vent, circulating the air as we laughed and whirled about. This was a fun break from sitting and doing math, and it became a winter ritual, passed on to the next teacher.

The school basement had a tall storage bin for firewood that could be filled from an outside door. The older boys would fill this with wood every few months. When I reached seventh grade, I came to appreciate that stacking wood in our basement was a real prize, for when we reached the top of the pile, we were next to the girls' cloak room. I recall sitting silently with my buddies in this privileged world, my head bumping the ceiling, holding my breath, enchanted by the magic of girls talking, hoping I'd learn something of their secret world.

Class started at nine, often later when blizzards possessed the land. During recess and lunch breaks, we played soccer, baseball, snow hockey and homespun games made up on the spot. In spring, we'd haul buckets of water to drown out the gophers that infested our schoolyard. We raced our bikes and used them for tag. Spinning around in mud holes was great fun.

During winter months, we built snow forts, igloos, caves and tunnels. Usually, there were large snow banks for sliding. We also played soccer in winter, and at times the north wind would sweep our ball across the yard to the grocery store, or clear to the church or railroad tracks. We'd fly after the errant ball, and once retrieved, on our way back we might hit the grocery store for a bit of candy.

In 1948, the year after Mother died, Helen, Phil and I joined our older sister Jean, riding the train to Sprague, in the southeast part of the province, about three hundred miles from our Norgate home. We thought of the Sprague area as bush country, as it had few open farm fields, and large forested areas with thick undergrowth and wild critters.

The Golden Branch School, five miles north of Sprague, like most schools, had one classroom, with the usual outhouses. Unlike our Norgate School, it was surrounded by woods and had a warmer, more rustic feel. When the McLeod family arrived, the student population jumped to over fifteen, and our sister Jean was the teacher. She had taught at other schools and ended up at Golden Branch, for that little enclave also had a church where they preached the only true gospel.

We learned quickly enough that this church had more and better truth than our fiery clutch of believers at Norgate. The church had a modest steeple with a cross on it, and was heated by the hellfire screaming sermons. When the headache-long services were over, we were happy to forget about hellfires and enjoy each other, along with meat, potatoes, gravy and pie for dessert.

My sisters, brother and I were silently grieving the loss of Mother, facing each day with a remarkable determination to get on with life. I had never heard whippoorwills before, and their mournful piping from the night forest deepened my grieving and comforted me. During those long nights, I'd fall asleep to their cries. They were voicing my grief for a mother lost—grief I could not express for fear I'd die too.

If we could transcribe sounds onto national flags, the sound of the whippoorwill and the loon, next to the maple leaf on the Canadian flag, would capture the two sounds so common in the north country. Both sounds are unique and filled with a soulful longing impossible to fill, and thus they go on and on.

After a year at the Golden Branch School, Helen, Phil and I moved back to Norgate to complete our schooling. Thus began the era when we batched at times, doing our own cooking and housework, interspersed with various housekeepers. Jean was away, teaching at various schools, and Helen would sometimes be with her, leaving Dad, Phil and I to fend as we could. Canned tomato soup, toast and cheese made up too many of our lunches and suppers. Oatmeal, toast, honey or jam, and black tea for breakfast.

After grade eight, each of us by turn went to Kelwood High School, five miles south. Depending on the weather and season we walked, rode our bikes or took the school van. Usually we rode in the van. It was nothing but a diminutive, wooden box with wheels. When the snow flew, a couple of men would sling the box onto a horse-drawn sleigh, like the ones used for hauling wood and other cargo. The sleighs had four wooden runners, usually with metal surfaces on the bottom, and were pulled by a team of horses—horses that were also ambivalent about school, and had to be urged on with shouts of encouragement and much snapping of the leather lines used to steer them.

The weathered van that housed our budding generation of scholars was perhaps twelve feet long, and seven feet wide, with a wooden frame covered with canvas. Inside, a narrow bench ran along each side of the van, and in the middle sat a small metal stove, about a foot wide and two feet high, into which we stuffed a lot of wood in an attempt to ward off the subzero temperatures. This was an honest-to-god, full gospel stove: hissing, puffing and glowing red, and a grim reminder of hellfires.

Kelwood school district had several van routes, each picking up six or ten students along the roads that fed into the school. Each route was five to ten miles long. Many van drivers stayed in town for the day, housing their horses in a warm barn. Sitting in school, struggling with math or geography, my monkey mind would inevitably wonder what the van drivers did during the day. Small town rumors were not as biting as blizzards, yet they had their own cutting edge, and swirled about with life-threatening gossip. We heard about excessive beer drinking, and illegal betting at the pool hall and more.

The prairie has many songs, and one of them was the squeaking, soprano notes made by sleigh runners when the thermometer mercury drops out the bottom. With the soft thrumming from the sound of the horse harness and the chatter of children, we were an orchestra, an unheralded choir, weaving across the snowy fields.

Occasionally, a horse would get spooked and a van would experience a runaway; apart from a few moments of panic, most students were happy to miss some school time. Stories of runaways were told and retold, becoming more runaway in the telling, offering respite from the routine flatness of prairie life.

The fiery gospel stove was a constant hazard. In our bulky parkas, we'd scrunch together, crowding our feet as close as possible to the glow, as the snow on our felt boots sizzled into the air. If our felt boots were too hot, they'd notify us with steamy smells. We also warmed our mittens by the stove, and if the fire was down, toss them on top of the stove for a minute or two. Inevitably a mitten would go up in flames, crying for help and smelling like a dying sinner.

Like hellfires, and indeed farming itself, our van stove balanced on the edge of survival and death, and all three invite a type of reckless tempting of fate. Often our roads were blocked by massive snowdrifts, and we'd turn around prior to getting to town. Each storm added new snowdrifts, and we'd look for new openings, new routes we might take. The navigation skills of Mr. Gower, our van driver, were tested over and over. Our laughter, our trail of steaming horse turds, and the smoke from our stovepipe marked our passing, as we plied around and over snow banks, teeter-tottering our way as well as we could.

After a northern howler, the drifts of snow guaranteed a challenging trip, depending on the skill of the driver and other things that could only be vectored out in physics class. When snow was piled high enough, we'd head for the open fields, which meant crossing fences—some buried in the snow, others showing a top strand that could snag the leg of a horse or the van. A few of us would leap forth, and using our heavy winter boots, stomp the barbed wire down and stand on it, while the horses and van crossed over it.

Barbed wire is sharp and has a sense of mischief, and as we stood on it, holding it down, it might slip from under our snow boots and pop up under the van, hooking it so that we could not proceed. If the wire slipped from underfoot at just the right moment, it would take time to untangle it, and that meant we'd miss some school time. I'd swear, but not too loudly, when this happened it was always accidental.

The snarl of the north wind, combined with a knot of kids in a small van with a hot fire is a dangerous combination, and reflects a lack of rules and regulations. That was characteristic of our lives: wild and unruly much of the time. Inevitably, the day came when the balance of life and death reached a tipping point, and fate threw some dice across our trail.

Mr. Irv Gower, our van driver, knew the value of silence and may have been a monk in a former life. He made a miscalculation one day and the van ended up precariously balanced on a precipice of a large snow bank. Because we lived on the edge a lot, and had an intimate knowledge of sledding, we automatically moved to the high side of the van to keep it from going over. This time things were more edgy than normal, and we held our breath, waiting to see what the next moment would bring. Breaking his vow of silence, Mr. Gower asked a few of us to slither out as tenderly as possible, to brace the van from tumbling over.

My brother Phil, Nels Arvidson, and I saw the possibilities and were quick to volunteer. We crawled toward the rear door as gingerly as we could, and eased ourselves into the deep freeze. As we moved to our task, our years of team sports meant we moved with one mind. As hockey players, we were especially primed for coordinated and explosive moves. Acting as one, without words, we moved to the high side of the van and wordlessly, with the merest touch of our milking fingers, nudged it over—just to see what would happen. It was another experiment. We were always doing experiments, some with better results than others.

When fields are blanketed with snow, silence is deeply sweet, and from my hunting days I know that the crack of a rifle sounds like the end of the world. On this snow-muffled morning, when the van tipped over all on its own, it was like a rifle shot: the smaller kids were screaming and crying and above that, all vows of silence forgotten, Mr. Gower's voice filled the prairies with curses and pleas.

Possibly because of gravity, the hellfire coals had spilled from the stove and the laughter that started in our throats died as we realized the danger. Ever-ready farmboys, we sprang to the task, opening the back door, helping the little kids out; then, like the gophers of summer, we bent over, and from between our legs blasted snow onto the coals. Smoke and steam poured from the van that now carried burn marks as testimony to the hazards of winter, and another hellish experiment.

Within a few minutes all was under control. The prairies and Mr. Gower had fallen again into proper silence. We righted the van, steadying it as we moved it from its balance place, then crawling back in, we proceeded on to school. Now we were fully awake and energized for a full day of studying history and the rest of the stuff.

We often faced danger, and surviving the fall of our van was not as scary as it might seem. Our guardian angels were once again on duty: none of us were *the worse for wear* as we often said. Mr. Gower, realizing he was responsible for the upset, broke silence again and asked us for the impossible: *Kiddies, I don't want you telling anyone. Let's pretend this never happened, eh?*

The rest of our ride was warm with whispered giggles and knowing smiles. Even the little tykes, with their limited knowledge of science, seemed to know why the van had fallen like humpty-dumpty, but none of us could voice the truth as long as Mr. Gower was present. As well as we could, we muffled the laughter and excitement that, with our first recess, would fill our schoolyard and ring across white fields all the way to the blue hills.

At recess and lunch hour we went over the story again and again, each of us adding details, as the snow bank got bigger and bigger, the fire hotter and hotter. When school was out, we went with our friends to show them the proud burn marks on the van, and to add more details about how lucky we were to survive. Like other wild adventures, this was part of our group lore for many days, until it was replaced by something else that set us spinning in new directions.

Despite, or perhaps because of all the ups and downs of life, we each find our way, as children and adults. Each of us face both open and closed doors, and they are equally challenging. I'm proud to say I graduated at the top of my grade eleven class, and have in my office an official piece of paper documenting the twenty-five dollar scholarship that came with that honor. If, like my family and friends, you get my humor, you'll ask how many were in my class, just to get a handle on how smart I really was, along with a chuckle.

I was pure country cream, risen to the top of a class of four. Some cream. Some milk. Four innocent country bumpkins, standing in a row, at the award ceremony. We were too old to suck our thumbs, so we just grinned as we wondered what might happen next. I was barely an average student. All four of us were gifted at milking cows, cleaning barns and stacking hay, with nary a scholarly bone among us.

Somehow I'd pranked, pimpled, parlayed and pondered my way through eleven grades, and accidentally won an award for my troubles.

It is an honor for me to relate the most important thing that happened to me at Kelwood High. More clear than the memories shared above are those of a great teacher who forever changed my life. My images of him are colored with love and gratitude, mixed with remorse and shame for the troubles I caused him.

Many of us were blessed to have a school teacher who inspired us in a special way, and as we recall that person we feel appreciation and love. Gifted teachers open a portal to the song of life, and when we find such a person we more fully join the great symphony, with our teacher as conductor and us piping along behind.

We know that even the most subtle daily experience makes some imprint on us, altering cells, genes and neurons. Gifted teachers literally alter our cells, and even when we don't consciously remember them, they are nonetheless recorded in the unconscious, ongoing operations of our brain, body, heart and soul. This is the nature of cellular memory.

The most important school teacher in my life was Jean Solomon Moreau. I say his name with reverence, and to honor him: Jean Solomon Moreau. His middle name captures his intrinsic wisdom, but says nothing about his dancing brown eyes, his radiant love, his lively wit and the playful smile that radiated from his face.

His loving influence on me can be measured in part by the way he continues to jump alive in my conscious mind, and I am startled by the clarity of his presence—images reinforced by the pictures of him that occasionally roll up on my computer. The wrinkles and warp of time have not altered him one whit: he stands in my inner classroom, inhabiting my soul as he did in real life, one hand on his hip, the other gesturing to make a humorous point or to raise a question, engaging me intently, inviting me to enter into a dialogue that was at once serious, playful and irreverent.

I watch him as he stands within: his back has a subtle and unusual bend, offset by weak stomach muscles that pooch out a bit, the result of many months in an iron lung as a youngster with polio. He has a flattop haircut and routinely dresses in conservative grays and browns. As I write this, I stand up from my desk and try to imitate his standing posture, and I feel inadequate in my attempt. At my age, I have a creeping belly, yet his had a unique curve I can't capture. As clear as he is in my mind, as fully as he inhabits me, I struggle to capture the way his body inhabited space and time.

As minutes, hours and days roll through us, we take much for granted, and can't see the larger impact of the present moment. Only later, perhaps years later, as we reflect back, we see more clearly and with more appreciation the impact of a person and of different events and stages in our lives. This has been my experience with Mr. Moreau. During the time I knew him, I simply could not see or appreciate how his life was altering mine.

He opened great doors in my life, and with his humor and word play, he stretched my mind and heart. Many times I've wondered why he reached out to my brother Phil and me, why we were so special, whey he loved us so. Even though I don't recall this, we surely must have been his favorite pupils, for he could not have had enough time or books to share with our peers, as he did with us.

September, 1955: I am sixteen, wearing my farmer's shirt and jeans, and stroll into his classroom. I'm disarmed by his goofy smile, and the way he slouches with one hand on his hip. His pants and shirt are clean, fashionable—a city guy for sure. He surveys me with his cow-brown eyes, taking me in all at once it seems, and I go shy, lower my head and take my seat. I cannot know it, but this is the first step, the first day of long journey that has no end. This odd man who radiates warm mischief and curiosity is a vital door to my future life. This mystery is secreted to both of us.

In the next few months, I don't want to acknowledge that he seems to favor Phil and me, lavishing us with attention over our peers for reasons I can't fathom. He reaches out, reaches out, over and over to us. I am not an easy reach, for I'm a trickster, punster, a mercurial, coyote character from early childhood, and Phil has these characteristics too.

In my inner conversations, with him as a listener, I've wondered: did he feel a kinship with me because of my playful humor? What, who did he see under the tricks and problems I caused him? Did he love us more because he knew we were motherless? Did he think we were more troubled than our peers, and thus offered a hand to help us out? I was puckish and prankish and he too had these traits, and this helped us connect.

These sorts of questions constitute a vital part my personal and professional passion in life. As I puzzle over the complexities of relationships, past and present, I'm filled with gratitude for the gracious tolerance of others, and the love that has been, and is extended to me, even when I've acted badly. My puzzlement hangs in the thin air of history, along with similar questions many of us have about the past when we attempt to fathom the twists of life.

As I see it, there can be no absolute or clear answers to such questions, yet we might have an answer in the form of a general knowing that is deep and sure, and with Mr. Moreau this is the case. With him, as with much of my life, I look back and choose to believe that I was truly lucky and blessed, and that a larger wisdom was guiding and calling me into his life.

His love and interest was such that he continued reaching out to Phil and me for twenty-some years after the one magnificent year he spent at Kelwood High. As with most of our teachers, one year in the boonies was enough, for they'd then disappear, happy to escape, never to be heard from again. The case was entirely different with Mr. Moreau; he left after a year, but he stayed in our lives for the next twenty-four years.

After he moved back to Winnipeg, his first letters began arriving at our little post office. His handwriting was pure art, done with a fountain pen, and with artistic flourishes. His letters were erudite, supportive and witty, and I still have a dozen or so and count them among my sacred objects from the past.

He insisted we come and see him, and as we did so, he shifted our relationship away from the formal rules of teacher and student, informing us we must give up the *Mr. Moreau* and call him Chuck. He took us to fancy restaurants and encouraged us to have a sip of wine with him. In the late 1960's, I was blessed to introduce him to my new bride, Samona Ruth, hoping he'd love her as he loved me—and of course he did.

One of my favorite pictures is of Chuck, Phil and me, sitting at an outdoor table in the Gatineau Mountains outside of Ottawa, where he had insisted on taking us on a picnic. As he routinely did, before our trip we shopped at his favorite farm market where he handled the produce with studied hands, checking for freshness and asking questions of the proprietor. That day in the Gatineau, we had special burgers with fresh veggies, and the picture shows the requisite bottle of red wine, wrapped in newspaper to disguise it from any patrolling wardens.

On that same trip, he took us to the famous Ottawa Tulip Festival, and several pictures show us amongst the tulips. My favorite photo shows Phil and Chuck, kneeling low to the ground, only their faces showing amidst the tulips—the sweet flowers of life.

Ruthie and I saw him several times in the sixties and into the mid-seventies, at which time we drifted apart. I superficially thought he was no longer in my life, and of course as I matured, I came to realize in many ways he was still quite alive in me. I'd pick up a book and think of him. I'd see his face, his smile, when I heard certain music.

It was obvious he was a *true man of letters*—to use a quote from him—a scholar of literature, fluent in both French and English, stunningly informed about history and many other things. He was familiar with a vast range of music, had over 3000 vinyl records in his home, could name any piece of music he heard and add footnotes about the composer and more. After his move to Ottawa, he helped start and became part of a TV program for high school students, in the form of a quiz show. He could quote many passages from literature, and was armed with a volley of jokes, some ribald enough to set my young cheeks blushing. He was a gourmet cook and a lover of fine wine and the occasional cigar.

I don't recall my first impressions of him, but before long, as happens when we enter loving relationships, he was a living image, a guiding voice in my head. Only a few months after he became our teacher, he started sending Phil and me home with various books numbering in the dozens, ranging from science fiction, to novels, to history books and classic literature. He had made paper covers for many of his books, and I've cherished and carried a few of these across the decades.

Two of the pieces of music he gave Phil and me continue to soften me, sometimes to tears. One of these was Kirsten Flagstad, singing Gounod's *Oh Divine Redeemer.* I played it repeatedly on my portable record player in the small, third-floor apartment Phil and I shared, at 864 Winnipeg Avenue. I was enraptured by the beauty of the music and her voice, and handled the recording with careful fingers. Just a few days ago this piece played on our car radio, and my wife and I fell silent, surrendering to the profound sweetness of that song. As often happens when we listen to sacred music, we both had tears of gratitude and wonder that anything could be so lovely, moving and inspiring.

The other most memorable piece was the violin concerto *Introduction et Rondo Capriccioso,* composed by Saint-Saens. This song had a repetitive, lilting quality that gave me images of the skipping stones we flung across our pond.

The most distinctive book he gave me is a hefty, green-clad, musty tome of the complete works of William Shakespeare, published in 1951 and 1376 pages long. I pull it from my bookcase as I write this, and again and I see Mr. Moreau's smiling approval.

The gift card that came with the Shakespeare book captures much of who he was, and of his love for me, and a few of his words I recall even today, for they imprinted themselves in me.

I pull the book from its shelf, and read the words that reveal much of him:

Christmas 1957. Merry Christmas Albert!
An English-speaking gentleman of culture begins his private library with the acquisition of three basic works: a Bible, a good English dictionary, and the works of Shakespeare. I am presuming much, but I hope this grain that I sow will grow into a fine collection, and above all, produce a well-furnished mind. I don't expect that this book will give you much "fun" just now, but over a longer period Shakespeare should provide you with as much deep pleasure as I constantly get from my own copy.

Following this is the embellished initial of his first name, *C*, written with a flourish in black ink.

As I scan the book, I find markings on the pages of only four plays, at least one of them for a college class, for I note the date of Feb. 27, 1962 at Evangel College. After high school and college, the only Shakespeare I've read are brief passages, usually a sonnet that springs like a rose in other contexts. While I've been happy to imbibe the fragrance of Old Bill Shakespeare (as I once called him to get a rise out of Mr. Moreau) I've not lingered in the garden—despite the gift of his book and the fact he also shepherded our class to see a few of the bard's traveling plays in Neepawa.

At the top of page 263, from *As You Like It,* I wrote a phrase from the play that gripped me: *We that are true lovers run into strange capers...,* and as I read this I smile, for I see how this line captures a core part of me, and how I've lived my life.

Another book from Mr. Moreau is authored by Bertrand Russell and bears the title *Mysticism and Logic.* As with other books he gave me, this one has a cover he made from special paper, and the title and author's name are in his handwriting. Inside on page ninety-five I discover his imprimatur pressed into the paper, made by an impressive personal metal stamp bearing his name. He marked his books with this stamp, and I sense this as symbolic of the lasting mark he made in my life.

A third book that stands out is a red leather-bound book of poetry, printed in England, but without a publication date. Mr. Moreau's inscription, printed in careful gold ink from a fountain pen, reads: *Presented to Albert McLeod, for best essay, Water for Kelwood, 1955.* His attention to detail is evident, for he inscribed this with special gold ink, now faded. The spine of the book needs serious repair.

The city fathers of Kelwood were thinking of building a central water system, and Mr. Moreau thought it would be a good idea to have input from students, so he devised a contest. On a good year we only had twenty or so kids in the four grades of high school, and I'm not sure if everyone wrote an essay. In any case, given the love and kindness Mr. Moreau had for me, he would not be an impartial judge.

I don't recall reading any of the hundred and more poems from this book, and it bears only a few of my underlines in the preface. As I leaf through it now, I want to pick a poem to help commemorate Mr. Moreau and the time we shared. My eyes fall on a poem entitled, *A Boy's Song,* by James Hogg. As I read this poem, it seems serendipitous, for it not only describes many experiences from farm days, it also refers to a boy named Billy, and in this way also honors our brother Billy.

Another special gift from Chuck to me, is a charcoal portrait of myself at age seventeen. He had many gifted friends, and one was an artist whom he commissioned to sketch my face. I felt honored as I sat there with a lovely female artist drawing my face; I've saved this sketch as another sacred gift from my great teacher.

Mr. Moreau gave me unabashed support in my athletic activities. I intuited that he never played sports, mainly due to his bout with polio, and also assumed he loved my athletic skills the more because of this.

I was fast on my feet, and though I was less than average in hockey, I scored more than my share of touchdowns and soccer goals. We occasionally traveled the short distance to either the towns of McCreary or Birnie to play football, and he'd come along with a pile of us in one of the cars, to cheer us on. I remember in one game, after I made a long run for a touchdown, as I went to the sideline he was laughing, and his eyes were beaming with love and pride for me and my skills. *Albert! How can you run so fast, and be so tricky?* His words inspired me to run faster, and to think of more daring plays.

Thinking back, another image arises, bringing a smile each time, for it involves a tricky baseball play, made in part because I knew he'd love it. I was playing third base and had a runner trying to nudge me off the bag—my bag. I wanted to get him out, and again fate helped me along.

When the next batter hit a ground ball right toward me, I scooped it up with a flourish, and made an exaggerated throw to first base—except I didn't throw the ball, knowing the runner standing next to me would take off for home. After my fake throw to first, I touched the runner who had left third base, then hurled the ball to first to score two outs. Just as I hoped, Mr. Moreau was convulsing with laughter. My bit of wizardry captured much of my coyote character, and was also a characteristic of Mr. Moreau and our playful relationship that darted here and there.

I've referred to the troubles Phil and I, and our fellow students created for our dear teacher, and I'm embarrassed to relate these, for some of them go far beyond casual mischief. All of the nasty things were done by boys, and I beg indulgence and understanding, for we were unruly farm kids, hormone-crazed hockey fiends, with an impulse for making rash moves and taking chances.

I begin with another coyote act of mischief: Mr. Moreau often brought an orange to lunch, along with a sandwich, and one morning I sneaked the orange from his lunch bag, filled our soccer pump with water, and injected it as copiously as I could at several points into the orange. My buddies thought this was such a funny idea, and we couldn't wait till lunchtime, when we surprised him by clustering close as he ate. We watched him eat the juiciest orange in the world, and his pants and the floor enjoyed the juice too. He must have known something was amiss, but he outfoxed us by not letting on. He likely suspected me.

In the face of my recriminations, I share some of our most reprehensible actions as a confession of sorts: one of the things we often did was to throw objects at Mr. Moreau as he wrote on the blackboard. These objects included bits of paper, mud from our shoes, bits of pencils and chalk. I cringe as I write this, and wonder: *what were we thinking?* On some days, the front of the class would be littered with our thrown objects, and Mr. Moreau, after an early round of reprimands that changed nothing, would go right on with his lecture. We were out of control, and he knew it and had no remedy, and we knew that.

In addition, we plastered the ceiling using the mud that clung to our heavy shoes. We'd roll the mud into small balls and toss them underhanded upwards, where they'd stick to the white ceiling. More fun was to use a ruler, drawing on Archimedes and his work with levers, properly explained to us by Mr. Moreau. We'd take our foot-long rulers, hang half over a desk with the mud ball on the opposite end. Then, holding the fulcrum point with a finger, with quick hockey hands, we'd smack the hanging end downward, launching the mud ball rapidly upwards, where it would stick on the ceiling. Because of what we were learning of physics, launching mud balls with rulers was not wanton mischief; it was an experiment.

It was tragic and comic all at once, to see our ceiling poxed with mud balls. As they dried they'd fall to the floor over the next few days or weeks. Mr. Moreau would be talking, and suddenly a mud ball would fall, and we'd either pretend nothing had happened—as he usually did—or we'd laugh, and sometimes he'd helplessly laugh along. These were days of high innocence, and we pretended to have no idea how the mud could have elevated itself to the ceiling. A piece of mud would fall to the floor, and we'd look at each other, our faces ripe with the question: *Where did that come from? How can mud fall from the sky?*

One day, when Mr. Coyote danced around in me, I created a cannon to launch real missiles, using the crutch that I used after breaking my ankle on the day of infamy, December eighth, 1955. On idle for a few moments in class, I had an insight equal to the most creative moments of Archimedes when I realized my crutch would have serious throwing power; not a lever vast enough to move our planet, as the great physicist thought, yet a tool that would sling something bigger than a mud ball.

I was not entirely devoid of wisdom. I waited until Mr. Moreau left class, then I popped my crutch into the inkwell hole at the top right corner of my desk. In the same moment, I placed a book at the top, and invited Bob Habing, my buddy across the aisle, to pull on the bottom of the crutch while I stood and pulled the opposite way on the book at the top of our launcher. When the tension on the crutch reached maximum, I released the book, and it flew across the room, with pages flapping like an eagle in a killing dive, crashing loudly into the wall just below the window. Luckily a few students in our line of fire had dodged the missile. The scary thing was my desk suffered collateral damage, for it had cracked all the way across from the inkwell hole to the other side. When Mr. Moreau came back to class, I sat for the rest of the period with my arms over the crack. Then, at the end of the school day, I exchanged my desk for a spare from the back of the room. Once again I was blessed to escape punishment, for no one said a word about the cracked desk.

Another of the cruel tricks we played was to nominate a young woman we considered among our least attractive classmates as a queen candidate for our winter carnival. If I had to bet, I'd bet this was my idea, and all of us quickly supported it. With our votes, she won as carnival queen. Like most things in life this had a mixed outcome: over the few weeks of the contest, the young lady in question began dressing nicer, coiffing her hair in a cute way and wearing some makeup. I remember the cute necklace she started wearing, and as she started to look truly attractive, the guilt I had for our twisted humor was reduced to a comfortable level.

One of my favorite and more harmless escapades occurred one afternoon in class when I was bored yet again, as Mr. Moreau tried to hold our attention. Boredom was a plague for many of us, and we boys dealt with this common problem by cooking up various hues of mischief. On the day in question, I was reaching across the aisle, tossing things, passing notes and whatever. Mr. Moreau, who had patience beyond my understanding, was finally exasperated and warned me: *Albert, if I so much as catch you moving one more time you are going to the principal's office!!* The tone of his voice was uncharacteristically harsh, and his wagging finger left no doubt he meant it. This sobered me up for a few minutes. Convinced of my new sobriety, Mr. Moreau returned to weaving his lesson on the blackboard.

Predictably, the little devils in me soon started jumping around, demanding a hearing, and one of the dark critters led me to lean across the aisle and say something to my buddy Nels Arvidson. I must have whispered too loud, for the good Mr. Moreau whirled about from the blackboard and faced me with a fury I'd never seen. In that same moment, one of my pesky demons seized control of me and I froze with one arm out to Nels, a leg in the air, and my mouth bizarrely agape with an unspoken word. I bugged my eyes out, staring into thin air, never blinking. He'd warned me he better not catch me moving, and I'd turned into eternal marble. A long moment of astonished silence ensued as he peered at me with genuine curiosity, through his horn rims. I was holding my breath, hanging silently in a weird position where gravity, time and space stopped. The classroom had stilled, hypnotized by this new weirdness.

Mr. Moreau stared at me, and then, as he realized I'd won this round, his inevitable sense of play began lighting up his face, and he turned back to the blackboard shaking with laughter, muffling it as well as he could. I think he knew again, in that moment, that his only recourse with me was to go on loving me, working with my trickster as well as he could. In that moment I felt so pleased with myself, along with a deeper love for him and the compassion he showed me.

Beginning some years ago, I became more aware of how Chuck had opened my mind, heart and soul. He'd appear in my head in odd moments, standing in his familiar posture, talking to me, eyes sparkling with mirth playing across his face. As my awareness increased, and I started to catch my thoughts and bookmark them, I started to see how often loved ones, including Mr. Moreau, stir about in my head.

Now I could see it: all along I'd been indwelt, inhabited by those who loved me, and now I was becoming more conscious of how aswim I was, how past tides had pulled me. The dancing liquidity of neurons, of thoughts, of soul images, running with time, printing out in my mind.

The more I thought of Mr. Moreau, the more I wanted to thank him with spoken and written words. During my long teaching career, the words of gratitude from my students had touched me deeply, and I wanted to—I needed to—let him know in written and spoken words how he had changed my life. And so began my search, over the years, on the internet and by telephone. I did not pursue my quest with sufficient intention, and found no trace of him.

Then came the day when I again googled his name, and was excited to see it jump up, loud and clear on my computer. Sadly it was his obituary: he had passed away on July 12, 2007 in Ottawa, Ontario. I was awash in sadness and regret that he would never hear my outpourings of gratitude. I was reminded again of the words of our wisest teachers who encourage us to routinely express our thanks to those we love.

To help me remember, mourn and celebrate, I bought a CD of Saint-Saen's violin concerto and for the next few weeks played it, along with a few other songs that helped me soften and let my tears flow. As I listened, his soul was alive in my soul. A few nights after reading his obituary, Ruthie made polish stew, based on a recipe from Chuck. As we ate it, we thought of him and our love for him, and how he had flung so many life doors open to me.

I conclude this tribute to my great teacher by noting that while he had loving mirth for everyone, he had a clear preference for men, and all his roommates were male. Given my restricted and religious environment, I could not imagine anyone being gay until I matured enough to open my mind to the many expressions of love, beginning in the early and mid-seventies. My professional readings had stretched my mind to see the astounding diversity of life and love, especially when in the early 1970's a beloved friend shared that he was gay. My wife and I listened closely to his story, and the struggles he had with being gay, and from then on we were accepting and compassionate for those of different sexual orientations.

This gave us another reason to love and honor Chuck, knowing how he must have struggled with being in the closet during a time of profound cultural repression towards anyone who was not heterosexual. As I reflect on how much he loved me, I now realize part of his enduring love for me may have had romantic overtones. Given all he knew about me, and how much he loved me, he never once made any offensive gesture or comment to me. I love him today, in retrospect, all the more for his bountiful love expressed in so many ways to me.

With farm kids around the world, I joined the migration to city living, leaving for my final year of high school in the fabled 'Peg—Winnipeg, our capital city, a distant 150 miles away, and light years away in terms of life style.

The siren call of Winnipeg sounded more loudly when the Red River flooded the city in spring of 1950. Families with children were encouraged to leave the city, and the Confrey and Frend families arrived to live with us on the farm. Our brother Bob had married a city girl related to both families, and we were happy to have them be with us.

The two families that fled to our farm opened an archway to the rest of the world, and for this I am thankful. They arrived with laughter, fancy cars and clothes, cokes and snacks, and invited us to join the party. One year, for Dominion Day, they brought not only lots of goodies, they also had bags of fireworks, and we generated our own lightning storm in our front yard. For me this was another sign we were a family going places. The city people were my heroes. I liked how they thought, talked and walked.

After their brief time with us, they continued to come and see us every few months, and we'd clean our home and stare down the lane impatiently, hoping to catch a glimpse of their shiny car as they rounded the turn into our yard. The wait seemed so long. When we finally glimpsed them turning into our lane, we were ecstatic: *Bud and Ev, and Bill and May are here….they're here! Here they come! Here they come!* We'd sprint out to meet them, screaming, arms open in greeting.

They insisted we visit them in the city. We were eager to do this, and it also meant we had to clean up our act, and maybe buy a new shirt or pants. At that time, the 150-mile drive was an adventure replete with unknown risks, over dusty gravel roads in cars of questionable character. Often we had flat tires and other breakdowns. One time, coming up the road into Neepawa, our old and wheezing Chevy demanded several of us get out and push her up the hill.

We visited our city families a few times a year, and my brain caught the fire of bright lights, professional baseball games, French fries doused with white vinegar and the peopled avenues. Then the Confrey family invited me to live with them for my final year of high school. They lived in East Kildonan, a suburb of Winnipeg, and I enrolled at Miles MacDonnel Collegiate. They were truly my second family.

Many of us can recall axial shifts in our lives, solstice moments when our souls tilted further to the sun, and springtime colors blossomed within. Leaving our farm was this type of experience for me. The flooding of the mighty Red River cut a channel in my soul, inviting me to sail away from our tough farm life, and at seventeen I began plotting my escape.

As I thought of leaving the farm, I was torn with guilt: how could I leave my dad and Phil with all the work? I felt I was walking out on them, turning away, betraying them along with my grandparents and the sacred sod of home. As I did the chores, many thoughts and emotions rolled through me. I'd been entranced by the bright lights, had eaten from the forbidden apple, and knew I could not ever, ever stay on the farm.

I feared Dad would not let me go, so ahead of time planned a big lie that I felt would shock him into releasing me. One evening after milking, I blurted out my plans to go and live in the city, and all in one breath, before he could resist, I told him I must go lest I get a girl pregnant. He was properly shocked and agreed I must go, and that was that.

Again, a surprising flood of memories and an emotion I've never felt before: as I write this I tear up, and I want to apologize to my father for lying to him. Since May of 1969 he's been silent in his grave in far off Neepawa, there beside his silent wife. But in my mind, as I see his face, I imagine apologizing to him and setting the record straight.

My eyes drift up and leftward where his picture hangs in my office, with him sitting between Phil and me shortly after Mother died. We are dressed in our church-going best, ties and all. Dad looks forlorn, and stares at the camera without even a forced smile. The photo is framed in wood from our old barn, and touching it helps me go back: this is the barn of ten thousand hours, where Dad had devoted much of his life, milking, feeding, watering and cleaning his animals.

I take the photo from my wall, and use the corner of my shirt—an old farm habit—to dust off our faces, and as I look at my father I feel the words forming in my chest, my throat: *Dad, I'm sorry...I lied to you, and I'm sorry...* Then I go on to explain what I've said above, letting him know the farm was too small for my dreams, that I could not carry on as he wished.

The move to Winnipeg was an archway, a rabbit hole, a secret passage out of the flat prairies into the mountains and valleys of life, bigger than any dream I could have dreamt.

If a fortune teller had sat me down at age seventeen and laid out my life before me, I would have laughed and run off to tell others how silly she was.

❧

We played a game as children where we'd lace together the fingers of our hands with all the fingers pointing inward and down, except our index fingers would point upward in a prayerful way. Then we'd say: *Here is the church and here's the steeple, open it up and here are the people...* This game was widely known, for my wife also played it growing up in Houston. Now the church, the farm, and our little town have emptied of people.

Since the mid and late 1960's, when we spent many weekends at our farm while I was teaching summer classes at the University of Manitoba, I've lost touch with most everyone. Many from our area moved away to places unknown. I heard about different marriages, but at this point have forgotten who got hitched to whom. And of course life goes on: babies are born, and faithful Mr. North Wind sings his cold songs, and the run-for-cover thunderstorms still own the land.

CHAPTER 17

—— ❧ ——

First Loves

Life is a series of open and closed doors. Glancing back, we might see that the closed doors were as vital as the open ones. Pregnant with life, damp with rain, we journeyed one night hoping to find shelter, and were told there was no room at the inn. A great door closed on us. We know the story for it is our story. Yet, think of how different the story would be if that door had opened.

We know what it's like to be banished to the barns of life. We also know that humbling experiences can stabilize us, can help us find our guiding star. Letting go of pretense, being close to the earth, we can birth ourselves into a new beginning. me, again!

❧

THE SUMMER STORMS that swept down from the Riding Mountains were like old friends, and we slept through all but the most violent ones. My childhood ended with an inner storm that blew out of nowhere, throwing me into chaotic and unfamiliar territory. No one had forecast this storm, and our secrecy and shame prevented us from talking about flooding hormones. We were blessed to have plenty of books in our home, but none dared say a word about the unmentionable areas below our belt lines. I needed a manual, an idiot's guide to puberty.

I had watched our older brother, Bill, and his friends transform from playmates to men. Before puberty Bill was happy to play with us and be a regular brother. After his inner storm blew in, he swapped his bike for a car, forgot about his little brothers, and roared around chasing girls.

Where had little Bill gone? I was confused, for it happened so quickly. In a few short months an odd growl was noticeable in Bill's voice, as his childhood tenor fell away. Hair began sprouting from his face. Soon he was making a big deal about slathering shaving cream all over his face and shaving with Dad's razor. He developed a swagger, started smoking and spending nights away. Then I noticed beer on his breath. With his new muscles, he could lift two, even three bags of wheat at the same time. We had lost our playmate.

After Sister Rachael, our holy roller housekeeper, arrived, we understood the vital need of inner transformation. Her fiery religion promised big changes to our inner lives, where we'd die to our old sinful selves and be reborn as pure children of God; yet as much as we struggled to be reborn, the changes in our souls were hard to see. Puberty couldn't be missed and didn't demand long altar calls and crying out to Jesus. We were cajoled into choosing Jesus and giving our hearts to Him; puberty assaulted us, giving us no choice.

I wanted to be grown-up, to be a real man, to take the same road as our brothers, Bob and Bill, and their friends. Sadly, I had to go through puberty to get there. Watching older guys sail through puberty was one thing; dealing with my own thunder and lightning shook my ground and scared me.

As usual, we secreted our emotions, saying not a word about the deeper stuff of heart and soul. We kept a stiff upper lip and worked hard. With the new hormones blasting through me, alone in the night, I not only worried that Jesus might come; I also feared the upheaval in my body. I was sure some of my growing pains were cancer and that I might die like our mother. At times, I no longer dreaded the coming of Jesus; I prayed he'd come and snatch me away. Yes, I knew I was a sinner, but I was ready to take my chances.

As a herd animal, I imitated others as well as I could, keeping my hand to the plow, milking the cows, cleaning the barns. I was proud of the way my muscles were growing and of my new strength. In one short year, I could hit a ball from our house up to the top of our barn, making a thundering sound on the wood. The snowballs and stones I fired were suddenly lethal. I could strike out my little brother at will, whistling the ball or a stone past his pitiful swings. Slinging manure from our barn, handling buckets of grain and water and helping in other ways was effortless fun. Cranking up the John Deere was something I relished. Heck, I was now stronger than Dad, and he seemed to like this too.

Most surprising, I had grown new eyes. My eyes, well tuned to the curve of a puck or baseball were now mesmerized with the curves of girls and women. This was the most amazing part of puberty. Until now, girls had been merely silly, boring in their own special way. Then, magic! They were now scientific specimens; my miracle eyes were telescopic, for I could spot a girl far across the prairie. At close range, I had the gift of microscopic eyes, using them to stare at their mesmerizing forms.

I'd heard stories of true Christians being called by God, to go as missionaries to darkest Africa, and I feared this might be my calling. Now I knew my calling was different. I was called to stay home and fall in love all over the place. I wanted nothing more than to flirt, touch, tease and dance with the girls. There was more than enough missionary work to do on the prairie, with lots of girls to be saved for the Lord—and for me.

I threw myself into my new life, using my tracking, snaring and hunting skills for this higher purpose. I felt reborn. Had Jesus really saved me after all? Sister Rachel had promised that Jesus would fill us with the energy of a mighty roaring wind, and now I believed it. Everything was new. Prairie skies were higher, horizons called more loudly.

The grand chase had begun all on its own. I dreamed of a shiny new car. Older guys had shared enough stories about cars and ladies, and I needed a car.

The first young woman who moved into target range was an outsider, not one of us, and without the gunpowder in my veins, I would never have looked at her twice. She was what we ignorantly called a *half-breed*, and those of us who had light skins and owned farms—never mind how small they were, or how broke we were—needed to feel superior to someone, and we sadly, regretfully, mistakenly saw her people as far below us.

From what I heard adults say, they were a mix of good white blood and bad Indian blood, and were contaminated by the mix. Any worth they had showed up only at harvest season when they'd arrive in old wagons, drawn by mangy horses. They'd see a crop ripe for harvest, and come knocking at our door.

They carried their home with them, consisting of a battered tent and some pots and pans. They were prairie phantoms; I never knew where they came from or where they went when they left our farm. We kids, bug-eyed, would stand back full of stares and wonderment as one of the gypsies walked to our door, bowed down, and begged for work.

Once a wage was agreed on, they'd ask where they might camp and Dad would wave a westward arm toward the creek. We hired them for several harvests, and one unforgettable time they camped near the old slaughterhouse on the west side of our farm. Within hours, with my hormones leading the way, riding my bike along the road near their camp, my eyes were riveted by a young girl tending their fire. Pure desire gripped me. My soul flamed up with no regard at all for who she was or was not. I didn't stare for long, as I was quite visible on the road, so I rode hastily home, threw my bike on the porch and ran west along the creek, completely unarmed, stalking the most exciting game I had ever spotted.

This was a time in our lives when Phil and I were captivated by a couple of books by Zane Grey with a hero named Wetzel. He was a border scout and spent his time alone in the woods, living on wild animals and berries while killing Indians. He had great eyesight, could dart through the forest without disturbing a fern, and was a marksman with his special long rifle. When Phil and I and other kids played cowboys and Indians, being Wetzel was our first choice, and God help you if you were an Indian.

Feverishly, I sped west along the creek toward the new center of my universe, taking all my short cuts. I became Wetzel again, darting between open areas, then moving slowly and softly, stopping behind trees to peer silently ahead. As I crept closer, I went snakelike to the ground, being careful not to snap twigs or rustle any underbrush, holding my breath when needed, my keen eyes dancing about, looking for movement. I was a shadow, a mere illusion in the woods, and if an animal or other human looked my way I'd disappear into thin air.

Crawling, sniffing the wind, I slithered undetected to a place near the campground where I had a good view of the ray of light that had burst into view. She had beautiful long black hair, and more fascinating were her breasts and hips. My heart rate had gone up, my body was shaking, and suddenly I was scared. This was unknown territory. Wetzel was dissolving into the ground, not wanting to shoot or leap out with a knife. Here I was after a successful stalk, and all I wanted was to talk with her, to have her smile at me, and, *Please, please God, let me touch her hair.*

Barely breathing, my heart hammering in my chest, I watched as she disappeared into the tent. I slunk back into the woods, springing home on new legs, surging with energy and with a song in my heart. I sneaked back a couple more times; one time she may have spied me, and from her glance I knew she loved me too.

Then, harvest ended. I was sad when my love left a few days later, and went to their campsite, picking up a few scraps of paper and bits of cloth, as though they might help me understand my spinning world and my setting sun of childhood. Abed at night, she lived in my imagination, and I'd drift off to sweet sleep as I thought of sharing a tent with her.

My second intense romantic love experience was more personal and up close; heart-shattering, perfumy close. Like many experiences of love, this one was unexpected and it blindsided me in the night. A year or so after my first infatuation with the young woman camped in the woods, my romantic impulses grew even stronger. I was fourteen and the testosterone that raged in my body was jerking me around like a runaway horse.

One summer evening we were playing hide and seek with our friends, Nels and Bill Arvidson, at their home. We were having so much fun we barely noticed how dark it was until I ripped into a barbed wire fence as I streaked for home base. I had a ragged tear a couple of inches long in my right thigh—a scar I carry still. I was bleeding and in pain, and after I got over the shock, I wanted only to go home. When I jumped on my bike, my leg hurt and started bleeding again.

Now comes the soul-tilting moment. God walks into His garden, and love, brighter than northern lights, shines full on me. Ramona offered, gushy voiced, to ride me home.

She was the sixteen-year-old sister of Nels and Bill, and for a few years we'd noticed she had hormones and liked to flaunt them, exciting us to giggle and fall about.

My childhood innocence had been bludgeoned, besmirched and besotted with hormones, and now I was about to fall out of Eden. Ramona held the bike and I jumped on the crossbar, and she put her arms around me. I said goodbye to my buddies, a goodbye more profound than I could know, as I rode off into my new life. We wheeled down the lane, riding into the skies, toward the north star of home.

I was a goner, wasted, irretrievably lost. I was melting down, melting in. I forgot all about Jesus. With the first dreamy whiff of her perfume, my bleeding legs and tears were healed. Her soft hair caressed my face as her breath warmed the back of my neck. I fell into the most fantastic reverie. I was on the ride of my life, wafting like a feather buoyed up by a divine wind.

In the dark, I'd charged into a barbed wire fence, and now I was swept up by the light, to heaven and the sweet wonder of womanhood. Embosomed by the planets and heavenly warmth, I let myself be carried home. My trembling? We agreed it was the shock of my cut leg. I was in the throes of an exquisitely new kind of pain, and had no words for it. I wanted that pain, that night ride, to last forever. I'd found a new altar on the crossbar of a bike.

The next love of my life was Janet Ohirko. Janet's family farmed just west and north of our Norgate school, and she was a year or two older than me. Her family had invaded our province with a swarm of other Ukrainians, and Dad and other old timers knew they were all communists. Sundays, when they gathered at someone's home for lunch, we'd drive on the far side of the road to avoid the long arm of the evil Joseph Stalin. All those parked cars! *They were up to no good that's for sure. They're going to buy up all our good land and take over. We won the war in Europe, now they're invading us.*

Happily, love knows little about such matters, and sends her arrows through us as she will. Communist, half-breed, Christian? Who cares? Only love cares. My new life force propelled me across the prairies with little concern for the color or creed of my loves.

I was fourteen and in grade eight when Janet started high school at Kelwood, five miles south of our farm. In the silly era before puberty she was just another girl, and I lobbed snowballs at her, called her names and stuff, with complete disregard for the future.

As can happen in love, one glance is all it takes. One wintry day as I casually looked out the west windows of our school, I saw her walking to the road where she caught the horse-drawn van to high school. She had made this walk many times, and I had seen her only with half an eye, but on this day, my energy reached critical mass. My telescopic eyes zoomed across the snowy field, drawing her in, making her larger than life.

There was a rhythm in her walk that called my name. The shape and movement of her hips hypnotized me with wonder and mystery, and set me reeling. In one moment, I realized I adored her, not because I wanted to, but because she was suddenly beautiful. I was envious that she went to Kelwood High with other big kids and their knowing ways, their secrets about life. I was sad to think she likely had a boyfriend, older and more experienced than me. My heart obsession fueled me for many weeks, and I thought of her continually, drifting off to sleep with her face smiling at me.

One night, as I prepared to attend a community gathering where I hoped she'd be, I wrapped a plaid scarf around my neck, convinced this would attract her and she'd see how handsome I was, and return my love. The clan McLeod Tartan: who can turn from its colors? I coiffed my hair, and looked in the mirror from different angles, posing with various movie-star looks. I really was handsome after all!

Indeed, she was there, and my fear and longings created a perfect storm in me: I wanted to reach out, talk and touch, yet was immobilized with anxiety. Finally we faced each other; I used my best Romeo pose and cracked a joke, and she gave a flirty laugh. I felt a rush of energy, a brief moment of nervous laughter, and was convinced she loved me too. I loved her, and if she was a communist I loved her still. Sadly, that was the only real contact we had; the following weeks of love were powered by my runaway imagination.

Eventually, my infatuations followed roving eyes far away from our farm, to the western border of our province, and a little town named McAuley. I've forgotten her name, but can still see her radiant smile and curly black hair. We were both in the 4-H clubs, and with a hundred or so other young people, gathered in Winnipeg. The city itself was romantic and charged with magical expectations, and we stayed in the ritzy Marlboro Hotel with its fancy chandeliers and carpets.

We sat next to each other at dinner, and watched the newly released movie *White Christmas,* with Rosemary Clooney, Bing Crosby and Danny Kaye. After repeatedly repressing my urge to hold her hand, I finally reached out, and the rejection I feared did not happen. As she clasped my hand, I trembled with excitement. Big city life. I loved it. Even though I felt the electricity, I was far too shy to attempt a kiss, but we swapped a hundred sweet glances. I was forlorn the next morning when we said goodbye. At the door of the famous Marlboro Hotel, we hugged and walked apart, vowing to write, hoping to reconnect. We never saw each other again, but for months she was alive in my imagination. For the next few years, I carried a picture of her, in my worn and nearly empty wallet.

Then, once again my life was touched by grace. In my middle teen years I was in love with a fully grown woman, a true queen of stunning beauty. Millions of other men loved her too, all at a safe distance, but of course, I had a special relationship with her.

The first time I saw a picture of Grace Kelly, the movie actress, I was stunned by her beauty, hypnotized by her face, her hair and long graceful neck. I spent hours thinking about her, creating scenes in my mind of how we might meet, and how and why she'd come to love me as I loved her. My lovely fantasies lasted many months, and my enchantment with her helped time fly as I worked the fields, cleaned the barns, and stared into the creek imagining how eventually we'd be married.

My logic had broken out of the stable and fled to the back forty. My infatuation with her was such it didn't seem improbable that she could fall for a pimply farm kid from the middle of nowhere. Why not? Heck, I'd go to Winnipeg and be cast in a play, where a Hollywood agent would see me as the new James Dean. Why not? James Dean had grown up on a farm much like ours. I'd grab the Greyhound to movie land and be cast in a film with a female lead by the name of Grace Kelly. At our first meeting, I'd be super nonchalant, asking if she spelled her name with two *L*'s or one, and so forth. I practiced my James Dean look, combing my hair, slouching around, making furtive glances like he did. I was getting the hang of it. I was unique, a rebel, a really interesting guy. Around Grace, I'd pretend she was just another woman, stilling my heart. I was a gifted actor and could pull this off. Because other men swooned around her, I knew being cool would charm her, and when she became intrigued, I'd warm to her, bring her flowers. We'd marry and live in a big Hollywood home and have kids. I loved her, and I knew love made all things possible.

Again, I kept all this secret, as our family often did, hiding in the furrows and creek beds of my heart. If I was with anyone else and we saw a picture of her regal highness, I'd blush and turn my head, fearful they'd discover my secret love. The song, *Once I had a secret love that lived within the heart of me...* played on the radio during this time, and I sang that song over and over as I thought of Grace, my love.

Then the unthinkable: she married some communist guy from Europe. The short guy with the weird mustache and fake uniform. Besides, he was too old. She needed a younger guy like me, a real guy who could make her laugh. True, he had more cash, but my charm would make up for that. I was so disappointed in her. I knew their love would be short-lived and went on loving her. Meantime I could pray for her and hope she didn't suffer too much, with all the rules and stiffness of palace life.

As my love for Grace impelled my soul, I became interested in Donna, a young woman in our high school. She had a round, sweet face, a sense of fun. A notch above me socially, her dad was the postmaster in Kelwood, and they lived in a charming home with running water and carpeted floors. The real deal. She wasn't Grace, but would do in the meantime. It actually felt good to put Grace on hold. She'd ignored me, now I'd ignore her. That might get her attention.

Kelwood was a real town with a few hundred people. Besides the high school, it had cross streets with names, a clutch of shops, and a sense of magic and romance. I was fifteen and Donna was a year younger, and even though she had a boyfriend, we started making eyes at each other. I did my petulant James Dean posturing, and things heated up.

With lots of encouragement from my good buddy, Nels Arvidson, I asked her if she wanted to go out, and she surprised me by saying yes. I was ecstatic, and also afraid that her boyfriend, Dwayne, might try to beat me up. Once again, love won out, and Donna and I went on a double date with Nels and Enid. After fries and cokes, we ended up parking on a road west of town. I was all jittery. We could hear Nels and Enid giggling and smooching, and I wanted to do the same, yet was frozen by fear. The chasm of car seat between us was bigger than the gulf between me, Grace and Hollywood. Loving Grace was easier than this. I summoned my courage, squirmed toward her, and she flew into my arms. Her perfume, her hair, the feel of her dress, the electricity of the night engulfed me once again. She was the first girl I ever kissed.

Ripples of our new love spread like prairie fire, and the next day Dwayne found out. Not good, for Donna and I had agreed to a date the very next night.

I relive the scene: Saturday night, I drive into town from the north in Dad's '48 Chevy, while Dwayne rides in from the east on his horse. Images of two cowboys walking down Main Street for a shootout buzz about in my brain.

Unknown to me, Dwayne has already fired the first shot by riding into town early. A buddy tells me he has spirited Donna away to the horse barn. While I stand around kicking dirt, they have a talk that never ends. What else are they doing? Donna eventually walks to my corner of the O.K. corral and tells me it is over for us, and that she's back with Dwayne. I climb back in the Chevy, heartbroken, feeling betrayed, crying at times, hitting every pothole in the road. As I turn down our lane I'm thinking of Grace. Grace! You are my real love. I'm sorry I've ignored you, but now I'm yours for keeps.

With my romantic love experiences, I was redefining the meaning of heaven. My love for Jesus seemed a bit jaded compared to what I felt for the ladies I loved. I began to see that Old Moses had a narrow view of the promised land, for I had discovered many promised lands and they were walking around with lovely hair, sweet perfume and charming ways.

Not that it was all ecstatic, for I was also feeling the pangs, the confusions of love. My passions brought waves of guilt, as my body mugged my soul. That old devil had me good. I felt like a big backslider, and begged Jesus for deliverance from the force that had nearly put Him in second place in my heart. Some days I wanted to go back, back to the days of childhood.

I left the farm for Winnipeg in summer of 1956, for my final year of high school. I had passing crushes on a few women, and then I gave my heart to a wonderful woman, also named Donna. Donna Seeley. I say her name to honor her. We dated for a year and a half, and talked seriously of marriage. Then something came up in our relationship that I was not big enough to handle, and I ran away.

At the time, I blamed her for much of what happened, for that is what we often did in our family—blamed others for our sufferings, and did not take responsibility for our own feelings and actions. I can see now the devastation I felt was due to my immaturity, and the inherited, severely narrow religious principles I clung to, for she was a wonderful person.

My heart was shattered after our separation. I barely ate for a week and was depressed for a few months during the summer of 1959, when I worked as a rod man on the initial survey for the new Winnipeg airport.

My separation from Donna threw me into a spiritual crisis; I spent hours praying to Jesus for help, crying with grief. Phil and I were boarding together at the time, and he fretted about me and supported me as well as he could. Given the shame and secrecy inherited from our family, I shared little with him. My desperation overcame my fears, shame and secrecy, and I went and cried my heart out to Pastor Barber, at the church we attended. I hoped he could heal my pain. I wanted him to raise me from hell, the way Jesus had done with Lazarus.

As my soul healed, I continued praying long and intensely, and out of my crisis I felt God was calling me to be a pastor, to minister His Word, and decided I must go to college. That fall an archaeologist came to speak at our Calvary Temple church. He was a professor at Evangel College in Springfield, Missouri, returning home after a dig in the holy land of Israel. His talk added fuel to the fire that was growing in me, and he encouraged me to apply to his college. Phil and I both did so, and were both accepted, starting our studies in spring of 1960.

That fall, before going off to college, I meet another woman named Gail, and we share love enough to think of marriage, but my fears win the day and night.

Because I still loved Donna and Gail, (in the larger sense of love with a smidgen of romance around the edges) we corresponded during my first year of college, for they had similar sentiments for me. We had shared sweet times, deep talks and enough tears, and wanted to stay in touch. I still hoard a sacred stash of their love letters, along with a few from family and friends. I've peeked nervously, shyly at a couple of their letters over the years, wondering about the young man they describe: who is he?

Reading their letters, I see myself anew, for they saw in me things of which I could not be aware. They are a mirror to me, letting me see who I was and was not, as they saw me. They could see my fears, my love, my shame and secrecy, as I could not. As the mist of memory lifts, I stand revealed in the sun and moonlight of their words. They were sometimes baffled by my lack of self-disclosure, and wanted to know more of me.

I read and chide myself: why could I not have shared more openly? Why these hints, these glimmers, and nothing more? Regrets surface along with my love and compassion for them and myself. Yes, I know I could not have been more than I was, and yet the wish shapes words in me. I want to see them again and pour out my heart; all my apologies, my love, my compassion, and then one last hug, yes, one last hug, please!

In college I dated a few different women, most not seriously, except for a woman named Carolyn. We shared special times, and dreamed of a possible future together. Again, I was not ready to commit. I graduated from college in January of 1963, and for no special reason, decided to stay in Springfield with friends before moving on. This decision, not based on logic or rational planning, shifted the axis of my entire life. This planet was ready to orbit around a new sun.

Here's what happens on the morning when the stars are perfectly aligned and God is on His throne tinkering with the cosmos: I am sitting in chapel, minding my own business, thinking I'm in charge of my life as a new college graduate, and then I look up. I look up, look up at just the right moment, and my life is graced. One fateful glance. A dream, a virtual Grace Kelly, a goddess with a white fox collar was gliding on air in front of me, and my soul flies upward to dizzy aeries, hoping to finally nest.

Ah! She walks with such grace, turning her neck regally, softly scanning the room with fluttering eyes. I pray, dear one, don't look at me, for I will die! My soul was, is, born for this, and verily I am undone. Ancestral soul voices are whispering, *She's the one you've been seeking, she's the one...* and I'm listening.

I tell people I fell in love in twenty-eight seconds, but it may have been thirty-nine. I was gone, swept up, melted down, smitten, mesmerized, entranced, hooked, bitten, Godsmacked and gobsmacked..

I had never seen her before, did not know her name. She was with, presumably, her parents, and I already loved them too. I could see this was a package deal for the ages, and I was already signed up.

I tiptoe behind them out of chapel, note their blue car, dial up my Grandpa's tracking genes, and follow them in my car. Then, I lose them. Oh, cursed red light! Oh, terrible fate! I've lost my love, and may never know her name, may never see her again. Oh, me. Where are you, oh God, when I need you?

I beat down my despair, and I go back to tracking, asking my dorm buddies if they know who she is. I have a quick hit, for Lew Welker, older than most of us and from Houston, Texas, had recognized Rev. and Mrs. Rice, also from Houston. Oh, Jesus! Thank you Jesus! I see the alarm in Lew's face as he spots my feverish eyes, then I turn away, hot on the trail.

As I write these words, I begin to doubt if it truly happened as I'm saying, and I fear my readers too, may also wonder, asking as we do today, *Really? Really?* I reassure myself and others that I made detailed notes of this historical shift in my life, and when doubt arises, I check my notes, and laugh again at the drama of that day of first beginnings. (Along with my notes, I have all our love letters—the ones that Ruthie's mother loved to read!)

As this new love energy cracked my soul, I felt finally free of my dogged hunt for the perfect woman. That I was graced to find her in our chapel seemed a perfect thing.

My journal of that ecstatic springtime reminds me that I called seventeen motels in the part of town where I last saw her car, asking if Reverend Rice from Houston was registered with them. On the seventeenth call, an answer to my prayer, as God stirs on His throne and turns my way: the lady who answers the phone is happy to tell me the good Reverend has just walked in, and promptly handed him the phone. His booming voice was all assurance, and I freaked out and hung up.

There by the phone, I sat myself down and gave myself a pep talk, working up my courage, telling myself aloud that if I didn't call back I was not only a wimp, I'd regret it through all eternity. My voice was stern, controlling and also hopeful. I called back, apologized for being cut off, and faking a true adult voice, informed him I was vice president of our student body and would love to introduce his daughter to my student friends.

Every word was true, so why did it all sound so hollow and fake? I didn't know. I was all shaky with love energy, as Ruthie's father launches his favorite expressions: *Joy, joy, joy, joy. Praise the Lord, Praise the Lord. My, my, my, my! Oh, this is such a blessing to have you introduce her to some students here...my, my! May God bless you!*

All timid and bumbling, caught in my farmer's mind, I met Ruthie the next day. Samona Ruth Rice from Texas. The yellow rose of Texas.

The only problem (well, one of the problems) was, she was a senior in high school and not interested in committing to anyone, let alone a college grad with a sociology major.

Her older brother Chuck was an engineer, and Ruthie a math major, so sociology cost me points. It took nearly a year for her to think I might be a suitable long-term partner, and during this time I lived in Toronto, then started graduate work at the University of Omaha.

While it took me only a few eye blinks to fall for her, she needed more time. 31,449, 600 seconds if my math is right—a year of ruminating, praying, reading my love letters with her mom and stuff like that. I take the Canadian view of things here, believing my quick love for her came directly from my hockey days, with the sudden moves intrinsic to that game. As I've noted, for Canadians, hockey is the ultimate cause of everything, and the most obscure events are seen as having obvious roots to that madcap game.

My wife has a decidedly slow sense of time and is late for most everything, so she naturally needed a year to take me seriously. I wrote her letters most every week, she'd write me back every three weeks or so, and I'd despair for the last two weeks. Then a letter would finally arrive and I'd be in heaven.

My great college friend, Glenn Lindsey, my roommate at that time, nearly wrenched himself apart too, as he watched me ride the holy roller coaster of love. Our small Omaha apartment glowed with joyous light after I received a letter from Ruthie, then went dark when she fell silent.

While I knew in my soul I loved Ruthie right from the start, and it was obvious to her and others, it took me a year to tell her I loved her. I simply could not say the words; I'd never heard these words back in the hard days of farm life.

Unlike her precious daughter, Ruthie's mother loved me right from the beginning. Later in life, she loved to repeat the story of our first meeting; she expected to see a tall dashing Mounty in a red dress tunic, on a white horse. Her first disappointment was fleeting, and she went for horseless, diminutive me. Once she learned I was a true Christian with honorable intentions, she opened the gates of her soul and took me in. Besides, I was Canadian, and she loved Canadians, God bless her.

She was smart enough to act as a broker for her daughter, secretly sending her grocery dollars to Omaha so I could buy a bus ticket to Houston. On my first trip to Houston, I grabbed the Continental bus south from Omaha, rolling through a moonlit night to see Ruthie for Thanksgiving, then passing through Dealey Plaza the day after President Kennedy was killed. Flowers and people were everywhere. With millions of others, we wept as we watched the funeral for President Kennedy.

The secret dollar transfer from Houston to Omaha became a full blown conspiracy when Ruthie's mother suggested I send some of her hush money back to Houston, so Ruthie could afford to come and see me. I embraced that idea too. I took delight in this money-laundering scam—not exactly identity theft, but close to it. Unknowingly, Ruthie used her mom's grocery money to buy a plane ticket to see me in Omaha. Glenn prepared a gourmet meal, and Ruthie started to think that with friends like him, I must be a good guy.

We were married August 14, 1965: fifty years, in this the Year of Our Lord, 2015. I jokingly tell people we've had forty-seven good ones, while Ruthie quotes a lower number. A few years after our courtship, I told Ruthie about her mom sending cash to me, and she had a secret to share back: her mom had been reading all my love letters and insisting her daughter write me back!

When I learned her mother had read my letters, (and hot off the press too, for Ruthie would read a page, then hand it to her hovering, misty-eyed mom) I turned fire engine red and sirens shrieked in my head, as I thought of what I might have shared in our letters. The obvious therapeutic conclusion for me was that Ruthie's mother was having a vicarious affair with me.

Later, in the hell of bankruptcy, (due to my greed with real estate investments) Ruthie was seeing a therapist, and he was happy to tell her she married me to please her mother. Ruthie thought this might have some truth, but did not take it as a defining truth. Had she really married me to please her mother? We bantered and danced with this idea, mainly as a humorous dialogue for us, and as part of my playfulness, I dismissed the entire idea as fanciful, Freudian poppycock and advised her to get a new therapist. To imagine she did not love me for my own dear self! Obviously, a misguided notion from a therapist who did not know me.

Ruthie's mother, in many ways, became my true mother. She could sense in me, as many have, hungry-child eyes looking for a lost Mother. After Dad Rice died in 1992, Mother lived with us for six years, and it worked out splendidly. Well, ninety-three per cent of the time, to tell the truth, and I figure that is quite impressive, given the notorious history of mother-in-law and son-in-law relationships.

I liked to tell Mother the joke about the guy who saw his mother-in-law fly off a cliff in his new car, and he wasn't sure if he should cry or cheer. We could make each other laugh to tears, and her tummy would jiggle all over the room. One time, eating out in a restaurant, she started to choke, and I leaped up and gave her an over-zealous Heimlich hug—which did the trick. I broke four of her ribs, and faked remorse as well as I could. Even the paramedics were fooled, and kept telling me to not fret, for broken ribs were common with older folks. No charges were filed.

I was careful to not crack any jokes until her painful ribs healed. Then I assured her I'd been waiting for years to give her a crushing hug, but promised I'd never do it again. And then her belly dance would begin, like the first tremors of an earthquake, and soon we'd be crying with laughter. *You'd just let me choke, right?* And I'd say, *Yes, 'cause I wouldn't want to crack your ribs again...it might kill you...* We slapped our knees, jiggled our bellies, shed mirthful tears, as we created new bits of zany dialogue, centered around her broken ribs.

Her immediate love for me, like mine for Ruthie, may also have been a matter of unconscious knowing, of sensing into the future at a level beyond conscious awareness. She may have known I'd love her back, and help look after her into her 90's. She was a most noble and wise woman—just like her daughter. Both of them have been sources of light, wisdom and laughter to our family, and most every day I feel gratitude for them. My friends like to say, *Al, you really lucked out!* And I so agree. If people have told Ruthie she lucked out with me, I've yet to hear of it.

Apart from my role as a professor, I've been noticed in life because I've followed my beautiful wife around. The way she dresses enhances her beauty, and people notice me after first being struck by her elegance and femininity. My imagined conversation when this happens has this theme: *he must be a good man, he must have something going for him to be with such a lovely woman.* And, more whimsically: *what's she doing hanging out with a guy like him?*

I'll share one last story about the two women I most loved romantically. In 1993 our young people's group from Calvary Temple, Winnipeg, had a reunion in Kelowna, B.C. My old love, Donna, was there. Ruthie knew how much I had loved Donna, and how I continued to love her in a non-romantic way, and included her on my prayer list.

The first night of our reunion Ruthie and I walked into a room full of people, and I was excited and nervous about seeing Donna after thirty-three years. I began a catch-up conversation with one of my friends, when I saw Donna walk in. I took a deep breath, and in a couple of minutes started moving across the room to greet her. My eyes finally spotted her again: she and Ruthie were hugging each other and crying! A big lump formed in my throat, as I neared them and hugged them both, and let my own tears flow. Ruthie told me later that she recognized Donna from pictures, and had gone to her, and said, *You must be Donna? Al has loved you his whole life, and I'm so happy to meet you!* What Ruthie said and did demonstrated the essence of her big heart, her

342

compassionate soul. And Donna, similarly, was ready to open her heart and receive the gift Ruthie had given.

The next day, helping in the kitchen, Ruthie and Donna peel peaches together. It is the best peach I've ever tasted, dripping with sweet symbolism, memories and meaning. Such a soulful peach: caressed and loved by my two great loves, it filled me with gratitude and wonder.

༄

I end this chapter by dedicating my favorite love poem to Ruthie. It was penned by e.e. cummings. He liked to break the rules about capitalization (including his name) and punctuation, and I quote it here as he wrote it. Endless gratitude to you, Ruthie, for enclosing me and helping me *unclose*.

somewhere i have never travelled, gladly beyond.

somewhere i have never travelled, gladly beyond
any experience, your eyes have their silence:
in your most frail gesture are things which enclose me,
or which I cannot touch because they are too near

your slightest look easily will unclose me
though i have closed myself as fingers,
you open always petal by petal myself as Spring opens
(touching skillfully, mysteriously) her first rose

or if your wish be to close me, i and
my life will shut very beautifully, suddenly,
as when the heart of this flower imagines
the snow carefully everywhere descending;

nothing which we are to perceive in this world equals
the power of your intense fragility: whose texture

compels me with color of its countries,
rendering death and forever with each breathing

(i do not know what it is about you that closes
and opens; only something in me understands
the voice of your eyes is deeper than all roses)
nobody, not even the rain, has such small hands.

CHAPTER 18

❧

Heaven and Hell: Legacies from Our Early Religion

Train up a child in the way he should go: and when he is old he will not depart from it.

PROVERBS 22; 6

The heart leans toward healing, just ever so slightly. You can notice if you look.

TODD MCLEOD

❧

IT WAS DEMANDED of us in those incomprehensible, windblown days of childhood, that we continuously scan our conscience, to properly note our sins, and to pray for the blood of Jesus to wash us clean. Our inner radars were finely tuned, and for me, this inward looking has stamped both my personal and professional life as a challenging obsession. Looking back, I see how this eventually led to my interest in the self-awareness practice of Buddhism, beginning in spring of 1993.

In the Buddhist tradition, self-reflection and awareness practice is wedded to detachment and compassion, a scanning of self with love and some objectivity, spiced with humor and dance. From this position, apart from the spinning cosmos of our inner worlds, the entire human zoo is a fascinating project to contemplate; this has been the central project of my life. (As a disclaimer, I must note that I am not a Buddhist, and know precious little of that courageous and Great Project. I've embraced only the aspect of self-awareness practice, and use this as well as I can.)

Self-awareness practice might seem like mere navel gazing and excessive self-absorption; it is much more than this. The guiding belief is that as we become aware of our inner propensity to cause harm, the more clearly we see this and have compassion for our sufferings, the more compassion we have for our families, friends and others. One of the challenges from the Buddhist tradition is to live harmlessly in the world, and for me this is as an ongoing struggle. Some scientists believe that with our destructive habits, our species is causing the sixth great extinction of life. The problems we create, for ourselves and others, in interpersonal relationships, are ongoing and not given to easy remedy.

Given my personal and professional interest, indeed my obsession, with the inner lives of our species, I've pondered the impact the hellfire religion had on our family, seeing patterns and connections. How did I become the person who sits and types these words on this sunny California morning? What happened to the McLeod family on the windswept prairies? Who were we? What events really impacted us? What do I most remember? We all inherit scars and gifts from our childhood, and my quest has been to heal my scars as well as I am able, and to have gratitude for the gifts from my first days.

I begin by sharing a few of the negative impacts of my early religious experiences on my life, since those long ago days, concluding with the gifts from that tradition. I've become aware that during my life I've had a deeply layered victim mentality, and given to excess whining, blaming and shaming of myself and others. As with most of us, this aspect of self—*my* self—was thankfully not often on public display, being well covered with the mandatory happy smile and a get-to-work persona. All good.

So my task here is to not dwell on the abuse we suffered, rather to make a few basic observations and be done with it. I think of, and relate to, the Buddhist story our son, Todd, likes to tell about the man who had a healthy life, and at age 95 as he is wheeled into the hospital, cries out: *Why me? Why me?*

As a general comment, I want to note that I'm intrigued with our profoundly human capacity to believe spiritual entities are in and around us. We have a remarkable ability to visualize disembodied personages and to make them real. Across our planet, beginning in childhood, we create imaginary creatures, and carry on conversations and other interactions with them. Angels, ghosts, gods, goddesses and dark beings make up much of who we are. We construct elaborate temples in which we hope to trap our most revered entities, and they often show up in our dreams at night. Images, hallucinations, thoughts, perceptions, projections: these make up who we are. Potent, soul shaking, 3-D spiritual visions are always lurking in the background wanting out, and can surprise us with their luminosity, literally sending us off in a new direction. Much has been written about all this.

It is not just a question of how we visualize nonmaterial entities: in everyday reality, the actual individuals we know, and have known, are composed of layers of images in our minds, and over the years we shift our perceptions of them. We commonly assume that our perception about another is who they really are, and not our fabrication of them. We might share common views about any one person, just as we do with a divine entity, yet each of us has a unique spin on every person, object and experience. The layers of our imaginations, the stories we weave about each other and all life, are multi-layered and difficult to call into awareness and articulate.

I trace the beginning of my inner awareness and healing to my early thirties, when, due to a series of circumstances, I started to glimpse how the toxic beliefs of our religious cult had wounded me.

More objectively, I began to realize that Jesus was real to us, to me, maybe even more tangible than the inhabited bodies of those around us. We absolutely believed that Jesus was in us, and indwelt our minds, hearts and souls. We might be alone, separate from others at times, but Jesus was always alive in us, in me. He was, we said, *closer to us than our breathing.*

I could see and sense Him in my mind and feel His presence in my heart every day; this seemed equally true for the sisters and brothers in our band of true believers. Indeed, even now, abed in the night, saying my lazy prayers, Jesus still shows up, either stretched on his terrible rack, or floating about in his ethereal body after his resurrection. These past decades I've wanted to delete the image of Christ on his cross, but despite my best efforts that awe-full scene arises in me.

Our Jesus-of-the-prairies was a living, dominant force in our lives, more intimate in some ways than the real people around us. He was us. His blood had washed us clean from sin; He was in our marrow, our souls. Our images of Him, we believed, were objectively true, inspired by God and the myste-rious Holy Ghost. Because such beliefs were poured into me, I could never imagine that my thoughts of the Divine Ones were partly my creation, unique in certain ways to my genetic and acquired propensities, crafted with passion-ate love and dedication, profoundly colored in the context of our family.

Because we believed our souls were a battleground of good and evil where God and the devil clashed every day, because we lived in occupied ter-ritory, we could not take full responsibility for our own actions. We regularly evoked favorite phrases: *Jesus told me to do this. I was led by God. The devil made me do it.* Passing the buck was the coin of the day. As I matured into adulthood, I often felt and acted as though I was at the mercy of larger forces in life, and could not take responsibility for my choices, my thoughts and feelings.

When I saw myself as a victim, I might feel put upon, unworthy and over-looked. I suffered with feelings of inferiority and hurt, and felt the need to defend and justify myself, my beliefs and actions. This led to the sometime need to angrily strike back at those I felt had hurt or ignored me. My wife told me sometime ago that in our early relationship she felt she was walking on eggshells much of the time. Like too many of us, I saved the best and worst for those I most loved. Like too many of us, I was the best and worst partner and parent.

The burden I've most consciously suffered from is the damage I did to my own family, with my shame, blame and anger. Most every day I experience sadness and remorse for the times I struck out at those I most cherish. How they survived me, and remained so loving toward me, is a mystery beyond my comprehension. How did they navigate those troubled waters? I have no clear understanding of this, but remain forever grateful. How I was as a par-ent is revealed to me most clearly through the loving light of how our son and daughter, and other families I know, relate to their children.

Feeling shameful and sinful are connected to my feelings of being a victim. Shame and blame are bedfellows: when we feel shamed we often want to blame another for our feelings of humiliation, and so we strike out at others. Shaming, blaming, powerlessness and anger are comrades in crime.

Shame is a universal human emotion, and we have a deep intuitive understanding of it. Feelings of shame vary in degree with each of us, and when shame is deeply rooted, we can think of such a person as being shame-based or bound. I put myself in that category, and am happy to report that over the years, as I've increased my awareness, I've been blessed to soften my emotions of shame, blame and anger. I still hear the old tapes, the old voices in me, and these days can detach from them with compassion for myself and others. I could cite other challenges from my past, but now want to focus on the positive legacies.

Along with occasional fighting, and the common shaming and blaming, our farm family was blessed in how we loved and supported each other. I see in my brothers and sisters virtues and strengths I believe are gifts from our childhood. All six of us have raised families of our own, 26 children in all, who've scattered to the four winds, each committed to their calling, each adding fragrance to the world.

I trace core themes from early childhood to the personal and professional interests that grip me as fervently as did my early religious training. Beginning in my early thirties, I developed a passion to understand myself and others as fully as I could, and started training as a therapist, undergoing therapy myself. In our training groups, under the supervision of an experienced therapist, we'd take turns being client and therapist, learning from each other as we went along. Along with my baptism into therapy groups, I also had individual therapy at different times.

My passion as an astronaut of the soul world was inexhaustible, and continues today, nearly five decades later; a fact that astounds me as much as anyone. My desire to understand the inner lives of others and myself has truly been a Holy Grail quest. I'm fascinated with how we become who we are, and how we continue to change through life. I've listened to the stories of many others, how they make sense of their lives, and the connections they make to their childhoods.

In our farm family, we couldn't share our hearts, our deeper thoughts and emotions, and so, of course, I flung myself headlong into the sacred enterprise of understanding others and myself in the clearest, deepest and highest ways possible. In addition to the therapeutic questing, for thirty-eight years I taught at California State University Fresno, centering on interpersonal relationships. The old expression fits: we teach what we want to learn. I'm still learning, and can see the wisdom road is long and without end.

As part of my evangelical fervor in helping others heal and find their way, I also led weekend workshops for nearly three decades. During my retreats I encouraged people to communicate their feelings as openly and clearly as possible, in one-on-one encounters, as well as in the circle of our whole group. I used my training in imagery, visualization and dream work to help lead us inward, and to facilitate reflective silence. My deepest teaching and facilitating happened during such workshops, and feedback from participants revealed the helpful discoveries they had. I continue to hoard select letters from those who had life-altering experiences.

My thirst for deeper truths led to an interest in dreams and spiritual visions, and to help others find their personal meanings in such experiences. Doing dream work invariably led to surprising discoveries, and left me filled with wonder and gratitude. I learned that while journeying with another through a dream, a new, waking dream or spiritual vision might ignite, flinging open a door to new possibilities.

When I reduce my core personal and professional passion to only one thing, it is my enduring interest in altered states of consciousness. I trace much of this to my early religious influences. Accepting Christ into our hearts often led to a change in inner life as well as behaviors. This was undeniably real, and is real for most religions. I wondered, and still wonder, how such an experience can cause such a shift in our lives.

As a child in church, I'd watch someone fall down in the spirit and flail about. Or someone might suddenly leap to his feet speaking in tongues, leaving me bug-eyed and bedazzled. I saw people laugh ecstatically, and a moment later, sob uncontrollably at the altar.

Back in the days of fire, I observed people accept Jesus into their hearts and be deliciously happy for weeks. A few weeks later some of them would crash back to earth. So of course! Yes, I'm fascinated by the astounding capacity of humans to shift gears, to move from one mental-emotional state to another. Our brain dance, our shifting images, moods, opinions and attitudes create many questions for me, and for science, and I'm delighted to be caught up in such a quest.

Because I've softened many of my childhood *truths,* part of me feels I've betrayed the faith of my farm family, yet in my own way I've carried on the tradition. As much as any missionary or evangelist, I've thrown myself into the study of altered states of consciousness and carried on the *faith of our fathers* in a secular way, as I taught and counseled people. Indeed, I no longer make an absolute distinction between sacred and secular, for in the yin and yang of it, I see each viewpoint contains elements of the other.

Most of my readings, and the few hundred workshops and seminars I attended and taught, pivot around the profound capacity of our human hearts and brains to dive deep and soar high. Over and over I noted that some individuals reported significant mental, emotional and spiritual shifts, as profound, they said, as any that happened in the context of religion.

The teaching environments, the learning fields I created were designed to help others become more aware of the layers of attitudes, emotions, opinions and the rest of their inner worlds. In my work with others, a core goal was to support students and others in discovering more of their depths, encouraging them to have more respect and love for themselves and others.

For me, this was and continues to be sacred work, and I have a sense of *the holy* when I feel others touching their own souls, and the hearts and souls of others. This is especially true when I travel with another into the world of dreams.

Thus, in my own way, I've continued the practice of *saving souls.* While my teaching occurred in secular settings centered on secular themes, the driving energy was more heart and soul centered, and not just focused on the more mental aspects. My students often reported this in their anonymous written feedback.

In my classes in the Sociology Department at CSUF, I wanted students to internalize the core concepts and theories of sociology and psychology. More vitally, I encouraged them to learn to question everything, including what *I* said—to be curious, and to challenge their opinions and beliefs, and be ready to change if that felt right. I supported them in being more aware of their values and emotions, and in using these to help understand who they were at the deepest levels, and how their emotional biases colored their thinking.

After my first years of teaching, I shifted from being the *sage-on-stage* to mini-lectures and talks, facilitating and coaching my students as they worked in small groups. Between classes, the co-scholars in my classes were required to write personal journals, connecting course concepts to their daily lives, and each week they read a peer's journal and gave helpful feedback.

I knew the research about the profound effects of teacher expectations on student performance, so I set the bar high for my students, creating the implicit assumption that they could always do better, reach higher. Most always, they did. Our co-created classrooms evolved during the semester; journal writings improved along with the tenor of class discussions. When I meet former students, they frequently tell me they've kept their journals from twenty or more years ago, and reread them at times.

I was passionate about teaching, and over the years came to think of my class as my mission field, for as much as any missionary, I hoped my students would rebirth themselves, not in a religious sense, but from their own self-inquiry and morality—their own desire to be the best persons they could be.

Just as the acorn wants to oak, early on I believed each of us has a restless desire to grow, learn and evolve into a higher state of being, and that if we give support, provide coaching and set an example, we can inspire others to reach upward. Through anonymous written feedback two or three times a semester, as well as face-to-face comments, students kept telling me of the positive changes they were experiencing in our classes. Reading their journals was a delight, and gave me such buoyant energy as I read their journeys of self-awareness and growth.

We called our end-of-semester journal a celebration paper and it truly was; I was often moved to tears and laughter as I pored over their words, giving them copious feedback in my written comments. I continue to treasure and hoard a few of the most astounding journals in my office. This entire process was due to our entire learning team, and in fact, I believe the students learned as much from each other as from me.

As I look back and ponder this, I see that one core root of my intense teaching energy was a gift from our family, and that I was, as the old hymn worded it, *bringing in the sheaves,* in my own way, using science to facilitate their evolution into more holistic states of being.

Working as a loving, cooperative team, during every class session my students and I formed a creative, bubbling learning field, and each day was richly rewarding. Our emotions would range from riotous laughter to occasional tears, and everything in between. One of my favorite moments occurred after a deep exchange, when a student stood up and said he couldn't take it any more. He was on fire, frustrated and laughing as new insights stormed around our classroom, and he walked out amidst applause. When he returned a few moments later, there was more applause. Because most of us experienced and understood the shaking and expansion of long-held positions, we celebrated his turmoil.

Given my missionary zeal, I received several awards for teaching, including, the 1999 Provost Award for excellence in teaching. Recently, reading the memoirs of our sister Jean, I note that our mother won an award for teaching around 1920. This may hark to a *teaching gene* passed on to my sisters and brothers, thence to Heather and Todd, our children, and some of my nieces and nephews who are gifted teachers.

Related to my teaching career, I had several psychic readings thirty-some years ago, out of fun and curiosity, and in each case made detailed notes afterwards. I've reviewed these files years later to learn that nearly all of what was *revealed* simply didn't fit or come true in my life. There is one notable exception. When Ruthie and I were in Amsterdam in the late nineties, after a dinner when I had a bit too much wine, we stumbled into a square where a young woman was doing tarot readings. For fun, I tossed down my seven dollars for a reading. I sat there stunned as she told me about my passion for teaching and for my students. This was astounding enough. Then she went on to be more precise, giving details on why I did what I did, the hunger and intention in my heart and soul, and more.

As part of my teaching load, I taught two courses on deviant behavior for over three decades, focusing on topics ranging from drugs, to various types of crime and prison subcultures. Slowly, I began thinking that my study of deviance was tied to the out-of-the-box religion of my childhood. It made sense that one of my core interests in deviance was the study of religious cults. In addition to my readings on this topic, I visited various cults, including one in northern Scotland (The Findhorn community) during a sabbatical in 1977.

I invited members and former cult members to come to my deviance class as speakers, and these sessions were exciting, even incendiary. Such class sessions, where none of us knew what might happen, ignited memories of my holy roller days.

Beginning in the 1970's, the writings of Carl Jung, the Swiss psychiatrist (1875-1961), were especially important in helping me move away from the limiting and damning aspects of our childhood religion. His reflections on the book of Job had a profound effect on me, opening an entirely new way of thinking about the mission of Christ in our world.

More than ever, I see that we all pass through different stages in our lives, as we grow and change. I see this among our family and friends, and it is also true for my wife and me. We rarely attend formal religious services anymore, yet feel more spiritual than we did in our high religious days. Based on my readings and talking with others, it seems in the past few decades many of us have let go of the idea of a vengeful, bookkeeping God and view *Him* as more loving and compassionate.

Like everyone, whatever their religion, we cherry pick the parts of holy scripture that suit us. Like others, I can think my ladder is highest, and my cherries the sweetest. I stand on my ladder: *Hear me, hear my truths. I am one among many billions, yet more than anyone, I have found the truth! Hear me, you underlings, as*

I shake the highest fruits from the tree of life. Is this not the belief many of us have? That we alone have somehow found the highest and best truth.

In spring of 1993 a special friend, Trish, gave me a book on Tibetan Buddhism, entitled: *The Tibetan Book of Living and Dying.* We had an *accidental* meeting one morning in a coffee shop. She immediately shared her joy about her latest book and insisted I must get a copy and read it. She then decided to walk me to the bookstore, where she bought me a copy. For several years that book was my *bible.*

The Buddhist teachings from that book provided me with moments of great joy, deep reflection and tears of recognition at the fundamental truths of life. My family, and many of our friends, have been influenced by the Buddhist wisdom, and our son Todd inspires me with his commitment to meditation and the teachings. We've attended Buddhist inspired retreats—one with five days of silence.

My current spiritual path is a heady, home-brewed elixir of Christianity, Buddhism and Jungian psychology, with a pinch of this and that, and is constantly emerging with new experiences and insights. Buckminster Fuller once famously said, *I seem to be a verb,* and that is how I see each of us. Much as we might like to freeze our sense of self, we are continually changing as the river of time carries us along. We are a process, a work in progress. It makes sense to me that in some religions, people change their gods and goddesses at different stages of life.

From my contemplative-awareness practice, as best I can, I strive to see the subtle levels of my emotions, images, ideas and thoughts—the vast inner cosmos of light and dark gifted to each of us. As I pray and extend compassion and best wishes to our loved ones, I also feel gratitude for our family and friends, and for the gift of life, of being able to share this time and space together. This, for me, is an immense realization and cannot be overestimated. Our universe, as I sense it, leans more toward light and love than toward darkness.

As with most of us, I don't pray enough, but when I do, along with my faith, I'm aware of my doubt, for it is real and often present, and I wonder if my prayers stop when they hit the ceiling. I smile as I think that if they can reach the ceiling, perhaps they can go around the world. My experience is that doubt can deepen faith. We may profess to know the mystery of the divine, but from my view, our minds are simply too small to comprehend the infrastructure of all life, which, for me, equates with the divine. It seems to me that nature—and all the gods and goddesses that have existed across eons—cloak themselves well. As we peer into the world of the atom, far out into the cosmos and into the depths of ourselves, we find limits beyond which we cannot go. We do indeed, *see through a glass darkly,* as St. Paul said.

Along with my introduction to Buddhism, spring of 1993 was life-changing in another way, for in March I made my first visit to Esalen Institute at Big Sur. This place of stunning beauty and wisdom has been a profound spiritual home since that time, and I continue to go three or four times a year for five-day workshops. Yes, that means I've been there seventy-five or more times, and each time I drink deeply from that rich well, it's been worth every penny. I've kept a file, recording my highest, deepest and most magical Esalen moments. I want to share one such experience, for it ties directly to the religious experiences of my childhood.

Most groups at Esalen are experiential, with limited talks and lectures, and include various exercises, meditative silence, music, movement, and other modalities to help reveal deeper layers of the self. After several days of such immersion, soul stuff starts to cook and bubble up. In one group with a distinct soul focus, we engaged in the familiar practice of moving into smaller groups of five or six.

Deep listening and sharing are core features of Esalen groups, and we each took turns talking about our most precious spiritual experiences. Without any forethought, a Jewish member in our group spontaneously started praying in Hebrew. This moving expression led an evangelical Christian in our group to begin speaking in tongues. The two soulful outpourings were in harmony, blending, rising and falling together. The rest of us were awestruck as we honored both spiritual paths, and drank in their songs of worship.

I knew again why I loved this place so much. *Esalen! You called my name! I was slow to answer, but in my fifty-third year I answered your call.* I tell people that the beauty of the place is worth the price of admission—to say nothing of the organic food, the open-hearted people (seminarians who come from all over the world), and of course, the dreamy, steamy tubs, perched above the pounding Pacific with the gift of hot water from mother earth. I don't have much to say about the place, so don't get me started.

Viewed through the religious eyes of my childhood, I'm a professional backslider, a reprobate, a lost sinner. I now think it preposterous that my farm family, that any small group of people, could believe they have the final, total and absolute truth about anything, whether in science, religion or politics. From my Buddhist readings, I've come to see that every moment we are spinning stories, watching and listening to our inner movies, and projecting them onto others. From this view, the challenge is to become aware of our stories and how we succumb to them, and then to compassionately detach and watch them as we might a movie, choosing the one that is most loving to self and others.

When I think back to childhood and our little group of true believers, I am amazed that we felt so superior to others, so pure, so special, compared to those around us, and see this today as a type of kingly ego inflation—as a rare, tragic and comical form of narcissism.

Back in our holy roller daze, drunk on the elixir of absolute truth, we forgot all about Christ's teachings on the importance of humility. As we bragged about our special love for and from Jesus, we were violating other holy teachings. We knew the Bible, and astride our high horses, used it as a sword to humiliate others. We delighted in running our swords of truth into the hearts of sinners. We cherished the verse telling us *pride comes before a fall,* on the dangers of being *puffed up,* forgetting this admonition before milking time. We well knew, and were warned of the sin of the Pharisees, the hypocrites who prayed loudly in public so others would see how religious they were. Yet, we were public pontificators in our own preposterous way. With our fixation on sinners, and our love for Jesus, we trampled on other holy teachings, our right hands unaware and innocent of what our left hands were doing.

When I reflect on our self-righteousness, our severe condemnations of the *sinners* subjected to our street meetings, I feel lucky we were not tarred and feathered, or maybe shot on the spot. If anything, getting egged and bombarded with firecrackers demonstrated the restraint of those we called evil.

The love, compassion and tolerance they showed us incite gratitude in me, and I can see they displayed many Christian virtues that we lacked. Most of the hard working farmers who enjoyed and put up with our bombastic insults were Christians too, blessed to not have the insufferably rigid views we had. Today, I cringe at how we shamed them, how we projected our darkness onto them. They must surely have viewed us as a joke, as an early version of Saturday Night Live. That's it. That's why we survived, why we were tolerated, why we were permitted to set off our truth bombs.

Many of us intuitively feel that passionate beliefs are fueled by the opposite, unconscious energy, and this type of overcompensation seems universal. I now believe that our boasting of being God's favorite children was a kind of reaction formation—a denial of our inner dark tendencies, especially our private doubts, which we hoped to banish with our hallelujahs. Having doubts, raising questions about our truths, was an especially dark sin. I think too, our insistence on being God's chosen little children may have buffered us from the shame we carried.

In our glory days down on the farm, I had some awareness I was not a spotless saint, superior to the evil sinners around me. Some of my confusion and shame was tied to this. I knew my own heart well enough, knew my own doubts, my own tendencies to *sin*, to ponder and do things that weren't right. I wanted to throw eggs back at those who threw eggs at us. I felt I had little choice but to go along with the powerful adults around me. From this view, I ended up violating my heart and sense of truth, and this helped create confusion, self-doubt and shame.

As with most religious fanatics, love and consensus can fracture a group when the *old devil* gets ahold of some of them, and they decide they have a higher truth than the others. This is the nature of absolute, either/or belief systems: they can divide us internally and in our relations with others. I recall several heated arguments between groups of true believers, each absolutely knowing they had the final truth and were more loved by Jesus. Invariably, someone would find an obscure Biblical verse, or reinterpret a familiar one, declaring they had a direct line to God, verified with prayer and fasting. They were happy to pronounce their sisters and brothers as wrong, lost sinners.

These fights for higher ground led them to walk away from the apostates and start a new church. The reprobates, those lost in darkness, could go straight to hell with their wrong-headed ways.

I playfully refer to Albert Einstein as *the other Albert*, and he allegedly said we each have to decide if the universe is friendly or not. The God I met, the God that assaulted me in childhood was more angry than loving, more filled with judgment than compassion, and our inner and social worlds reflected this. We espoused the love of God, but knew little of it. Too often, we felt surrounded by sin and sinners, and viewed the world as hostile.

In Genesis, the first book in the Holy Bible, after His acts of creation, God declares His creation to be very good, even excellent. I think God meant it. A phrase from the past smites me: *If the Bible says it, it's good enough for me!* So I cheerfully, cleverly, cheekily, cherry pick and embrace the idea that creation is essentially good, that the world is more friendly than not. The daily sordid headlines, focusing on violence, give us, as I see it, a distorted view of life. Evil and suffering are real, very real, but do not define who we are. This accords with the Buddhist notion that under our terrible actions, we are loving, compassionate beings.

I believe most of our sufferings come from our own unkind thoughts and actions, rather than from any supernatural force. Every time I choose my grasping hand of greed and selfishness over my open hand of compassion, when I act unkindly toward another, I create suffering for myself and others. Some Buddhists talk about how difficult it is to be simply harmless in the world, and I'm learning how true this is.

One more note on Einstein. He went through an intense religious period from age nine to twelve. Then, in his twelfth year he had a surprising, opening experience, and in a short time shed his traditional religious views. He described this as a wonderful feeling of freedom and release, and as a turning point in his life. He launched his mind to roam the universe and to walk into the heart of the atom. Free of his confinement, he could think thoughts that had never been thought before. On the web, I've just learned there is a Russian word that captures much of Einstein's thirsty brain. The word is *prostor* and notes it is the desire for spaciousness, to move freely in the expanses of self in a creative and spiritual way. Einstein used his active and radical imagination to ride a light beam into space, and to notice that time slowed down and the light wave bent as it went by large objects. As we reflect on our own lives, we can see that we too, have passed through stages and have rebirthed, regrouped in our own way.

Genius may require a certain hubris: when a friend asked Einstein how he'd feel if one of his theories was proven wrong, he said he'd feel sorry for the Lord. He believed too, in a universe of symmetry and order, as revealed in another of his famous quotes: *the Lord does not throw dice.* We see in this quote the seamless integration of his science and spirituality.

For the rest of us who fall a light year or two below the level of genius, it can take decades to release habits and patterns from childhood. The way his brain sprang open at age twelve was surely part of his genius. He birthed himself into a new world, a parallel universe that opened within, revealing secrets about time and space, the atom and the cosmos.

As our world becomes more secularized, partly due to science, we begin to see that people of all faiths are equally sincere and passionate. This allows us to be less fanatical, and to see that our own beliefs are a small part of an ancient puzzle in our quest to know the divine. This viewpoint can reduce our religious wars so that we are less ready to kill *infidels* and can lead us into a larger, and I believe, deeper spirituality where love, compassion and acceptance are dominant. I'm convinced had I been raised in a different culture, I might be Buddhist or Hindu, or something else. We are herd animals, and early in life learn core, cellular truths about the divine.

Given the intensity and severity of my early religious training, it took many years to come out of the religious trance-state of childhood. Slowly I came to see the inevitable truth of our human condition: we all see the world in our own way; we put our unique stamp and spin on everything. Just as we did on the farm, with clinched fist, I've held up a handful of certain Bible verses into the prairie sky, releasing them slowly as we did with wheat, blowing away the chaff, as the good seeds fell into my other hand. If I blew hard enough, I'd end up with some Manitoba premium, hard winter wheat. One handful was more than enough to chew on for a lifetime.

Over the centuries, thousands of Christian cults and churches have been born, many with a short life span, all proclaiming to have the real truth, so help me God, about God. I'm part of this colorful parade, and choose scriptures that make sense to me, puffing away the chaff as much as I can. Other religions have their own factions, as the great search goes on. Yes, we all like to feel superior to at least someone, so it is natural we think our religion is the highest and truest.

As part of his spiritual journey, the American President, Thomas Jefferson, literally took a razor to the New Testament, cutting out words he thought were uttered by Jesus, eliminating all the rest. He then pasted the teachings of Jesus in a book known as the *Jefferson Bible*. He had a high ladder, did some sweet cherry picking, took pride in them and shared with us. I have more than ten versions of the Bible, and value my Jefferson Bible as one of the most interesting.

We sit together in temple worshipping the same God, but not quite. As a psychological reality, even when we belong to the same religion, each of us has somewhat unique images, thoughts and emotions about the divine. With our eighty-billion-plus neurons, and our greater array of synaptic connections, each brain and mind are unique, each created only once in the long history of time and space.

Like the characters in the mythic story, *The Wizard of Oz*, we are all seeking something bigger, something more. When our journey leads us to the wizard, we might find he is a pretender, a humbug of sorts, and we are free to enlarge our view of life and the divine ones. Once we see that the goddesses and gods have many masks and names, we are no longer confined by our original beliefs, and like Einstein, we let our minds spring open.

The made-up God of my childhood, I now see, was a pretender of sorts, an angry bookkeeper of the sky, a paranoid keeper of grudges. He was the god of summer thunder and lightning, bringing the night terrors. He was a god that had been made up by those closest to me, and as children, we inhaled the stories and believed them. A vital part of my journey has been to deconstruct such a vengeful deity, and many of us experience a similar process as we encounter open and closed doors along our path.

I often think of myself as a Christian mystic, believing our logical minds can only understand so much, and the rest truly is a leap of faith. My faith is uncertain, yet I trust that a wondrous intelligence is afoot in the cosmos. I am one of nearly eight billion humans alive on our planet, and there is no way I can know the final and complete truths about life.

Is my God better than yours, and more true? Does your God keep watch in the night while mine does not? Is my faith more genuine than yours? In the great scale of life, how do we weigh such matters?

In 2014, I wrote a five page piece inspired by an Esalen workshop, equating the divine essence with light (attached as an appendix). Here I quote a few sentences from that, for it captures one way I see the interpenetration of spirit in atoms, molecules, cells and the singing cosmos:

> *It is wise to meditate, to say our prayers, bang our drums and light our candles, for these can deepen us into the light. Yet, if we do none of these we are still indwelt, caught fast in the web of light. Our sweat lodges, synagogues, temples, mosques and cathedrals and other attempts to trap and focus light, help us know and remember. But let us not suppose that when we walk from our place of worship, we leave the light behind. That is pretense. The divine light of being cannot be trapped or left behind. Light is. Light is the source of all life. It pumps our blood and fires our thoughts. Light is here, there and everywhere.*

Our sister Jean died in 2002; throughout her life she remained faithful to the straight and narrow path of childhood, as did our brother, Bob (who died in March of 2015). Bill, as I noted earlier, rejected the full gospel. Helen, Phil and I have modified our early religious indoctrination, in ways compatible with our larger view of things, folding in life experiences as we went along.

I continue to have a passionate interest in spiritual issues, and see this as an enduring imprint from farm days. This passion has led to decades of reading from various spiritual traditions, and attending spiritual talks, seminars and retreats. I know bits and pieces of this and that, and am an expert on nothing. Who can know the whole of anything?

As I've noted, my teaching was dedicated to helping others find their own center, their own truths, their own soul and path. That has been, and continues to be my calling, and this book is part of my passion.

CHAPTER 19

—— ৎৡ ——

Soul Journey: Thawing Frozen Grief

He who wants to enter the divine realm first must enter his mother's
body and die herein.

PARACELSUS

Don't come here looking for answers. In this pub where we drink
there are only questions.
The answer is that there are no answers.
When you stop seeking, you will have found.
When you no longer want things to be different
Then they will finally, at last, be very different.
When you no longer demand for things to change
That will be the greatest change of all.
....you've lived small for so long harbored in the shelter from the
storms.
What was there to fear and is it worth the price of not knowing the
world?

TODD MCLEOD

ৎৡ

NOW I SHARE some intensely intimate experiences I've had, as I've faced my grief about Mother's death. I'm a teacher, and I take the risk of sharing what

I do, hoping that others will understand how deeply pain and trauma can scar us. My hope is that some who read what follows might be encouraged to more fully explore and heal their souls. I strike the Buddha bell again: beneath our happy smiles lies suffering. No exceptions. Not even for the perfect people in our glossy magazines. The theme carries forward five hundred years after the Buddha, to Christ, the suffering lamb.

My path to healing has involved both training as a therapist and being blessed in receiving both individual and group therapy. Because everything is two-sided, at times I've felt therapy was a curse. Waking up, becoming aware is fraught with challenges. Passing through the eye of the needle is not easy. One joke about California is that when you go to a party, every third person you meet is a realtor, and every fourth one, a therapist. My wife is a realtor, so we fit the joke. An intriguing majority of our family and friends have a therapistic bent: some are therapists, nearly all have had therapy of one form or another, some too much, some not enough. Just saying. Not wanting to name names. Most of us have made the four-hour drive to Esalen Institute, to ride that beautiful holy roller coaster into our minds, hearts and souls. Here on the western frontier, where exponential change rules the day, we need all the help we can get. I got on the therapy ride at age twenty-nine, and have yet to get off.

In therapeutic circles, one term we use is *deep work*, referring to those moments when we shift from our happy selves into the suffering that dwells within. Some of our suffering is universal to our condition and hard to word, hard to identify. Part of our pain is personal and tied to the unique trauma that each of us has experienced. Words and thoughts in silent skies circle round, seeking contact, wanting grounding, wanting to be shared. As we slow and surrender to what sleeps within, we grasp for words to help us connect to our depths, and to help others understand.

A fundamental assumption of most therapy is that suffering impacts our lives in one way or another, and if we touch into it and bring it into consciousness, we can lessen the unconscious impact it has on us. An additional therapeutic belief is that our pain is stored in our emotions and bodies, more than our conscious minds, thus working with feelings and body sensations is vital to healing ourselves. We think too, that greed, anger, sadness, jealousy, fear, hatred, and other toxic emotions that blight our aliveness, are compacted forms of energy, stored in our cells and emotions. Our brains and bodies are electromagnetic energy systems; this seems especially true for our emotions.

As we summon negative emotions and body states into our awareness, making them as conscious as we can, we can at least partially defuse them and tap into more positive energies.

Diving into our pain, witnessing our suffering scares us and demands resolute courage. Over several decades, what I've seen again and again, in myself and others, is that when we touch our deepest pain, equanimity, peace, joy and other such emotions are released. I like to say that diving deep leads to soaring high.

In my years of diving and soaring, I've discovered ongoing layers of memories, emotions, thoughts and images in myself, and most every day I unearth something new. We are all complex and infinitely high, deep, and mysterious. As we drill through our most obvious stories, emotions and images, we discover endless, subtle levels that impact daily behavior. The process is unending, and this may be one reason some Buddhists say we need seven lives to get it right.

I'll share a few of the most painful therapeutic encounters I've had, hoping again, that my sharing might inspire others to be warriors in their own way. For me, it is entirely clear: facing my wounds has helped heal me, and has added more creative energy to my life. Plowing up my inner fields, exposing my soul to the light of day, has been a passionate personal and professional quest. And I love to help others do the same. This has been my north star. This star that arose within, birthed in the mystery of ancestral memories and more.

I left the farm with all of me, and in my thirties started becoming aware of how my anger, grief, shame, and fear were harmful to myself and others. I've seen this same trajectory in others: the vitality of youth can shield many of us from early pain. As we grow older, we may be startled by a sad memory that comes out of nowhere, as with the lauded author, Margaret Laurence (also noted in the first part of my chapter on Mother's death) who after five decades is inundated with grief for her mother.

At the everyday work level—my teaching and other duties related to that—I managed quite well, as most of us do, even if we're packing around a ton of pain. In fact, in my public life I was playful and optimistic, and my coyote-trickster self was in full bloom. As a teaching professor I loved my students, and they respected and loved me and my classes. As many of us do, I expressed the best and worst parts of me in our family. I was both a good husband/father, and I also expressed too much anger, shaming and blaming. Below the surface were my pain and my enchantment with the sacred spiritual part of life. One of my big challenges has been to understand and reconcile my divergent selves; this integration is ongoing.

In private, when I slowed down and dropped in, fear, sadness, paranoia and anger could arise. As I started to read about shame, I realized I engaged in many self-shaming and blaming thoughts every day. My first reaction to others was often to blame, shame and criticize. Beginning in my middle teen years I'd often break down, sobbing in bed, for reasons that were out of proportion to events in my current life. This pattern persisted after Ruthie and I were married, and she'd hold me in the night as I cried. What was this well of sadness and grief? It took me some time before I could explore these waters. I was a mystery to myself, and frightened to put myself under the microscope.

Watching and listening to my wife, I began to realize I might live my life more like her, with her stable, patient, predictable loving kindness, a fact we attributed to her loving and stable home life. My friends and colleagues also inspired me to take inner inventory. I was beginning to wake up, to be more conscious. I was following the light of consciousness along a dimly lit furrow that lead to the earth of me.

Until my early thirties I was terrified to think of Mother, so I never really knew where my sadness—and all the rest—was coming from. When I thought of her, as quickly as I could I'd dismiss her death as a thing long past, and of little consequence. I could not consciously know it, but I was preparing to enter the valley, the well of tears. I never thought of her, or called her Mom, for that implied an intimacy I did not, do not know.

Important in my awakening process was the extensive literature focusing on the disturbing effects of the loss of a parent early in life. When I first started reading this research I was not connecting it to my emotions—reading it, rather, as part of my academic learning. Before long, I began to see that I was one of the *kids* traumatized by a mother's death, and it became increasingly difficult to read about the pain tied to parental death. I've recently read that memory scars from the death of a parent in childhood are genetically passed on to the offspring of other living creatures. It is sad and sobering to know that painful memories are passed down through generations, and that this stream of suffering wounds us and our children, through no fault of our own.

As I continued my inner quest, I plunged into a variety of experimental groups that popped up in the late sixties, including encounter, sensitivity, somatic and gestalt groups. I fell into my first therapy group *accidentally*—something I now see as a soul-guided thing, as divine leadership, or perhaps the gentle, pre-conscious guiding of Mother.

Over the years, I'd occasionally remember Mother, but this was limited most of the time to thoughts, rather than the deeper reality of emotions. And of course, my emotions would sometimes surface, wanted or not. Until very recently, when I smelled flowers, with few exceptions, I was back at Mother's funeral, and I'd be gripped with sadness; my voice would break and on my turned face, tears might drizzle down.

I was in my early thirties the first time I talked about Mother with a therapist. As I formed my first words about her death, in a quick moment, my words were blocked by a lump in my heart and throat. I sat there shaking, shaking, crying, shivering like a cold baby.

In various therapy groups, my pain over Mother's death has unexpectedly surfaced. In one group at Esalen Institute, as my grief came up, the leader asked if I could pretend I was eight and talk with my mother, to say goodbye to her, and tell her how I loved her. I could sense words forming in me, but was terrified to speak them for fear that I'd die.

In a different session I dive deep into anger: anger at life, at God, at the cancer that killed my mother. I surprise myself with my rage, and sense how it sources much of my suffering. The therapist asks if I want to be angry at Mother for leaving me, and I can't do it, for it seems so wrong to yell at her.

The therapeutic process of holotropic breathing is another method that can help us move from our everyday brain centers into altered states that draw more on our emotional centers. This procedure occurs in a group context of anywhere from 20 to 300 individuals. Willing warriors lie on a mat for two to three hours, taking deep and rapid breaths for much of the time. This tweaks brain chemistry and can lead to some remarkable experiences, ranging from ecstasy, to fear, grief, anger, stillness, peace and compassion. During a few of these sessions, grief for my mother has surfaced, along with many other feelings.

In one such group, as various feelings, images and words rise and fall away, I'm going for the gusto, the big breakthrough where ego and suffering are transcended once and for all. I want to be a Buddha. After an hour or so with many emotions, the old wave of mother-grief floods into me. The leader comes over, cradles my head, asking me to imagine I'm eight years old, with my dying mother holding me. As well as I can, I imagine I'm my mother talking to little me: *Albert, you are a good little boy, and you have strong legs to carry you through life. I see you running and leaping about, and see how strong and quick you are. You have a good heart, and can help look after our family. I'm leaving soon, but you must not worry about me. Albert, I'm going to a place far away, and some day you can join me.*

This is only the first half of it: the therapist next invites me to be my eight-year-old self and to talk to Mother. As I imagine Mother holding me, I can, for the first time, feel her long-forgotten embrace, and I force excruciating words: *Mother, Mother, why are you sick, and where are you going? I don't understand why you are sick, why you must leave. I want to go with you, I want to go with you!! Please take me with you, take me with you.*

I'm heaving with pain, curled in a fetal position on my mat—a mat wet with sweat and tears, and littered with Kleenex. I sob until my ancient well is dry. As often happens with such a plunge into the dark night of soul, I end up in a new place, a place of profound calmness and peace. I feel an unfamiliar life energy for weeks afterwards. I went in, I surrendered, I emptied and filled.

In another Esalen group, using body-focused therapy, I lie on the floor with others in our group and dreamy music in the background. With eyes closed we are encouraged to sense into our bodies, and see what emotions and images come up. After several minutes I notice my hands, all on their own, have drifted up and are caressing my stomach, centering on my belly button. Images of Mother leap up as I realize this is my last physical connection with her. Grief and gratitude arise in me.

Unconscious cellular memories are potent and real: at age forty-seven, I suffer acute abdominal pains. I drop into my silent prairie place with night terrors, knowing I will die from cancer just as Mother did at age forty-seven. After several days I let Ruthie know, and she, too, is fearing the worst. Our doctor seems unconcerned, and eventually the pain goes away. I feel reborn; my life will go on. Gratitude and faith infuse my days.

As I mentioned earlier, in March of 1993 my friend, Trish, gave me a book on Tibetan Buddhism, and again my soul cracked open. That book was my bible for several years, and the pages carry tear stains, underlines, double underlines, multi-colored underlines and marginal notes from those rending years. Those too, were the years when I dived deep and soared high. I found such comfort in the Buddhist view, and part of this was the acceptance of the idea that all lives, all life, is scarred with suffering. Important too, was realizing there is a way to ameliorate suffering, through right thought and action.

I draw inspiration from others, especially my sister Helen, two years my senior. In a 2004 letter she writes that she lights a candle every year, honoring the death of Mother. She recalls: *How terrible it was for me to see them throw dirt on her casket at the burial sight… it seemed wicked and cruel and so very final. I always have some depression on these days, but this year I have more a sense of acceptance and thankfulness for God's good grace that carried us on, and helped fill the void as we learned to open our hearts to others…we are the persons we are today in part because of our loss. I am strong, loving, caring and nurturing, sensitive, tender, wise, brave and understanding while also fearful, insecure and highly vigilant. I'm loving myself more with all my weaknesses and so better able to deal with them…*

Helen also remembers the secrecy around Mother's illness and death. She writes how, at age eleven, she tried to help Phil and me cope with Mother's passing, and how lost she felt in this task. She knows she did as well as she could, yet also feels the need to forgive herself for not loving and guiding us more.

She also describes her denial of grief and pain, and how this made her afraid of many emotions. Like me, in prayer times and therapy sessions, she eventually faced her pain and says: *I found a great deal of healing...and the process goes on and always will...* She feels like she is a stronger person because of her struggles, and that she has met her challenges with *grace,* and is no longer a victim of her past. My heart is warmed by all she says, especially when she talks about spreading her wings, and seeing God in all of life! Exclamation point indeed.

Part of her healing was working for several years with children who had lost a parent, making it safe for them to grieve. She believes too, that her sadness about Mother not living to see her grandchildren has given her an increased love of her own grandchildren. Her actions verify all she reports. Thank you Helen! I hold onto your words and feel your courage, your love and light, carrying me.

In 2012 I return to therapy, seeing a Jungian dream therapist, to explore a series of vivid, complex dreams. As we process my dreams, we embrace the Jungian notion that losing a mother is the loss of the feminine aspect of life, a sundering of half of the soul. Then the bomb. After several sessions she is pleased to announce that Mother's death is the pivotal event of my life. I don't want to hear her crowning insight—after all, I've spent serious money on therapy, and am decades removed from the farm. But there it is. Her words hang in the air, and I, unhappily, take them in. I wonder: is there no end to this? I walk dejectedly from her office, random tears marking my way.

If we could press a button and delete our painful memories, our current suffering, most of us would do so. The core issue is we don't understand how memories are recorded in our brains, thus are uncertain how to soften and reframe painful memories. Based on my readings, some recent lab experiments with psychoactive drugs—especially psilocybin —may be the most immediate way of breaking up the symptoms of P.T.S.D and similar trauma. I've lacked the courage to follow this path.

Around our planet, we've used many practices to help us heal, some very successful. The list of healing rituals and processes is a long one, and most are part of the thousands of religions and spiritual paths we've created.

Our farm family honored the healing power of prayer, singing and worshiping with others. At Esalen, I've had the chance to study and participate in some of the earliest, indigenous healing traditions of shamanism, including sweat lodges and vision quests in the native North American tradition. Fasting, chanting, dancing, meditation and multiple other rituals and practices can heal and restore.

Wisdom writers have suggested that when we lose a parent early in life we spend the rest of our lives looking for them, and this has been my experience. I was blessed to find a second mother—my wife's mother, Mrs. Samona Rice. She loved me from the first time she saw me. Perhaps she sensed my mother-hunger. She later told me that prior to our first meeting, she expected a tall Mounty to ride in on a white steed. No matter. She had a love of all things Canadian.

She was a gifted violinist, using her instrument to glorify God in churches large and small. Tragically, she lost her hearing at age 43, but this did not dampen her sense of humor or love of life. She was a noble woman, and we lived with her for six years prior to her passing. She told me more than once I was a true son, and I my spirit took flight when I heard such endearments.

I watch nature programs on TV, including documentaries showing elephants returning to gently nuzzle the bones of dead family members. At times they will carry a bone and place it near a tree, perhaps to protect it, perhaps using the tree as a monument to those who no longer walk about. We may be more like the elephants than we imagine. Like them, we are unwittingly called by a deeper knowing that leads us to return along unmarked paths to honor loved ones.

For such a return, no compass is needed, nor do we have to check the wind; we simply do what we do, putting one foot in front of another. We say our prayers, we trust in life, we have faith we'll find our way. Intentions, planning and scheduling are not the most vital part of this journey, for it happens below awareness, in our old brains. Our deeper intelligence is often beyond our conscious knowing, is beyond words, and we don't embrace it—it embraces and carries us along, even in the nighttime, across land and ocean. Our inner deserts and jungles are vast, and if we want, we too, can find our way; we can return to honor the bones of loved ones, and in the doing learn something of ourselves.

There at the sacred spot we stand; we say: *Here I am. I've returned to honor you. May my tears nourish the flowers I leave on your grave. I have not forgotten you and you are often in my thoughts. You live on in my heart. I've come here to also honor myself, to remember who I am.*

With reverence, we've called this ground-intelligence by many names— names not needed by the geese or by the salmon as they return home. Without planning, we stand one day in a place unremembered for a long time, now as clear as the cry of a morning lark. We are awed, surprised we arrived here. We stand as supplicants, uncertain, eyes wide open. We wonder: did we find this place or did it find us?

Returning to our core question: do we have a part of us that is separate from our molecules, our marrow? My incessant scientist takes the podium again, to stake another claim: he tells us the science of microchimerism informs us that the cells of mothers live on in their children. After a child is formed in the womb, a few cells from this new individual pass into the mother's body, and some of her cells pass through the placenta into her child. This means too, that cells from older siblings, resident within mother's body, can be passed on to younger children.

Families are not mere concepts: blood is thicker than water and we are linked, mothered, fathered, sistered, and brothered at the cellular level. We are continuous with the past and future; we are embedded creatures, part of a web we are only beginning to fathom. I am most decidedly not my own man.

When we grieve others, are we not also grieving our own future death? This is a literal truth when we realize that when mothers pass, they take some of our cells, part of us, with them. In grieving them, we grieve the part of us that dies with them.

As I visualize Mother's cells within, I believe her quiet voice has guided me more than I can ever consciously know. Do her cells find voice through me? Are the words I seek here partly shaped by her? *Mother! Do you look through my eyes—the eyes you bequeathed to me? Your long, long prayers for us, for me, have helped me chart my course. This is my faith and my gratitude.*

Given the odd decisions our species has made across time, we might conclude we are not as conscious, as logical and intelligent as we like to think. We pride ourselves on our big brains, pretending we are superior to the critters around us and the trillions of bacteria within. In fact, our lives and our decisions are driven in vital ways by the hungry ghosts that inhabit us; by atoms, genes, hormones, bacteria and nerve cells that vibrate within, carrying out their own plans and guiding our waking minds. Each gene, each bacterium, carries a trove of information stored over the centuries to be read, to speak in its own time.

Here is one of many examples from my own life. It is fall of 2015, and our family is walking in the park, looking after our two-year-old grandson, Oliver, while his mom and dad have a break. Oliver takes a little fall and cries for his mother, *I want my mommy, I want my mommy,* over and over, for several minutes. As we console him, out of the mists of memory, an unspoken voice arises in me: *Well, Oliver I want my mommy too!* With the voice, comes a burst of micro-images of our farm, our family and of Mother, along with a wisp of sadness and longing.

I'm a bit surprised by the upwelling of ancient images and my mother longing. A few moments later, I share my ghostly voice experience with my wife and daughter, and they share back that they heard no such inner voice. So there we have it. For those of us who've lost a parent early in life, decades later we carry the soul-longing for the mother or father who has crossed the great divide.

I engage in another imagined conversation with Mother: *Mother! I've not forgotten you. All of your daughters and sons remember you. My memory is mainly of your suffering and death. I keep the faith that your prayers for all of us have guided and protected us.*

Some nights, in an elephant frame of mind, I think of your bones, of you and Dad, lying serenely in the cemetery in far off Neepawa, and I'm thankful not only for your souls, but also for your bodies, the bones that carried you and birthed us. And, Mother, something you might not know: after your chains fell away, someone cut off a bit of your hair. Reddish brown it is. I'm pleased to tell you that I have a few sacred strands of your hair in my desk drawer. I love you Mother.

One Buddhist teaching says that when we leave our bodies, it's like running into the arms of mother. *So Mother, wait awhile, and I'll come running.*

Epilogue

Life must be lived forward, but can only be understood backwards.

KIERKEGAARD.

༉

Though absent long,
These forms of beauty have not been to me,
As is a landscape to a blind man's eye:
But oft, in lonely rooms, and mid the din
Of towns and cities, I have owed to them,
In hours of weariness, sensations sweet,
Felt in the blood and, and felt along the heart....

....Though changed, no doubt, from what I was, when first
I came among these hills; when like a roe
I bounded o'er the mountains....and the lonely streams
Wherever nature led.....(the coarser pleasures of my boyish days,
And their glad animal movements all gone by,)....

....For I have learned to look on nature, not as in the hour
Of thoughtless youth, but hearing oftentimes
The still, sad music of humanity,
Nor harsh nor grating, though of ample power

To chasten and subdue. And I have felt
A presence that disturbs me with the joy
Of elevated thoughts; a sense sublime
Of something far more deeply interfused,
Whose dwelling is the light of setting suns.....

LINES SELECTED FROM : WILLIAM WORDSWORTH,
TINTERN ABBEY.

ာ

IT SEEMS INEVITABLE, given how our brains work, that we look to both the past and the future. We can't be certain of the future, but as we reflect back in time, certain memories stand out. Our accumulated past makes up most of who we are. Each of us is a monument of life, built on the foundation of childhood.

Our lives share much in common, yet each is also unique in less obvious ways. While this has been my story, it is my hope that you, who've read it, or parts of it, have experienced a quickening of your memories of childhood, and that such memories have not been too sad or painful. My tale is but one story among all the billions who've passed, and those yet alive. Each life, each journey, each story is important.

I also hope that in reflecting on our roots, each of us has arrived at a more clear understanding of who we are, and the meanings of our lives. Most importantly, I hope that with this has come gratitude to those who birthed us, and guaranteed our survival.

We are graced by the gift of life, and we also drink from the well of suffering. As we look back to our first steps in life, if we choose, we can move away from our complaints, our feelings of being left out, and have more appreciation for the gift of life. This has been my inner change as I've recalled our farm family. We had hard times, we had good times.

We humans are a small part of a vast and complex web of life and relationships, each of us with fulfilled and broken dreams. As we embrace the past, we might think of the doors others opened for us, the love extended, the smiles offered. We are birthed and suckled by our mothers, and then helped along by other family members, friends and teachers.

As we think back, we remember not only open doors; we might also think of the doors that closed on us. Facing a closed door can wound deeply, leaving us lost and angry. Plans, schemes and dreams might shatter when our way is blocked. When a door closes we can make up *if only* stories, and regretfully, I've done this too much in my life. Now, writing my story, I've seen the closed doors were gifts I could not receive at the time. Like others, I stared at the barrier in front of me, felt my heart breaking and heaven receding away.

More than an open door, a closed door invites us to take inventory, to question our core assumptions, and the stories we weave. When others close a door to us, we have the chance to open inner doors, to reflect and make changes, to head off in a new direction more suited to our lives. As we open the doors to our heart, mind and soul, light streams in.

Inescapably, we dwell within the bosom of time, space and gravity. We are carried along by our turning planet, adrift in a cosmos of staggering size. We are indwelt, pregnant with atoms, molecules and cells too small for reckoning.

Those of us who make it to the autumn of life have been given the gift of more time. Each of us is a small arrow point on the tip of time (some of us sharper than others) and each of us leaves a mark, a memory of who we were, of how we lived, what we did or did not do.

If we have children, they carry our essence and memories forward. Those of us with grandchildren, and even great grandchildren, are profoundly blessed. My wife, Samona Ruth, and I have been graced with a son and daughter, their spouses, and three grandchildren.

We, I, leave this late harvest of leaves to you, family and friends, and especially to you precious grandchildren, Somerset, Oliver Hawk and Lillian Skye. And to all who read this, may your lives be blessed, your days marked with grace.

───────── ❧ ─────────

Refractions On The Nature Of Light, Life, Longing

I am the light that is over all things. I am all: from me all came forth, and to me all attained. Split a piece of wood; I am there. Lift up the stone and you will find me there.

WORDS ATTRIBUTED TO JESUS, FROM GOSPEL OF THOMAS,
LOGION 77

Where is the way where light dwelleth? And as for darkness where is the place thereof……By what way is the light parted, which scattereth the east wind upon the earth?

GOD, SPEAKING FROM THE WHIRLWIND, TO JOB. JOB 38: 19 & 24

❧

THE FOLLOWING SUMMARIZES an experience I had in Miranda MacPherson's group at Esalen, March, 2014. During the week, we engaged in various spiritual rituals, including meditation, this one beginning with the question of what lies under our ego, what is our essence as deeply as we can know it?

My experience was oddly devoid of emotion, subtle, and just as oddly, sneaked up on my soul through the *backdoor* of science. It had the simple quality of *is-ness*. My thoughts went to the atoms, molecules and cells in me, and all their busyness. At one point, I felt my fingernails growing and realized I was not doing that; that some force deep in me was sustaining, growing me. I realized this was the life force of light. During our week, we were blessed with visitations by many dolphins and whales and the dance of light from them and the ocean helped me *sea* what follows.

Miranda's soul energy and that of our group was the womb that birthed this experience. Miranda believes in and teaches a *non-dual* view of life, and the insights that arose in me, I believe, are genetically true to that vision. Non-dual, as I understand it, means that under all the faces, the looks life gives us, is one essential, unshakable thing.

In the past, and even today, many believe the world is composed of two distinct parts: the world of objects/things—often seen as secular—and the world of spirit, the sacred, diaphanous realm, imagined as the dwelling place of the gods and goddesses, known by many names. Our planet has spun along, split in two, for all these years.

Another view is that life is continuous, that no part is completely separate from any other part. This perspective of wholeness and oneness has been embraced by spiritual masters and mystics over the centuries and is now emerging on a wider scale, driven in part by science.

If we care to believe it, we've learned (mainly from the gospel of Einstein,) that matter and energy are equivalents, that they are interchangeable. We've discovered that the atom is the bedrock of everything, but it is not the solid matter we've thought it was, for it is a bundle of shimmering, secret energy—the thing behind the thing.

The raw energy in the elusive heart of each atom keeps our cosmos running, and if we split it apart we get a blinding yield of light that in reckless moments can lead us to think of the *divine light* written about since we walked out of Africa. Paradoxically, our final spiritual revelation may rest on the dogma of Einstein which informs us that energy equals mass times the speed of light squared. That's a lot of light—more perhaps than the old masters who talked of divine light could have imagined.

The cosmos, from atoms out to dim galaxies, to you and your neighbor, is filled and fueled with light, and none of it is made of two things, not sundered, for everything is compressed light.

The discovery of light as essence, as prime mover is an embarrassment for all of us, whatever side of the great historical divide we occupy. Those on the religious side of things, when they perceived the divine ones as distant, often missed or misunderstood the imperative and immediate reality of light that *dwells in and moves through all things,* while the tough minded materialists could scarcely imagine that *solid objects* are charged with pulsing energy—energy that today remains a mystery. And so the headline for today: because everything is sourced in light, you are an enlightened, light-filled being. More startling, so is the person you live with, and all those you know, even your enemies.

Interestingly, we hang in equipoise at precisely the right distance from our sun. The continuous infusion of light flowers our earth, sustaining us, birthing our air, our food, water, our cells, our brains and these words and the images that spring up as you read these words. Light is. Light is inescapable. Light is us, and *we are light.* Thanks be to the sun.

Like it or not, light is inevitable, invincible. We slosh around in photons—light particles—and they slosh around in us. As dolphins swim in ocean, we swim in light waves, and those waves swim in us. Our skin, which we think makes of us an island, does not, cannot, for our skin is thinly veiled light, and like the rest of us, lets the light in and out. Light photons pour through us as we breathe and energize us through the water we drink and the food we eat. And the coffee! We can see only because light bounces off objects, pours through our eyes, refracting from our inner mirrors forming words, images, dreams. This paper, these words, your reflections on these words, are all birthed from light. We can never be separate from the light.

From ancient times our species has revered the light, carefully naming and assigning meanings to the stars, planets, and constellations. Sun, moon and star worship is in our light-fueled genes. It is no accident that our spiritual teachings have seen and continue to see light as divine, as spiritually infused, for they are refractions of light. Across time, light-filled visions have inspired both scientists and spiritual seekers. Einstein walks away from the clock tower in Bern and has a new vision of the nature of light. After their potent infusions of light, Buddha and Black Elk both awaken to greet and be greeted by the light of the morning star. Light filled visions have fired imaginations since the time of our first shamans.

And now the creation story of monotheistic science tells us that everything, every first and last thing, began with a blinding flash of light: every quark, atom and molecule, all birthed in light. Time, space, and gravity and the strong and weak forces of life, dark and light, were all born on that morning long ago. And the energy from this light continues to sustain us. If our sun goes out, we go out.

Science and religion are equally created by light, and make one in sight. Our fantastic pursuit of truth and our longings for the divine have led both to the same inevitable altar. Both are fired by light, invincible, all encompassing, all absorbing light. From the microbes, to the worms, to the ponderous whales, we are solar beings, inexorably fueled by the sun. Science, religion and each of us drink from one communal cup.

When we notice the similarities of religion and science, we see the light more clearly, for now, beyond our traditional places of worship, we can pay homage in the labs of science, and most recently, to the large hadron collider embosomed in Mother Earth. There, at nearly the speed of light, we break the bread of atoms, hoping to discover in the smallest crumbs a *God particle* that will help light our way. And for science, as new facts are unearthed, the mysterious unknown expands.

We may or may not believe in light, yet light abides, light is. The electromagnetic energy of light is the life pulse of everything, including our brains; the hormones and chemicals are, themselves, forms of light. The synapse is that holy point in our brain, where light leaps from the hand of a giving neuron to the welcoming palm of another. In this secret recess, all thought—this thought—is born, as well as the thoughts that leap up as you read this. We did not create ourselves in the womb of our mother, nor do we create our thoughts. Everything is the dance of light and shadow, of light reflecting, mirroring back on itself. This can be viewed as the fountainhead of all spiritual teachings, of science, of the light and dark that marks our path.

Again: we, and all life, are fueled by the invincible fabric of light, a *ground of being* that simply *is,* and my or your belief cannot alter this. I, we, are along for the ride.

We are birthed and carried by beams of light. We can choose to see light as only or purely physical, as particulate matter, yet this view is not supported by either science or religion, for we know that all matter is a pulsing, mysterious form of energy of unknown origin.

Thus we are all enlightened beings, from microbes to bumble bees, our ants and uncles, the two-legged, the four-legged, the many-legged, the plants and trees. We are all inescapably creatures of light. Light is the raw energy of our planetary system and manifests as earth, as water, as leaf, as wispy thought. Given the magic of science, today more than ever we are blessed to refract light in a way to let us see this, to be conscious and reflective.

The ego, the self, the id, the you, the me, the I, are all interesting refractions of light. It is not necessary to believe that light is the essence, the core energy of all life. We can know and believe this or not, even as the light sustains us. It simply is.

Because we are creatures of light, we also have shadowy, dark tendencies. Shadow is birthed by light. Light begets shadow, shadow cannot beget light. Shadow is diminished light. Dictators who've tromped through time have cast dark shadows birthed by their love: their love of country, of power and greed, and by their voracious dreams. The dictator resident in each of us, seen in our grasping, our love of power, fame and riches, is born in light. Light casts shadows, and thus shadow contains light. When the sun goes down, when the light dims, a million suns come out.

Each of us uniquely refracts both light and shadow that shifts from moment to moment, and day to day. Our wisest wisdom teachers and scientists reflect light in a peculiar, gem-like way, and the light in us is fascinated, humbled by their light. Yet we are all equally fueled and infused with light—enlightened beings in that sense. We all have unique refractions of wisdom and insights: our children, and so-called *simple folk* can startle us in any moment with their insights.

Thus endeth the old guru shame game of *I'm enlightened and you're not, I'm enlightened and you're not!* Now we can see that we're all teachers and students with each other. Here we fall silent and open our ears. Light-inspired wisdom resides inevitably in each of us.

Most of us desire more wisdom, more truth, more light, yet excess light burns. We are cautioned by the moth that flies into the flame, by Icarus and his high flight. We are like sister moon; we have our cycles, daily, hourly, and our dark side, our occasional eclipse, our lover's quarrel with the divine, our love of and railing against science. All our hungry ghosts are incorrigible creatures of light.

Just as the Divine Ones—the gods—have many faces, so does light: light itself dances between particle form and wave form. We naturally believe our God is the highest and wisest; now we can see that our old tribal gods and goddesses are birthed by the same light, each a uniquely amazing refraction inviting us to kneel.

When we see this, there is no escape, nowhere to hide. Light has infused itself inescapably into the cells of history, playing a mad game of light and shadow, of hide-and-seek. The looking-glass gods. Like the photons of light that switch between particle and wave, we too play hide-and-seek, furiously seeking and running from the divine light and the light of science. Our arms that reach for truth and the bunkers we build for hiding are, themselves, made of foolproof light. We doubt and believe, we trust and fear, we love and hate, and all of this is an inescapable play of light and shadow.

Our pretenses, doubts, and beliefs about science and religion are all interesting reflections of light. My feelings, my thoughts of light cannot alter the nature of light, for it simply is. I can curse the light or the darkness, yet both are born of light. All the words, the emotions we feel about light, circle round as a wonderful, sometimes painful sun dance.

Light is all, and where light is, there are no insiders or outsiders, no us and them, no self and other. The priest, philosopher, poet, and prostitute, those who march and don't march: all creatures of light. Knowing this, there is no need for crucifying ego, or self, no need to despise ourselves for our sometime wicked thoughts, our nasty emotions, our relentless judgments. All of these are amazing, inescapable reflections of light and can only be sourced in light.

Our recriminations, our loathing, our crawling on our knees—all desires to slay the self—are curious reflections of light. The hand that receives the nail, the hand that drives it in, the hammer and nail themselves are made of light. Here there is no escape, no hiding place, no rock, no tomb safe enough. Light is; light cannot be buried or wished out of existence. Here there is no need to die to anything, no need to be reborn. No need to clip coupons, or take the garbage out.

From these judicial reflections we might wish to recuse ourselves, but where would we go? All the courtrooms brim with light, and our yammering prosecutors, our ego defenders, the law itself, all birthed in light. Rumors of jail abound, yet none are found.

It is wise to meditate, to say our prayers, bang our drums and light our candles, for these can deepen us into the light. Yet, if we do none of these we are still indwelt, caught fast in the web of light. Our sweat lodges, synagogues, temples, mosques and cathedrals, and other attempts to trap and focus light, help us know and remember. But let us not suppose that when we walk from our place of worship, we leave the light behind. That is pretense. The divine light of being cannot be trapped or left behind. Light is. Light is the source of all life. It pumps our blood, fires our thoughts and sources our dreams. Light is here, there and everywhere.

What is odd is that we ever felt separate, unenlightened, ungraced. Around this thought we wrap prayer shawls for reflection. Are we not carried by the same earth, do we not breathe a common air? Were we not born from our mother's wombs, the larger tree of life, and is not everything infused by one light? We did not ask for any of this, did not create any of this. None of this is manufactured, imported or exported. Earth is. Air is. Our planet turns, the sun shines, our moon rises and sets. It is remarkable that we've chased and fled the divine light as though it could be anywhere other than here. To think we ran in circles!! That we thought the honeymoon was over. Let us light a candle here. We were delightfully crazed creatures and now we see it. To this, we raise our glasses to catch more light. Now we can rest in and embrace the light that has embraced us, infused us all along.

And we will surely forget all of this. Then, at the rising of the sun, we'll remember again. And then forget again. Inevitably, a waxing moon will call to us, and we'll look up and remember once more. All these things are gifts of light.

Finally: Death! You! Our constant companion; who then art thou? You are the magical midwife to our next birth; you lift the veil from our precious particularization of light. When you happen along, we dissolve into wave form—the dematerialization of photons, the great diaspora, the scattering into the eternal light field around us, to reform again as it will. There is no escape. Light is, light is in us and all about. Inescapable, inevitable light.

The Last Perilous Particle

Vitriolum: visit the interior of the earth

ෆ

WE LIVE IN interesting, if not dangerous, times, and one of the most interesting tension points is the one between science and religion, for these are the bones, the mythic infrastructure, the foundation and energy source for who we are and for daily action. The tension vibrates in many of us, but especially so between the keepers of the faith in the spiritual traditions, who see spirit as primary and are nervous about science. Scientists, meanwhile often feel constrained and misunderstood by the guardians of religion, throwing up their arms in despair as they plead for more understanding.

This tension, the danger is ancient. Our human history is the story of shifting loyalties to different gods, of hammering out theologies, spinning new stories that seem more advanced than the old. We love our old altars, but also have the need to create new ones. Those who hold onto the past are especially stressed, sensing that the accelerating pace of change will leave them homeless, lost in a space and time they no longer recognize. There is a widespread sense that we are at a radical place in this process, a break off place, where *the center cannot hold,* a wild time when everything might be spinning into a nameless vortex, a time where the arrow of our hunger might strike a target in some parallel universe. Some speculate about a meltdown of science and theology into one new element unpredicted by any periodic table.

One of the core issues is this: all of science rests on the assumption that some particle, some fragile, wispy, perilous bit of matter serves as the foundation on which all reality is built. This latest scientific creation story informs us that some 13.7 billion years in the past, an infinitely small, and infinitely pregnant particle erupted with a BIG BANG, and birthed everything that is, both within and without. Because most of us don't like explosions, it is enough to make us run right back into the arms of God.

Without the existence of such an obsessively small, and marvelously pregnant piece of matter, science does not, cannot exist, for it then falls into the realm of the old theorists: the wisdom/spiritual traditions that posit the existence of pure spirit, without any material substrate, without any matter at all, as the source of all things.

More than ever, the world of data, of science, meets the diaphanous world of spirit. And more than ever, the attempt to keep these two at arm's length appears doomed to failure. The diaphanous and the data, like many polarities, may be doomed to a strange reconciliation, now only dimly glimpsed.

As the questions about the origin of that first pregnant particle become more demanding, some physicists believe there may well have been infinite big bangs, and thus, infinite universes, with big bangs continuing like cosmic popcorn over trillions of years, even to infinity. This is the dangerous place in which we scientists find ourselves, for as much as the old spiritual masters, we too want to understand origins; yet as we do so, we threaten the basis of science.

At times, the idea of infinite big bangs and thus infinite universes, can feel like a desperate escape clause, a flight to some cosmic hole-in-the-wall, a last refuge housing our secret suspicions about the implausibility of the BIG BANG. Late at night, busy in our labs, the suspicion arises that our big bang creation theory serves only to make the old creation stories more believable. Our creation stories are also nearly infinite: we were birthed by a great dragon, or we walked out of the dream time, or once there was a Garden of Eden through which we walked with God. Parked next to the idea of infinite big bangs, all these stories seem reasonable, doable. So it may be that in this way, the new theoreticians lend gravity to the older ruminations.

As scientists work to imagine the size of the first necessary particle, infinitely small and infinitely pregnant—as we realize it is far too small to haul into any laboratory, to put under any microscope, our incredulity and wonder are raised to a quantum level. At this level we can say most anything and have it believed. Measured against this tentative, wispy beginning, a grain of sand is taller than Everest, an ant is a giant cosmic earth-moving machine reaching as far as the Andromeda galaxy. The scope of this makes beggars of our 80 billion neurons, our 100 trillion synaptic connections, leaving us reeling, incredulous.

Old and new theoreticians alike: we are all humbled and stretched by both the power of the small, the atom and all her particles, and the first big bang particle, dwarfed too by the large, the cosmic dimension of things 13.7 billion light years to the edge of our universe and counting.

Now, with the discovery of dark energy (DE) and dark matter (DM), the situation between science and religion has a startling new edge, for both DE and DM appear real enough, yet neither demonstrates any atomic structure or basis. Present calculations figure that DE and DM make up 96% of all the energy and matter of the universe, and neither of these are yet measurable by any of our instruments. These partners in crime seem happy to ignore the photons that populate our planetary system, delighted to stay below our radar, unwilling to give us any feedback. And yet, our most powerful mathematical models state that DE and DM must be real, otherwise the cosmos would collapse or explode. Not good.

The hypothesis is that DE and DM must have a different particle structure from all the matter we know. Again, even though we cannot see or measure these particles, they must be assumed to exist, otherwise science is in the business of mucking in spirit, something that will never do. Science is forced to posit that all things are rooted in material particles, whether detectable or not. The sooner such particles are found, the better for science.

If only four percent of the universe is made of the energy and matter we can detect with our senses and instruments, this leaves us a decidedly narrow band of awareness, similar to the limited band of light we can see, or the limited range of sound we hear. It means too, that our grandest mathematical theories and laws of physics apply to a truly narrow slice of the universe. Once again, we see that the realm of the unknown towers over the world of the known, and suggests we will never be able to explain most of what is going on *out there* in the cosmos, or *in here* in the atom, and especially inside our brains, now generally seen as the most unexplored frontier.

New scientific advances open a Pandora's box to the unknown, for our explorations only increase the proportion of the unknown to the known. If this is true, then the more successful our science, the more we know, the larger the unknown becomes. This points to an interesting and diminishing role for science. This limitation in our brain's production of high math and physics points to what may be the final barrier beyond which we cannot go, a new Heisenberg limitation not restricted to the atom, but stretching like a new iron curtain between the world of known and unknown. Like it or not, we all end up as mystics. The old mystics must be smiling.

Survey data informs us that nearly half of scientists embrace some wisdom/spiritual tradition, and I number myself with them. Along with most everyone, part of me is in love with matter, with the hardware of everyday life. I am attached to my body, even as I see it running down. Bread, water, my home, car and computer all serve me well. The other half of me, my soul, adores nothingness: the spirit and soul of life, the suspected thing behind all things, the sparkle in the eyes of others, the unseen energy which seems to stream though life. With many other scientists, awake at night I launch my prayers, hopes, wishes. And the scientist in me wonders if I am fooling myself, if my prayers only make it to the ceiling. Today, more and more of us appear to have this lively inner dialogue between our inner scientist and our faith in an ancient god or goddess.

I am honored to be part of the scientific community that adores little particles, for they are the last stronghold into which we drive our claims. All of us who pledge allegiance to science are required to hammer pitons into any particle we can find, as a necessary place from which to hang our entire scientific apparatus, our creeds and lives, hoping not to fall into thin air. At night the fears come up: we fear either the particle or our pitons might disappear, and the whole edifice collapse into the chasm of the unknown, into the world of pure spirit. It is an image that must cause the old spiritual shamans and masters to rub their hands in glee.

And thus it is a dangerous time for science, clutching as it does to the belief in the existence of gossamer particles that often behave more as waves. If a magician were to happen along and make these particles disappear, science would also go up in smoke. No particles at all?! Ipso facto, no science. The magician waves his hand, but without applause from the scientists in the audience.

Given the insistence that science is built on matter, on atoms and even smaller particles, we can see that the old wisdom model is twice as wide as that of science, for it includes both spirit and matter, with spirit as the source of all. This model believes that spirit hungers for matter, wants to become flesh, to press itself into our sensory world in many forms. Thus across eons, blossoming across our planet, ancient gods showed up with many faces, in many forms, their dwelling places our oceans, forests, upon our mountains, in our skies, and of course, resident within our very selves. We are indwelt! I am not just me, you are not just you, for behind our eyes is infinity, is a larger presence. The diaphanous divine lives in everything. Indeed, this is perhaps our deepest, most ageless and most pleasing belief: spirit is first and final cause, with matter as a necessary manifestation of the divine. In the face of science the myth endures. We walk under night skies and fill with awe. We say our prayers at dawn. We ascend our mountains and feel we've touched the face of a cosmic lover. A lover who touches back. We are noticed, embraced, touched and loved by the infinite One. What could be more human, more filling than this? Believing this, in dark nights hope endures, and even some scientists release their hold on that last particle.

It is not that science and the wisdom traditions are entirely different, for they share some things in common. Like other bits and pieces, they might seem disconnected, but inevitably have a yin-yang relationship. Along with the old spiritual masters, science too, is driven by the same engine: the infinite desire to know, to answer our deepest questions. Viewed this way science can be seen as a fantastic historical expression of our soul's desire to probe the unknown, of our quest to understand more of ourselves, perhaps even of our gods. Science as a critical high point of soul urgency, and now, after a long historical struggle, we have new eyes, a beginner's mind beyond our wildest dreams. The eyes we have today include powerful electron microscopes, along with Hubble and all the other probing, curious eyes we have launched into space. Surely, none of these are intended or designed to capture any gods, but a few harbor the secret belief that we might also, incidentally, discover the essence of the One, both in the small and large places.

When we let our neurons out to play, as we are doing here, we create a potential trap for ourselves, and even for the spiritual masters; this might cause them to wring their hands not in glee, but distress. If we let our neurons dance enough, we can see our scientists as the latest order of priests, of shamans, of many spiritual orders we might name.

Let us, then, look again at the face of Einstein, seen by many as our greatest scientist. Why does his face intrigue us? Why does his face keep showing up on posters? What is it about that wild hair that probes into time and space? That smile that suggests he knows something we don't? How can we understand the outpouring of new books which explore his mind and soul, along with his theories? Is this only about science? Are we only about science? As we ponder his face, engaging in thought experimentation as he did, we can perhaps see that he is also a shaman. In one of the most famous pictures of Einstein, he sticks out his tongue at us. That is an old shamanic trick par excellence: startle us with something unexpected, something that will force new perceptions, that will cause a frenzy of neurons. To upset old perceptions, to bring a radical shift in consciousness, is the core work of shamans: to trick us into seeing a whole new way. This is Einstein, loose in the world, shattering old perceptions, teasing us into our beginner's minds.

The irony of it all: those of us on the religious side of the great divide insist Einstein is outside the fold, that he is not one of God's children. How then, did he get here, and what is he doing on our planet with his fantastic brain, and his reading of the Lord's blueprints? Why are religious scrolls part of God's handiwork, and mathematics the inspiration of infidels?

Aside from his role as early scientist/priest/shaman, he was the most uncanny prophet; his theories predicted things decades ahead, and even today, as we devise new tests, we find his future insights stunningly accurate. In 2015 we finally measured gravitational waves, and they have an uncanny fit to his theories of one hundred years ago. Is he a prophet or not? In his reverential pursuit of truth, he discovered vital workings of our cosmic clock and the layout of our universe dating to the day of creation.

His theories upset the old order of science, inciting new ways of thinking that continue today. It is widely known that he brought his whole self, his soul, to science. At different times he expressed the belief that his sense of wonder, awe and reverence were prime motivators for all he did.

It is not blasphemous to think of him as a high priest, prophet and shaman in the new order of things, for he had an enduring faith in a grand, impersonal intelligence in the universe, a sense of order underneath the seeming disorder. *The Lord God does not throw dice* he said. We can count on the predictability in the divine order of things; his creed was such that he spent his life proving this to himself, higher math and physics as his scripture. And most of us, even though we will never understand his theories, believe in him. We laugh as we talk of him and say, *it's all relative,* implying maybe we can relax a bit, maybe even jump out of our box. Indeed, what are we to make of our reverence and awe for him? We don't understand his theories; he ignites our intuitions, our souls.

Like an impudent child he stuck his tongue out at us, on his 72nd birthday! This man who had flown into other dimensions of time and space, who heard the angels whisper on his shoulder, and maybe chatted with God. When someone asked him how he would feel if his core theories were wrong, he said he would feel sorry for the Lord. He woke us up like few have done. We can speculate that he changed our consciousness as much as the teachings of the wisdom masters. And if so, what do we make of this?

Thinking of our scientists as our new priests and shamans, we might ask what is our new altar? Travel not too many miles from Stonehenge, even fewer from the Cro-Magnon art paintings in the caves at Lascaux, France, and there it is, buried deep in the secret earth, there in the heart of mother, our new altar. We call it the large Hadron Collider, and we have thrown twelve billion dollars into the offering plate to see what new truths it might reveal. At the conscious level, it is predicated only to the interest of probing matter, with, officially, no thought of trapping spirit. This collider is dedicated to smashing particles in the hopes of finding new ones, the most intriguing referred to as *the God particle*. Take the reverence out of it, and the particle is properly called the Higgs boson, named after another scientist/prophet who foresaw it decades in advance. The God/Higgs particle has impressive gravitas: it is believed to give mass to everything.

It is written. It is written that even our most brilliant scientists smile when they use the term *the God particle* to describe what they might unveil when they rend the curtain, when they pulverize atoms in the large Hadron Collider. Calling it *the God particle* reveals much about the complexity of who we are as humans. There inside the most magnificent scientific machine ever built, science is taking us back to the first seconds of creation, the moment perhaps when a creator reached out and sent a spark of life into the world. Our Hadron Collider is shaped like a circle, the same form that shows up repeatedly in our sacred traditions. It is a mandala that calls us to center.

The bones of the old alchemists shiver and dance as they feel the vibrations from our high tech wonder, for it is the stunning fulfillment of their wildest dreams. Now we can see it is the greatest cooking chamber, the vas, where matter is melted and transformed. It is a sacred vessel seventeen miles round and full of flashing light.

And more: along with protons, the collider uses lead—a substance much favored by the alchemists—as one of the substances, hammering this dense material into yielding up the secrets contained within. It can also be seen as a mandala that guides us into the inner world of soul and matter. The alchemists, and other ancient wise ones, believed that transformation arises out of our darkness: to fully know ourselves we descend into caves, sweat lodges and dreams that arise in the dark of night. In such places we cook our souls, our cells, and thus expand the light. It is no accident that the Hadron Collider is buried hundreds of feet in the darkness, embosomed in the rich loam of mother earth. More than ever, mother earth, the eternal feminine, gives us treasure.

There in the soul of that machine, eager scientists probe back to the beginning of our universe towards what our spiritual traditions think of as spirit. There in a magnificent machine, sitting atop thousands of years of evolution, the word goes forth, and the god particle is found and named.

The whole Hadron smashing enterprise is so ironic, for it now seems our scientists are as intent on discovering the ultimate ground of things as the theologians were and are. This odd situation points to an ongoing reconciliation of science and religion. The particles we smash into smaller and smaller fragments move closer and closer to the world of spirit, of energy without any matter. These particles are ghostly indeed, for they don't show their faces, only a hand wave, a trace of light indicating they passed through our time and space frame for less than a trillionth of a second, arising from *the void* and falling back into *the void*. Here in this new altar, where light dances and matter fragments, the world of matter and spirit approach unity. And what happens after we've hammered our particles into the smallest possible pieces, after all the gluons and quarks have been finely rendered? At some point, can we say that infinitesimal particles merge into nothingness, into pure spirit? Is this what we mean by *the void*?

Would it not be more fitting if the old spiritual masters were trying to destroy the evidence, trying to show that matter is merely a cover, an impostor for spirit?

Yet, it seems clear our spiritual traditions would not do away with matter either. On the soul side of things, who can ever imagine living in a world without our bodies? Without our senses, our sensuality? How else can a soul be informed, if not by our senses? Were we not born to inhabit materiality, and does not spirit want to be move downward, into flesh, to marrow out in bones? If we did not have faces, if we were only glimmers, ghosts afraid of this time and space, what then? This seems to not be what we crave, either.

The ancient teachers tell us we were formed by the breath of the Divine Ones; out of pure nothingness they breathed life into us. There was no original particle, only spirit. We not only breathe, we are breathed. It may not be completely absurd to think that science and religion, the new and old musers, along with the rest of us, might someday embrace the similarities between the two, rather than defending the differences.

Some scientists believe there are parallel universes, all about and even within. Even gravity, some think, leaks in from another universe. Is this not similar to the ancient, near universal spiritual belief in a spiritual realm both within and without? Many spiritual traditions have embraced the idea of infinite time, and now science also posits this. Viewed from one angle, the progress of science seems to inevitably lead to a kind of pure energy underlying all things. This seems dangerously close to the idea of spirit and soul, of the living essence that broods through, and moves through all things. At the quantum level, some scientists now believe our minds influence, if not determine, what goes on in the atom as we probe into it. This belief is, again, dangerously close to the old notions of the gods, with their far-seeing minds, their divine intelligence creating, inhabiting and informing all of life.

We can also note that both the wisdom paths and high science encounter a barrier that simultaneously hides the gods and the soul of the atom. What lies behind the veil in the temple? This reduces all of us to the status of mystics, truth be known. This reality is not easy for some scientists to accept, yet we can see a creeping softness, a reverence in the way our hardest, most rigorous scientists talk about the unknowns in the distant cosmos and within the atom.

So it is not only science that needs that one last particle; soul and spirit do too. The cosmos and atom are bigger than we are, whether due to some intentional spiritual design, or evolution without soulful intention. Life is given to us; we are birthed into it, either from stardust, or from the breath of a divine entity, or both. Either way, we are ancient. From the viewpoint of science, we are born from the stars. Our spiritual traditions say that spirit came first, and Divine Spirit created everything. Spirit and matter: both are honest legacies.

What does it mean to be human then, to live this life? We are inescapably caught up in the tension between particle and soul, between body and mind, between matter and energy. The laboratory, the synagogue, the cathedral and mosque, the Hadron Collider, the sweat lodge, are different altars on which scientists and the wisdom teachers can feel a primary and universal impulse to surrender and revere the mystery of life. We hush to hear *the God particle* speak.

If it is a dangerous time for science, it may be more so for those of us who cling to the spiritual side of life. Science as a new theology? Einstein and others our high priests? A new altar in old Europe? These are the challenging ideas that confront us.

Based on the thoughts above, it is possible science and the wisdom traditions are moving to a place where both are held as simultaneously true. The melding of science and religion into one larger source of truth might partially fulfill the dreams of scientists for parsimony, for the desire to have one theory that explains everything. Not the unified theory that science dreamed of, but maybe in the long run, one possible answer to our wholeness.

We've been found alive under mysterious circumstances, and our grand inquest to discover what happened is a drama beyond what kings and queens ever witnessed. Here on the cutting edge of history, moving at warp speed, we are honored to be carried along by both old and new thought streams.

APPENDIX C

⚜

Where Do We Go After We Die?

⚜

Where did Mother go? Where does anyone go when they die? Of the thousands of spiritual traditions we've created on our planet, past and present, most believe in life after death, and many in life before birth. This is also true for many myths not tied precisely to religious traditions. Out of the millions who've believed in immortality, are we ready to dismiss them all as dupes and idiots? As victims of hope and faith? Science, too, rests in part on hope and faith. Shall we also throw out that baby with the bathwater?

Some theories of the afterlife propose horrific scenarios. The Christian tradition of our farm family painted a terrifying portrait of hellfire if we did not believe in the right God. Eternal hellfire. Not for a year, but forever. As a child, I'd get a headache thinking about *forever*. We kids woke up at night terrified we might be consumed in flames. Not until decades later could we talk about this.

The other scenario was eagerly embraced, for it said if we *were right with Jesus* we'd go to heaven after our short time here on earth. Of course, I think Mother went to a place of love and peace, perhaps not precisely with the pearly gates and all, but who wants to think, who can possibly believe their mother has gone to hell?

In addition to the spiritual traditions I've read about and explored, I also value the insights offered by science. It is common to perceive of science and religion as opposites, but if we think about it, we can see this is not absolutely the case. I like to find the similarities between science and our spiritual traditions, and in what follows, I draw on science for intimations of our immortality.

I begin with the scientific findings with what we call *the mind-brain problem*. Here I expand this to include how we use our minds to think about our sense of self, spirit, soul and life itself.

The standard scientific model believes that our minds, our thoughts, are produced by our brains. This includes all ideas, thoughts, images, dreams, hopes, meanings—in short, that which makes us human. These endless productions are believed to happen at the point of synapse where complex biochemical and electrical impulses leap across a space only nanoseconds wide. I think of our cascading images as trapeze artists, flying across this tiny space, and leaping into consciousness. Here is the fountainhead of all poetry, math, dance, love and hate—and all the rest. The synapse is where our human experience happens, and this makes us who we most are.

I like to ask family and friends what their thoughts and images are made of. For most of us this question is perplexing, for it probes into who we most are, and what we most take for granted. Invariably, most of us see images and ideas as airy and non-material. We share widespread agreement that thoughts and images happen so fast, sometimes randomly cascading, it feels as though they aren't at all similar to the hard objects of our everyday world. Images pop in and out of existence in seconds, to be replaced by other thoughts that do the same. This is happening as I write this, and as you read it. Often we feel the Niagara Falls of images and emotions are happening to us, rather than our making them happen.

Perhaps because we think of our self, our feelings, images and thoughts as non-material, it is easy for us to imagine our spiritual essence, our *souls,* as a kind of energy that is not anchored in the hard, material world. From this, it is only a short step to thinking we are, or have some part of us that is eternal, not bound by time and space.

This becomes even more complex when we think of how we capture thoughts with speech or the written word. We simply can't describe how we do this, and in fact don't know where to begin. Of all things human, thinking, feeling, speaking and writing are most native to us and most taken for granted. At times, we can steer and choose our thoughts, with the part of us we call *self,* and at other times images and thoughts seem to choose us, especially in our dreams at night. Again, this is happening in real time as *I* manufacture these words, and as *you* read them.

Our mind-brain discussion is made even more complex when we think of our sense of self, of who we are. Researchers have found that when they ask people where their *self* is located in their body, most of us pick our heads and hearts, while others choose their feet or hands. Again, when we think of our *self*, we usually don't think of it as a material object. It is not unusual that on some days we might say, *I don't feel my usual self*, or that a sudden, hurtful action *was not really me*.

Perhaps because of the illusive and airy qualities of self, we conceptualize our self as non-material, and can equate this as being similar to our essence, to our soul or spirit. Additionally, we can think of our personality or character as part of this complex, ever-shifting life energy within us. We resist all attempts to think of this dynamic energy as a material object of any kind. We are not objects in the same way as furniture, and neither are the thoughts and feelings that pass through us. Even Costco doesn't sell emotions or thoughts.

Another complication: science has no clear or consensual definition of what life is. We can agree that life is an animating, vitalizing force within all living creatures, yet we can't get a good handle on the origin point of life, or how it animates us in our days and nights. When I ask others to distinguish between life, soul, mind, spirit, thoughts and images, most of us agree they all seem much alike, and certainly not molecular or material. We inhabit a strange place of uncertain latitude and longitude.

Where then, are the deep roots of our self, our thoughts, images, soul and spirit—all that is most us? Because science deals only with our known material realm, the answer must point to the electromagnetic, biochemical brain as the source of our diaphanous existence. From this view all our long, long thoughts of self and soul are created by atoms and molecules, by brain neurons that dance like the northern lights. Our holy grail quest at this point can leap in many directions.

For example, a few scientists believe that, compared to other forces, gravity is weak because it leaks in from another universe. I grab this idea and think that our souls might also dwell in another realm—a realm of existence that has been both in us and around us all along. This line of thinking leads me to imagine that our minds, our selves and souls, might be part of another realm, at the cutting edge of what we now understand with science. We know our brains are partly driven by electromagnetic impulses in our nerve cells; we know too, that our earth is a potent electromagnetic field, and this suggests to me that all thoughts are influenced by this field.

When Van Gogh moved the few hundred miles from Paris to Arles, he noticed the angle of light was different, and his paintings changed in response to this. Only the keen eye of a great artist would notice such a subtle shift. It may also be that the electromagnetic forces were different in his new home, and this, too, may have altered his brain, his moods and perceptions.

Science recognizes that all life depends on the light from our sun. Living cells are created by light, and nourished by light, so, literally, light is the essence of us and all life. Many spiritual traditions honor light as the mystical presence of the divine, and I adhere to this view. (As an appendix, I've attached my five page essay on light, which I wrote following an experience I had at Esalen Institute in spring of 2014. In that short piece I conclude that we and all living things are inevitable creatures of light, and when we leave our material forms, we simply merge back into a larger field of light.)

Continuing with what we can extract from science, I note too, that despite all we've discovered about the atom, it veils itself in mystery: in the heart of the atom, time, space and cause and effect don't follow the laws of everyday life. We are rooted in atoms, and thus we remain a mystery to science and ourselves. So, in certain moments I imagine that our wispy essence finds a lasting home in the timeless space of the atom.

Some spiritual teachers believe that the part of us that watches the rest of us, our *witness,* exists in eternal time. When we think about our physical brains, it seems as though our brain is not the watcher, not the investigator watching the firing of neurons. How can the physical brain watch itself? It is similar to the weatherman, reporting the weather (and some days we are adrift in inner fog.)

Our common experience seems much like this: It is the *I* part of me who watches my brain...my self—and this witnessing self seems to hang suspended above our physical brains. Apart from our two physical eyes, we seem to have an inner eye that can scan in many directions at once. We can *see* back in time, imagine the future and alternate versions of history, and so forth. Our inner eye seems surprisingly free of time and space. It may be, as some claim, that our inner eye is not fully produced by our brains, and is more connected to the quirky realm of the atom, where time, space, cause and effect, along with gravity, violate everyday laws.

At night our inner witness stands once removed, watching our dreams just as scientists watch an experiment in process. We have the distinct impression that we are not our dreams, that they seem independent of us and happen as they will, and that we watch them with our everyday self. When we enter the dream realm, it seems not quite to be us, and we watch that unbidden world with interest, and sometimes fear and awe. A surprising number of us have dreams clearly recalled decades later. What is this about? Recurring dreams are also common, and can be stopped by taking thirty minutes or so to connect the dream with everyday consciousness. When someone keeps knocking at the door, it may be wise to let him in.

One of the essential features in the Buddhist practice of self-awareness is to increasingly observe the many subtle layers of all that lies within, and to do this with compassionate detachment and love. We have thousands of stories about who we were, who we are, and who we want to become. Our inner *watcher* and *witness* seems ethereally suspended above the rest of us, tied potentially to the timeless realm of the atom, streaming perhaps from the same universe where gravity originates.

The fact we can *transcend* time in our minds, observing past, present and future all at once, suggests a link with the timeless realm of the atom. The emerging field of quantum biology explores the connection between quantum processes in the atom, and the operation of our cells. Photosynthesis appears to be an example of such a process, for it appears that electrons within the leaf follow many pathways all at once, in a process that can readily lead us to think of the cascading, overlapping thoughts of our everyday brains.

As we increase our self-awareness, making our inner witness more robust, we see that the stories we tell ourselves are complex creations, made up of inherited memories and especially of early formative experiences. We continue to revise our viewpoints and stories as we live, and some stories are so much better than others. Who and what then, is this seemingly transcendent part of us?

The science of psychology has helped us become more aware of the thousands of our species who have had visions and near-death experiences where they believe they entered a unique realm of existence. Indeed, those who have had such experiences not only think or believe, they **know** they have tapped into another dimension. These experiences cannot be trivialized, for the everyday lives of many who have had spiritual visions are altered in observable ways. For some, the trajectory of life is permanently altered.

Such experiences can also be triggered by psychoactive drugs. Our brains, our minds have the capacity for wondrous leaps and travels, some seemingly transcending time, space and causation as we know it. It is difficult to dismiss the impressive library of such experiences as lies and fabrications, or as mere hallucinations. Most everyone who experiences a laser-clear vision knows immediately and intuitively that it is not a hallucination, or anything other than a vision. If we must call these three-dimensional visions *hallucinations,* what are we to make of civilization and its discontents?

There are thousands of books and articles on brain pathology, focusing on our fall out of normal consciousness into mental illness. Just as real, our brain also has the capacity to move into higher, healthier states, sometimes slowly, sometimes in a dramatic and sudden way.

Millions, if not billions of us, know this: we have had bursts of inspiration, deep insights, an *aha* experience, perhaps a spiritual vision. Such experiences are the infrastructure of our spiritual traditions, and also account for a few of the breakthroughs in science. There are many triggers for sudden, elevated, ecstatic experiences: being in a special place in nature, sitting with a master teacher or guru, deep times of chanting, meditating, praying or dancing. The list is rather endless, for our brains seem *born ready* and genetically open to jumping to a higher level of functioning.

We need not go outside ourselves and look to the radically altered visions of others, for every night in our dreams we enter another realm, remembered or not. Given my personal and professional interest in dreams and my work with clients, I know that dreams, too, can be life altering. In rare cases, dreams are precognitive and point to future events; these can be disarmingly real when they have precise markers. Out of the few thousand of my own recorded dreams, I've had only two that pointed to precise future events. Again there is ample evidence that our brains can transcend time and space, and in a similar way we can think of scientific theories that cannot be proven until years later.

Science also informs us that information is never lost; it only changes form. The atom contains an infinite library of information. Science has enabled us to extract information about he atom, and the elusive complex behaviors of sub-atomic particles. The large Hadron Collider is the most recent technology that lets us peek deeper and deeper into the buzzing realm of the atom, in our long quest for the *god particle*. As we look at the pictures of the explosions of protons within the collider, we can see the ghostly trails of particles that emerge *out of the background* and disappear in trillionths of a second. From what womb are they born and where do they go? The standard answer is that the shimmering sub-atomic particles emerge from the background radiation left over from the big bang. That we emerged out of an explosion, that we were once stardust, is difficult dogma for many of us to embrace.

In addition to mining information from the atom, we have looked outward and learned much about the cosmos. Exploding atoms and exploding stars change forms, but no information is lost. All animals, ourselves included, are born with enormous information stored in our genes, and we acquire new information across our lifetime. We know now that our daily experiences, and the way we gather and process information, alter our bio-chemicals, our bio-genome and even our genes. Where does this information go when we are no longer chained to our bodies? I tempt myself with possibilities.

Loved ones live on in our memories. In everyday life, the images we have of those we love make up much of who they are. Loved ones, past and present, move around in us, show up and inhabit our hours. As we begin to notice this more keenly, the reality of this can surprise.

When the body of a loved one falls away, a vital part of our relationship goes on. Again, the part of us we call *me* and *I,* our diaphanous essence, is birthed in the holy cleft of synapse, the mysterious fountainhead where thoughts and images leap up. The web of spirit, of self, is stretched across time-bound bones that fall away to dust and ashes. Who can know where the jellyfish ends and water begins? I also read that at the microscopic level it is difficult to know where tree roots end and mother earth begins. We are not islands; we are always connected to the larger universe by light, by electromagnetic energy and more. And yet we cling to the pretense that we are alone, that we live only in our bodies.

We tell ourselves many stories, and of the most basic ones is this: do you, do I, see the universe as continuous, or discontinuous? Is anything absolutely and finally disconnected from anything else? If we think that all things are connected in some way, as with the cosmos and the atoms within, then we can imagine that the realm of time and space we know is also in some way tied to a timeless realm where cause and effect work in ways we don't understand from our tiny niche in life. We are trapped in ourselves, can only see with human eyes. If we could communicate more fully with the dolphin, the bumblebee or any other species, we would have surprising insights into other ways of being in the world.

As science and religion evolve, we can draw on both to answer our ancient questions about life and death.

The author can be contacted at almcleodme@gmail.com